O God, our Father, Thou Searcher of human hearts,
help us to draw near to Thee in sincerity and truth.
May our religion be filled with gladness and may our worship of Thee be natural.

Strengthen and increase our admiration for honest dealing and clean thinking,
and suffer not our hatred of hypocrisy and pretence ever to diminish.
Encourage us in our endeavor to live above the common level of life.
Make us to choose the harder right instead of the easier wrong,
and never to be content with a half truth when the whole can be won.

Endow us with courage that is born of loyalty to all that is noble and worthy,
that scorns to compromise with vice and injustice
and knows no fear when truth and right are in jeopardy.

Guard us against flippancy and irreverence in the sacred things of life.
Grant us new ties of friendship and new opportunities of service.

Kindle our hearts in fellowship with those of a cheerful countenance,
and soften our hearts with sympathy for those who sorrow and suffer.

Help us to maintain the honor of the Corps untarnished
and unsullied and to show forth in our lives the ideals of West Point
in doing our duty to Thee and to our Country.

All of which we ask in the name of the Great Friend and Master of all.

AMEN.

The Warrior's Character

LEADERSHIP WISDOM
FROM WEST POINT'S
CADET PRAYER

DR. DON M. SNIDER, EDITOR

NEW YORK CHICAGO SAN FRANCISCO
LISBON LONDON MADRID MEXICO CITY MILAN
NEW DELHI SAN JUAN SEOUL SINGAPORE
SYDNEY TORONTO

The McGraw-Hill Companies

1 2 3 4 5 6 7 8 9 10 DOC/DOC 1 8 7 6 5 4 3 2

ISBN 978-0-07-180261-1
MHID 0-07-180261-4

e-ISBN 978-0-07-180262-8
e-MHID 0-07-180262-2

Design by Lee Fukui and Mauna Eichner

This book is printed on acid-free paper.

CONTENTS

ACKNOWLEDGMENTS

This book is the product of several stout hands, the absence of any of which would have prevented its creation. They are the USMA Class of 1946, which initiated a project to bring renewed emphasis to the Cadet Prayer at West Point; the USMA staff and faculty, which responded with alacrity to the opportunity to strengthen character development of cadets and officers; the Academy's leaders, who provided an environment richly receptive to intellectual inquiry; and, lastly, those who sacrificed personally so that this volume could come to fruition.

In the fall of 2002, three members of the USMA Class of 1946 banded together to seek renewal of the traditional prominence of the Cadet Prayer in West Point life. Though the three represented different religious faiths—Roland Catarinella, Protestant; John Donahue, Roman Catholic; and Jesse Cohen, Jewish—their life experiences all converged on a common conclusion. Each believed that their lives, their very essence, had been shaped profoundly by what they had internalized from the moral precepts so eloquently set forth in the Cadet Prayer. They sought the same outcome for future generations of graduates. In the words of Catarinella:

> I was disappointed to learn in 2001 at the 55th reunion of my Class that the Cadet Prayer was unknown

> to some cadets. They had never read it and knew nothing about it. When I discussed this matter with my classmates John Donahue and Jesse Cohen, they agreed that if the Academy continued without the Cadet Prayer, West Point would have lost a powerful force with which to develop leaders of character committed to the values of Duty, Honor, Country.

With Catarinella in the lead, they approached the USMA Chaplain with the general idea of underwriting the production of a book about the prayer. Sensitive to the current status of church-state relations in America, particularly as affecting the service academies, they offered on behalf of the Class of 1946 to provide enough copies for a substantial initial presentation to cadets without charge. Remarkably, more than a score of their classmates have since joined them in this endeavor.

When I returned from medical leave in the late spring of 2005, the USMA Chaplain, Colonel John Cook, asked me if I would take on the project of creating a book about the Cadet Prayer. That request coincided with my own abiding interest in the Cadet Leader Development System (CLDS) which, in the cadet developmental reforms of 2000 to 2002, had specified a new domain—the domain of the human spirit—as one of the three areas in which the Academy facilitates the formation of character in future Army officers. In the ensuing years, however, as little had been done to advance cadet development in that new domain, I became ever more convinced that the Academy's faculty, effectively the professoriate of the Army profession, would itself need to create the expert knowledge necessary to supp development of the spiritual domain.

I therefore agreed to undertake the task provided that I could assemble an interdisciplinary team of thinkers from the USMA staff and faculty who shared my interest in character development. We were all enthusiastic over the opportunity to combine in common cause the Class of 1946's Cadet Prayer initiative and the Academy's own initiative to buttress cadet moral and character development. In aiming to address this developmental void at West Point and within the Army, we sought new ideas, models, and language that would enhance the ability of future officers and their mentors to analyze and critique their own moral and character development, particularly those entering the Army from Generation Y.

Gratifyingly, my stipulation was quickly met, as attested by the many members of the USMA faculty, both past and present, who eagerly stepped forward to do the arduous work involved. Such enterprise was an outgrowth of our professional calling—it certainly wasn't dictated by anyone's job description. As the Army's "university at large," West Point is privileged to have had some very remarkable scholars and professionals among its staff and faculty, some still at West Point, some retired. Of singular mention as one such remarkable scholar and former Army professional is the editor of this book Lloyd Matthews. This is our third book together since 2002, and one of the delights of my days has been to hear from Lloyd and see what he and his gracious wife Phyllis have been able to do with the often hurried prose we provided them.

Contributors to the original publication cooperated so wholeheartedly because of the uniquely hospitable intellectual environment that prevails here at West Point. It is one that encourages honest inquiry into topics critical to the Army profession, even if they are as potentially controversial as the subject of the warrior's spirituality. The flourishing of such an environment is testimony to the wisdom of the leader teams assembled there in recent decades by the Academy's Superintendents—Lieutenant Generals Howard Graves, Daniel Christman, William Lennox, and F. L. Hagenbeck.

As with all such endeavors, someone has to pay the bill in terms of the fugitive moments wrested from crowded days in completing such an undertaking. Each author has his or her own story to tell of relationships and endeavors that were encroached upon to make room for this book. So far as I personally am concerned, Caroline, my Army wife of 47 years, once again unstintingly shared my load. That said, however, we have both been richly remunerated by the satisfaction that comes from serving the cause of West Point and the Army in this manner, which we are both so privileged to do.

Don M. Snider
Carlisle, Pennsylvania
Summer 2012

FOREWORD

My generation arrived on the world scene late in the first half of the 20th century. We grew up in the shadows of giants, those who fought and won World War II and saved our Nation and the world from tyranny. Born in Hawaii about a year after the attack on Pearl Harbor, I was raised on the fringe of what was called the Pacific Theater of Operations. My personal heroes, whose shadows touch me even today, came from the 100th Infantry Battalion, the 442d Regimental Combat Team, and the Military Intelligence Service, those highly decorated Nisei units whose soldiers also fought to prove the loyalty of Americans of Japanese ancestry. On the heels of World War II came Korea. Once again, I sensed what preserving freedom and liberty meant, this time on the Korean Peninsula, and internalized the great sacrifice, courage, and heroism displayed by the Americans who fought there.

Following my graduation from the United States Military Academy (USMA) and commissioning with the distinguished Class of 1965, I deployed to Vietnam for my own tours in a war zone. A first tour, without benefit of the Officer Basic Course, and a second tour, during which I dealt with a combat refusal, provided early grounding in the leadership challenges of the profession of arms. Service in Europe followed, the first time at the height of the Cold War and the second during its final days, when the Berlin Wall was breached and the Iron Curtain fell on November 9, 1989. Then Lt. Gen. Fred Franks, Commander of VII Corps, taught all of us about courage and toughness and seeing one's duty clearly, no matter what the General Defense Plan mandated. During this period of uncertainty, when the outbreak of freedom was preceded by indicators of an impending military invasion, he and his chain of command, with characteristically cool heads, held us in our garrison locations rather than take the provocative step of marshaling our units and deploying them to defensive positions along the interzonal German border. For leaders, the harder right usually involves risk, sometimes significant risk.

When I retired from the Army in August 2003, young Americans were fighting once again, this time in Afghanistan and Iraq. I had come full circle in a life that began at the height of World War II and an Army career that concluded during America's first war of the 21st century.

Throughout my 38 years as a soldier, the responsibilities of leadership were underscored time and again by the words of the Cadet Prayer—words I was inspired by when I first heard them 46 years ago. They remind us that ethics is about the unwavering demand of duty—our responsibility for knowing what needs to be done, for understanding the difference between right and wrong, and then for doing what is right without fail. They still reflect some of the finest insights into ethical leadership I have ever encountered:

> Strengthen and increase our admiration for honest dealing and clean thinking, and suffer not our hatred of hypocrisy and pretence ever to diminish. Encourage us

> in our endeavor to live above the common level of life. Make us to choose the harder right instead of the easier wrong, and never to be content with a half truth when the whole can be won. Endow us with courage that is born of loyalty to all that is noble and worthy, that scorns to compromise with vice and injustice, and knows no fear when truth and right are in jeopardy. Guard us against flippancy and irreverence in the sacred things of life.

For those who listen, these imperatives drum an insistent cadence. All these many years later, the words from the Cadet Prayer still resonate with me because they foster ideas and actions that not only reinforce the fundamental values of the profession of arms, but also remind us of our sacred duty to uphold them.

In February 1997, the Army's senior four-star generals gathered at a Winter Senior Commanders Conference in the Pentagon. The conference was organized around a select number of 30-minute decision briefings tightly managed by the Vice Chief of Staff. One briefer mentioned in passing the Army's new institutional values. Time seemed to stand still as the senior generals confronted one another about those attributes—for over three hours. "Why isn't Competence on the list?" asked one General. "What do you mean by Honor?" asked another. "How do we measure integrity?" asked a third. And on it went until they had addressed their concerns. I sensed that they understood they were defining their Army for generations to come, and they wanted to get this right. They seemed to think that, if they were able to do that, all else would follow. They were right. Today, those seven Army Values—Loyalty, Duty, Respect, Selfless Service, Honor, Integrity, Personal Courage—define our Army and its service to the Nation, both in peace and in war. Sitting in on that conference as a note taker, I wondered then, as I've wondered on other occasions since, whether similar discussions occurred in other institutions and other militaries around the world. I felt incredibly good about my profession, and I have always believed that those general officers treated me to a privileged moment.

Dick Cavanagh, the highly respected President and CEO of the Conference Board, once described a dinner party that took place in 2001 at the Four Seasons Restaurant in Manhattan. Peter Drucker, the distinguished "Father of Modern Management," and Jack Welch, the former CEO of General Electric, led a discussion about who best develops leaders. In Cavanagh's words, "To my surprise, the usual suspects so often cited for finding and training leaders didn't figure—not the Harvard Business School, or Goldman Sachs, or McKinsey & Company, or General Electric, or IBM, or Procter & Gamble. The enthusiastic choice of both of these management legends was the United States military."[1] He went on to remind us that the high regard in which the military is held represented a recent reversal in standings between military leaders and their business counterparts.[2] Discussions like this one led to a partnering endeavor between the Army, the Conference Board, and the Leader to Leader Institute, led by its inspirational Chairman, Frances Hesselbein, to find common ground in developing inspired and *inspiring* leaders across the various sectors of America.

This growth in respect was important to the U.S. Army, which had left Vietnam some 28 years earlier, after having fought successfully at the tactical level without achieving the strategic outcomes desired by a Nation that had lost its way and its will in that brutal conflict. We were led out of the dark days of Vietnam by tough, smart, and determined military leaders, who saw their duties clearly. Their mission was to rebuild the Army quickly into a force capable of dealing with the massive threat presented by Warsaw Pact forces in Europe. Many gifted Soldiers had a hand in rebuilding the Army and its noncommissioned officer corps, but the men who led this turnaround were the Army's successive Chiefs of Staff. It was the continuity of their investments in leader development that produced the conclusions that were arrived at in the Four Seasons Restaurant during that evening in 2001. At the heart of the Chiefs' determination were the skills, knowledge, attributes, and values underscored by the words of the Cadet Prayer.

Eric K. Shinseki
General, U.S. Army Ret.
West Point, NY
September 2006

INTRODUCTION

The Army profession, like all others, creates its own expert knowledge. That knowledge is then mastered and embedded in professional Soldiers in the form of expertise to be practiced whenever and wherever the American people direct the Army to serve, in peace or in war. This book is a part of that evolving expert knowledge of the U.S. Army, but also a way for civilians to better understand the ethos of the Army profession in regard to character and leadership.

The specific knowledge addressed herein is the modus operandi for developing moral character in the Army's officer leaders, particularly those who are commissioned at the U.S. Military Academy each spring after completing the 47-month West Point experience. Our mission at the Academy is "to educate, train, and inspire the Corps of Cadets so that each graduate is a commissioned leader of character committed to the values of Duty, Honor, Country and prepared for a career of professional excellence and service to the Nation as an officer in the United States Army."

We understand the development of our graduates, including their moral character, to be the result of carefully integrated activities fulfilling all three of the verbs in the mission statement—educate, train, inspire. And it is the third of these, to inspire leaders, that serves as the focus of this book—the inspiration to do their duty as Soldiers and leaders regardless of circumstances or obstacles to mission accomplishment. Such inspired motivation comes from the leader's human spirit.

Having commanded the 10th Mountain Division in Afghanistan and subsequently served as the manager of the Army's human resources as the Deputy Chief of Staff for Personnel–G1, I am very well aware of the unique demands this Long War against radical Islamic terrorists is placing on our Army's leaders, particularly its junior leaders. These terrorists are an adaptable, cunning, and utterly immoral enemy whose tactics and techniques in battle flout all the international laws of war. In the desperate straits of battle, then, the urgent temptation for our forces to respond in kind is thwarted only by Soldiers and leaders of such high moral character that they can be relied upon to "choose the harder right instead of the easier wrong."

That quotation is one of the seven nonsectarian moral precepts within the Cadet Prayer, written in 1924, to illuminate for all, regardless of faith, denomination, or spiritual disposition, the type of moral character they needed to acquire in order to become maximally effective leaders throughout life. This humble fragment of military lore has become a transcendent didactic and cultural force at the Academy. Its moral precepts have inspired and guided generations of West Point graduates in peace and war, and continue to do so to this day, including, with all humility, myself.

But even if the inspiring words of the Cadet Prayer point to the necessary behavioral outcomes, how are these particular

PART

I

The ROLE *of*

CHARACT

DEVELOPM

in th

WEST P

EXPERIEN

outcomes, as manifested in strengthened moral character, developed? And how should our faculty, staff, cadets, and leaders outside the Academy think about the relevant developmental processes, and with what ideas and words should they discuss their own development within the domain of the human spirit? Our inability to achieve such development with sufficient conceptual clarity sparked the interest of our faculty in explicating for the Army profession how moral character can be further strengthened in the newest generations who come to West Point from diverse cultural backgrounds and spiritual assumptions.

Thus, an interdisciplinary group of USMA staff and faculty under the leadership of Dr. Don Snider has produced still another landmark text for use not only within the Army profession itself, but within any institution of higher education and leader development, and in everyday life and business, where the character of the leaders produced is the paramount concern. Given that West Point understands the significance of the human spirit in preparation for war, it should not be surprising that the disciplines of cognitive psychology, social psychology, leadership theory, philosophy and ethics, theology, political science, and Islamic studies are represented in the eclectic group of contributors.

Obviously, we have no pretense that what our contributors have produced is the last word on the theory of moral development, which remains a dynamic and rapidly evolving field of research. But in elaborating the methods currently employed at the U.S. Military Academy to produce leaders of character—methods validated daily by reports reaching West Point from more like a governmental bureaucracy. It had been a difficult time for the Army, called upon to do more with less as its end-strength and its budget were reduced by over one-third during the decade. This change in the institution's culture and behavior produced an exodus of captains and contributed to a loss of professional self-concept among the remaining officers of the middle grades. Thus, it was recommended to General Christman that the Academy address this malady directly by instilling more deeply in future Academy graduates an explicitly professional identity, one based on the understanding that the Army is to be a vocational profession and each officer within it an aspiring or practicing professional.

As to the second added role, servant of the Nation, the committee was responding to several factors. First and foremost, the concept of a graduate's duty to the country had long been a part of the Academy's ethos, most recognizably in the Academy's traditional motto, "Duty, Honor, Country." Thus the committee wanted to codify formally in the new development system that long-term aspect of the Academy's, as well as the Army's, ethos. But in the nearer term, the Academy was resetting its developmental system in the midst of the economic bubble of the late 1990s. Hypermaterialism was rampant at that time in America as members of the boomer generation were "getting theirs" before the bubble burst. Throughout the Army, attractive offers, many by former Academy graduates themselves, were being made to graduates at the rank of captain as they approached the end of their five-year mandatory service obligation. Such recruiters argued that graduates had "paid their contractual obligation" to the Academy and the Nation for their "free

PART I

The ROLE *of* CHARACTER DEVELOPMENT *in the* WEST POINT EXPERIENCE

CHAPTER ONE

Developing Leaders of Character at West Point

Don M. Snider

In his book titled *Honor Unvarnished: A West Point Graduate's Memoir of World War II* (2003), General Donald V. Bennett, USA Ret., who earlier served as the Academy's 47th Superintendent, spoke these eloquent words: "It is to the Point that I shall finally return and where I shall rest. . . . Nearby will be the Chapel, where long ago I heard the words that shaped my life." Then, General Bennett quoted in full the Cadet Prayer:

> O God, our Father, Thou Searcher of human hearts, help us to draw near to Thee in sincerity and truth.

May our religion be filled with gladness and may our worship of Thee be natural.

Strengthen and increase our admiration for honest dealing and clean thinking, and suffer not our hatred of hypocrisy and pretence ever to diminish. Encourage us in our endeavor to live above the common level of life. Make us to choose the harder right instead of the easier wrong, and never to be content with a half truth when the whole can be won. Endow us with courage that is born of loyalty to all that is noble and worthy, that scorns to compromise with vice and injustice and knows no fear when truth and right are in jeopardy. Guard us against flippancy and irreverence in the sacred things of life. Grant us new ties of friendship and new opportunities of service. Kindle our hearts in fellowship with those of a cheerful countenance, and soften our hearts with sympathy for those who sorrow and suffer. Help us to keep the honor of the Corps untarnished and unsullied and to show forth in our lives the ideals of West Point in doing our duty to Thee and to our Country. All of which we ask in the name of the Great Friend and Master of all. Amen. (Italics added by author of this chapter)

Following the Prayer, General Bennett continued: "As long as those words are spoken, acted upon, and believed in, I know that all of the sacrifices of those who sleep the eternal sleep on the Plain of West Point will not have been in vain."[1]

As the moral precepts italicized in the Prayer make clear, there is a unique character required of the members of the Long

Gray Line of West Point. Not all attain it, but the vast majority of them do, and it bonds them together in a manner unlike that of the graduates of other elite colleges and universities in America. In those institutions the bond is more tenuous, focused on the individual graduates and their storied achievements across the many vocations that make up the various sectors of American life, public and private. West Point graduates, however, are not being prepared for those activities, though they may pursue them later in life, applying all they have learned. Their preparation is to enable them to serve as commissioned officers in the U.S. Army, leading America's sons and daughters into the crucible of mortal combat, to fight the nation's "wars" wherever and however the society they serve chooses to define a war. Thus, the bond among the members of the Long Gray Line is focused on their common understanding of their duties and whether they, individually, have the attributes of moral character necessary to fulfill those duties. To betray their commission, the Army, and America's soldiers, and thus the Nation, by poor individual leadership is also to betray the other members of the Long Gray Line. The quality of moral character counts in an officer, and thus it counts in all Academy graduates, but it is also imperative to any leadership position.

General Bennett knew of what he spoke when he noted that the moral precepts within the Cadet Prayer must be "acted upon and believed in" if the necessary personal character in West Point's graduates is to be built. After graduation and commissioning with the Class of 1940, he deployed to North Africa in 1942, then to Casablanca, Tunisia, and Sicily, then on to England and across the Channel, landing on Omaha Beach on June 6, 1944. He led his soldiers through the killing zones of the beach, through the breakout, across the lowlands, and, with his battalion, held the northern shoulder of the Bulge during the terrible winter months of 1944. They then crossed the Rhine and by May of 1945 had fought on to the Elbe River in Czechoslovakia.

Then, after three years of war, he observed the start of another war—the Cold War—as, under the terms of Yalta, Russian troops moved up to the demarcation line along the Elbe and rounded up the columns of wretched humanity fleeing the occupation. He watched as they were marched eastward toward the gulags. He watched as what Churchill would famously call the "Iron Curtain" descended between Eastern and Western Europe.

General Bennett's story demonstrates, as do the many thousands of other silent narratives of wartime officers, that military leaders in war need a very special quality of personal character. In a deeply self-directed way they must discern their duties rightly and fully and then manifest the courage and resilience to persevere in fulfilling them, often under the most adverse of conditions for months and even years at a time.

Great military leaders have commented frequently on this inner quality of personal character that is a necessity for combat leaders and their soldiers alike. General of the Army George C. Marshall noted:

> The soldier's heart, the soldier's spirit, and the soldier's soul are everything. Unless the soldier's soul sustains him, he cannot be relied on and will fail himself,

> his commander, and his country in the end. It is not enough to fight. It is the spirit that wins the victory. Morale is a state of mind. It is steadfastness, courage, and hope. It is confidence, zeal, and loyalty. It is élan, esprit de corps, and determination. It is staying power, the spirit which endures in the end, and the will to win. With it all things are possible, without it everything else—planning, preparation, and production—count for naught.[2]

More recently, another well-respected leader General Colin Powell used the metaphor of the heart in describing the quality of character requisite for effective military leaders. Speaking to the Corps of Cadets in 1998, he noted:

> Our Army is truly a people's Army. This simple code [Duty, Honor, Country] is not something West Point gives to you. It is something that West Point helps you give to yourselves. For all its beauty and history, West Point is a pile of stone until you bring it to life everyday. You can inscribe Duty, Honor, Country, on every granite block and it would mean nothing unless those words are engraved in your heart. You bring the code alive every day by the dozens of decisions you make. . . . Always live by the code inscribed in your heart.[3]

While developing the moral character of its graduates is accepted as a necessity at West Point, that is not the case for many elite colleges and universities in America today. They simply do not see this as a task for themselves. For example, in 1997 during the well-known "Aims of Education" oration presented annually to incoming freshmen at the University of Chicago, Professor John Mearsheimer observed:

> Not only is there a powerful imperative at Chicago to stay away from teaching the truth, but the University also makes little effort to provide you with moral guidance. Indeed, it is a remarkably amoral institution. I would say the same thing, by the way, about all other major colleges and universities in this country. . . . Today, elite universities operate on the belief that there is a clear separation between intellectual and moral purpose, and they pursue the former while largely ignoring the latter. There is no question that the University of Chicago makes hardly any effort to provide you with moral guidance. . . . I am not saying that moral questions are unimportant and that you should pay them little attention in the years ahead. On the contrary, individuals and societies they live in constantly run up against troubling ethical questions, and they have no choice but to wrestle with them and attempt to find the right answers. However, for better or worse, we do not provide much guidance in sorting out those issues. That burden falls squarely on your shoulders.[4]

Subsequently, Mearsheimer's faculty colleague Professor Andrew Abbott, confirmed Mearsheimer's point in 2002 in a similar oration to freshmen, but with a very interesting twist:

> My friend John Mearsheimer had the guts to stand where I am standing four years ago and argue forcefully that college education is not moral education. Theoretically Mearsheimer may have been right—he argued from a strong libertarian and positivist viewpoint—but empirically he was dead wrong. Willy-nilly moral learning will be central in your college experience. You will do a lot of moral learning, even in the classroom, much of it learning to dissemble your real views in discussions that are more apparent than real. . . . Now my point is that for you as individuals, your responsibility for finding education is not limited to the cognitive matters to which the University—following Mearsheimer's argument—largely restricts itself. You need to become educated in morals and emotion as well. And in those areas, I am sad to say, we do not really provide you with anything like the systematic set of exercises in self-development that we provide on the cognitive side. So you are on your own.[5]

What Abbott recognized, and Mearsheimer did not acknowledge, is that postadolescent students are conducting their own search for moral meaning and their own understanding of truth, irrespective of whether the university recognizes that to be the case or not. Fortunately, at West Point, that fact is well understood and, even more importantly, is being acted upon. These lessons may be unique to the Academy, but are useful for any individual seeking an understanding of moral meaning.

IN THE WAKE OF THE COLD WAR: WEST POINT RENOVATES ITS APPROACH TO LEADER DEVELOPMENT[6]

As the Cold War came to a close and the full implications of this historic tectonic shift in relations among nations began to dawn on attentive thinkers, it became apparent that both the type of wars in which the Army would fight and the demands placed on future Academy graduates had fundamentally changed. The first Gulf War in 1990–1991 had shown that American Army divisions were the most professional and devastating land force ever to fight, particularly in armored battles in open terrain. But it was also clear that the Cold War era of great power conflict was at least in a state of strategic pause, and that America no longer faced any real land-power threats. This development had produced much debate, both within the Army and outside it, over the employment of Army forces in Haiti, Rawanda, Bosnia, and Kosovo in the mid-1990s in what were called "humanitarian interventions." At its core, this debate went to the root of the self-concept of the Army officer. Was he or she in the late 1990s a war-fighter or a peacekeeper; and were the demands on the leader the same in both cases, or were they so specialized and different that an Army officer could be competent only in one or the other, but not both? For officers who believe, rightly, that professional competence is in fact a moral imperative, this was a matter of deep concern, and so it was for those who led and served at the Academy during that period of change.

It was at this point that Lieutenant General Daniel Christman entered the scene as Superintendent of the Academy, serving in that capacity during the critical years 1996–2001. For roughly two years a faculty committee established by Christman studied with the Academy's leadership team the Nation's external security environment on one hand, and the internal processes by which cadets were developed into officers on the other. In brief, how should the new security environment affect the Academy's development goals for cadets? The committee's conclusions were straightforward, accompanied by four major recommendations for the Superintendent. First, it recommended that the Academy adopt a broader self-concept as the developmental goal for its graduates, moving well beyond that which had been used at the Academy during the Cold War decades—one in which graduates had seen themselves as confined to the roles of "war-fighter" and "leader of character." The larger debate within the Army had already convinced many senior Army leaders, including those at the Academy, that "war-fighter" was too restrictive to describe the martial role of future graduates, with "warrior" becoming the preferred alternative. But even with this refinement, "warrior" and "leader of character" formed too narrow a goal according to the analysis presented to General Christman.

To create this broader officer identity, the committee recommended the addition of two additional roles—those of "member of a profession" and "servant of the Nation." With regard to membership in a profession, concurrent research, some of which was done in the field among active-duty Army majors, had shown clearly that during the force drawdown of the 1990s, after the first Gulf War, the Army had lost many of the attributes of a profession and was coming to behave in many ways more like a governmental bureaucracy. It had been a difficult time for the Army, called upon to do more with less as its end-strength and its budget were reduced by over one-third during the decade. This change in the institution's culture and behavior produced an exodus of captains and contributed to a loss of professional self-concept among the remaining officers of the middle grades. Thus, it was recommended to General Christman that the Academy address this malady directly by instilling more deeply in future Academy graduates an explicitly professional identity, one based on the understanding that the Army is to be a vocational profession and each officer within it an aspiring or practicing professional.

As to the second added role, servant of the Nation, the committee was responding to several factors. First and foremost, the concept of a graduate's duty to the country had long been a part of the Academy's ethos, most recognizably in the Academy's traditional motto, "Duty, Honor, Country." Thus the committee wanted to codify formally in the new development system that long-term aspect of the Academy's, as well as the Army's, ethos. But in the nearer term, the Academy was resetting its developmental system in the midst of the economic bubble of the late 1990s. Hypermaterialism was rampant at that time in America as members of the boomer generation were "getting theirs" before the bubble burst. Throughout the Army, attractive offers, many by former Academy graduates themselves, were being made to graduates at the rank of captain as they approached the end of their five-year mandatory service obligation. Such recruiters argued that graduates had "paid their contractual obligation" to the Academy and the Nation for their "free education," and it was only fair for them to earn something for themselves in the booming private sector. The effect on retention rates of Academy graduates was distinctly negative. Thus the recommendation to the Superintendent was to counter this environment of materialistic self-centeredness by reinforcing explicitly within the new developmental goal the servant concept with its inherent suggestion of self-sacrifice in a noble calling—that of spending a lifetime in service to one's countrymen. This addition also brought the newly broadened developmental goals directly in line with the Academy's mission:

> To educate, train, and inspire the Corps of Cadets so that each graduate is a commissioned leader of character committed to the values of Duty, Honor, Country; professional growth throughout a career as an officer in the United States Army; and a lifetime of selfless service to the nation.[7]

Note that within the mission statement, the objective—the target of the Academy's efforts—is to be a "commissioned leader of character." While quite accurate, this is a rather wordy way of saying, "Officer," but it does indicate clearly that the mission focus at West Point is to be on the officer's commission and character rather than on the Academy's diploma and the graduate's intellect. To accomplish such a mission, the Academy must produce graduates of such competence and character as to be able to fulfill the obligations of a commission in line with the Nation's expectations of what it means to be an Army officer. Thus, the third recommendation to General Christman was to renew at the Academy use of the term "officership" as the inclusive self-concept subsuming the four individual roles, and making it—officership—the new developmental goal for the Academy entering the 21st century.

Originally coined by Professor Samuel Huntington in the 1950s, the term "officership" had served quite well the early generations of officers in the Cold War.[8] But, with the push toward egalitarianism in America and her civic institutions in the revolutionary post-Vietnam era, the term had fallen out of favor in the Army as being too elitist. The committee recommended reversing that trend by making clear the unique role that commissioned officers play in the Army's and in the Nation's civil-military relations by instilling a deeper understanding of officership in the Academy's future graduates. The Superintendent agreed and subsequently promulgated as strategic guidance for all developmental programs for the decade, 2000–2010, the definition of officership:

> The practice of being a commissioned Army leader, inspired by a unique professional identity that is shaped by what an officer must KNOW & DO, but most importantly, by a deeply held personal understanding and acceptance of what an officer must BE. This unique self-concept incorporates four interrelated roles:
>
> Warrior
>
> Servant of the Nation
>
> Member of a Profession
>
> Leader of a Character

Thus, USMA Strategic Vision–2010 envisioned future Academy graduates as officers "prepared for the uncertainty and ambiguity of military service . . . because they will have reflected upon and developed *a personal understanding of the unique characteristics of their chosen profession and the principles that govern the fulfillment of their office*."[9] The italicized phrase captures the essence of officership—a self-concept, a professional identity, and a personal understanding of the unique characteristics of what it means to be an Army officer within a unique profession. Moreover, the phrase also acknowledges a set of principles that "govern the fulfillment of their office." The Oath of Commission charges an officer to "well and faithfully discharge the duties of the office I am about to enter." But since cadets have not yet served in a commissioned status, the definition of officership was augmented with a set of eight principles intended to guide the cadets' personal development and conduct day by day, both at the Academy, later on active duty, and in their lives moving forward. As the vision document states, "To meet these responsibilities, commissioned officers are guided throughout their lifetime of service, from lieutenant to general to civilian-servant, by the following eight principles: Duty, Honor, Loyalty, Service to Country, Competence, Teamwork, Subordination, and Leadership" [10]

THE PRINCIPLES OF OFFICERSHIP

Duty. Professional officers always do their duty, subordinating personal interests to the requirements of the professional function. They are prepared, if necessary, to lay down their own lives and the lives of their soldiers in the Nation's interest. When an officer is assigned a mission or task, its successful execution is first priority, above all else, with officers accepting full responsibility for their actions and orders in accomplishing it—and accomplishing it in the right way. The officer's duty is not confined, however, to explicit orders or tasks; it extends to any circumstance involving allegiance to the commissioning oath.

Honor. An officer's honor is of paramount importance, derived historically from demonstrated courage in combat. It includes the virtues of integrity and honesty. Integrity is the personal honor of the individual officer, manifested in all roles. In peace, an officer's honor is reflected in consistent acts of moral courage. An officer's word is an officer's bond.

Loyalty. Military officers serve in a public vocation; their loyalty extends upward through the chain of command to the President as Commander in Chief and downward to all subordinates. Officers take care of their soldiers and their families. This loyalty is central to the trust that binds together the military profession for its public servant role.

Service to Country. An officer's motivations are noble and intrinsic: a love for the technical and human aspects of providing the Nation's security and an awareness of the moral obligation to use that expertise self-sacrificially for the benefit of society. The officer has no legacy except for the quality of his or her years of service.

Competence. The serious obligations of officership—and the enormous consequences of professional failure—establish professional competence as a moral imperative. More than proficiency in the skills and abilities of the military art, professional competence in this sense includes attributes of worldliness, creativity, and confidence. Called to their profession and motivated by their pursuit of its expertise, officers commit themselves to a career of continuous study and learning.

Teamwork. Officers model civility and respect for others. They understand that soldiers of a democracy value the worth and abilities of the individual, both at home and abroad. But because of the moral obligation accepted and the mortal means employed to carry out an officer's duty, the officer also emphasizes the importance of the group as against the individual. Success in war requires the subordination of the will of the individual to the task of the group. The military ethic is cooperative and cohesive in spirit, meritocratic, and fundamentally anti-individualistic and anticareerist.

Subordination. Officers strictly observe the principle that the military is subject to civilian authority and do not involve themselves or their subordinates in domestic politics or policy beyond the exercise of the basic rights of citizenship. Military officers render candid and forthright professional judgments and advice and eschew the public advocate's role.

Leadership. Officers lead by example always, maintaining the personal attributes of spiritual, physical, and intellectual fitness that are requisite to the demands of their profession and which serve as examples to be emulated.

Returning to the Academy's mission statement, we must also note that it emphasizes three verbs—"educate, train, and inspire." Taken together, these three verbs define human development—the holistic means by which the Academy accomplishes its mission, the processes by which cadets are introduced to, experience, reflect on, and internalize the defining fundamentals of officership. The committee was well aware that the Academy had always educated and trained its graduates quite well. But, as discussed earlier, educating and training them for "what" was now less clear. Thus we accepted that the Academy must do much better at "inspiring" them to service in whatever future might eventuate.

Thus, the fourth recommendation of the committee was to embed the redefined goal of officership within the Academy's educational and training programs in a manner that was consciously, effectively, and systematically developmental.

This may sound like mere common sense, but in fact the issue was much more urgent at the Academy during General Christman's tenure than it might now appear. Other faculty studies and internal assessments of cadet life had indicated clearly that cadets had become overcommitted and overscheduled. Many cadets were going from activity to activity over their four years, from academics and sports or club activities to summer training and back to academics, in such a hurried and frenetic manner as to preclude the essential processing necessary for human learning and maturation. They had little time, opportunity, or encouragement to reflect on their everyday experiences, often to the point that many activities that should, and otherwise would, have been developmental for them simply were not.

Thus in 2001, the Academy initiated the implementation of a new Cadet Leader Development System (CLDS), one that was specifically tailored to implement the "officership" goal. Far more than in the past, the approach taken was to unify the efforts of staff and faculty across the breadth of the Academy and the vast number of very different activities they led and mentored—from football team, to chapel choir, to physics class, to debate team. The single, common, unifying goal for all was to develop graduates who, as noted above, had thought carefully about what it meant to be an officer and had internalized as their own the fourfold self-concept of officership.

The term "officership" provided the vision, a common developmental goal. But the greatest challenge to the implementation of the new CLDS was to get the institution's staff and faculty to understand that the new goal concerned far more than education and training per se. More important, it dealt with inculcation, inspiration, and transformation. The new goal of officership would be attained only to the extent that all activities worked to change how cadets saw themselves and their place in the world and to bring them to accept for themselves the new meanings that these changes entailed for their lives.

The staff and faculty thus needed to have more than a goal; they also needed a common understanding of human learning and maturation. Moreover, they needed a conceptual framework or model for officer development. Not surprisingly, no such common understandings existed at the Academy at the time (nor were there models describing the process of human development in any published Army doctrine). To be sure, those responsible for individual components of the Academy's programs had their own conceptions of how cadets developed—intellectually, physically, and militarily. But there was no integrating concept, nor was there any documented understanding of how cadets developed morally in terms of their individual character.

Therefore, the final version of the CLDS manual provided for the staff and faculty such a model, one built around what it calls the "five keys to human development":

1. The individual readiness of each cadet to be developed, understanding that they do not all develop at the same rate either by age or class

2. A series of experiences that are meaningful, varied, and marked by difficulty and conflict such that individuals are moved out of their comfort zones to challenge their own worldviews, understandings, and capabilities

3. Consistent support and feedback from staff and faculty acting credibly as role models and mentors to enable individual cadets to make sense of their world in new ways as they transit the demanding and potentially developmental experiences

4. Facilitated reflection on these experiences to allow the cadets to become more self-aware, both of themselves and where they are in the development process as apprentice officers

5. Availability of time, recognizing that while education and training are normally rather short-term interventions, human development is a continuous and open-ended process that will extend well beyond the tenure of cadets at West Point.[11] In fact, for the aspiring officer, such development and commitment to lifelong learning is a true mark of a professional.

The CLDS redesign, and particularly the conceptual model outlined above, were deliberately made to accord with the Army leadership doctrine that has long been cast in the BE-KNOW-DO framework. The Army defines leadership as influencing people by providing purpose, direction, and motivation while operating to accomplish the mission and to improve the organization.[12] The BE-KNOW-DO framework sets forth the characteristics necessary for an effective leader in terms of character, skills, and actions. Attributes and values describe personal character (BE); professional knowledge provides the foundation for, and is manifested in, skills and expertise (KNOW); and the result of BE and KNOW is ultimately seen in the leader's actions (DO). To be authentic to their followers, the actions of leaders (DO) must be an accurate reflection of who they are (BE) and what they have learned professionally (KNOW). In other words, a leader's "walk" must match his or her "talk."

Given this framework, it was clear that, far more than in the Academy's past, the redesigned CLDS focused intentionally on the BE component. The reason for this was straightforward to the committee and quite explicit in their discussions with General Christman. Their studies had shown that in an information-age Army, the rate of technological advance would cause rapid and continuing changes in the American way of war and thus in what a leader must KNOW and DO. Constant reeducation and retraining were to be the norm now that knowledge and skills once learned were increasingly perishable in information-age warfare. But what would remain constant within this welter of change was the necessity, particularly in combat, for a deeply moral character in the commissioned leader, the BE component of Army leadership.

Thus, given the Academy's unique opportunity to develop cadets over a 47-month period (no other full-time educational or training experience for an Army officer exceeds 12 months save for civilian graduate schooling), it was logical to place greatly increased emphasis on the BE component of developing leaders. The officership concept with its four interrelated identity roles provided, by design, specifically for such emphasis.

To move now from the abstract to the concrete, let me offer an example of how this intentional focus on the BE component was implemented in the Academy's developmental programs. The first example is known as the cadet's "cemetery walk," which was intentionally focused on the third verb in the Academy's mission, "to inspire." To help cadets personalize what it means to join the Long Gray Line, sophomore cadets were given the name and obituary of a graduate who had made the ultimate sacrifice for his or her country. They were assigned to go to the Post Cemetery, locate the graduate's headstone, and meditate on the life and sacrifice of their assigned graduate, answering such questions as what he or she accomplished by military service and whether or not the graduate's death was in vain.

They subsequently wrote a reflective essay, to be discussed with a mentor, as to what meaning they could attach to such a life and how it might help them understand their own evolving commitment to officership. Mentors were often astounded at the insights that young cadets displayed, especially given there were no "right" answers. Meaning is what the individual cadet made it to be, but in the process of meaning-making, terms like sacrifice and service lost their hazy abstraction and took on flesh-and-blood significance. At the same time, the cadet's moral character took another stride forward along the path of realization and maturation.[13]

INSIDE CLDS— DEVELOPMENTAL DOMAINS FOR COMPETENCE AND CHARACTER

There are two fundamental ways to describe the total developmental process at West Point, the sum of all those scheduled and unscheduled activities that offer the potential for human learning and change over 47 months. One is to describe it as experienced by the cadets; the second is to describe it as it is organized, planned, and implemented by officials at the Academy. I will use here the first approach, covering the six developmental domains within which cadets experience targeted growth opportunities: the intellectual, military, physical, spiritual, ethical, and social domains. While each domain has been designed to facilitate a particular aspect of growth, to the individual cadet the experiences tend to blend together holistically. However, to the Academy, it is recognized that growth must occur within each discrete domain if the institutional mission of producing commissioned leaders of character is to be accomplished.

Within the Army, leadership, and specifically officership, has always been understood to be a combination of individual competencies and character. Thus three of the domains—the intellectual, military and physical—are associated with the development of professional competence, while the remaining three—spiritual, ethical, and social—relate to the development of personal character.[14]

Compared to past conceptions of leader development at West Point, there are now two new domains—spiritual and social. The Academy has long promoted leader development in the other four domains, that produce attributes essential to all military leaders—the intellect, military skills, physical capabilities, and an internalized ethic. But now, consistent with the committee's recommendation to refine graduates' understanding of what it means to BE an officer, the Academy has two new domains.

This step was not taken without considerable debate, usually focused on why a spiritual domain was needed when the Academy already had an ethical domain.

The Spiritual Ingredient in Character Development at West Point

Human spirituality is a subject of increasing interest to American society today, not only with regard to individuals but also regarding its role in institutional life as well. Of particular interest to the Academy is the research proceeding in three areas—higher education, leader development, and the American workplace. Each of these areas intersects with the mission of the Academy and the roles its graduates will fill.

Definitions of human spirituality abound. Here is an example proposed by a group in higher education:

> Spirituality points to our interiors, our subjective life, as contrasted to the objective domain of material events and objects. Our spirituality is reflected in the values and ideals that we hold most dear, our sense of who we are and where we come from, or beliefs about why we are here—the meaning and purpose we see in our lives—and our connectedness to each other and to the world around us. Spirituality also captures those aspects of our experience that are not easy to define, the mysterious, the sacred, and the mystical. Within the very broad perspective, we believe spirituality is a universal impulse and reality.[15]

Then we have an example suggested by a prominent theorist on leadership in the workplace:

> Our individual sense of who we are—our true, spiritual self—defines us. It creates our mindset, defines our values, determines our actions, and predicts our behavior. As such, spirit is a part of leadership and always has been, whether the individual leader knows it or consciously uses this fact in developing his or her leadership approach. As our work world expands in importance

> and becomes, for many, the central activity of our lives, relating personal spiritual values with work values becomes the central task of leadership. Leaders must get in touch with their own spiritual nature. They must sense the spiritual essence of their followers and must deal directly with the task of creating an organization—defined as a group of people in voluntary relationship—where the essential spiritual needs of each member are considered and made part of the group experience.[16]

For its part, the Academy has newly included the spiritual domain in CLDS, consistent with the increased focus on the BE component of leadership, that is to support development toward the fourth identity of the officer—the Leader of Character. As portrayed in the CLDS manual, the Leader of Character is defined as follows:

> **Leadership**—the process of influencing others to accomplish a mission.
>
> **Character**—those moral qualities that constitute the nature of a leader and shape his or her decisions and actions.
>
> **Leader of Character**—seeks to discover the truth, decide what is right, and demonstrate the courage to act accordingly . . . always.

This definition was carefully crafted to unite both dimensions of this role—capacity to lead and character—in a vital and indivisible whole.[17] All leaders, and leaders-to-be, must come to understand that their actions will flow naturally from their moral character. Only leaders of high moral character can be expected consistently to take actions that the profession and the client it serves will consider ethical. That is the essence of their personal integrity, taking actions that are consistent with and motivated by their own beliefs and fully consistent with the ethics, now internalized, of the profession they have chosen to embrace.

The definition also carefully arrays the full range of moral development required for a leader's actions to be integral with his or her own and the profession's values and beliefs. If leaders are not looking for the truth, if situations resonant with moral implications are not recognized as such, then leaders may base decisions on purely expedient grounds with potentially unethical results. But moral sensitivity alone is not enough. Once leaders know that they are facing a decision with a moral component, they have to invoke moral reasoning and judgment to decide what is right and just. Even then, moral sensitivity, reasoning, and judgment do not always produce ethical behavior. Without the courage to follow through and take the right action—the DO component of leadership—such discerning and reasoned assessments may go for naught. The final element in developing the leader's character, then, is molding the fortitude to do the right thing over and over in the course of a duty day.

One brief but effective method of illustrating this necessary range of moral development is set forth in the following linked sequence:

Personal Truth => Professional Ethic => Leader Actions

Starting from the right, a leader's "walk" (the leader's visible actions) must match his or her "talk" (the leader's spoken or written affirmation of the profession's ethic). One reason it is so easy is that history offers all too many examples of leaders whose walk has not matched their talk and who are therefore rightly disregarded as role models. Toss such an example to a group of cadets for discussion and the heuristic effect is remarkable. They literally teach themselves.

The walk-talk connection also lends itself to edifying discussion because of persistent questions as to what the professional ethic really is. Over the years, the Army has not seen fit to codify the ethic into a single document for officers; rather, parts are to be found in the Declaration of Independence; the Constitution; the officer's Oath of Commission and other legislated statutes that govern the services, particularly the Uniformed Code of Military Justice; the Army's own Seven Values; and the Army's deeply engrained customs and traditions, particularly the now broadly assimilated West Point motto, "Duty, Honor, Country."

Thus, the uncodified nature of the Army's ethic is initially challenging to young officers and apprentices as they seek to find out exactly what "the rules" are. Though it is far too general to be a complete ethical prescription, a useful base for them to touch is the "Requirements of Exemplary Conduct" in the United States Code, Title 10—Armed Forces (3583) which establishes as a matter of law the commander's responsibility for the moral and ethical stewardship of his unit:

> All commanding officers and others in authority in the Army are required:

1. To show in themselves a good example of virtue, honor, patriotism, and subordination
2. To be vigilant in inspecting the conduct of all persons who are placed under their command
3. To guard against and suppress all dissolute and immoral practices, and to correct, according to the laws and regulations of the Army, all persons who are guilty of them
4. To take all proper and necessary measures, under laws, regulations, and customs of the Army, to promote and safeguard the morale, the physical well-being, and the general welfare of the officers and enlisted persons under their command or charge[18]

But how do young cadets develop in a few short years to the point of being able to fulfill this very demanding set of legal duties and obligations, which are far more stringent than the relativistic, postmodern value structure that in many cases characterized their education and acculturation prior to arriving at West Point? The Academy believes that in order to do so, they must continue, while at West Point, the individual search for meaning, values, and personal understanding of truth that is a natural part of postadolescent maturation.

Glancing now at the left side of the Truth=>Ethic=>Actions sequence discussed earlier, we note the results of that search, i.e., the individual's conception of his or her personal truth and beliefs. The challenge, then, is for individuals to continue that search while also reconciling any differences between their own beliefs and the values inherent in professional ethic. In the Army, once commissioned, officers are expected to enforce the norms of the professional ethic, even in the most desperate straits of mortal combat. Long experience, validated by scientific research, has taught the Army that young officers cannot do this well if they have assimilated the profession's moral virtues in a shallow manner due to dissonance with their own beliefs.

Returning to the two additional developmental domains identified by the faculty for inclusion in CLDS—the spiritual and the social—we note that they were added specifically to amplify, for cadets and staff and faculty alike, the full range of character development needed in Academy graduates—particularly to fulfill the role of the leader of character. The previous approach simply lumped together the widely dispersed elements of requisite moral-ethical development as a single entity, often thought of as a mere penumbra of the traditional domains of competence. However, such an approach failed to provide the needed degree of definition and saliency to moral inquiry within the totality of cadet development.

Leaders must be aware of their human spirit and essence, knowing who they are, what they believe, and what they personally understand "truth" to be. They need a personal worldview that is solidly informed and purposefully evolving, thus the addition of the spiritual domain. They also must be grounded in the ethical domain of development. And they must lead through the interpersonal relations they develop with others, thus the social domain. Such development requires leaders to seamlessly join a personal search for meaning—which is inherently a spiritual and moral endeavor—with ethical norms and expectations, and to take actions within a social context. Indeed all leadership activities themselves, occur within a social context.

THE SPIRITUAL DOMAIN

For many West Point cadets, and other future leaders, the search for moral truth will be faith-based.[19] But that is not the case for all. Moreover, as a U.S. Government institution the Academy has no official interest as to whether that is the case or not; the Academy is not in the business of telling cadets that they must be religious or, conversely, that they may not be so.

There are generations of cadets who have freely chosen not to pursue a faith-based approach to their moral development, but have, according to their own testimony, found profound meaning, guidance, and inspiration from the moral ideals so eloquently stated in the Cadet Prayer.

I believe readers will agree after digesting the contents of this book that the moral precepts written into the Cadet Prayer in 1924, its year of composition, are as relevant and apt today as they were then. The Prayer serves equally for all, whether developing the moral character of warriors like Donald Bennett and his classmates graduating in 1940 bound for the bloody fields of World War II, or those deploying to Afghanistan and Iraq during the period 2003–2012. Civilian business leaders, government officials, and younger students of all vocations can also learn from the Prayer on the path to their own professional and personal development.

They had no right to win. Yet they did, and in doing so they changed the course of a war . . . even against the greatest of odds, there is something in the human spirit—a magic blend of skill, faith, and valor—that can lift men from certain defeat to incredible victory.

—Walter Lord, Inscription,
Battle of Midway Panel, World War II Memorial

CHAPTER TWO

The Domain of the Human Spirit

Patrick J. Sweeney, Sean T. Hannah, and Don M. Snider

Anyone with experience in close combat knows that in the face of the paralyzing fear that it brings, not all soldiers, sailors, and airmen acquit themselves with the same degree of inner strength. This is not just a phenomenon of wars past. By one recent account from Iraq, American land forces have conducted in Anbar Province alone over 200 firefights within the confined rooms of concrete houses. In contrast, in Vietnam during the Tet Offensive of 1969, at the height of the urban battle for Hue, U.S. forces conducted only two confined firefights of such intensity.[1]

Today the outcome of such close combat is still determined as it was in ages past, by the will, courage, and perseverance of the stronger combatants and the society they represent. To prevail,

Army leaders need to be individually strong of spirit, called to their professional service, and fortified by the support of the American people. Notwithstanding the advantages offered by modern high technology, we see no chance that the nexus between soldierly spirit and success in close combat will weaken in the future. And neither did those who redesigned the developmental processes for the cadets at West Point.

Americans also accept the primacy of spirit, taking care to enshrine it in their most prominent war memorials. The epigraph at the beginning of this chapter recounts for all visitors to the National World War II Memorial in Washington, DC, that the Battle of Midway would have been lost save for the indomitable spirit of those who fought there. The inscription by Walter Lord makes clear that our servicemen not only won the battle, but also changed the course of history in the Pacific theater of that war. On the other side of the Memorial's ellipse, where the war in Europe and the Atlantic is portrayed, is an inscription for the Ardennes. During the Battle of the Bulge fought in that area, soldiers of the 101st Airborne Division—men of equally indomitable spirit—held out against overwhelming odds even as divisions on both their flanks crumbled under the harshness of freezing blizzards and the German Army's winter offensive.

Today, the Army expects all of its soldiers, and particularly its officer leaders under commission, to manifest the Warrior Spirit and to adhere to the demands of the Warrior's Ethos:

- I will always place the mission first.
- I will never accept defeat.

- I will never quit.
- I will never leave a fallen comrade.[2]

As emphasized in the Memorial inscription alluded to above, this ethos reflects accurately the expectations of the society the Army profession serves. In turn, the Academy is vitally concerned with how best to instill such an indomitable, winning spirit in its graduates, a goal pursued by the various developmental activities cadets experience during their 47-month preparation to receive their commission to lead.

From the time in 2002 when two additional domains of development—spiritual and social—were added to the Cadet Leader Development System (CLDS), a major challenge has been to create among cadets and their faculty mentors a common understanding and language for development within these new domains.

Simply stated, human spirituality is a topic with which many Army officers and other nonmilitary leaders are not viscerally familiar, particularly as it relates to leader development. Regardless of its central role in the warrior ethos as enacted in and out of the combat zone, it is fair to say that the topic is seldom seriously addressed in Army and nonsectarian schools, let alone in the workplace. All too often this is because of concerns that it might be misinterpreted as institutional support for religious spirituality, with any number of church-state issues attached thereto. Thus, neither the Army nor the Academy currently has such language or other tools of pedagogy for development of the human spirit broadly construed.

But it is not just within the Army profession that understanding of the human spirit is needed. An interview was recently conducted with the parents of the first Naval Academy female graduate to be killed in Iraq, Marine Maj. Megan McClure. The journalist conducting the interview was at a loss for words to explain what he learned from her parents. When he offered condolences, Megan's mother replied that "she had died doing what she believed in and that's a great gift." The journalist continued:

> There's an incredible eloquence and depth in these words. . . . There are certain irreducible elements in a person's essence that cannot be separated out and conveniently lent to arguments over politics and war. One of the irreducible elements of Major McClure's life was her belief in the cause, her dedication to the mission. That's military talk that a lot of people don't understand, but it's a point of view that should be draped in honor. I'm not talking about medals or other trappings, but the honor of being true to one's self.[3]

In this chapter, then, we seek to explain that ineffable something the journalist could only describe as "military talk." We do this by presenting briefly a proposed framework to further understanding of human spirituality and what it means to "be true to one's self." We hope that such a framework will assist cadets, faculty, staff members, and leaders of all types, across any industry, in discussing their own development in these newly defined domains.

NARROWING THE TOPIC

Obviously, the subject of the human spirit is immensely broad. The etymology of the word spirit indicates a source in the Latin *spiritus*, meaning breath, later moving to the English language via the Old French esprit, from which we derive esprit de corps to mean the élan or spiritedness of a military organization.[4] The spirit has traditionally been understood to be the animating force, or the energy, within living beings. It has therefore been strongly linked with the occurrence of life itself, distinguishing a living from a nonliving person.

More recently, the subject of the human spirit and its role in mortal combat has been usefully adapted within the Army's own professional literature. As two respected soldier-scholars deeply versed in psychological studies of soldiers following the terrorist attacks of September 11, 2001, and Operation Iraqi Freedom have written: "All soldiers have human needs and most have spiritual needs broadly defined, and converting these needs into strengths of will and character is an important part of combat leadership."[5]

Thus the Army profession has historically considered it important to understand how soldiers could persevere, as at Midway and the Battle of the Bulge, under the most daunting and demoralizing circumstances to produce victory in battle when all rational calculation seemed to indicate that defeat was inevitable. And what the profession has learned is that soldiers who have strong, indomitable spirits can face the unimaginable dangers, horrors, and hardships of combat and still persevere to complete the mission.[6] Indeed, it is the spirit that drives soldiers to self-sacrifice and to prevail. The result that flows from the presence or absence of such spirit can be contrasted across armies, as for example the case of the Iraqi soldiers during the first Gulf War, whose readiness to surrender caused their lines to rapidly fold, leading to a swift defeat.[7]

A leader's spirit imbues in his followers the purpose, direction, will, and courage to do the right thing in any complex and chaotic environment. Nowhere is this more apparent than in the Army profession when faced with combat, where life, death, and strategic interests of the country hinge on the leader's decisions.[8] Leaders who nurture their own and their followers' spirits are preparing to meet the harsh rigors and stresses of combat, literally and figuratively. In doing so, the combat power of a unit or team is enhanced, promoting the growth of the leaders' followers as humans. In its published doctrine, the Army has recognized the critical importance of developing the human spirit, incorporating it, among other places, in its master plan for promoting soldier well-being in its totality.

We have reduced the complexity of spirituality so as to establish a common framework, one that can be implemented and utilized in various belief systems. We recognize some limitation to this model as it may relate to any specific belief system, but do hold that it captures many of the innate core processes that produce a leader's spirit. We acknowledge that some individuals, such as those whose moral quest in based on a specific religious faith, may find this model insufficiently complete to encompass their full definition of spirituality. We believe, however, that it is a model which they can individually add to, thus accommodating it to their own value systems.

Development of the human spirit is thoroughly manifested in who we are now, in who we seek to become, and in most of our thoughts and actions in between. In other words, our spirit represents our evolving human essence from which we cannot divorce ourselves; it will always be an integral part of our being, our actions, and our social interactions.

A DEFINITION OF THE DOMAIN OF THE HUMAN SPIRIT

We can define spirit as "the vital animating force within living beings; the part of a human being associated with mind, will, and feelings; and the essential nature of a person."[9] According to this definition, the human spirit influences how one thinks, acts, and feels about life. Thus, the development of the human spirit should form the cornerstone of any leader development program.

To advance our understanding of how the human spirit develops, we revisited the literatures of humanist psychology and human spirituality. The humanist psychologists view such development in terms of realizing one's full potential, or self-actualization. To do so, people must determine their purpose in life, discover who they truly are, and develop the strength to pursue activities that will develop the true or authentic self regardless of any contrary expectations from others.[10] Similarly, scholars of spirituality, particularly as regards college students, view individual spiritual development as the inward quest to discover one's identity, purpose, meaning, truth about the world and life after death, and how to live a life that matters.[11]

Integrating the concepts from both the humanist psychology and spiritual literatures, we offer the following definition of the development of the human spirit:

It is an individual's search to find:

- One's true self in terms of core values and beliefs (character)
- Meaning and purpose in life, making a difference and thus making life worth living
- Truth about the world, enlightenment
- Relationships that bring fulfillment
- The autonomy to pursue realization of one's full potential[12]

Psychological Components of the Domain of the Human Spirit

To discuss the development of the human spirit, we focus on identifying the psychological structures and states that comprise an individual's spirit. Common themes found in both literatures were the following:

- To develop the spirit, one must engage in self-reflection and introspection; self-awareness is critical.
- Increased self-awareness allows one to solidify his/her values and belief system (character), which forms the foundation of one's personal philosophy or worldview.

- One's evolving worldview is used to determine truth and make meaning out of experiences.
- Spiritual development is the individual's responsibility; institutions can only provide conducive conditions.
- In order to establish positive relationships and further refine one's worldview, one must develop social awareness (empathy and respect), which is necessary to understand others' emotions and viewpoints.
- An individual must have a strong conviction (faith) that living according to one's values and beliefs and striving to realize one's potential will lead to a fulfilling and satisfying life.

Since development of the human spirit is universal and occurs in all cultures,[13] we accept Abraham Maslow's proposition that innate human needs drive the process.

We propose that the domain of the human spirit consists of the psychological components as depicted in Figure 2-1: a worldview, self-awareness, a sense of agency, social awareness, and faith. These components are interrelated, and taken together they foster the growth of the human spirit. We believe that an understanding of these components and the relationships between them can facilitate individual's journeys toward spiritual development while also providing leaders and mentors insights as to how best to contribute to or otherwise facilitate these explorations.

Before we proceed, we need to clarify the semantic distinction between *human spirit* and the complementary noun *spirituality*. While we view the former as a product—i.e., the vital animating force or essence defining us as uniquely human—that one may choose to develop over time, the latter can be viewed as the degree of receptivity one feels toward undertaking such development. Specifically, the human spirit is a leader's current state as it relates to possession of the components of the framework (Figure 2-1). At any point in his career apprenticeship, a leader has a certain level of agency, faith, self-awareness, and social awareness, and his aim should be to gradually increase the level and integration of these qualities. *Spirituality*, by way of comparison, can be seen as a leader's inclination and orientation to pursue such development and enlightenment within the domain of the human spirit.

In certain contexts, it is useful to use the noun *spirituality* (along with its adjectival cognate *spiritual*) in a second sense, that is, as applying to the *process* whereby the components of worldview, self-awareness, sense of agency, social awareness, and faith interact to promote growth of the human spirit, as depicted by the bidirectional influence arrows in Figure 2-1. Thus, the ameliorative transformation we seek in the human spirit of leaders can well be described as a *spiritual* quest or an adventure in *spirituality*.

We turn now to a description of each component of the domain of the human spirit.

WORLDVIEW

A person's worldview can be understood as being the lens through which he/she views the grand stage of human existence. It is an individual's personal life philosophy used to make meaning out

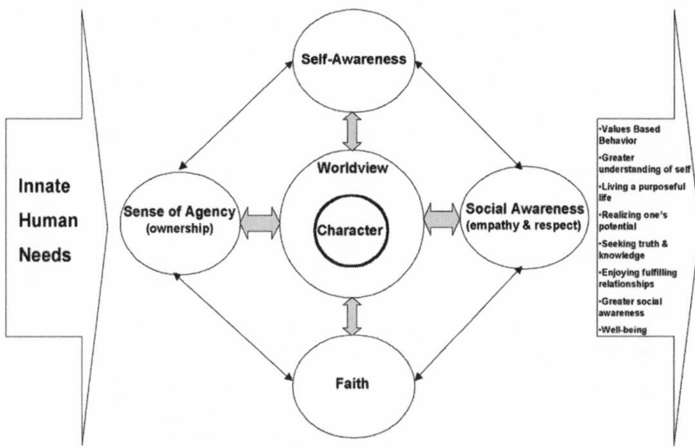

Figure 2-1 **Conceptualization of the Domain of the Human Spirit**

of experiences and to provide direction and purpose in life. This complex cognitive framework determines what one attends to, how one interprets information and events, the knowledge and experiences one seeks out, and how one behaves. Not static, but dynamic, a person's worldview actually influences every aspect of his/her current life and future goals. Thus, a person's worldview is the foundation upon which the development of the human spirit rests.

This cognitive framework contains at any point in time an individual's collection of knowledge and assumptions about how the world operates; truths about the world based on learning and experiences; a system for determining truth and meaning; values and beliefs that one should live by; a vision of a life rendered worth living by making a meaningful contribution;

reflections on one's mortality; and beliefs about what comes after death. Individuals continuously refine and develop their worldviews through the acquisition of new knowledge, reflection on their own and others' experiences, introspection concerning their values, beliefs, and meaning-making systems, and discussing with others topics about their human essence.

Worldviews are largely shaped through the socialization processes of the mediating institutions of family, school, and church, among others. Parents' childrearing techniques, the community's cultural expectations, educational and life experiences, and religious or philosophical practices all play a role in the development of the early worldview of children. The cornerstone of a person's worldview, as depicted in Figure 2-1, is one's values and beliefs system or character. This system defines who the person is and what the person stands for, serves as a guide for determining behavior—especially in ambiguous and chaotic situations—and also provides the courage and will to act in accordance with one's beliefs and values. For most people, adolescence is the time they begin their struggle to discover their own identity and character and to establish themselves as independent and unique individuals. Thus, the college or post-high school experiences are critical periods in which to establish coherent and soundly evolving worldviews.

From the military perspective, the soldier's character provides the physical courage to fight in close combat and the moral courage to act in accord with, and to enforce, the profession's ethics. A major insight offered by Lord Moran in his classic book *The Anatomy of Courage* is that "a man of character in peace is a man of courage in war."[14] A strong character provides a person with a sense of continuity and stability in one's day-to-day life.[15] It is here that the moral precepts of the Cadet Prayer resonate so strongly, serving as a moral compass for guiding future behavior. The compass points are the attributes that all leaders require, e.g., "Make us to choose the harder right instead of the easier wrong and never to be content with a half-truth when the whole can be won."

Finally, in the interpersonal realm, a leader's worldview is central to his/her leadership as it provides the cognitive lens through which to experience and make meaning of personal experiences as well as those of followers. It is this ability to make meaning and communicate that meaning to their followers that enables leaders to provide purpose, motivation, and direction amid times of stress.

SELF-AWARENESS

Reflection and introspection are the processes individuals use to enhance development of their human spirits. Through reflection and self-examination people gain insights into life's most pregnant questions, such as: Who am I? What is my purpose in life? What is a life worth living? Who do I want to become? What can I believe in? How do I live a life that will make a difference? and How can I be happy? Answers to these pressing introspective questions help form and shape one's worldview and identity.

Indeed leaders cannot separate their own self-concept from their concept of the external world. The self-concept is in fact an idiosyncratic "construct" leaders develop over their lifespan as they interpret and encode their personal experiences into memory.[16] In essence, leaders learn who they are as they interact with and receive feedback from their social environment. It is through dedicated reflection about these experiences that the self with its human essence becomes "known" to the individual. We argue that to the extent leaders' developmental experiences contain elements of the spiritual, the more they reflect on these elements the greater will be the growth of their own human spirit. This drive for reflection and self-awareness—to know oneself—is part of one's spiritual orientation, a part of one's *spirituality*.

Reflection and introspection allow leaders to make sense out of their own and others' experiences and in the process create new meaning or knowledge. Reflection and introspection also help organize and integrate the content of their worldviews. Therefore, everyone, especially young adults, should set aside time for reflection, particularly in solitude, to gain a penetrating view of their inner lives. Leaders can use various activities as opportunities to facilitate reflection and introspection: journaling, sitting in a quiet location, writing a paper on a topic that requires introspection, listening to music, walking, hiking, trail running, meditating, biking, praying, participating in a retreat, watching the sun rise or set, and lifting weights. The venue or type of activity is not important; the keys are solitude and quiet time to reflect and assess one's inner life.

These periods of reflection and introspection provide leaders with the opportunity to question and evaluate aspects of their worldviews, which were shaped for them mostly through early socialization and learning processes. It is through continuous reflection and introspection that leaders gain the ability to step outside those handed-down worldviews shaped largely by parents and culture, and then to self-author their own unique worldviews. These processes of enhancing self-awareness provide leaders with a greater understanding of who they truly are, who they want to become, how to determine truth and meaning, and how they should lead their lives. All of this promotes the development of their worldview schemas. It is thus through self-awareness that leaders gain the ability to chart and focus their quest to develop their human essence.

Such spiritual self-awareness is critical to leadership. Before they can provide value-based leadership and facilitate idealization and inspiration in others, leaders must have a firm grasp of who they are, what their core values and beliefs are, and their self-concept as it relates to their role as a leader. It is only the self-aware and resolute leader who can operate effectively when faced with challenges and provide the moral compass for his/her followers' actions.

SENSE OF AGENCY

The development of the human spirit is an active, dynamic, and personal journey that the individual owns exclusively. Agency involves assuming ownership of and responsibility for one's spiritual development and having a sense of confidence that one can successfully guide this developmental quest. Individuals who assume responsibility for such development and actively engage in activities that foster the growth of their spirits tend to live satisfying and contented lives.[17] Those who fail to take responsibility for the development of their human spirit are forced to live with the worldviews that society imposes on them, which can cause extreme psychological distress.

A sense of agency empowers people to reflect, evaluate, and self-author their own worldview. It provides the independence of thought to chart their own path for the development of their spirit and to step away from the expectations of others.[18] In a sense, such agency provides them with essential control over their own destiny. Individuals with a sense of agency will actively seek out activities that impart new knowledge, create new experiences that reinforce or challenge their existing worldview, and promote self-reflection and introspection in order to develop and strengthen the human spirit.[19] These empowered individuals will demand the freedom to develop their spirit in the way they see fit. Freedom of thought and action are necessary conditions for one's sense of agency to grow.[20]

SOCIAL AWARENESS

Social awareness is important to the development of the human spirit because without respect and empathy a person will have trouble forming connections with other people and ideas. This will in turn hinder the ability to form new relationships and to gain new knowledge about diverse cultures and ideas. Without such experiences there can be little broadening or refinement of one's worldview.

Thus, the quest to develop the human spirit requires people to develop the social skills necessary to establish positive relationships with others. Respect for others is the first social skill one must develop. Respect is simply recognizing and acknowledging that others have the right to hold different values, beliefs, and customs and that one must, without giving up one's own beliefs and values, show them due consideration and be open to learn from alternative views. This form of toleration is bedrock to democratic pluralism, the Constitutionally founded form of government that the Army profession is sworn to defend. Respect also entails the ability to appreciate others and their beliefs without immediately judging them as being inferior because they differ from one's own. Showing respect for others' views communicates that they are acknowledged, valued, and accepted as humans, which sets the conditions for positive interactions and learning from each other.[21]

Moreover, to truly understand others an individual must have the empathic ability to place himself/herself in the shoes of others and view the world through their lens. Social awareness enhances empathy by increasing the person's capability to recognize emotions in others.[22] Empathy allows one to see the situation as others see it, to feel the emotions that others feel, and to experience the motivational forces that compel behavior by others as they experience these forces.[23] This is a daunting challenge for all of us! But a person can use insights into others' perspectives to expand and refine his/her own worldview and to develop positive relationships that communicate understanding, acceptance, and care for others.[24]

Such social awareness is central to effective leadership. We discussed at the beginning of this chapter the importance of the military leader's human spirit in facing the perils of combat while behaving within the bounds of the warrior ethos. To be able to do so, leaders must be aware of, accepting of, and able to leverage and draw upon their followers' inspired motivations, their human spirits. Indeed, we suggest that such leadership should be seen and valued as a unit combat power multiplier.

FAITH

Faith is defined in *Webster's Universal Encyclopedic Dictionary* as "something that is believed especially with strong conviction; allegiance to duty or to a person; a firm belief in something for which there is no proof; complete trust; or fidelity to one's promises." Such faith is critical because it provides the direction and will to persist in the continuous, often arduous, journey of life and the trust and hope that the journey will produce a life worth living.

Simply stated, faith is what keeps us striving toward life's goals, the striving that fuels our hope for a successful, meaningful life. For many soldiers and cadets, such faith will be grounded primarily in one of the world's religions, but if not that is a personal choice to be respected by all. As mentioned earlier, many individuals place their faith in several belief systems at once, especially during the intense interactions between higher education and spiritual awareness and growth.

For the purposes of this discussion, then, the kind of faith we are interested in is intrapersonal; it is a person's confident belief in and commitment to a life-long quest to develop and to live in accordance with one's values and principles—to be true to oneself as was Maj. Megan McClure. Otherwise, what motivation leads us to live and strive, or even more, to serve others? As the epigraph to this chapter reminds us, such faith was an element evident in the indomitable spirit of those who won the Battle of Midway and other battles critical to national survival.

At the intrapersonal level, then, such faith provides a strong sense of conviction or expectancy that there is a path which, if followed, will lead to enjoying the experiences of truth, happiness, fulfillment, and, if one so believes, nonworldly rewards such as eternal life. That path consists of living by one's own values and principles; continuously refining knowledge of the inner self through reflection and introspection; striving to develop one's full potential by seeking out new knowledge and experiences; working for noble pursuits that have a positive impact on others; developing positive relationships with family, friends, and associates; and appreciating and respecting others. Thus, the kind of faith we are addressing here keeps the person moving forward to develop his/her essence, to seek truth, and to live above the common level of life out of the firm belief that it is the right thing to do.

For the Army officer in particular, such faith works in the same way except that it does so within the context of the profession's service to the American people. Such faith provides officers the courage to behave according to their values and principles and according to the profession's ethic in the face of bureaucratic pressures to do otherwise; to seek growth experiences that stretch capabilities instead of "playing it safe" with the next assignment; to explore and understand new cultures despite initial discomforts; to engage in self-reflection and introspection even when it is painful; to join a noble and prosocial profession such as the Army instead of pursuing financial wealth; to focus on the good in the world when the news media focus on the negative; and to continue to strive to have a positive influence when others do not seem to value or appreciate it.

INNATE HUMAN NEEDS

As we mentioned earlier, people from every culture are engaged in the quest to develop their essence, so it is logical to accept the hypothesis that innate human needs drive the development of the human spirit. In his theory of human motivation, Abraham Maslow proposed that the following hierarchy of human needs, ranging from the most basic to the most advanced, drive the development of the human spirit:

- Physiological (survival needs)
- Safety or security (control and predictability)
- Belongingness and love (affiliation)
- Esteem (efficacy and respect)
- Knowing and understanding (curiosity and insights)
- Experiencing the aesthetic (order, symmetry, and closure)
- Self-actualization (reaching one's full potential)[25]

It is in striving to satisfy these innate needs that the development of the human spirit is advanced. According to Maslow's theory, as each level of need is met, the need at the next level of advancement becomes more dominant as a source of motivation. Thus, once a given need is mostly satisfied (e.g., safety), that need diminishes as a source of motivation, while advanced-order needs (e.g., belongingness) take over as more dominant sources of motivation. If an individual is working to satisfy advanced needs and satisfaction of a more basic need is threatened, the person may redirect efforts to meet the basic need.

Development of the Human Spirit

Ultimately, assisting developing leaders in their spiritual growth toward the most advanced level, self-actualization, will be facilitated when leadership development experiences provide broad opportunities to advance through the complete hierarchy of human needs in a progressive manner. We turn now to a discussion of how an individual's striving to meet the various needs contributes to development of the psychological structures and states that, as earlier posited, comprise the domain of the human spirit.

NEED FOR SAFETY

Beyond the most basic need of all—survival—a person's need for safety compels him/her to develop a worldview or personal life philosophy in order to understand and accommodate to the immediate environment. There are two aspects of the safety need: physical and psychological. The physical aspect is met when people feel secure and protected against threats from criminals, nature, and anything that could do them harm. Regarding the psychological aspect, people feel safe when they have a means to organize circumstances in an orderly and predictable manner so that unexpected, unmanageable, and dangerous events are less likely to happen. Thus, they innately seek a sense of control over the events of life.[26]

A leader gains a sense of control over such events through the establishment of a worldview, enabling prediction and sound expectation as to what is coming. This schema contains knowledge and assumptions about how the world operates, a values and beliefs system, ideas about one's role or purpose in the world, and a vision of who the person is striving to become. Thus, a worldview provides the ability to reasonably extrapolate to a provisional view of future situations and how others will act and react, thus providing a sense of control and predictability in life.

NEED TO BELONG AND BE LOVED

The innate affiliation need manifests itself in a desire to connect to something, or someone, outside and more powerful than the self. The key to meeting this innate need is the ability of individuals to transcend the self and subordinate their own interests. This transcendence involves the humbling realization that one is but a small actor in this vast universe and that a connection with a more powerful force can empower, enrich, and inspire one's life. The source of this connection could be an individual, a group, a supreme deity, an idea, a philosophy, or a calling to vocation such as the officer's calling to the Army profession or the businessman's call to a certain industry.

This innate desire to connect with someone or something more powerful than the individual serves an adaptive function because it contributes to one's sense of safety through physical and psychological support and also enhances one's worldview by serving as a source of new knowledge and inspiration for one's purpose in life. Being loved, valued, and accepted by others reaffirms one's perceptions of self-worth and also contributes to feelings of wholeness. Thus, individuals need to seek connections with people, groups, ideas, or deities outside of themselves to help shape and develop their human spirits.[27]

The military profession has long recognized the empowering benefits of a greater sense of confidence, safety, and purpose gained from meeting soldiers' innate need for affiliation. This is why the U.S. Military places such great emphasis on unit heritage, unit integrity, promoting selfless service and teamwork, and demanding loyalty in terms of taking care of one's buddy and the unit. For example, a soldier who has established positive relationships (connections) with other members in the squad has eight other people looking out for his/her safety and sharing the burdens of combat, which boosts his/her sense of confidence and safety and also greatly increases the soldier's probability of survival.[28] In addition, the connection with others provides a social support network that helps the soldier deal with the fears and stresses of combat.

Through such a social network, an individual can learn new knowledge about how to deal with stress; express fears and other emotions; receive understanding, acceptance, and validation for emotions experienced; learn combat survival techniques; and, most important, learn new ways to come to terms with traumatic events.[29] The collective meaning-making that takes place in any social network tends to enhance a person's worldview. Thus, by forming these connections with others and their group or team, each individual gains a greater sense of confidence in his/her own ability as well as the team's to successfully complete the mission, or task, at hand. In fact, in a military setting, soldiers who fail to make connections with others tend not to last long in the combat zone. They either succumb to stress or are injured or killed early in their tours because they are not fully connected to the social support system in the unit.[30] Most important, these connections between soldiers serve as the primary source of motivation for them to fight.[31] Cohesion continues to play a critical role in individual and team performance.

NEED FOR ESTEEM

The innate need for esteem plays a significant role in the development of a person's sense of agency (responsibility for and ownership of one's destiny) and also impacts the development of one's worldview. Maslow proposed that the innate need for esteem entailed two interrelated components: self-esteem and gaining the esteem of others. Self-esteem consists of a person's feeling that he/she has the ability to act independently to achieve life goals and to handle life's challenges. Thus self-esteem is very important in the development of a sense of agency. Individuals who feel confident that they can chart and master their own life journeys are more likely to assume the responsibility for developing their human spirit. They will actively seek out and engage in activities that promote the development of their worldviews. On the other hand, people with low self-esteem are more likely to have a lesser sense of agency regarding the development of their human spirit because they do not feel they have the ability to control their destiny. Individuals with low self-esteem are more apt to let society and others influence or even dictate the development their human spirit.

Receiving the esteem of others in terms of praise, recognition, status, and appreciation provides external verification of one's abilities and worth to others. This validation of one's value to others enhances self-esteem and a sense of agency, and facilitates positive emotions and human flourishing. In addition, Maslow explained that being valued by others provides individuals with the sense that they are important and that their presence in the world makes a difference, all of which bolsters faith in their developmental journey and their evolving worldviews. Individuals must be imbued not only with such personal esteem, but also with pride and esteem in their job and team, which promotes cohesion and a collective sense of purpose.

NEED TO KNOW AND UNDERSTAND

The innate human need to know and understand significantly contributes to the development of a person's worldview and feelings of safety. Individuals' curiosity and desire to seek out and learn new knowledge helps them gain a greater understanding of how the world works and how people live in it, which adds to the richness and complexity of their own worldview. In turn, a more refined worldview helps them to perceive more orderliness, meaning, and predictability in both themselves and the world, thus contributing to a greater sense of safety.

The innate need for knowledge and understanding also contributes to individuals' motivation to engage in self-reflection and introspection with the hope of discovering insights about themselves. This increased self-awareness helps people answer life's pressing questions concerning identity, purpose, worthy contributions, and how to achieve happiness.

Lastly, the need for knowledge and understanding plays a role in promoting a sense of agency in people to develop their own essence and inner strength. Such people will likely attribute their knowledge-seeking behaviors to internal states, thus providing the perception of agency or self-directed development.[32] Particularly during stressful times, leaders and their teams must find a level of coherence and acceptance, hence satisfying the innate need for understanding.

NEED FOR SELF-ACTUALIZATION

Self-actualization is the most advanced level of Maslow's hierarchy. The need for self-actualization contributes to the growth of the human spirit by motivating people to develop themselves to become "who they must be" in order to have a life that is meaningful and makes a difference. Carl Rogers, a noted humanist psychologist, proposes that the need for self-actualization is the "mainspring of life" that propels people to seek out activities that cause them to grow, mature, and become autonomous in their quest to reach their full human potential. According to Rogers, to achieve self-actualization a person must:

- Determine his/her purpose in life
- Live a responsible, moral, and self-restrained life (positive values and beliefs system)
- Be confidently proactive in initiating change to promote growth and independence (agency)
- Engage in reflection to develop one's self-awareness (introspection)

- Form connections to sources outside of the self (affiliation)
- Learn to enjoy the simple pleasures of life (achieving happiness).

Thus, according to the views of both Rogers and Maslow, the innate drive toward self-actualization will develop a person's full human potential and, as well, one's human spirit.

Self-actualization is central to the identity of development as a leader. Leaders tend to envision their current self and also a more distant possible self which they would like to become—their ideal self.[33] It is through envisioning, most likely by use of a role model, and by lucidly visualizing the "gaps" between the current and possible self, that leaders will be motivated to develop and actualize that possible self.

To the extent that leaders and their followers envision a possible self with higher capabilities for faith, agency, self-awareness, and social awareness they will have greater drive toward development in the domain of the human spirit. More specifically, this drive and its developmental manifestations will be experienced as a heightened sense of spirituality.

EXPERIENCING THE DEVELOPMENT OF THE COMPONENTS OF THE HUMAN SPIRIT

In the last portion of this chapter, we present various emotional, cognitive, and behavioral indicators of how the development of the human spirit is manifested and experienced. Indeed, we believe these indicators should serve both as a rudimentary road map to chart the development of the human spirit, and as milestones to chart progress toward the possible self. Research has shown that development will occur through vicarious learning such as observing role models and imagining instructive experiences, e.g., having followers imagine themselves successfully engaging in positive spiritual behaviors and achieving their own envisioned possible selves.[34] More than likely, multiple indicators from each one of the three areas—emotional, cognitive, and behavioral—will apply. The more indicators that do apply, the greater will be the progress.[35]

Emotional Indicators

Development of the worldview manifests itself in feelings of safety, orderliness, and peace. The growth of a more complex worldview provides individuals with a greater ability to predict and make meaning out of their experiences. Thus, events do not surprise and/or shock them as much as they did earlier, and individuals no longer feel naïve regarding how the world operates. The cornerstone to one's sensation of safety and peace is the feeling that one has the correct values and beliefs (character) to function effectively in the world and to live a life that makes a difference. As individuals experience progress in becoming who they want to be and realizing their potential, they assume a sense of well-being and contentment with life. Furthermore, individuals know that their sense of agency is developing when they feel a sense of empowerment to self-author their own values and beliefs and to control their journey to realize their potential.

Individuals feel they own and have control over their destiny because they have the capability to create the lives they seek. Growth in social awareness manifests itself with feelings that one has the ability to read and understand other people, see the world from others' point of view, and establish positive relationships with them. Individuals feel a greater sense of respect and appreciation for human life and also a greater sense of compassion toward others. They feel that their own lives are enriched by other people, who aid them in their journey of self-actualization.

Growth in self-awareness manifests itself in feelings that one is getting to know and understand oneself better. Such individuals are not afraid to reflect on and evaluate their inner lives because they feel increasingly comfortable with who they are and what they want to become. Finally, they know their faith is developing when they feel a strong conviction that living a life based on one's values and beliefs is right and will lead to fulfillment in spite of social pressures to live otherwise.

Emotional Indicators of Development of the Human Spirit

INDICATOR	HUMAN SPIRIT COMPONENT	INNATE NEED
You feel a sense of safety, peace, orderliness, and understanding in life.	Worldview	Safety
You feel that you are on the right path in life.	Worldview/Self-awareness	Self-actualize
You feel that you have a greater ability to make meaning out of your experiences.	Worldview	Know and understand

INDICATOR	HUMAN SPIRIT COMPONENT	INNATE NEED
You feel that your vocation contributes to your sense of purpose in life.	Worldview	Self-actualize
You feel that you have created a good and true set of values and beliefs to guide your life.	Worldview/Self-awareness	Know and understand
You feel a sense of confidence to interact with people from different cultures.	Worldview/Self-awareness	Safety
You feel driven to seek out new knowledge and experiences.	Worldview	Know and understand
You feel that you have the power to achieve your goals and dreams in life.	Sense of Agency	Esteem
You feel that you control your journey to develop your spirit.	Sense of Agency	Esteem
You feel that you are making progress toward becoming the person you would like to be.	Sense of Agency	Esteem
You feel a sense of curiosity for and excitement about learning.	Sense of Agency	Know and understand
You feel that you have the power to author your own values and beliefs and not have society or others dictate them for you.	Sense of Agency	Esteem
You feel that others accept you for who you are.	Social Awareness	Affiliation
You feel connected to and understood by others.	Social Awareness	Affiliation

INDICATOR	HUMAN SPIRIT COMPONENT	INNATE NEED
You feel that others respect, value, and trust you.	Social Awareness	Esteem
You feel a greater sense of self-control.	Self-awareness/Sense of Agency	Safety/ Esteem
You feel more integrated as a person.	Self-awareness	Know and understand
You feel that you have a greater understanding of who you are, your purpose, and direction in life.	Self-awareness	Know and understand/Self-actualize
You feel that your values and beliefs are right and will lead you to a fulfilling life.	Faith	Self-actualize
You feel commitment to living a principle-centered life and developing your potential.	Faith	Self-actualize

Cognitive Indicators

Individuals know that their worldview is developing when they generally understand how the world operates, accepting the existence of both good and evil. They become more open to, and not threatened by, new ideas, experiences, cultures, and beliefs. They develop a thirst for knowledge. Such individuals increasingly consider their own values and beliefs when making decisions because their need to maintain integrity to self outweighs the desire to meet the expectations of others. When this occurs, individuals have the autonomy to control their journey to develop their human essence.

Moreover, such individuals know they are developing their self-awareness when they regularly reflect on their strengths and weaknesses, their life goals, and the progress they are making toward developing their potential. They question and evaluate their values and beliefs because they want to know truth. They reflect on experiences to make meaning out of them and evaluate the implications for their worldview. The cognitive indicators of social awareness entail a greater understanding of people and a willingness to view others as individuals rather than applying prejudicial group stereotypes. One also develops a greater understanding of the frailty of human nature, resulting in a greater sense of compassion and desire to help others (altruism). Individuals understand and accept that others have a right to have different viewpoints, values, and beliefs, and that just because these views are different, they are not necessarily wrong, bad, or inferior.

Cognitive indicators of the development of one's sense of agency are thinking routinely of activities to develop the spirit, monitoring the progress of the journey, and making adjustments as needed. Individuals know and accept that they are fully responsible for and in control of their own spiritual development. As discussed earlier in connection with the emotional indicators, they feel a sense of autonomy enabling them to step away from the expectations of others and pilot their own journey with an increasingly strong belief, or faith, that the quest to develop the spirit will lead to a meaningful, noble, and fulfilling life. Such a person more and more lives a principle-centered life, even in the face of social pressures to do otherwise, because such is the right thing to do to be true to one's self.

Cognitive Indicators of Development of the Human Spirit

INDICATOR	HUMAN SPIRIT COMPONENT	INNATE NEED
You possess a greater understanding of how the world operates.	Worldview	Safety/Know and understand
You have more realistic expectations about what is coming your way.	Worldview	Safety/Know and understand
You are more open to new ideas, different cultures, and different belief systems.	Worldview	Know and understand/ Affiliation
You consider your own values and beliefs when making decisions regarding behavior.	Worldview/Self-awareness	Safety
You have less need to impose control in relationships with others.	Worldview	Safety/Affiliation
You have a sense of curiosity about the world.	Worldview	Know and understand
You think of activities to develop your spirit.	Worldview	Know and understand
You refine your developmental plan frequently to ensure that the direction of your life is on track.	Sense of Agency	Self-actualize
You have autonomy to develop your own values and beliefs.	Sense of Agency	Esteem/Self-actualize
You believe that you have the ability to control your own journey to develop your spirit.	Sense of Agency	Esteem/Self-actualize
You believe that you are capable and talented enough to accomplish your life goals.	Sense of Agency	Esteem

INDICATOR	HUMAN SPIRIT COMPONENT	INNATE NEED
You believe that others have the right to hold differing views and that different does not mean incorrect or bad.	Social Awareness	Know and understand
You have a greater understanding of how others and groups operate in the world.	Social Awareness	Know and understand
You have the ability to read people's emotions.	Social Awareness	Know and understand
You understand that all humans have needs for being valued, accepted, and respected.	Social Awareness	Know and understand
You can understand others' perspectives when making decisions.	Social Awareness	Know and understand
You have fewer negative evaluations (prejudices) toward groups of people.	Social Awareness	Know and understand
Since all humans have value, you are more compassionate in your dealings with others.	Social Awareness	Know and understand
You accept others who differ from you and do not judge them because they are different.	Social Awareness	Affiliation
You are open to questioning and evaluating your own values and beliefs.	Self-awareness	Know and understand
You periodically reflect on and evaluate your values, beliefs, and life goals to ensure they are true and lead to a life worth living.	Self-awareness	Self-actualize

INDICATOR	HUMAN SPIRIT COMPONENT	INNATE NEED
You possess a greater understanding of who you are and who you want to be in the future.	Social Awareness	Know and understand
You believe that your developmental journey will produce a meaningful, noble, and fulfilling life.	Faith	Self-actualize
You continue to consider your values and beliefs when deciding what is right even when others are encouraging you to do otherwise.	Faith/Sense of Agency/Self-awareness	Know and understand/Self-actualize
You are optimistic about realizing your full human potential and creating a satisfying life.	Faith	Self-actualize
You look at obstacles and setbacks in life as a means to grow and become stronger.	Faith	Esteem

Behavioral Indicators

Individuals know that their worldview is developing when they find themselves behaving in a more authentic manner based on their own values and beliefs. They engage naturally in activities that promote learning about new subjects, people, and cultures, such as reading about or experiencing different philosophical and religious beliefs in a search to find truth. They realize their sense of agency is growing the more they engage regularly in activities that help realize their full potential. Likewise, their self-awareness is growing when they take time routinely to engage in reflection and introspection, particularly regarding their experiences, values, beliefs, and goals in life. This can take the form of journaling, documenting life visions and goals, carrying on internal, positive dialogues with themselves, praying, or meditating on life's eternal questions.

Behavioral indicators of a developing social awareness are treating all people with respect, engaging in volunteerism to help others, cooperating with difficult people, and being more understanding, tolerant, and forgiving of others and their weaknesses, including being less judgmental. Greater social awareness is also manifested in the formation of positive and cooperative relationships. The main indicators of the strengthening of an individual's faith is a more consistent, daily striving to live a value-based life, and taking action to follow one's developmental journey despite the arduousness of the task—more often doing "the harder right instead of the easier wrong," as enjoined by the Cadet Prayer.

Behavioral Indicators of Development of the Human Spirit

INDICATOR	HUMAN SPIRIT COMPONENT	INNATE NEED
You act in accordance with your beliefs and values to do the right thing.	Worldview/Sense of Agency	Safety/Self-actualize
You are authentic when dealing with others.	Worldview/Sense of Agency	Safety/Self-actualize
You seek activities to learn new knowledge.	Worldview	Know and understand
You associate with diverse people.	Worldview/Social Awareness	Know and understand/ Affiliation

INDICATOR	HUMAN SPIRIT COMPONENT	INNATE NEED
You engage others in discussions about the meaning and purpose of life.	Worldview/Social Awareness	Know and understand/ Affiliation
You feed your passion for learning.	Worldview	Know and understand
You write out goals and objectives as part of a developmental plan to develop your human spirit.	Sense of Agency/Self-awareness	Self-actualize
You actively seek out and engage in activities that develop your spirit (meditation, prayer, self-reflection, new experiences, etc.).	Sense of Agency	Esteem/Know and understand
When confronted with situations you cannot make meaning of, you seek out new knowledge or talk to friends, parents, or mentors to help.	Sense of Agency	Know and understand
You look for and take advantage of opportunities to gain exposure to differing viewpoints.	Sense of Agency	Know and understand
You take advantage of the opportunity to study abroad.	Sense of Agency	Know and understand
You make time for reflection and introspection.	Worldview	Know and understand
You regularly evaluate your values, beliefs, and life goals to ensure they are true.	Self-awareness	Know and understand/Self-actualize
You periodically reflect on your progress in developing your full potential.	Self-awareness	Know and understand/Self-actualize

INDICATOR	HUMAN SPIRIT COMPONENT	INNATE NEED
You keep a journal of your inner thoughts.	Self-awareness	Know and understand
You reflect on new experiences to determine meaning and lessons learned, and to assess your strengths and weaknesses.	Self-awareness	Know and understand
You attend retreats to get in touch with your inner self.	Self-awareness	Know and understand
You join groups that have noble purposes.	Social Awareness	Affiliation
You associate with people for who they are and not for what they can do for you.	Social Awareness	Affiliation
You treat all people with respect and dignity.	Social Awareness	Affiliation
You act in the best interest of the group and its members.	Social Awareness	Affiliation
You volunteer your time or give money to help others.	Social Awareness	Affiliation
You work hard to establish positive relationships with others, especially family and friends.	Social Awareness	Affiliation
You actively listen to understand others and learn.	Social Awareness	Affiliation
You show more kindness toward others.	Social Awareness	Affiliation
Your behavior demonstrates more tolerance of others because of your greater appreciation for the frailty and vulnerabilities of being human.	Social Awareness	Affiliation

INDICATOR	HUMAN SPIRIT COMPONENT	INNATE NEED
You are more forgiving of others.	Self-awareness	Affiliation
You strive to develop your full potential because that is the path to satisfaction, happiness, and well-being.	Faith/Sense of Agency	Self-actualize
You live your life in accordance with your values and beliefs.	Faith/Sense of Agency	Safety/ Self-actualize

DEVELOPMENT OF THE INNER SELF

By applying a model for the domain of the human spirit, we believe anyone can achieve a needed level of commonality in understanding and articulating the development of the inner self. Individuals can understand what psychological components and states are involved and how they interact as they develop. These tools will provide the ability to tailor individual developmental efforts, targeting specific components of the human spirit and using applicable indicators to track progress.

With diligent application of such tools, we believe that at least five outcomes are feasible, all clearly supporting the development of leaders of character:

1. An increased self-awareness by each leader, most often enhancing the ability to understand and to self-author the values and beliefs that define his/her character

2. An evolving worldview or personal life philosophy that seeks truth and justice, appreciates diversity, and

continuously seeks out new experiences and knowledge to promote growth

3. A growing social awareness that fosters respect for others' viewpoints and the ability to see and understand the world through the eyes of others, an attribute critical to understanding subordinates, allies, and enemies
4. An empowered sense of control and responsibility for one's own being, existence, and development, thus fostering inner strength and fortitude
5. A sense of conviction or faith that one is part of a noble profession, providing intrinsic motivation to service and a fulfilling life

We have outlined spirituality as a central facet of a leader's existence and a key driving force in the behavior and meaning-making systems of both leaders and followers—especially under conditions that most try the human spirit, such as close combat. Development of the human spirit must therefore be recognized as inextricable from any development program for leaders or leadership. We propose that such development should be purposive and that it can be made so by application of this model.

The military requires its members to have a strong inner strength to withstand the stresses and rigors of combat and also to achieve psychological well-being; therefore, it is absolutely imperative for military leaders to understand how to develop their own human spirit, thus facilitating the moral journeys of both themselves and their soldiers toward full possession of the Warrior's Character.

CHAPTER THREE

Reflections on Moral Development at West Point

Erica Borggren and Donna M. Brazil

The Cadet Leadership Development System at USMA recognizes that one of the developmental mandates of late adolescence and young adulthood is the search for a worldview. It is at this point in young people's lives that they begin to question many of the assumptions they have held since childhood. An individual cadet who might have grown up going to church with her parents each week now has the opportunity to question the value of church attendance and the very assumptions upon which this behavior is based. She might no longer blindly accept the tenets espoused by her parents and instead seek to determine for herself what "truth" is. While the search for a worldview often involves redefining one's own religiosity, a young person who has no religious affiliation will still find herself searching through these years to determine her connectedness to the world and her place in that world.[1]

Across the field of psychology theorists explain this stage of life in varying ways. One school of thought focuses on identity development, others on changes in cognitive development, and still others on stages of moral development. While approaching the phenomenon from different angles, all acknowledge that there is a developmental imperative—namely, to determine who "I really am" and what I personally value—that is met head-on in the late adolescent or early adult years.

THEORIES OF DEVELOPMENT

Perhaps the most well-known developmental psychologist, Jean Piaget, posited that the prime developmental mechanism throughout childhood is one of active construction. Through active construction, individuals learn and develop by interacting with their environment and by building mental models that explain the outcomes of those interactions. While the complexity of the mental models is constrained by age during the early years, Piaget believed that it is in meeting these challenges that an individual changes, redefines, and develops more complex mental models. This can be seen in the 10-year-old child who can order his world and think systematically, but only when confronted by concrete issues and challenges. However, if this child is never challenged by disorder or allowed the opportunity to organize thoughts, she will not develop in this domain at the same speed as a child who is so stretched. The child who is challenged has the opportunity to build more and more complexly differentiated structures by interacting with the environment. In this way, the child grows to understand her world and develops a view of how she fits into that world. Throughout the first three periods of development that Piaget posits, children are unable to comprehend abstract thoughts.[2]

With regard to the final period of development addressed by Piaget, he suggested that sometime after the age of 11, individuals begin to mature into what he referred to as "formal operations," a developmental stage that continues on into adulthood. This period of development is marked by the ability to engage in abstract and hypothetical thought. It is here that a young adult can begin to go past the simple black-and-white rules and question the environment she lives in. This new-found power to question the world sometimes leads adolescents and young adults to be focused on themselves and to have illusions of their own importance in the world. It should be noted that Piaget did not believe that all adults actually reach the level of formal operations, or that all those who do reach it function in this way all of the time. The late adolescent search for a worldview that is seen in the college years seems to occur as individuals are struggling with advanced formal operations.

Lawrence Kohlberg continued the work of Piaget, reaching the conclusion that Piaget's stages, while accounting for a great deal of cognitive development, stopped short of describing the changes in moral reasoning and moral development that also occurred as this cognitive development increased. Kohlberg noted additional differentiated moral development stages that continue where Piaget's formal operations ended. In these continued stages, individuals are able to acknowledge the presence of a law or precept but then decide to obey or disobey it for a greater good—understanding that punishments might be imposed for disobedience but believing they can present their case for lesser sanctions if need be. The sixth and final stage of development described by Kohlberg is that of attaining an appreciation for universal justice. Reasoning and acting in this stage require that an individual be able to look at a situation from the point of view of all concerned and seek out a solution that meets the higher universal need. As they embark on their search for meaning and a worldview, young people, especially students, struggle with their ability to see the world through different lenses and points of view in these last two stages.[3]

Robert Kegan describes the later stages of development as a struggle to be included in something bigger than oneself and yet at the same time to be independent. In Kegan's second stage individuals begin to form a self-concept, but in this early stage the self is still highly egocentric; in stage three an individual begins to acknowledge the needs of others and is able to work toward mutually beneficial outcomes. In stage four the individual begins to be able to reflect on personal roles, norms, and self-concept. Finally, in stage five individuals are able to see themselves as a fabric of many personal systems; they begin to understand that their roles are simply "what they do" and that these roles are constructs which can be distinct from "who" they actually are. Development in Kegan's framework is driven by meeting and resolving disequilibrium as individuals search back and forth between inclusion and independence.[4]

This human struggle can be looked at as tasks of cognitive, moral, and identity development. Though approached from different perspectives and focusing on different challenges, all serve to describe continual challenge, sense-making, and reflection as essential for developing deeper moral reasoning, cognitive complexity, and sense of self. The college experience in general, and the West Point experience in particular, provide fertile ground for exploring these issues and facilitating the struggle necessary for individual growth in these areas.

In what follows, the authors, as former cadets, share our own developmental journeys, both describing our postadolescent search for meaning and how we found it at West Point. We hope that our personal journeys, narrated in the first person, will illustrate many of the tenets for growth and maturation that we as authors discussed above.

ERICA'S JOURNEY

Late in the afternoon one day in my junior year of high school, I received a phone call that would prove to be life-changing. The tennis coach at West Point wanted to talk to me. Although I had only vaguely ever heard about USMA, I was immediately intrigued. Months later, during a recruiting trip to West Point, my interest became a lot more than intrigue. I would say I fell in love with the place, but more likely I fell in love with the idea of West Point. I loved the unity of purpose that radiated out of 1,000 cadets wearing identical uniforms, walking subconsciously in step. I loved the idea of service, and the nobility that seemed attached to this particular form of service. And I loved the fact that values at this place were normative and lived out, not just verbally batted around in a sea of equally viable values that would be "okay for you." For a girl with no military background in her family, this was all new and, for me, refreshing. Here, the values similar to those I grew up with were not thought of as quaint or blandly relative—they were instead something to be lived up to no matter the cost.

When I arrived at Beast Barracks in the summer of 2002, it was largely because I was won over by that for which West Point stood. I was in for the quick discovery, however, that West Point was about a whole lot more than ideas and values. Despite my preparation, Beast shocked my body, drained my emotions, and challenged my resolve with its physical and mental demands. I often found myself wondering, was all of this seemingly excessive challenge worth it? On top of all this, there was the fact that our cadre often led forthright and challenging discussions on the sacrifices required by military service. What got me was the frankness of the acknowledgment that one could die in this service! Was such sacrifice worth all this travail? I found that the crucible of the West Point experience pitched me headlong into the typical undergraduate search for "who I am."

The commencement of this search coincided with attendance at weekly chapel services (mostly, at first,

> because Sunday services were a refuge from the loud intensity of the rest of the week), encounters with an incredibly intelligent and loving chaplain, and an inexplicable feeling of peace at the thought of a higher power. This "coincidence" is something for which I will always be grateful. Thus began my earnest search into the question of who God was, if anyone. Because of the death of a friend during my senior year in high school, the question had already arisen. I had been to church a few times with a girlfriend, mostly out of desperate curiosity. My search intensified during Beast and my plebe year, however, fueled as it was by two important discoveries. First, I found that the Christian community of West Point had an unavoidable appeal; I really felt that the Christians I encountered had something I did not, something that made their faces shine with joy and their smiles radiate with sincerity and love. Second, and most important for a young woman with a very rationalist mindset, I found that at West Point conversation about God, no matter how dubious the tone or irreverent the questions, was encouraged and even welcomed.

Erica's search for meaning had begun before she entered USMA. Like many adolescents she was beginning to question her "fit" in high school. She was still concerned with belonging but beginning to question what that entailed. She had begun to define herself and her values and found, on arriving at West Point, that she was comfortable in the atmosphere provided there, namely, an environment where values are spoken about and freely questioned—not attacked. The West Point experience, from the classroom to chapel services, from the tennis court to the company area, was filled with open and lively debate about God, about right and wrong, and about the seriousness of commitment to serving your profession, and more so, your country. This openness of the community to challenge and discussion was critical to Erica's journey of faith and moral development.

> After nearly a year of wrestling with the God that my heart felt despite the intellectual objections that my head catalogued, my search was rewarded. Long and intense conversations with the chaplain and others had helped me address enough of my rational objections to reduce the size of the leap of faith required. Finally, the bridge of heartfelt conviction that my heart offered was long enough to span the now smaller gulf of doubt that had separated me from genuine belief. Finally, God had brought me to true knowledge of Him.
>
> As a brand new Christian, I probably did not yet relate the values demanded by West Point to the kind of life demanded by God. The ideals to me were still "shiny" and appealing in and of themselves. And while I believe drawing the association between being a good officer and being a faithful Christian was ultimately inevitable, the faith community and faith institutions in which I participated at West Point did much to urge along the process of linkage. The values of West

Point—honest dealing, clean thinking, harder rights over easier wrongs, whole truth, loyalty, duty—were the very things that God wanted and had enabled me to live out.

In Wednesday evening chapel during Beast Barracks and in regular Sunday chapel services, these values and the challenges related to them were regularly underscored, not only in the Cadet Prayer but in the consistent messages of the sermons themselves. God had called us, they emphasized, to this more difficult life. Just as God willingly sacrificed in service to us, so also must we be willing to do so in service to the nation and to our soldiers. As the sermons acknowledged, it might seem impossible to be truthful when there are repercussions, to always fulfill the tiniest of duties when sometimes things seem trivial, and to always give our best when sometimes energy is difficult to find . . . but God calls us to and through Christ, giving us the strength and willingness to do these very things. Naturally, then, my prayer life at West Point was filled with these issues.

Thanks to these sermons and related conversations with chaplains, mentors, and friends, the tenets of the Cadet Prayer were the very subjects I began naturally to pray about as I worked out my new faith. At the time, I believed my impulse to live out these values stemmed not from my desire to be a better cadet or officer, but from my yearning to somehow be a bit more like Christ, to be close to God and as pleasing to Him as I could be. Regardless of what West Point asked, these were the kinds of things I wanted my mind transformed to be, my will conformed to do, my heart formed to love. Looking back, though, I recognize that it was never as simple as this bare dichotomy would suggest. God had called me to be a cadet and eventually an officer, and thus He and West Point were asking the same things of me. In a sense, then, my identification with the concept of officership (and its inherent moral tenets) was not just a by-product of following God but was rather an integral part of the calling toward which He had brought me.

Erica experienced the struggles of reconciling different roles and norms. As a Christian, she was called to be like Christ. She sought to emulate Christ in her actions and in her dealings with others. At the same time, she was being called to be an officer, to lead others and ask great sacrifices of them. She worked through each of these roles individually and came to the realization that the roles were completely compatible and complementary.

For me, one of the most important aspects of moral development through faith at West Point is that faith was never just a matter for Sundays and sermons. Instead, it was allowed to be part of my everyday interactions and conversations. At weekly gatherings of the Officers Christian Fellowship, in informal conversations with friends, and even in academic settings with professors and classmates, real life and God were freely allowed to relate. In short, God was allowed to be woven into every aspect of cadet life for all who desired Him to be. For me, it was particularly important that outside their classrooms professors were willing to discuss faith with me. There were those who encouraged faith and helped me reconcile intellectual dilemmas, and there were those who challenged it and forced me to challenge myself and God for answers and understanding. All of this exploration allowed God to be about not just the heart but also the mind (for is not one of God's primary gifts to us our rationality?). The more God can be about the mind, the more freedom one has to intellectually work out dilemmas and doubts with Him; this is particularly important in the age of postmodern doubt, cynicism, and relativism. Because West Point allowed me the space and provided me the resources to know God with my head as well as in my heart, I emerged with a faith more able to withstand the relativist pressures that exist even within the Army. I certainly found this to be important when, just months after graduating from West Point, I found myself in the midst of an environment at Oxford University where the only espoused values were those of learning and tolerance.

As I've mentioned, I entered West Point as a young adult with a definite value set but not one very clearly thought through. Looking back, I think that those values appealed to me for the same reason that God appealed to me. It always seemed to me that God imbued us with a certain nobility in serving something higher.

> A living God whose love I could feel seemed such a better thing to serve than a faceless ideal or value itself. An important link clicked in place as I connected in my mind the values I had always espoused to something that gave me a reason to espouse them—God.

Erica understood the many roles she was asked to enact—cadet, Christian, leader, friend—and she fulfilled these roles well. Through her developing relationship with God and her working through the challenges posed by fellow cadets and mentors, she began to discern who she was, apart from these roles. In her mind, she found that the values and virtues that she believed were required for the roles she had assumed, were the same as those she already had developed in her faith journey. While the journey to faith and the journey to moral development are not always parallel, for Erica they seemed to be mutually supporting.

> Now, when I step back and analyze what guides my moral choices, I find that the continuing and difficult daily decisions involved in living out the tenets of the Cadet Prayer are something that takes place in the space between me and God. I have discovered that there are many more ethical dilemmas in the Army than I faced at West Point. Although they are never enjoyable, each is an opportunity to actually be the person that God and country have asked me to be.
>
> Even while I was at West Point, though, there were plenty of such opportunities. In the summer of my first

year, I stood face-to-face with an event that made quite clear to me just how important my faith was in living out the value of courage. The moment you are told to jump out the door of a flying plane is inevitably a moment of truth, no matter how much you trust your equipment and your training. That first step out the door, I found, required a definite knowledge of who I was and where I was (a child of God in His hands) and what would happen if the parachute did not open (I would go to be with Him). Had I not been able to accept that death was not the worst thing that could happen, somebody may have had to push me out of the plane. Every soldier must know how to find courage in the face of life's worst what-ifs; for me, I find that that courage comes from my identity in Christ. Whatever one's answer, it surely must be believed in the heart as well as the head.

The many Honor Classes we had during Commandant's hour at West Point were all geared toward enabling us to anticipate the types of situations in which we might be tempted by others or the system to deviate from truth. These classes encouraged us to precondition our reaction to that challenge. At the time, I thought these classes were a bit overdone, a bit too frequent, and at times forced in their overly serious tone. I have definitely found since, however, that these situations arise frequently in day-to-day Army life. When, as the Executive Officer for my company, I faced a decision of whether to raise the issue of false reporting occurring in my unit, I certainly felt for a moment like I was back in a West Point dayroom.

This, however, was the first time the possible consequences of a moral decision would be actual and mine to face. I could and did weigh the costs and benefits of reporting a commander to a senior commander. I could and did rationalize, dread, and worry through the decision. But when it came down to it, there really was no choice at hand, and I don't believe I ever really thought there was. Truthfulness and what is right could not be compromised. When I think about what causes me to cling to those guiding precepts so strongly, I conclude that it is because I have a God who Himself embodies the perfection of these ideals and who lovingly asks that I attempt to do the same. This highlights the importance, I believe, of being able to answer the question of why a value is important. I am not sure adherence would be such an absolute requirement, such a given, if there was not a why beneath the values themselves; for me, that value comes from my foundational beliefs in who I am, where I come from, and Whom I serve.

Accepting and meeting challenges are common requirements for development in each of these domains. Erica's experiences were indeed stretching for her, and challenged the earlier mental models she had developed. In meeting each of these she developed a deeper, more refined, and more complex sense of purpose and identity. It is interesting to note that development continues throughout our lives. Erica reflects on classes taught at West Point that seemed "overdone" when presented in the somewhat sterile classroom, but are now increasingly relevant as she meets new challenges.

> Finally, there is the issue of servant leadership itself: never ask your soldiers to do something you would not do yourself, always keep in mind that you are there to serve and guide your subordinates, and always put the welfare of your soldiers before your own. These ideas were so constantly emphasized at West Point that they could seem harped on to the point of tedium. Even I, one of the least cynical people I knew at USMA, would roll my eyes at times. However, now that I am in the Army and have soldiers under me, I find to my satisfaction that these precepts are deeply ingrained. Sometimes the extent to which I take this concept makes other officers around me laugh; who else, they ask, would feel uncomfortable taking an extra 20 minutes at lunch just because others in her office did not have that option? Even I can recognize at times the apparent triviality of some of the issues I actually create. But when it comes down to it, nothing feels too trivial to consider. I joke now with my friends and mentors that there is more "West Point" in me than I thought, but in actuality I think it is the foundation of my admiration for and calling to servant leadership—Jesus Christ—that underpins it. Servant leadership is what Christ did and is thus what a good officer does.
>
> Refusing to jump out of the plane, ignoring false reporting, getting out of a requirement my soldiers

could not get out of—in the crucial moments, I found that these were all nonoptions, for the values underlying the decisions I made were simply a part of me. In the Cadet Prayer, we beseech God to give us the strength to "live above the common level of life." Living at that higher level, I believe, takes place in the small and numerous decisions of daily life just like these.

Erica's journey is a stirring tapestry of many of the cognitive, moral, and identity development theories described at the beginning of this chapter. She came to West Point with strong values and beliefs but could not fully explain the reasoning behind them. Throughout her Academy experience, mentors, chaplains, professors, and peers challenged her to achieve a deeper understanding of who she was and what she truly believed. That search brought her to understand Christ and in doing so to better understand the values that guide West Point.

DONNA'S JOURNEY

My journey was a little different, though Erica and I traveled on the same roads and studied in the same buildings—Washington, Cullum, and Thayer Halls. Though we each entered college searching to find our identity and to understand our world, we entered with different backgrounds and different starting points.

Our military experience has also been different. I prepared for the Cold War and an attack across the Fulda Gap; she has been called on to fight the Global War on Terror. However, despite our differences, there are many similarities in our personal development that occurred at West Point.

I am, in cadet terms, an Old Grad. For the cadets I teach, I find that I am old enough to be their mother and sometimes feel differences in the generations that define us. However, while I do not listen to the music they listen to nor watch the same movies, more often than not I find that real differences are not great and that the developmental journey they are traveling is quite similar to the one I traveled more than 20 years ago.

I was already a senior in high school in 1977 when I saw an advertisement for West Point. I remember commenting to my guidance counselor that "they don't let girls go there." She told me that they had changed the rules and that the first class of women had started the year before. Growing up in the Bronx, I had visited West Point as a child and been enamored of the grandeur, the strength. I viewed it as separate from the rest of the world, at least as I knew it. West Point was less than an hour from New York City, yet seemingly lifetimes away.

When looking for a college, I wanted to make something better of myself; to try something new, out of the ordinary. I was raised Catholic, attending Catholic schools through high school. I laugh now to think that I have been in uniform since I was 5 years old. I was the second oldest of six children, raised with four brothers and a sister by my parents and grandmother. By all accounts, I was a bit wild growing up, always pushing the limits but somehow always managing to stay just within the lines. In my mind the schools I attended gave me the much needed lines. I credit St. Barnabas and Mount St. Ursula with structuring my development in those early years when I needed it most. I was attracted to USMA at first because it offered both challenge and clearly defined lines. I had read about the honor code and the strict regulations at West Point and believed that once again having these regulations as lines would keep me balanced and on target. What I did not know was that as part of my development at West Point, the lines that I once thought so clear and defined would be blurred, and I would have to decide for myself where the hard and fast margins were—if they existed at all.

I was very comfortable with lines, with having a higher authority define for me what was right and wrong. I had experimented in high school, pushing against the lines to see how far they would give, but I think that I only did that because I felt confident that the lines were out there somewhere and that I would not stray through the hole I might have created. In hindsight, I realize that I was yearning and searching for the real limits, and beginning to question the origin of the rules. I would argue for hours in order to understand the rationale behind a decision or perhaps in the hopes of getting it changed. West Point continued to provide the environment for that search—once again with lines, but they were not as clear now. I was free and even encouraged to question my faith, to question my identity, to question my values and my reason for being. In developmental terms, in my first years at West Point I struggled both to belong to something bigger than myself and to be independent.

During plebe year cadets learn the rules, and the Academy acknowledges that often cadets obey the rules simply to avoid negative repercussions or to obtain small extrinsic rewards. However, over time and with a growing understanding of the premises supporting the rules, cadets come to identify with and eventually to internalize the values of West Point and the Army. As I reflect on my experiences and development, I can see how I followed such a course. First, I was very comfortable with the lines that kept me in check. Then, as I developed at the Academy, I grew both in my faith and in my understanding of the underlying values that define the Academy and its graduates. I gradually grew from complying with the rules and sometimes resisting those rules, to adhering to them because the people I admired did so, to finally internalizing and acting out the rules and the values underlying them simply because they are right.

Many developmental theorists identify critical or crucible moments that have the possibility of accelerating one's development. Our reaction to these moments determines the trajectory of that development. As a sophomore, I was faced with the knowledge that a friend and fellow cadet had violated the Cadet Honor Code. I knew that I was likely the only person who had this knowledge. I struggled and prayed, knowing all along the "right" thing to do, yet not being confident enough in my own identity and my own internalization of the rules to actually do it. In the end, after a very difficult night, I confronted her and she acknowledged the violation and turned herself in.

Two years later, as a senior, I used a study guide for a course that I was struggling in. After taking a particular exam, I became concerned that the study guide, while commercially available, might not have been authorized, as many of the questions on the exam were similar to those in the guide. I spent another night thinking and praying. Had I violated the Honor Code? Had I inadvertently gained an unfair advantage over my classmates? Who would know? I had worked so hard and was scheduled to graduate in a few short months. In the end I knew in my heart that all of this did not matter. If I had violated the Honor Code, I had to report it. Though a difficult decision, it was no longer about getting caught or being punished. It was about violating what I believed, no, what I knew, to be the foundation of who I was. I reported it to the Honor Committee. A representative looked into the matter and discussed it with my instructor, who determined that there was not an unfair advantage since the guide was available to anyone. In the end, there was no board and no threat to the future I envisioned for myself as an officer in the Army, but there was real growth. Through the struggle I came out stronger in my faith and in my understanding of the values and beliefs that had been kindled in me as a child and reinforced at West Point.

The issues of whether I had violated the Honor Code and whether I should confront my friend over her honor violation were crucible moments for me, and I was fortunate to have friends and mentors who supported me and helped me to grow through these challenges to my worldview. Before those experiences, though I am quite sure that I could have spoken to someone about the values of West Point and explained the tenets of the Honor Code, I did not yet fully understand that acting out the tenets of honor truly defined who I was. While this second incident was also difficult, I grew because of it and emerged better prepared for the challenges of the future.

In addition to those two crucible moments during my cadet days at USMA, I had many opportunities to grow that were not as dramatic, yet were sufficient to gently nudge me along in my developmental journey. As a plebe I was invited to attend a retreat that focused on the mystery of the Passion—the sufferings of Christ between the Last Supper and His crucifixion. I signed up for the retreat, though I must admit now that my intentions were far from religious. As a plebe

I was eager for any excuse to get a weekend away from West Point. What I found at this retreat was amazing. I found a group of cadets and local college students who shared a common faith, yet all had vastly different backgrounds. I found individuals who wrestled with the same issues that I did, who were also trying to find their place in the world, an identity similar to yet distinct from the one I was establishing. I found a values-based environment that encouraged this questioning and in fact made not questioning seem as if I didn't care about the issues.

This retreat and the many more I attended in the next few years gave me the opportunity to reflect on my struggles, my growth, and my development while I was at West Point. Once a semester, through the West Point Chaplain's Program, I was able to take a weekend retreat in order to help make sense of these changes and experiences. During these opportunities, I continued to struggle to find my place at West Point and in the Army and to question the changes I was experiencing. All the while I was surrounded by officers, cadets, and individuals from the local community who were willing to talk about the issues and help me reflect on their meaning in my life. As I advanced through the years at West Point, I took on leadership roles in this group. I became one of the mentors and leaders who assisted other cadets in their journey. My own development continued through this leadership experience. As is often the case, in attempting to help others find answers and meaning, I was forced to continually re-evaluate my own identity and values.

Through these experiences and many more that are now so much a part of my being that I am unable to recall them as single events, I slowly grew from a teenager looking for answers to a young adult who had found meaning in who I was and in what I chose to do. Through these struggles I came out stronger in my faith and rock solid in my belief in the values and tenets of West Point. I learned that the values the Academy stood for are not simply rules, but instead are a way of life. As the USMA Chaplain says each year at new cadet reception day, "'Duty, Honor, Country' is not a way to see certain things, but a certain way to see all things." Though a simple motto, it is a rather complete worldview. The values of West Point are not rules or even lines—they just are. I understand that we are dedicated to doing the harder right. I understand that what is not corrected is condoned. I understand that when I say to myself, "Someone ought to take care of that"—I am that someone.

The other night I was driving in a storm and noticed that a traffic cone had blown away from the hole it was supposed to be warning motorists about. I asked my daughter to get out of the car and move it back in place. As she was getting out of the car, she muttered something like "Why do I have to have do-gooder parents?" The answer is simple—it's because both her dad and I "grew up" at West Point.

The Cadet Prayer, while not an overt part of my faith and life journey while I was a cadet, has become so in the years since I have returned to the faculty. Sadly, I have had the honor of attending far too many military funerals at West Point in the past few years, and at each of those services, no matter what denomination, the prayer was always part of the service. During these new moments of struggle and sense-making, I have had the opportunity to read and reflect on this prayer and the meaning of it in my life then and now.

THE TRANSFORMATIVE POWER

Despite the generations that separate old grads from new grads, like Donna from Erica, the precepts embodied in this prayerful petition are timeless and denominationally nonspecific. They reflect basic truths and values that the common experience at USMA allowed individuals the time and opportunities to inspect, dissect, and identify with, and eventually to own and internalize. Thanks to the unique developmental process that they were ready for upon arrival and for which USMA provided the groundwork, these values now describe not only how they act but who they are. It is fitting to end this chapter by recalling some of the language that lends the prayer such transformative power:

- Strengthen and increase our admiration for honest dealing and clean thinking.

- Encourage us in our endeavor to live above the common level of life.
- Make us to choose the harder right instead of the easier wrong.
- Endow us with courage that is born of loyalty to all that is noble and worthy.
- Guard us against flippancy and irreverence in the sacred things of life.
- Help us to maintain the honor of the Corps untarnished and unsullied.

PART

II

The ROLE *of* CHARACTER *in* MILITARY LEADERSHIP

If leaders are not looking for truth, if situations are not framed as having moral implications in the first place, then these leaders make decisions based on other criteria alone, often with disturbing results. Moral sensitivity alone is not enough. Once leaders recognize that a moral problem exists, they then have to decide what is right. This requires moral judgment—discerning which action is most justifiable based on a set of ethical criteria. However, even moral sensitivity and judgments do not guarantee moral behavior . . . without the courage to take action.

USMA Circulari-101,
Cadet Leader Development System
(West Point, NY: Defense Printing, 2002), XX.

CHAPTER FOUR

Frameworks of Moral Development and the West Point Experience

Building Leaders of Character for the Army and the Nation

Sean T. Hannah and Patrick J. Sweeney

This chapter integrates the sciences of leadership, moral decision making, social, cognitive, and developmental psychology, and organizational behavior, relating these theories to both the formal and informal developmental processes of leaders. Drawing from theories of authentic leadership development and moral leadership, we will then provide recommendations for accelerating moral development in cadets, students, and employees in the future. By authentic, we are describing the creation of lasting, positive change in these future leaders or officers so that their morality is internalized, and their moral decision making and actions are natural manifestations of their true self rather than the result of social sanctions or expectations. Authentic moral development is thus intertwined with the development of leaders' human spirit and drive toward self-actualization.

Specifically a leader's worldview and character are at the center of his/her human spirit, and are reinforced through agency, self-awareness, social awareness, and faith. It is this core that provides leaders the independence to author their own values and belief systems. This form of development is part of the larger leadership development process, entailing positive alteration of self-concepts, social perspectives, capacities for moral decision making, and ultimately motivation and confidence for taking moral action—thus developing true leaders of character.

We begin this chapter with an overview of what we call the "triad of moral capabilities" that we hold to be central to moral development: (1) moral complexity, (2) moral agency, and (3) moral efficacy. We then relate these three capabilities to the process of moral decision making and behavior, showing how the leader's level of moral development enables the effective processing of moral dilemmas.

AUTHENTIC MORAL LEADERSHIP DEVELOPMENT AND THE WEST POINT EXPERIENCE

We propose that authentic moral development occurs in leaders through targeted developmental events, such as exposure to key moral/ethical experiences, coupled with coaching and periods of dedicated reflection.

The English terms ethics and morals are derived from the Greek term *ethos* and the Latin term *mores*, respectively, which refer to the shared beliefs and practices of a people. The West Point experience is critical in this developmental process, because ethics are learned and practiced here as a part of living within a culture of professionals. Such organizations teach members the profession's ethics and values through the social learning processes. These processes are known to be particularly critical during the formative college years.

Moral development is, however, a lifelong journey; for example, an officer's commissioning from West Point should not be looked at as an end state. In fact a longitudinal study investigating the psychological development of West Point cadets found that officers in the rank of major averaging in excess of 10 years of service were still developing morally, and that on average had not yet achieved the highest levels of moral development attainable.[1] These highest levels of moral development provide officers with the psychological autonomy to author their own system of values and standards. Such autonomy empowers leaders to make moral decisions and lead in a moral manner in the absence of social support and in situations involving competing expectations from others or their organizations. Therefore, the developmental objective at the Academy is to accelerate such moral development and to set the conditions for leaders to embrace their own self-directed and lifelong development plans to search for moral enlightenment. This search for meaning is central to individual moral development and, more specifically, to the spiritual domain of character development found in the Cadet Leader Development System (CLDS).

We believe that moral development should be largely focused on three key capabilities, namely: (1) moral complexity, (2) moral agency, and (3) moral efficacy. We propose that this triad of moral capabilities is at the heart of high-impact, moral leadership. Ultimately, leaders with these enhanced capabilities will bolster ownership and engagement in their moral experiences, increase the depth of contemplation during moral decision making, and boost their personal confidence and courage to take the "right" actions in the face of adversity or social pressures. Many West Point experiences, such as reflection on the moral precepts contained in the Cadet Prayer, are influential in the development of this triad of capabilities and the creation of leaders of virtue and character.

MAKING THE "RIGHT" DECISIONS

Nowhere are moral development and ethical enlightenment more critical than at America's national military academies. To lead in combat, young men and women must have developed a highly accurate moral compass in order to navigate the constant currents of tension between personal morality and their role as a member of the profession of arms—a profession that must manage violence on behalf of the greater good. The dilemmas faced by young military officers today are like those always faced in battle—morally ambiguous situations where leaders have to choose between imperfect solutions, all of which may have questionable moral overtones. Does a leader expose his soldiers to enemy fire to save an innocent young child? Does the leader order her soldiers to fire on a car filled with a civilian family that does not appear to be slowing for a traffic control checkpoint? In garrison situations, does a leader punish a soldier by reduction of pay knowing that his family already has financial problems?

These examples should make clear that it is more important for the Academy to focus on how young leaders should think about and resolve such dilemmas than it is to focus on what the specific outcome should be. It is more critical to enable leaders to process ambiguous dilemmas autonomously, without supervision, and to come up with the best moral and ethical solutions. This developmental philosophy is also evident in the Superintendent's introduction to the CLDS manual:

> CLDS introduces the concept of Officership and focuses primarily on the Be component of the [Army leadership doctrine's] Be-Know-Do paradigm. . . . Influencing the Be component is a significant challenge. It entails affecting an individual's core beliefs: what one

stands for, how one views oneself, and how one views the world. It is an individual's character.[2]

It is precisely at this point that it becomes critical to address the importance of the human spirit in leader development. Inclusion of spirituality is a major dimension of character development in CLDS. Human spirituality, according to CLDS, is defined as one's drive to find personal meaning in life and to realize one's full potential.[3] It is in seeking an understanding of their evolving spirituality that all future leaders will form and reinforce their self-identity, find their sense of purpose and meaning in life, form their own philosophy for viewing the world, and develop the standards that define for them what it means to live good. Regardless of one's approach to addressing spirituality, whether it is through religion, the study of philosophy or ethics, or other means, all leaders must establish clear core beliefs and values and uphold those beliefs with conviction to be a moral leader—a leader of character—a leader who brings meaning to his or her missions, organizations, and work.

Regardless of any differences in their teachings, major religions can serve as catalysts for spiritual development. They provide important structure and discipline in the process of spiritual growth for the members of their congregations, and offer as well increased opportunities for spiritual experiences, mentoring, and reflection. At West Point, all cadets are encouraged to seek their own self-determined avenue for developing the human spirit as a centerpiece of their leadership development. At the Academy, both religious and nonreligious opportunities abound. We expressed in Chapter 2 the importance of the human spirit in human flourishing, and even more so in effective, principled leadership. Thus, as public institutions such as West Point continue to secularize, it is critical that they avoid the error of despiritualizing their developmental environments. Rather, we believe they must facilitate such personal searches for moral meaning. Professional callings, such as Army officership, require a sense of purpose and meaning and a sound view of how one relates to the larger group and society. For example, by cadets' commissioning day, the Army's new officers must know that their moral compass is highly functional and guiding them along the path of character-based leadership.

INTRODUCTION TO THE MORAL DEVELOPMENT MODEL

It is well established that a leader must first recognize that a situation contains a moral issue, process that issue to form a moral decision, transfer that decision into an intention to act, and then carry that intention through to actual behavior. Due to their sequential nature, a failure to navigate any one of these steps may derail the leader from taking the right actions. Leaders who are specifically developed and equipped to face the morally dynamic realm of leadership will be better able to perceive and recognize the moral implications of issues, process the relevant factors to come up with better solutions, form intentions to act on those decisions, and, most important, summon the courage and conviction to act morally and do the right thing in the toughest of situations.

We turn now to a detailed discussion of our model for the development of authentic moral leaders. The heart of this model is the triad of moral capabilities:

1. Moral complexity
2. Moral agency
3. Moral efficacy

We propose that these three moral capabilities are the foundation for moral development in authentic leaders.

Moral Complexity

The first element in the triad is moral complexity, the ability of the leader to attend to, store, retrieve, process, and, most important, make meaning of moral information. As the English philosopher John Locke noted, "No man's knowledge here can go beyond his experience." Our knowledge as a basis for contemplating moral issues is limited to our education and experiences. We must therefore first broaden our moral education and reflection. Moral complexity, as a capability, is based on high levels of cognitive development and one's ability to monitor moral thought processes, i.e., metacognition. We propose that cognitive development and metacognition together provide the leader with a capacity for moral experiences and for translating experiences into knowledge through guided coaching and recognition and making judgments.

Cognitive Moral Development

Theories of Cognitive Moral Development by Lawrence Kohlberg and Robert Kegan propose that over their lifespan individuals develop cognitively through different levels. They begin with a focus on the self (ego) and gradually move toward an understanding of their interactions and interdependency with the social world in which they are embedded. Developmental growth often takes place when people are confronted with situations in which their current meaning-making systems are inadequate, such as a child made to recognize the harm of her/his actions to others, thus triggering a conflict with her/his own values and meaning-making system. These situations cause people to experience a state of cognitive disequilibrium, which prompts them to develop more complex meaning-making structures to restore this equilibrium (in the example of the child, perhaps by the child's better linking its behavior and the expected consequences with her/his value structures).

Jean Piaget, a famous developmental theorist, called this developmental process accommodation. As people move toward the highest levels of development, they eventually transcend social expectations and constraints and begin to strive for universal values and principles in the decisions that they make. At what Kohlberg calls the postconventional levels, and Kegan the institutional and interindividual levels, people achieve the capacity to go beyond the norms and authority of social groups and pursue virtue through their own moral regulatory processes and internal standards—i.e., what we have previously referred to as their internal moral compass. Thus, these internalized values of people define their character. Higher levels of cognitive moral development have been positively related to moral behavior in numerous studies.[4]

Scholars of ethics such as James Rest have argued that levels of cognitive moral development are related to the mental representations people hold in long-term memory.[5] These representations store and organize our knowledge and are formed through life experiences as people learn "how things work" (processes and structures), "what leads to what" (hypotheses about causality and consequences), "who we and others are" (self and person-concepts), and other similar mental representations that are central to processing moral dilemmas. These mental representations are critical, since they determine what people pay attention to in their lives, how they perceive and process information, the quality of their decisions, and ultimately their behavior.

Focusing developmental experiences on creating a capacity for robust moral complexity enable us to conduct more comprehensive assessments of moral dilemmas and achieve more optimum solutions. A leader's complexity is central to the stage of moral reasoning or processing known as moral recognition. Individuals attend to information that is relevant to and consistent with their existing knowledge, while ignoring or discounting incongruent information.[6] In essence, people find that consistency and predictability enhance their comfort zone. They have difficulty processing information when they cannot relate that information to existing cognitive frameworks.

Since people attend to consistent information, the more their cognitive frameworks are marked by moral complexity, the more likely they will be able to recognize the moral components of leadership issues. Knowledge structures about one's self are also critical. Leaders who have worked hard to develop a self-identity marked by strength of character, and who accept responsibility for the moral aspects of their leadership's influence, will be more likely to attend to and process moral information and take action. As complex mental representations of an individual's moral self are developed and integrated with representations of other people, their organizations, and moral concepts, they become the moral compass to guide the one's future cognitions and behaviors.

These complex mental representations are held in long-term memory, and thus can be developed through a broad range of life and educational experiences that serve as developmental trigger events, moments that create moral disequilibrium and force the accommodation of new information, as discussed earlier. It is critical that these experiences be coupled with dedicated reflection and coaching to make meaning of those experiences.

MAGNITUDE AND COMPLEXITY OF MORAL KNOWLEDGE

All leaders, quite simply, are limited by the information they can retrieve from memory to make moral evaluations. Further refining the concept of moral complexity, we hold that leaders who have more complex mental structures can take in greater information from competing sides of an issue and create better linkages between different or perhaps conflicting information that may often characterize the moral dilemmas being faced.

More cognitively complex individuals are also better able to acquire new knowledge, since they can more easily make meaning of and relate new information to what they already know. They also tend to spend more effort and time interpreting new information and resolving complex dilemmas.[7]

Leaders with a greater capacity for moral complexity also have fewer extreme or polar attitudes that can often lead to selective or biased information processing and resistance to change.[8] These leaders are less set in their ways—they take the blinders off and assess the full breadth of moral dilemmas using their greater complexity. Studies have directly tested and found that higher levels of moral knowledge were related to more frequent resort to moral reasoning and moral behavior. We are not saying that any kind of increased information leads to moral development. For example, we know that exposure to high levels of antisocial or immoral information can lead to grave consequences for a young person. Indeed, the primary goal of character development at West Point is to align the character of the individual cadet with the role and moral principles of officership. Thus, although we believe it is more important to teach cadets "how" to think morally, one should not underestimate the importance of instilling certain core character tenets in young leaders to provide the foundation and strength to make the right decision in ambiguous moral situations, especially when lives are at risk.

Beyond the amount of moral knowledge a leader must possess, the second component of moral complexity is metacognitive ability, that is, the ability to effectively access and process this robust knowledge. Metacognitive ability can be thought of as the capacity to "think about thinking," allowing leaders to effectively monitor and control moral processing and to regulate their own cognitive processes.[9] Metacognitive ability has been directly related to both more acute moral reasoning and greater moral content in actions.[10] Metacognitive processing is more than thinking about the specific aspects of a moral issue; it is assessing how one is thinking about and processing that information. During metacognitive processing, the leader may ask whether all relevant sources of information are being assessed, what information is missing, what personal emotional responses are influencing the assessment, and whether the leader is applying his or her core values and beliefs in the decision.

The components of moral complexity are mutually supporting. Whereas high levels of cognitive moral development and the associated creation of rich and robust moral knowledge provide the database that leaders can access when faced with a moral dilemma, heightened metacognitive ability, or the ability to "think about moral thinking," is the human central processing unit that raises their ability to select from, access, and modify this database to drive conclusions for application to the moral dilemmas at hand. Thus coupled, the components of moral complexity truly transform the leader by providing greater capabilities for moral recognition and inquiry. Referring to the conceptualization presented in Chapter 2, these capabilities would bolster the human spirit by broadening leaders' worldview, capacity for self-awareness, and social awareness, and by increasing their ability to achieve coherence with their faith as they process moral dilemmas.

DEVELOPMENT OF MORAL COMPLEXITY AT WEST POINT

We hold that it is through the vast number and types of experiences cadets undergo at the Academy that they develop a higher level of cognitive moral complexity. These experiences may include for some their exposure to the moral precepts in the Cadet Prayer—e.g., to rise "above the common level of life," to discern the "whole truth" through the lens of their complex moral knowledge, and to weigh all options in electing the "harder right over the easier wrong."

We propose that there are at least five primary methods to develop such enhanced levels of moral complexity in West Point cadets: (1) guiding them through a series of moral experiences or trigger events with assisted reflection to enhance their interpretation and understanding of those experiences, (2) providing mentors and role models who personally model moral behavior, (3) placing cadets in situations that create cognitive disequilibrium, forcing them to challenge what they know in order to occasion deeper inquiry into moral dilemmas, (4) teaching specific moral decision-making skills and processes; and (5) having cadets live in a culture that requires and supports moral behavior.

Academy leaders such as instructors, coaches, and mentors, through deliberately planned trigger events, can expose cadets to moral dilemmas and assist them in their interpretation of such encounters through guided reflection. Cadets and their leaders must also be alert to the occurrence of unplanned trigger events, taking the opportunity to pause and engage in guided reflection. Such experiences do not necessarily have to be direct and personal; vicarious experience through observing others will also provide robust moral information for preservation in memory, thus to be called upon during the processing of future moral dilemmas.

Cadets must be exposed to moral conflicts in order to help trigger the development of heightened moral reasoning. We have stated that humans prefer consistency and therefore tend to discount or ignore occurrences that do not match their schemas. To alter and develop moral complexity, Academy instructors must expose cadets to opposed views and arguments that challenge their core perspectives, basic assumptions, and uncritical beliefs, thus assisting them to adopt an entirely new way of thinking about moral issues. This level of analysis and internal discovery requires facing the hard issues. After their first year or so at the Academy, cadets still tend to view moral issues such as lying, cheating, and stealing as black and white categories. Although there is value in discussing them to heighten sensitivity to those issues, such discussion does little to advance the ongoing transformation or development of cadets. The Academy must instead place cadets within a series of increasingly complex and ambiguous real or virtual situations that require hard decisions among less than perfect choices, decisions replicating what lieutenants face every day in Iraq such as during urban search-and-clear operations. These dilemma-laced decisions create cognitive disequilibrium, motivating cadets to reassess their knowledge and incorporate new information to restore balance.

The importance of role models and mentors in this process cannot be stressed too strongly. We know that leaders, as exemplars, can alter the value structures of followers. When individuals have moral discussions with mentors who have higher moral reasoning levels than their own, they are more likely to reflect on their values and beliefs and experience moral growth.[11] The more leaders are seen as role models by their followers, the more followers will identify with the leaders and be motivated to self-reflect on the examples they set. These role models show how things should be done, including the proper systems and processes. Some of the knowledge structures people hold are temporal—they have a sequence of events that unfolds through time, such as one's conceptualization of the proper steps in processing a prisoner of war. These structures, called scripts, are developed through experience, as one learns certain strategies when dealing with his or her environment. These strategies are recorded in memory, and subsequently reinforced over time. Training and role modeling are critical in the development of effective moral scripts. Through observation, cadets essentially learn "what works and what is right" and tend to repeat the same sequence of events later, a process that becomes habituated over time. It should be clear by now that moral experiences, or trigger events coupled with periods of guided reflection, are central in attaining higher levels of moral development.

Education has also proven effective in the development of moral complexity as long as that education teaches methodologies for analyzing the merits of various competing moral choices. Again, we focus here not on inculcating in cadets what to think, but how to think. To be effective, ethics classes must not be lecture-oriented since cognitive growth is best stimulated using opportunities for role playing, discussion, support, challenge, and guided reflection. In a study reviewing 23 different ethics training programs, those using group discussions of moral dilemmas produced on average an astounding four and half times more positive effects on moral development than those without dedicated moral discussions.[12] West Point's ethics training programs could thus profit from focusing even more on guided processing of increasingly difficult and ambiguous moral issues.

Leaders must observe through multiple lenses as they reason to moral judgments in the dynamic and ambiguous context of military operations. Such an approach induces them to access and exercise their various moral mental structures and develop an inherent metacognitive ability to achieve maximum coherence in their decisions.

We propose that cadets be prompted to examine moral issues through three lenses or perspectives: (1) what is right by the laws, rules, norm, or duties (deontological), (2) what produces the best consequences (teleological), and (3) what is the most virtuous action (areteological). Each one of these three lenses may produce a separate and distinct moral solution if viewed in isolation, so cadets must learn to simultaneously view moral dilemmas through all three lenses to understand the complete dynamics of an issue and determine the best course of action.

Rigidly employing only one lens is problematic when trying to resolve a moral dilemma. For instance, let us assume a soldier refuses to go on a combat patrol led by a squad leader who does not have the necessary training or experience to lead the patrol competently. If the commander views this situation only through the lens of "rules, regulations, duties, and laws" (deontological), he will most likely take action in accordance with the Uniform Code of Military Justice to punish the soldier's disobedience. However, the commander realizes that punishing a soldier who had compelling reasons for refusing to participate in an operation in which the institution had failed to properly develop the leader could have adverse effects on the unit's morale, cohesion, and trust in its leaders (teleological). Further, viewing this situation from the perspective of what would be the most virtuous action (areteological), the commander may place a competent leader in charge of the patrol to ensure all the soldiers are properly led, thus addressing the reluctant soldier's concerns and assuring that discipline and trust within the unit are maintained. As can be seen in this example, the three-lens approach provides leaders a systematic means for processing a moral dilemma in order to determine the best solution to resolve it. In sum, the Army needs leaders who can view moral issues from all three perspectives.

Moral Agency

Cognitive models of moral development, by themselves, are insufficient to explain moral behavior. To reason through complex moral dilemmas to a judgment and then take action on that judgment, leaders must have strong, directed motivation to be a moral actor. Moral agency concerns taking ownership of and assuming responsibility for one's own moral experiences. As the philosopher John Stuart Mill stated, "Over himself, over his own body and mind, the individual is sovereign." Such ownership by a leader of his/her moral experiences is a central element proposed in the conceptualization of the domain of the human spirit (presented in Chapter 2).

Heightened moral agency provides the motivation for a leader to be more aware of moral issues and to explore more fully the span of complex information surrounding those issues. We all know, however, that people often do not take action on their moral inclinations. Although they may determine that something is wrong, leaders, whether business, military, or otherewise, without high levels of moral agency will often fail to act. Moral agents, however, do take responsibility for the moral signature of their domain of influence and do the right thing. For example, the Cadet Honor Code's injunction that cadets do not lie, cheat, or steal, nor tolerate those who do, is a clear expression of the moral agency cadets are expected to assume, not only over their own personal moral domain but also within their social environment.

Noted psychologist Albert Bandura states that agency is the capacity one holds to exercise control over both the nature and quality of one's life—it is, in fact, the essence of humanness. Being producers as well as products of their environments, leaders cannot be passive; instead, they must own their own experiences and those of their followers and associates. As an active concept, moral agency includes both refrainment power (inhibition to keep from acting immorally) and proactive power (the power to intentionally behave morally). Bandura proposes that agency includes four major facets directly related to moral leadership: (1) intentionality—that one's actions are done intentionally; (2) forethought regarding consequences—that people anticipate the consequences of their actions and thereby select what they feel to be the best courses of action; (3) self-regulation—the ability to motivate and regulate one's self as a moral actor; and (4) self-reflection—the capacity to reflect upon the quality and impacts of one's thoughts and actions. Focusing on these four elements of agency accelerates the development of morally-engaged leaders-to-be, who take command of their moral domain.

Moral agency is central to developing truly authentic leaders of character. When making moral judgments, followers tend to comply with what they deem to be the moral desires of their higher authority and thereby often eschew personal ownership and agency. This phenomenon explains why under immoral leaders ethical disasters can plague organizations. For example, a disengagement of moral agency by followers under immoral leaders was a contributing, if not the major factor, in the My Lai village massacre in Vietnam and in the Abu Ghraib prison abuses in Iraq.

The Army needs to develop leaders who have the capacity (moral complexity) and ownership (moral agency) to challenge their organizations and their own leaders to greater levels of morality, and who have the internal fortitude to take charge and address ethical issues regardless of the will of their peers or superiors. The Army also needs to develop authentic leaders who invite dialogue openly and encourage their own followers to question the leaders' positions and decisions—a form of moral empowerment, allowing the leader, the follower, and the organization to grow morally.

IMPACTS ON MORAL RECOGNITION AND JUDGMENTS

We start with the influence of moral agency on the first two stages of moral reasoning, i.e., moral recognition and moral judgment. When we presented earlier the first concept in the triad—moral complexity—we described it as providing an enhanced ability for a leader to both recognize and process moral dilemmas, but were silent as to the motivation for conducting such deep reasoning during those stages. We now state that it comes from agency. Authentically developed leaders with high levels of moral complexity and moral agency search for and are more likely to perceive moral issues within their environment. Moreover, they increase their depth of cognitive processing once they recognize an issue.

In Chapter 3, Captain Erica Borggren and Colonel Donna Brazil discussed their personal experiences in internalizing West Point values and beliefs in their identity and self-concept. This step is a critical one in moral development and the formation of agency. The likelihood of recognizing a dilemma as a moral issue is dependent upon the amount of issue-related thinking expended by the individual. People who have internalized moral values in their identity are more likely to process more penetratingly and with genuine metacognition those situations that have potential moral issues. This is so because their self-concepts—who they believe themselves to be and their core values—are actively involved. In turn, these leaders who conduct deeper processing are then more likely both to recognize the complexities of the moral issues present and to process more effectively these complexities during the phase of moral judgment.

Deep, controlled processing requires a significant investment of one's precious cognitive resources. Leaders' sense of agency, i.e., responsibility to behave morally, will motivate them to make this investment of energy and cognitive resources.[13] Although people seek validity in their decisions, they are generally "cognitive misers" who tend to use the lowest level of processing possible once initial hypotheses about a particular situation are confirmed.[14] In essence, once people have a sufficient level of information confirming what they already believe, they tend to accept those beliefs as true even when conflicting information may be present. Again, we emphasize that it is engaged leaders, those with higher degrees of moral agency, who take ownership over their domain, who will most thoroughly deal with the moral dilemmas.

IMPACTS ON MORAL INTENTIONS AND BEHAVIORS

By itself, mere cognitive processing is inadequate. Moral recognition and judgments must lead to the last two stages of the moral reasoning process: moral intentions and moral behavior-Leaders must fully own their moral experiences. They do not have the option to determine that something is morally wrong and not take action to correct the problem. Such leaders must see it as their ultimate responsibility to act in a moral manner on behalf of a greater good within, and possibly even outside, their unit or organization. They must hold their own and the profession's virtues as part of their core self-concept.

Leaders with a highly developed sense of moral agency view themselves as moral actors, indeed exemplars, responsible for their moral environment and committed to maintaining and enhancing core values in their and their followers' self-concepts. The leader's self-concept is so critical to moral development because it is the largest and most elaborate of knowledge structures a person holds. Simply stated, as people constantly experience their "self," they gain and hold more information about their self than anything else in their environment. Although individuals may differ in the degree of accuracy of their self-knowledge—i.e., self-awareness—it is largely this knowledge that determines what tasks people engage in and how strongly they persist in those tasks.[15] The self-concept is also temporal—it changes across time. Leaders identify not just with their current self-concept (current self), but also with a more distant image of a possible self, or who they want to become. It is this vision of a possible self that drives a leader's goals and development and is thus central to both moral development and action.[16] At West Point, it is through guided exercises to identify their current self through reflection, and then through additional exercises to envision a possible self (through such as the reflective essays required in the core leadership course), that cadets focus their development and internalize the four identities of officership as specified in CLDS: warrior, servant of the nation, member of a profession, and leader of character.

DEVELOPING MORAL AGENCY AT WEST POINT

We turn now to a discussion of ways Academy leaders can better develop moral agency in future officers—authentic leaders of character who "own" their moral experiences and the honor of their institution. One way is by reflection on the moral precepts within the Cadet Prayer, e.g., "Help us to maintain the honor of the Corps untarnished and unsullied and to show forth in our lives the ideals of West Point in doing our duty to Thee and to our Country." This single tenet from the Cadet Prayer alone encapsulates much of the sense of moral agency. As noted earlier, moral agency has four components: intentionality and forethought in one's moral actions, and self-regulation and self-reflection with regard to one's moral thoughts and actions.

Much of the developmental effort at the Academy should continue to be devoted to inculcating core values in the self-concept of each cadet. The more mentors can focus cadets on the self-reflection aspect of agency—envisioning their possible self as a moral leader—the more cadets will be goal-driven and motivated to realize that possible self. Mentor-cadet discussions should not be entirely abstract. They must go beyond the purely theoretical and compel serious personal empathy and engagement so as to uncover and then challenge the cadet's core values and beliefs. Academy leaders must guide cadets individually in their reflection on both their current and possible self, discover the "gaps" that exist between the two, and coach and mentor cadets to create a tailored developmental plan to fill or bridge these gaps.

Academy mentors can also employ another moral developmental tool, facilitating the inclusion of group values in cadets' self-concepts. The self-concept is multidimensional in that people conceptualize themselves at the individual, interpersonal, and collective levels. In essence, all people have a concept of who they are; who they are in relation to others (e.g., who am I in my relationship with my platoon sergeant?); and who they are in various social groups (e.g., who am I/what is my role as a leader of my platoon?). Leaders can activate these various "levels" of the self in their followers to increase identification with facets of social morality. For example, the more leaders can inspire cadets to identify with the institution of West Point and internalize the values and beliefs of the institution, the more cadets will perceive their self-identity at the collective level. They come to see themselves not just as moral individuals, but as a responsible part of a larger moral community, first the Corps of Cadets and later the Army profession. They will then be more likely to internalize and act in accordance with these collective values (such as enforcing the Honor Code and the values of Duty, Honor, and Country) because the reputation of the organization increasingly becomes central to their own self-concept.

Imagine the inspiration and sense of identification felt by cadets when General Douglas MacArthur famously addressed the Corps on May 12, 1962, saying as he made his final departure from West Point that his "last thoughts will be of the Corps, and the Corps, and the Corps." Through such forms of inspirational motivation which link cadets' self-concepts at the collective level to the larger institution's moral identity, cadets come to accept their central role to lead with altruism and exemplary behavior within their organization.

Development of agency must also focus on building the capability for self-regulation. Self-regulation is the ability to control one's thoughts, emotions, and behaviors, with those having higher levels of this ability being better able to align their actions with their core beliefs. Those lacking in a capacity for self-regulation may practice moral disengagement, thus preventing their self-regulatory mechanisms from activating. They therefore forfeit agency and control over their impulse for immoral conduct (or fail to act when faced with a moral dilemma). It is through moral disengagement that people find excuses for their passivity, rationalizing that moral action is "not their job." For example, people conduct moral disengagement by dehumanizing the victims (e.g., calling their enemies demeaning names in times of war); using euphemisms and sanitizing language to discuss killing (e.g., "neutralize" the target versus "kill" the enemy); transferring responsibility (e.g., "I was just following orders" or "everyone else does it"); discounting the injurious effects (e.g., "only a few may suffer"); and blaming the victims (e.g., "they started it" or "they deserve it"). Resorting to these forms of disengagement allows leaders to protect their self-concept through self-delusion while conducting immoral acts or refusing to act to prevent moral transgressions by others.

It is a leader's role to determine when such coping mechanisms are dysfunctional to the extent that they rationalize or act as cover for immoral behaviors. Academy mentors should talk cadets through these human tendencies in the face of morally problematic stresses, raising cadets' awareness of and ability to control such impulses in themselves and in their future followers.

In addition to direct leader-on-follower developmental techniques such as mentoring, counseling, and inspiring, the organization's culture also plays a key role in developing agency and ensuring that members, especially leaders, do not disengage morally. The culture of the organization is the total aggregation of commonly held values and expectations regarding how members should think, feel, and behave. Thus, the organization has tremendous influence over the behavior, values, and attitudes of its members; and the organization's leaders play a pivotal role in developing and maintaining culture. Disengagement by leaders is less likely to be found in organizations whose cultures value moral engagement and reject moral disengagement. For instance, the Academy's Honor Code has the nontoleration clause which, as a reinforcement of the culture, demands that cadets accept agency over their peers, morally engaging and reporting fellow cadets who violate the Code.

Leaders can also increase agency, and thus moral engagement, by highlighting the consequences—or what has been called the "moral intensity"—of leadership issues. Among other methods, leaders can raise moral intensity by emphasizing (1) the degree of harm or benefit likely to result from an action, (2) the probability that the consequence will actually occur, (3) the short period it may be from the moment of their actions until the estimated consequences occur, and (4) how close the follower is to the victims or beneficiaries of his actions. In this case, "close" may refer to social, physical, or psychological distance rather than spatial. An extremely simplified example would be a leader who, during planning for an operation, states: "If we do not hold closely to the rules of engagement, we have a high probability of killing 30 or so combatants and up to 5 noncombatant civilians during the operation, and may displace many other civilians from their homes. These noncombatants are not sympathizers with the enemy, and we should view them as we would expect our enemies to view our own families." Statements from such a leader would trigger greater moral awareness, activate moral indignation toward inflicting collateral damage during the operation, and increase the propensity for subordinates to take greater ownership of their actions. Moral development may often occur more successfully when embedded in active field-training exercises, rather than in passive classroom settings that lack context and realism.

Over time, as Academy mentors and cultural influences expose cadets to analytical encounters with numerous moral dilemmas—particularly those involving elements of both moral engagement and moral disengagement—cadets will develop their own ability to perceive these facets themselves. In turn, their capacity for and inclination toward moral self-reflection and self-regulation will be increased.

Moral Efficacy

Saint Thomas Aquinas has declared: "The soul is known by its acts." It is true that the character of leaders will ultimately be reflected in their actions. Having outlined the processes of moral complexity and moral agency, we turn now to the third and last of the triad of capabilities: moral efficacy (confidence). This third element is necessary since junior leaders can have increased ability for moral complexity (recognition and judgments), and even see it as their place to adopt moral agency (engagement and intending), but still fail to act because they lack the courage and resilience to see their intentions through to action. A central precept in the Cadet Prayer implores, "Make us to choose the harder right instead of the easier wrong."

Often doing the "harder right" opens leaders to ostracism or alienation, or requires them to overcome strong social pressures. Leaders may even have to confront the moral indiscretions of their own superiors, advisors, or bosses, "speaking truth to power." To spur such moral action, a leader needs a strong sense of moral confidence and courage. Lawrence Kohlberg's theory of cognitive moral development alluded to earlier echoes our position that moral reasoning does not link directly to moral behavior, but rather is mediated through factors that increase or decrease the likelihood that the person will act on their own moral reasoning. These factors include the leader's felt confidence to realize moral ideals using his or her own intelligence and problem-solving capabilities.

Moral efficacy is essentially one's confidence in his or her capabilities to organize and mobilize the motivation and cognitive resources needed to attain desired moral ends while persisting in the face of moral adversity. This conceptualization includes not only one's confidence in her- or himself, known as self-efficacy,[17] but also confidence in his or her means, known as means-efficacy.[18] Self-efficacy includes those facets of personal confidence that enable one to believe that he or she can succeed as a moral actor, i.e., that one has the interpersonal skills to interject himself or herself in a moral dilemma, overcome whatever resistance is present, and make a positive difference. Means efficacy, on the other hand, includes the belief that the environment will allow one to obtain that success. These external elements may include such factors as other people, policies, culture, or equipment. Means efficacy highlights the huge impact organizations have on the moral behaviors of their members. Organizations and companies must generate cultures in which young leaders are immersed in a supportive, highly developed moral organization that encourages its members to be moral actors through such devices as rewards, positive reinforcement, empowerment, etc. Espousing given values within an organization is relatively easy, whereas creating a supportive, value-laden organizational climate is difficult and time-consuming, requiring authentic moral leadership at all levels.

Conversely, an organization that explicitly or implicitly punishes people who raise moral or ethical issues, thus "rocking the boat," or who challenge the morality of the actions of their leaders, will weaken the confidence of junior leaders to step forward. To develop and sustain moral leaders, organizations must solidify junior leaders' beliefs in both self- and means-efficacy—the type of moral efficacy displayed by the cadet who first stepped up to report the Military Academy's football team cheating scandal in 1951. Imbued with knowledge, principle, and confidence in both himself and his institution to face this issue and to maintain cherished ideals and virtues, this cadet put himself on the line and overcame enormous social pressure.

One's self-efficacy is not just a determination of the skills one has, it is rather a judgment of what one can do with those skills in specific contexts and tasks. For instance, one may feel that he or she can successfully intervene as a cadet platoon leader in the moral dilemmas existing in the platoon. When this cadet is on a summer detail out in the Army, however, he or she may lack the confidence to step forward and address a moral indiscretion of a noncommissioned officer/drill instructor. Once the cadet processes the drill sergeant's indiscretion through the first three phases of the moral reasoning process (moral recognition, judgment, and intention) as enabled by the cadet's cognitive complexity and moral agency, the cadet must decide whether and in what way to act. This decision will likely hinge on factors such as the cadet's self-perceptions of whether he or she has the interpersonal skills to reprimand and counsel a seasoned NCO, whether the cadet feels able to bring the issue to the chain of command and receive support on the matter, and whether the cadet's peers, other drill sergeants, or the chain of command will condemn or ostracize him or her for such actions. A morally confident leader will have the courage to go forward in the situation and the resiliency to face any resistance to achieve success.

As leaders experience moral dilemmas in varying situations and are successful in those experiences, they begin to establish a domain of moral efficacy across a broader spectrum of tasks and contexts. Over time these successes transform the leader into an increasingly confident moral actor in even more diverse situations. Junior leaders with higher degrees of moral efficacy will be more likely to act on their beliefs and moral judgments and thus carry intentions through to actual behaviors. In essence, they become leaders who carry action through to do in the Army's leadership philosophy of Be-Know-Do.

DEVELOPING MORAL EFFICACY AT WEST POINT

Given the demands of combat, it is paramount that the Academy develop leaders who face moral adversity with courage, thus embodying the following precept suggested in the Cadet

Prayer: "Endow us with courage that is born of loyalty to all that is noble and worthy, that scorns to compromise with vice and injustice and knows no fear when truth and right are in jeopardy."

There are numerous ways to develop efficacy. First, efficacy can best be built through enactive mastery experiences, i.e., hands-on encounters where cadets practice their moral leadership and succeed. These leaders will then be more likely to use such approaches to address future challenges of a nature similar to those already successfully employed. Not all experiences are the same, however. Leadership development experts Bruce Avolio and Fred Luthans opine that some experiences can be, as noted earlier, "triggering events" that jolt people out of their complacency and into a period of deep self-reflection, thus paving the way for exceptional individual development. A triggering event invokes the deep metacognitive processing outlined earlier, enhancing the likelihood that the person will reflect on the nature and adequacy of his or her own knowledge structures. Iteration of such events over time makes those structures more robust by incorporating the new experiences, increasing cognitive complexity. Following this logic, as the Academy subjects cadets to a succession of moral jolts that are progressively more difficult to handle, cadets will achieve an ever-heightening level of success and strengthen their moral efficacy. The Academy's honor and ethics training programs can best be accomplished by providing such jump-starts for deeper moral reflection. So long as they are reinforced by a supportive organization and guided in timely reflection by capable mentors, acquisition of confidence for moral thought and action will be accelerated.

It is critical that these trigger events allow for initial success and then be ratcheted up in their degree of difficulty at a pace such that cadets continue to succeed, thus avoiding the reduction of efficacy that can occur from failing. We know that moral efficacy can be raised through incremental goal-setting, since research shows that individuals will raise their level of motivation and persistence toward major goals of great difficulty if subgoals along the way are seen as more obtainable. Leaders can develop followers by assisting them in their moral goal-setting and illuminating realistic enabling pathways to their moral development. It is critical, however, that trigger events eventually begin to challenge the moral core of these emerging leaders and force deep reflection.[19]

Although ethics discussions in classrooms serve a useful function, they will not normally provide a sufficient level of challenge. Cadets must be immersed in experiences reflective of the real world, even if they are virtual or vicarious. Although some of these experiences can be brought into the classroom through well-planned, role-playing scenarios and similar formats, they are perhaps better embedded in other training, such as tactical training missions. Further, all trigger events do not have to be planned—leaders can seize upon fortuitous events cadets face as part of their normal life experience by assisting and coaching their reflections on those events. It is critical that leaders have the ability to recognize "moral moments" that have developmental potential. At that point, they can "pull up a chair" and talk cadets through the issue at hand. Fortunately, West Point has more than its fair share of such leader-developers in the rotating faculty (captains and majors with five to eight years of relevant leadership in the Army and then two years of graduate school just before joining the faculty) and staff.

Moral trigger events can also be vicarious experiences in which cadets view other leaders' actions and responses to moral dilemmas, with the stipulation of course that they be coupled with dedicated and guided reflection. These vicarious experiences are most effective when the actor being modeled is perceived by the cadet to be similar to himself. The more a cadet thinks "he is like me so I can do it too," the more effective the modeling will be. Efficacy can also be built through social persuasion, such as senior leaders inspiring junior leaders to believe that they are in fact moral actors and capable of uncommonly challenging moral action.

Moral self-efficacy can be increased through psychological and physiological arousal—essentially "firing people up" about moral leadership and moral action. For instance, when leaders experience a strong emotional response to a moral dilemma, their strong feelings will evoke firmer determination toward addressing it, and their moral efficacy will accordingly be heightened. Thus one method leaders can use to fire up cadets is to show passion themselves toward moral issues and through framing those issues in moral terms. A leader's moral intensity begets moral intensity in his or her followers.

Finally, in developing moral efficacy in cadets it is essential that the Academy continue to articulate the quality and utility of means and support offered by the organization. This support cannot just be declared, it must actually be placed in use by the organization. A social fabric, a feeling of moral support, must permeate the culture in every nook and cranny. In essence, an organization must provide psychological safety to its members. Senior leaders must reinforce to cadets, through word and action, that the organization's leaders and members will support them in their moral initiatives. Leaders must ensure that existing organizational policies encourage, support, and protect those members who come forward to report potential moral improprieties. Supportive leaders will provide cadets with a sense of means efficacy needed for moral efficacy. Foremost, cadets must totally assimilate the value of creating a supportive culture so that they can replicate it in their own units when they are leaders.

AUTHENTIC LEADERSHIP DEVELOPMENT

Moral development is a vast and complex topic that requires integration of such sciences as moral decision making; social, cognitive, and developmental psychology; positive psychology; organizational behavior; and leadership to form a holistic moral development plan for accelerating character development. This chapter has provided an overview of what we consider to be the three major elements of such a developmental plan, those we call the triad of moral capabilities, i.e., moral complexity, moral agency, and moral efficacy.

We have focused here on authentic leadership development, which is evidenced by a true transformational change in the leader so as to enhance his or her self-sustaining capacity to be a moral actor in the absence of social sanctions or reinforcements. A recurring theme throughout this discussion has been the central role of robust moral trigger events, experiences that challenge the moral core of a young leader at ever-rising levels of difficulty. Coupled with mentored reflection and meaning-making sessions, these experiences will broaden and deepen the knowledge structures and cognitive abilities of young leaders and enhance their levels of agency and confidence. Reinforced by a strong sense of agency, they will own their and their followers' moral experiences across their domain of influence, raising their orientation toward altruistic interpersonal behavior.

An increased level of moral efficacy will provide confidence in the ability of young leaders to act and make a positive difference when faced with a moral dilemma—to do the "harder right instead of the easier wrong" as is so memorably expressed in the Cadet Prayer. If the foregoing factors are coupled with perceptions of supportive leaders in an organizational climate that values morality and provides the necessary means, the stage will be set for these leaders to engage fully as moral actors.

For you as an Army leader, leadership in combat is your primary mission and most important challenge. To meet this challenge, you must develop character and competence while achieving excellence.

—FM 22-100, Army Leadership Manual[1]

CHAPTER FIVE

High-Impact Military Leadership

The Positive Effects of Authentic Moral Leadership on Followers

Patrick J. Sweeney and Sean T. Hannah

The epigraph clearly declares that character development plays a central role in preparing leaders to meet the challenges of leading in combat. In fact, character is one of the three pillars in the Army's Be-Know-Do leader development framework. Character corresponds to the Be pillar of the framework, entailing the values and attributes that define a leader. The Know pillar pertains to the competencies (knowledge and skills) leaders must possess, while the Do pillar deals with the application of these competencies to leadership. Each pillar is necessary but not in itself sufficient to provide effective leadership, especially of soldiers in battle. Young leaders must not just be tactically and technically skillful, knowledgeable of leadership skills, and able to use these abilities—they must be imbued with strong character in order to use these abilities in positively and ethically influencing their followers and organizations.

The Army leadership manual mandates that leaders must continuously develop all aspects of their physical, mental, moral, and professional repertoire to become competent leaders of character. A key aspect of this overall development is internalizing the Army's seven primary values: loyalty, duty, respect, selfless service, honor, integrity, and personal courage. The Army values also reflect the values embodied in the U.S. Military Academy's motto of Duty, Honor, Country and the precepts of the Cadet Prayer. The Army and West Point believe that the internalization of these values would provide leaders with a solid character foundation essential for seeking the truth; applying values and principles in their decisions and actions; and displaying the courage, self-discipline, and commitment to do what is right in all situations. Such self-aware and virtuous leaders are authentic leaders of character.

In Chapter 4, we introduced a framework for moral development and discussed how it advances understanding of the Cadet Leader Development System. The focus was on the "how" of moral development. In this chapter, we focus on the "why" of moral development by highlighting the positive and synergistic impact that leaders of character have on their followers and organizations. The intent is to explain why the Army and West Point place such great emphasis on character development.

An authentic leader is one who is morally developed and has internalized the Army and West Point's values as opposed to one who acts ethically merely to comply with social rules and norms or to avoid sanctions. These authentic leaders are highly self-aware and able to regulate their behavior to stay true to themselves and exercise their core moral beliefs in the domain of leadership.

AUTHENTIC MORAL LEADERSHIP'S IMPACT ON TRUST AND INFLUENCE

Leaders' character plays a central role in earning followers' trust. For the purpose of this chapter, trust is defined as one's willingness to put life and limb at risk in the confident expectation that others—subordinates, peers, and leaders—can and will meet their end of the group's cooperative bargain. How, then, does a leader's character impact the development of followers' trust? According to a trust development model based on interdependence theory, set forth in Figure 5-1, trust develops through a reciprocating cycle in which each person in a relationship acts to reduce the other's fear of exploitation and to show that the relationship will be mutually rewarding.

A leader can reduce the followers' uncertainty about the relationship by taking action to show that he/she is dependable and has the ability to make the relationship rewarding. The leader earns his reputation for dependability by demonstrating

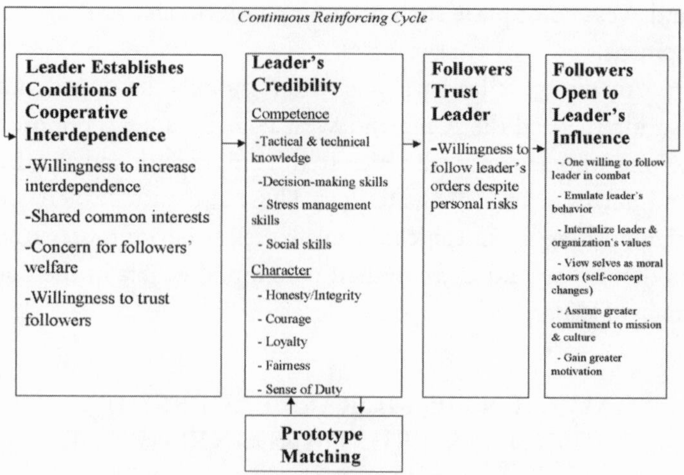

Figure 5-1 **An Interdependence Model for the Development of Trust**

his intentions to trust followers, his willingness to act out of concern for all involved in the relationship, the habitual sharing of common interests, and his willingness to depend on followers. These behaviors serve to establish cooperative interdependence in the leader-subordinate relationship.

Followers infer the leader's values and underlying character traits from the leader's demonstrated cooperative behavior. Thus, the leader's character influences perceptions of dependability. If soldiers think the leader's cooperative behavior is the result of sound and stable character traits, then the leader is perceived as dependable. A leader possessing good character is more likely to behave in a moral and ethical manner and not exploit the relationship. Further, followers' judgments concerning the leader's ability to make the relationship rewarding depend on an assessment of his or her skills, knowledge, and motivation to meet the responsibilities of the position. If individuals believe that a leader's demonstrated competent behavior was due to authentic skills and knowledge, then they will be more likely to believe that the leader will most likely behave in a competent manner in the future. Taken together, the perceptions of a leader's dependable character and competence form an overall evaluation of the leader's credibility. Credibility leads to the development of trust. The model in Figure 5-1 further proposes that trust increases one's willingness to accept influence. Therefore, the processes of developing trust and influence are linked.

This model can be applied to understanding the development of trust and its positive impact on a leader-subordinate relationship. To establish a cooperative interdependent relationship, leaders must trust their followers to do their jobs; genuinely care about their followers; emphasize how the accomplishment of organizational objectives is linked to the obtainment of followers' personal objectives as well; and willingly increase their dependence on their subordinates.[2] A cooperative and interdependent relationship helps provide group members with a sense of confidence that the relationship will be safer and more rewarding, that all members are working to ensure that everyone benefits from the relationship to the maximum degree, and that leaders trust and respect group members. Leaders who extend trust and respect, and demonstrate a willingness to work as a member of the team, prompt subordinates to reciprocate in kind. Followers will infer underlying character traits, such as loyalty, respect, and caring, from the leader's cooperative behavior. This is why the establishment of cooperative interdependence in leader-subordinate relations bolsters perceptions of the leader's credibility.[3]

To determine leaders' credibility, followers will assess both their character and competence. Leader competence entails technical and tactical knowledge, intelligence, decision-making skills, and interpersonal social skills.[4] A leader's character is the combination of values and attributes that define who the leader is as a person. Thus, leaders' characters will influence their interpretation of situations, their approach to leadership duties, their decisions, and most importantly how they behave as leaders.[5]

Leaders who internalize the moral principles embodied in the Cadet Prayer—honesty, the courage and motivation to live with integrity, loyalty to higher moral causes, service to country, maintaining honor—are more likely to behave in an ethical and reliable manner, especially in tough situations, such as combat. Knowing in advance that their leaders will display reliable and ethical behavior in tough and dangerous situations is very important to soldiers, for example, because their lives depend on their leaders' ability to function effectively under the stresses of combat while protecting their welfare. Leaders will be perceived as credible if they possess good character and are competent in meeting the role requirements of their leadership position.

The strength of leaders' character (Be), the extent of their competence (Know), and the establishment of a cooperative and interdependent relationship with followers through leader behaviors (Do), combine to develop trust. As shown in Figure 5-1, the level of subordinates' trust in their leaders in turn determines the extent of leader influence the followers will willingly accept. Followers are more willing to submit to the will of competent leaders of character because these leaders are more likely to fulfill all duties and accomplish all missions in an ethical manner, while at the same time protecting to the maximum degree the welfare of group members. Importantly, subordinates will allow a trusted leader of character to influence their beliefs, values, attitudes, motivation, and behavior.

Thus, trusted leaders will not only have the ability to lead followers effectively, they will also have the ability to change who the followers are as people, a central concept of transformational leadership theory.[6] Transformational leaders induce their followers to internalize their values, beliefs, and visions. Numerous studies have shown that these followers in turn excel beyond expectations.[7] In essence, followers will personally identify with such exemplary leaders and will over time internalize these leaders' values and ideals. This is the ultimate level of influence made possible by the establishment of trust, which is based on the leaders' good character and competence. Leaders who practice authentic moral leadership will earn their followers' trust, providing them with the ability to exercise the high levels of influence necessary for leading effectively.

Illustrations from Studies Conducted in the Iraqi Combat Zone

Results from two studies conducted in the Iraqi combat zone provide new empirical support for the propositions that leaders who practice authentic moral leadership will earn their followers' trust and that this trust provides them a greater ability to exercise high-impact leadership. The studies were conducted by the first author in May 2003 after the end of major combat actions in Operation Iraqi Freedom. The first study tested the validity of an interdependence model for the development of trust (Figure 5-1) using the responses from 315 Army soldiers. The results from this study indicated that the model provided a plausible explanation of how leaders earn their soldiers' trust in combat, that is, by establishing cooperative interdependent relationships, extending their own trust, demonstrating good character, and being competent. Followers' trust in their leader was highly predictive of their willingness to accept that leader's influence. The fact that findings from this study were based on data collected in a combat zone makes the results even more compelling.

This increased level of influence can be partially explained by prototype theory. Previous research had shown that through life experiences in general and through exposures to various leaders in particular, followers build their own *implicit leadership theory* (ILT) over time. An ILT is essentially a prototype of the skills, character, and other physical, emotional, and psychological attributes that followers determine a good leader must hold. This prototype is a form of schema, that is, a mental representation people form in long-term memory. Researchers have shown that a follower's ILT becomes the "lens" through which they view and judge any leader—as shown by the "prototype matching" box in Figure 5-1—and those leaders who best meet one's ILT prototype will be granted more influence.[8]

Importantly, research has shown that the components of moral character are common across the vast majority of followers' implicit leadership theories as to what makes a good leader—Army leaders are expected to be highly morally developed and to lead prosocially. Research has shown that immoral leaders are actually deemed antiprototypical and will be greatly limited in their ability to influence followers.[9] It is also of interest that ethical character is not only a common factor in the prototypes of an ideal leader held by members of the American culture at large, but has been noticed in cross-cultural research to be a universally and internationally held expectation of leader character.[10] This suggests that highly ethical officers, and general leaders, will also have greater influence over members of foreign militaries or organizations attached to or working with U.S. forces and over leaders of local civilian populations they must influence.

The effects of follower vision of the ideal leader were tested by the first author of this chapter in a second study. Seventy-two Army soldiers voluntarily reported, in their own words, the attributes they look for in leaders who could be trusted in combat, discussed why each attribute influenced trust, and rated the relative importance of each attribute to the establishment of trust. They also shared their perceptions of how trust and leadership were related. The two main purposes of the study were to map the prototype of a leader who can be trusted in combat and to explore soldiers' perceptions regarding the relationship between trust and leadership.

The prototype of a trusted combat leader that emerged from the study is outlined as follows:

1. Competence
2. Loyalty
3. Honesty/Good Integrity
4. Leadership by Example
5. Self-Control (stress management)
6. Confidence
7. Courage (physical and moral)
8. Practice of Sharing Information
9. Personal Connection with Subordinates
10. Sense of Duty

Analysis of this prototype clearly indicates that leaders' competence and character are the foundations upon which trust is built. The individual character traits most frequently mentioned by soldiers as important for trust development in combat were loyalty and protectiveness with regard to subordinates' welfare; honesty/integrity in word and deed; physical and moral courage to do the right thing; and a sense of duty to fulfill responsibilities in the toughest situations.

Subordinates' views of the character trait of loyalty were narrowly defined, focused on the leader's concern with and commitment to looking out for their welfare. Responses indicated that loyal leaders look out for their followers' welfare by planning, executing, and accomplishing combat mission objectives with the least possible risk to the lives of their soldiers.

Also, loyal leaders genuinely care about their soldiers, support them, and place their soldiers' welfare before their own. These leaders look out for their subordinates' well-being even if it incurs risk or cost to themselves, which allows soldiers to proceed with their duties in the sure knowledge that their leaders will protect their best interests at all times, especially when the risks are great. It is thus an adaptive process for soldiers to trust leaders who are loyal to them, because it helps ensure their own survival in combat.

An episode related by an artillery lieutenant, serving as an Infantry Company Fire Support Officer, illustrates how his commander's willingness to defy a directive in order to protect his soldiers' welfare demonstrated loyalty and served to bolster trust. The company was conducting an attack in An Najaf while wearing full Nuclear, Biological, and Chemical (NBC) suits in conforming with the battalion commander's guidance. The NBC suits were very heavy and hot. The temperature during the attack was high, and the unit suffered two heat casualties early into the attack. If the unit continued to attack with the NBC suits on, the soldiers would suffer and combat effectiveness would decrease. In the artillery lieutenant's words,

> The Company Commander made the commonsense decision to wear just t-shirts and roll the pants to mid-shin. This may seem like an obvious decision, but it was going against command guidance, and the First Sergeant wanted to remain in uniform. However, it greatly increased the trust in the commander across the company because it was a decision that put the soldiers

and mission first, and not the all-important image depicted through the attached news media.

In the situation described above, the company commander made an adaptive decision based on the combat situation. His willingness to incur risk by defying command guidance to stay in chemical suits demonstrated loyalty to the soldiers' welfare and also enhanced the unit's combat effectiveness. The commander's willingness to hazard his personal standing with his commander in order to protect his soldiers' welfare boosted their trust in him. Research has repeatedly shown that leaders willing to take such personal risks or make self-sacrifices are seen as more charismatic by their followers, further increasing their influence and ability to be high-impact leaders.[11]

Soldiers tended to view leaders' truthfulness in word and deed as exemplifying the core character trait of honesty/integrity. Because soldiers had to take action and risk their lives based on information their leaders provided them, they demanded that leaders be absolutely honest in presenting information. A sergeant who served in an artillery unit provided a statement that captures the importance of leader honesty in combat: "Honesty in my opinion is what makes an effective leader. The Executive Officer of this unit kept us informed and never 'sugar-coated' anything. If we were headed for some rough times, he flat out told us. He always kept us informed and that is what soldiers need."

Leaders with such integrity provided soldiers with reassurance that in the extreme stress and chaos of combat, their welfare would be looked after and the mission accomplished according to the rules. A leader's integrity serves as a foundation for the moral and ethical execution of missions, which sustains his or her subordinates' moral justification for fighting and their will to win. Possessing a sound moral justification for fighting helps soldiers manage both the immediate and long-term psychological stress associated with killing.

Soldiers viewed the critical character trait of moral courage on the part of the leader as possessing the strength to act according to their values and beliefs (integrity), thus doing the right thing. Moral courage often entails taking risks by standing up to authority to protect soldiers' welfare or to defend the leader's decisions. Soldiers trusted leaders who had the moral fiber to take a stand for what they believed in and for the decisions they made, and who possessed knowledge of the proper way to conduct missions. Authentic moral leaders have high levels of moral agency, that is, ownership of and acceptance of responsibility for their moral experiences. Those with high levels of moral agency value living with integrity more than they fear the consequences of taking a stand to fight for what they believe is the right course.

Moreover, authentic leaders also possess the physical courage to face the dangers and hardships and still perform their duties. Leaders must be able to manage their fear—even the bravest will experience fear at times—without betraying it through their looks and manner. A leader's physical courage enhances subordinates' perception of credibility, which facilitates trust because followers can depend on courageous leaders to fulfill their responsibilities in the toughest of situations. An Artillery Battery Executive Officer in Mosul, Iraq, succinctly captured how physical courage influences the development of trust and subordinates' willingness to follow in combat: "I trust leaders who volunteer to share in any potential danger."

Authentic Moral Leadership at My Lai

Captain (USA, Ret.) Hugh Thompson's actions at My Lai epitomized moral agency, moral courage, and moral efficacy. These three qualities drive an authentic moral leader in combat. On March 16, 1968, then Chief Warrant Officer Thompson witnessed American soldiers killing the civilians of the Vietnamese hamlet My Lai as he piloted a helicopter over the village. He became morally outraged at what he was seeing and landed his craft between the American soldiers and the villagers in an attempt to stop the atrocity and evacuate the wounded civilians. He ordered his gunner to open fire on the American soldiers if they continued to shoot the civilians. Thompson was aware that he was risking his own life, the lives of his crew, and a possible court-martial for ordering his gunner to fire on American soldiers in his effort to stop the killing of noncombatants, though he knew his action was the morally right thing.[12]

Further, Thompson had the moral courage to report the incident up the chain of command, to testify before Congressional and military inquiries, and to testify at the court-martial of Lieutenant William Calley. In the face of death threats and ostracism, he steadfastly voiced the truth to the Army and the American people about what happened at My Lai on that March morning.[13] Captain Thompson's action during the My Lai massacre and his subsequent quest to ensure that the truth about the tragic incident was heard, exemplified the principle of moral courage found in the following lines of the Cadet Prayer: "Make us to choose the harder right instead of the easier wrong, and never to be content with a half truth when the whole can be won. Endow us with courage that is born of loyalty to all that is noble and worthy, that scorns to compromise with vice and injustice and knows no fear when truth and right are in jeopardy."[14]

Captain Thompson's strong moral values and his courage to live by these values enabled him to exercise high-impact leadership at the hamlet of My Lai. More important, his authentic moral leadership set the example and served as the moral conscience for the army at large when some members of the Army's leadership tried to cover up this sordid episode. He was truly an authentic moral leader.

The Link between Trust and Combat Leadership

The role of trust in combat or other high-risk or high-stress situations cannot be overestimated. Leaders on a dynamic battlefield cannot do everything alone, so functions need to be spread around and power shared. Effective leadership becomes a system of relationships across all levels of an organization, and these relationships must be sustained through trust, respect, and reciprocity. Leadership research prior to the 1960s tended to view followers as being passive in the leader-follower relationship. Researchers focused more on leader traits or the "position powers" of the leader. These are the authorities they are assigned by virtue of their position, such as the various rewards and punishments that can be employed to influence their followers. More recent research, beginning with contingency models of leadership in the 1960s and continuing with current research on charismatic and transformational leadership, has increased attention on the active role of the follower in the leader-follower relationship.[15]

This more active role of the follower focuses not on leader position powers, but on the "person powers" of the leader, i.e., those powers that must be "earned" by the leader such as referent and expert powers. Referent power exists when subordinates accept a leader's influence because they identify with the leader, use the leader as a role model, and seek the leader's approval.[16] It is the nature of these powers that they can be proffered by followers or denied entirely within their own discretion. We hold that it is these person powers that will have the greatest impact on followers, particularly in a life-threatening combat environment where the efficacy of incentives (reward power), threats of punishment (coercion power), or "because I am in charge and I told you so" (legitimate or formal power) may be seriously diluted. Major General John Schofield in his famous definition of discipline makes this point about as well as words can express:

> The discipline which makes the soldiers of a free country reliable in battle is not to be gained by harsh or tyrannical treatment. On the contrary, such treatment is far more likely to destroy than to make an army. It is possible to impart instruction and to give commands in such a manner and such a tone of voice as to inspire in the soldier no feeling but an intense desire to obey,

> while the opposite manner and tone of voice cannot fail to excite strong resentment and a desire to disobey. The one mode or the other of dealing with subordinates springs from a corresponding spirit in the breast of the commander. He who feels the respect which is due to others cannot fail to inspire in them regard for himself, while he who feels and hence manifests disrespect toward others, especially his inferiors, cannot fail to inspire in them hatred for himself.

The incidents involving "fragging" leaders in combat in the Vietnam conflict are extreme examples of the result when position powers are no longer recognized by followers in a combat environment.[17] In such extreme situations, followers will impute greater influence to leaders who have demonstrated high competence (and thus earned expert power) and have demonstrated the character and values that engender high levels of trust, in essence leaders who are credited by their followers with substantial referent power.

The role of referent power was evident in the second study conducted in Iraq. When asked to describe in their own words how trust was related to leadership, a majority (78 percent) of the respondents indicated that trust was necessary and essential for a leader to exercise influence in combat.[18] Or, to put it simply, subordinates' trust in their leaders determined their willingness to accept leader influence and to risk their lives to achieve the organization's objectives. This was a very powerful finding because the results suggested that in extreme situations, where the subordinates assume the greatest risks, trust is the psychological mechanism that persuades them to willingly accept leader influence, to downgrade their self-interests to a position secondary to the organization's interests, and to step into harm's way. As discussed earlier, competent leaders of character exercising authentic moral leadership will shine forth in their subordinates' eyes as role models, thus earning their followers' trust, which in turn enables them to exercise effective leadership in combat.

Below is a series of actual statements by subordinates that add up to a compelling story of how important trust was to their acceptance of leader influence in combat in Iraq:

> *I think trust is leadership. Leadership is the act of influencing soldiers to accomplish the mission by providing purpose, direction, and motivation. If soldiers don't know that they can trust you to feed them, let them rest, tell you what they are afraid of, then how in the hell are they going to follow you in any situation?*
>
> —Sergeant, Artillery Gunner, Mosul, Iraq

> *If you trust your leader, you are willing to go to hell and back if need be.*
>
> —Sergeant, Artillery Gunner, Tall Afar, Iraq

> *Soldiers first have to trust you to follow you. Following a leader and following orders are two different things. If they trust you and believe in you, there is nothing they won't do for you.*
>
> —Second Lieutenant, Infantry Company Fire Support Officer, Qayyarah West Airbase, Northern Iraq

Trust to me deals a lot with leadership. The more I trust a leader, the more I allow him/her to influence me.

—Specialist, Artillery Computer Operator, Mosul, Iraq

If you trust in your leaders, the soldiers will do more. On the other hand, if they do not trust their leaders, the soldiers will always second-guess their leaders before they do what they have to do.

—Sergeant, Mechanic, Mosul, Iraq

It is like a Field Manual. The Field Manual is the leader. If I do not trust it, I would not read it. I would not take information from it or apply it or risk any lives. Trust in a leader allows you to listen and do what is expected of you. And because you trust the leader, you know that he will not foolishly risk your life and that of your peers/subordinates.

—First Lieutenant, Platoon Leader, Mosul, Iraq

The responses above indicate that subordinates who did not trust their leaders would follow the leaders' directives only reluctantly, would question orders, and also would be unwilling to assume the risks of combat, all of which could put unit members' lives at risk and have a detrimental impact on organization effectiveness. The lack of trust in a leader would cause subordinates to fret about their personal safety and at the same time cause anxious doubts as to whether the leader's directives would result in accomplishment of the organization's objectives. This questioning of leader directives and focus on personal safety could result in subordinates' adopting a protective or timidly passive attitude, which would decrease their aggressiveness and the will to face the rigors of combat. Subordinates will look for ways to change or avoid a nontrusted leader's directive in an effort to minimize risks to their own safety, probably complying with his orders only as a last resort. In extreme cases, subordinates may even disobey orders of leaders they do not trust. The responses below illustrate how the lack of trust in a leader decreases subordinates' willingness to accept leader influence:

If you do not trust your leaders, it can be difficult to follow orders, especially if death or dismemberment is [a likely] result.

—Sergeant, Infantry Company Forward Observer,
Qayyarah West Airbase, Northern Iraq

If you cannot trust your leader, you are going to have doubts about your safety as well as the safety of your fellow soldiers. You will not perform at 100 percent for your leader if there is not trust.

—Specialist, Artillery Gunner, Mosul, Iraq

If soldiers do not trust their leaders it leads to second-guessing and possible disobedience of orders.

—Staff Sergeant, Chief Fire Direction Computer,
Mosul, Iraq

You can tell a man to fight as his leader.
If he doesn't trust you, he will change the things you want.
If he trusts you, he will do what you want.

—Sergeant, Supply Noncommissioned Officer,
Qayyarah West Airbase, Northern Iraq

Trust is the most important thing that can relate to leadership. Because if I don't trust my leader, I will question every order in my head, which can make me hesitate and may get me killed.

—Specialist, Infantry Company Armor,
Qayyarah West Airbase, Northern Iraq

The main foundation for leadership is trust. If you cannot trust the person or people who lead you, then basically you are lost. How can you be influenced to do something if you cannot trust the person telling you what to do?

—Sergeant, Artillery Gunner, Mosul, Iraq

A soldier who does not trust a leader will question decisions the leader makes and will not be willing to follow the leader into a dangerous situation.

—Staff Sergeant, Platoon Sergeant, Mosul, Iraq

As verified by the examples above, subordinates view trust in leaders as a necessary condition for their willingness to accept leader influence and the risks of combat. Subordinates in Iraq willingly followed the directives of leaders they trusted and seemed willing to put forth extra effort and assume a greater degree of risk to accomplish the mission—in essence these leaders were high-impact leaders. On the other hand, subordinates who did not trust their leaders did not willingly follow them, questioned orders, and seemed to take measures against orders to minimize the risk to their personal safety. The results clearly confirm that in order to lead effectively, especially in extreme situations such as combat, leaders must earn their subordinates' trust.

Higher trust will give leaders greater "negotiating latitude" with their followers under stress. Under the time constraints and dynamic nature of combat, leaders must often be very task-oriented and transactional in their leadership. Particularly during enemy engagements, there is rarely time for full explanations or mutual participation in decision making. Followers must "blindly" follow their leaders under such situations and, as we have noted, unquestioningly put themselves in harm's way as ordered. The latitude that allows leaders to be directive in combat and still gain commitment of their followers must be built over time and prior to "game day" through the exercise of consistent and trust-evoking moral leadership. This type of leadership is an accurate reflection of the character of the moral leader.

AUTHENTIC MORAL LEADERSHIP'S IMPACT ON FOLLOWERS' MORAL DEVELOPMENT

Authentic moral leaders bolster their followers' moral development through modeling, persuasion, and establishing a moral and ethical culture in the organization. Highly developed leaders play a critical role in the development of their own followers and organizations. In fact, it is these leaders who in their turn lead others along the moral development processes.

Followers who trust their leaders are more apt to identify with these leaders and use them as role models by emulating their behaviors. These leaders of character serve as exemplars of an ideal leader whom group members want to emulate. The ideal leader is defined by the set of attributes, values, characteristics, and behaviors that reflect what the members of an organization or profession commonly believe makes such a leader. The prototype of an ideal combat leader that emerged from the Iraqi studies, clearly established that a leader's competence and character form the basis of trust. Further, the results from these studies indicated that individuals will trust and willingly follow leaders who are competent and possess the character attributes of loyalty, honesty, integrity, courage, and a sense of duty. Thus, the ability to lead arises from a leader's competence and character.

Followers who view themselves as leaders or have the desire to become leaders are more likely to incorporate the prototype of an ideal leader into their self-schema or future self-schema (their envisioned "possible self") because it pictures what they aspire to become. Once followers internalize the prototype of an ideal leader into their self-schemas, they will start to define themselves as moral-ethical leaders. This view of the self as a moral-ethical leader causes followers to view situations in a different perspective, increases the salience of moral and ethic considerations in their decision making, improves their behavior, makes them more attentive to the moral-ethical behavior of others, and provides them purpose and focus in their developmental journey to become authentic moral leaders.[19] Therefore, authentic moral leaders as exemplars serve as both sources of developmental information and motivation for followers.

Followers will use leaders of character as exemplars and sources of information to learn moral-ethical behavior, learn attitudes pertaining to morals and ethics, gain ideas on how to develop needed attributes, and, most important, form comparative standards for their development. Through focused observation, subordinates will learn moral-ethical behavior, attitudes, and decision making skills from trusted leaders. By observing leaders who are in fact moral exemplars, followers learn to identify cues that frame a moral-ethical situation, infer decision criteria for measuring and comparing courses of action, and gain an appreciation for the first- and second-order effects of the decision both inside and outside the organization. Observational learning also provides followers with insights to the specific techniques and strategies that authentic leaders use to develop and maintain the attributes necessary to lead in a moral and ethical manner. Thus, by serving as role models, authentic moral leaders exercise an impact on the development of their followers' moral complexity and efficacy.[20] As discussed in Chapter 4, moral complexity refers to the extent of development of the followers' moral schemas (cognitive frameworks by means of which they make moral decisions) while moral efficacy pertains to the followers' degree of confidence and courage to engage in moral-ethical behavior.

This is why the military faculty at West Point, especially the rotating faculty, plays such an essential and pivotal role in the moral development of USMA cadets. They serve as exemplars of warriors who are leaders of character that cadets should strive to be like at the end of their four-year developmental journey toward officership. The military faculty engage cadets in moral and ethical discussions both inside and outside the classroom. Besides teaching, the vast majority of military faculty members serve as cadet mentors, cadet sponsors, and officer representatives for cadet sports teams and clubs, and they attend cadet activities, all of which roles provide numerous opportunities for cadets and the military faculty to interact. These out-of-class interactions allow cadets to observe military faculty members behaving morally and ethically in all types of settings, provide opportunities to discuss the profession; and most important, provide opportunities for military faculty to help cadets work through and/or make sense of moral and ethical issues. This extensive cadet engagement, both inside and outside of the classroom, by the military faculty plays an essential role in the development of cadets' moral schemas and efficacy.

Subordinates use authentic moral leaders as benchmarks to chart their developmental progress toward realizing their self-concepts and becoming leaders of character through the process of social comparison. By comparing themselves against authentic moral leaders who possess the desired skills and attributes of an ideal Army leader, followers gain developmental insights.[21] They can use these insights to make adjustments to their developmental plan by shifting priorities and directing efforts to developing attributes or skills that are not up to the exemplar's standard. Serving as the comparison standard for followers' self-concepts is a high-impact effect of authentic moral leadership.

Followers using exemplar leaders of character as the standards by which to modify their own self-concepts is one of the noblest forms of influence leaders can exercise. Therefore, authentic moral leaders, whom followers use as comparison standards for their self-concepts, contribute to the development of their subordinates' moral complexity, moral agency, and moral efficacy through the social comparison process. Observational learning and the social comparison process not only provide group members with developmental information, they also serve as sources of motivation. Followers can gain inspiration by observing exemplary leaders being rewarded in terms of praise and respect for behaving in a moral-ethical manner. Observing a role model's moral-ethical behavior being rewarded increases the likelihood that one will learn and enact a similar behavior in the future. Subordinates' motivation to enact learned moral-ethical behavior rests with the perception that this behavior is rewarded by the organization for the right reasons.[22]

Thus, leaders can foster moral and ethical behavior in their organizations by ensuring that it is recognized and rewarded. For those followers who have a lower level of moral development, they have to see that behaving morally and ethically leads to external rewards such as recognition, praise, or promotions before they will learn and enact this type of behavior. On the other hand, followers who possess higher levels of moral development can experience vicariously and thus profit from the intrinsic rewards in the offing for leaders behaving in a moral and ethical manner. This vicarious experience alone might be sufficient to reinforce future moral-ethical behavior in followers with high levels of moral development.[23]

The social comparison process can also serve as a source of self-motivation for followers. Group members' developmental motivation will most likely increase when they compare themselves against an authentic moral leader and perceive progress. This perceived developmental progress or movement toward becoming one's possible-self as an authentic moral leader bolsters followers' motivation because it demonstrates growth and affirms their abilities to reach their goals.[24] This is especially true if followers perceive that exemplary leaders are similar to them, because that similarity makes the example set by the exemplar appear more obtainable—it validates their self-concept, indicates a smaller developmental gap, and boosts their confidence that they may become an exemplary moral leader themselves.

PERSUASION AND MORAL DEVELOPMENT

Leaders of character can use persuasion to enhance their followers' moral development. Research in the area of persuasive communication has confirmed that credible communicators are far more persuasive than those who lack credibility. A credible communicator is a person perceived as honest or trustworthy and possessing expertise in the subject matter. People will listen to and trust information from credible sources and thus be more likely to be persuaded.[25] Authentic moral leaders are credible communicators when it comes to moral development and can better influence the development of their followers' moral complexity, agency, and efficacy.

Leaders of character should take the time to talk followers through their decision processes as they resolve, or after they resolve, a moral-ethical dilemma. This exercise would help group members gain insights into the thought processes needed to identify and successfully resolve moral and ethical issues. This in-depth exposure to the authentic leaders' thought processes in resolving a moral-ethical issue reinforces and enriches the information followers gain from observational learning, in the process promoting the development of the complexity of subordinates' moral schemas. From leaders sharing their moral-ethical decision processes, subordinates may gain useful new perspectives, e.g., for viewing or framing moral-ethical dilemmas, structuring a decision-making process, learning important criteria for evaluating possible solutions, acquiring techniques for implementing a moral-ethical decision, and gaining a greater appreciation for the implications of moral and ethical decisions. All these new perspectives serve to increase the subordinates' moral complexity. Moreover, by providing followers with the insights and tools to analyze and successfully resolve problems in a moral-ethical manner, leaders are bolstering their followers' moral efficacy.

Similarly, subordinates will seek out authentic moral leaders to help them resolve personal moral-ethical issues. Leaders should help these followers by guiding them through a moral and ethical decision-making process to successfully resolve the issue. The salience of the personal issue, along with the follower's trust of the leader, would advance development of the group members' moral schemas. Once an issue is thus resolved in a moral-ethical manner, leaders should encourage the subordinates who dealt with the problems to share their thoughts and decision-making process with the team if the issue is appropriate for outside discussion. Group members are more likely to attend to and learn from information presented by a peer.[26] Group sharing and discussion about moral-ethical issues promotes the moral development of all team members. The insights followers gain from these open discussions reinforce development of their moral schemas, and in seeing peers successfully resolve moral-ethical issues through such discussions, followers experience a further boost of their own moral efficacy.

ESTABLISHING A MORAL AND ETHICAL CULTURE

Beyond individual identification with the leader as a role model, at the collective level authentic moral leadership has a tremendous impact on the establishment of the moral and ethical culture in any organization, group, or business. An organization's culture consists of a shared collection of implicit values and assumptions regarding the appropriate way members should perceive, think, feel, and behave in dealing with each other and in external functioning to reach goals. Thus, an organization's or business's culture has a significant influence on the values, attitudes, beliefs, and behavior of each of its members.[27] The circular that explains the Cadet Leader Development System stresses the importance of organizational culture to the development of members' character: "Character is shaped in communities where members practice virtuous living and pass those virtues on to others."[28]

In addition to observing the behaviors of its members, one can assess an organization's culture by looking at the artifacts or observable objects associated with the organization, for example, the USMA Honor Monument cadets walk by on a daily basis at West Point. Leaders, who live the Army values and demand that followers do the same, establish the moral and ethical aspects of the culture in their organizations and reinforce values through consistent behaviors. Eventually, all members will understand that the organization and its members expect them to behave in a moral and ethical manner and perceive that it is correct to do so in all situations. Reinforced over time, these moral and ethical values and expectations will become incorporated into the organization's culture, which is passed on to new members of the group through socialization processes. Authentic moral leaders can significantly influence the moral development of their subordinates by properly shaping the organization's culture.

Building Morality through Social Identity Processes

Organizational members gain much of their identity from the groups they belong to through social identity processes.[29] When people are asked to define themselves, they will normally include the main groups they are members of, such as American, female, infantryman, or Californian, and often various subgroups of attributes associated with a group (e.g., warrior as a subset of infantryman). Soldiers in particular, due to long work hours, the strong military culture and cohesion, and a shared common danger, interact and thus bond with their units more so than with any other social groups, sometimes including even their families, and are thus more likely to extract identity from their units. Social identity theory states that we identify with groups both to assist in categorizing ourselves and to gain esteem and psychological well-being. When one joins a prestigious country club or becomes a member of a profession, he or she is able to assume the positive identity of that group and incorporate that identity into his/her self-schema.

Leaders who create a moral culture in their organization increase the likelihood that aspects of moral identity will be internalized by their followers.[30] For example, West Point is known throughout the world as a bastion of honor and integrity, bolstered by the Honor Code and other ameliorative cultural artifacts. Cadets, regardless of their level of moral fortitude prior to arrival at the Academy, are able to incorporate honor and integrity into their self-schema and almost immediately transform the way they look at themselves as leaders of stronger character. Moral improvement through identity with West Point becomes so central to cadets that they will strive to maintain the organization's codes in order to maintain their own self-schemas. Any stain on the code will be seen as a stain on their own identities.

In combat it is imperative that Army leaders exemplify the professional ethos and execute operations in accordance with the Rules of Engagement (ROE), the Laws of Land Warfare, and the Geneva Convention. By setting high ethical and moral standards for the unit, leaders reaffirm the organization's cultural values and clearly delineate the moral and ethical boundaries for subordinates to operate within. These boundaries are important for keeping the distinction between socially sanctioned and morally justified application of lethal violence, on one hand, and unlawful murder on the other. Leaders who ensure that their units conduct combat operations in a lawful manner uphold the sacred trust the citizens of this country have in the military profession and affirm the country's values and moral justification for fighting, all of which serve to sustain soldiers' will to fight.[31] The moral application of force also limits our enemy's ability to assail the integrity of our nation, our military, and our motives for engaging in war. We have all seen how the moral failures of leaders at Abu Ghraib Prison in Iraq empowered our enemies to deride the United States in order to justify their own acts of terrorism and other atrocities, and to gain support of noncombatants against the U.S. and allied forces. Ethical lapses also demoralize our own soldiers. Soldiers' resolve to fight will remain strong as long as they believe that the cause is just and that combat operations are being executed in the most ethical manner possible.

Highly Developed Moral Leaders in the Military

Two examples demonstrate the importance of highly developed moral leaders and how these leaders' actions clearly establish and reinforce the importance of adhering to the moral and ethical boundaries governing combat operations. As witnessed by the first author of this chapter during V Corps' march to Baghdad during Operation Iraqi Freedom in 2003, the commanding general received intelligence that large formations of vehicles were moving from northern Iraq toward Baghdad. The conclusion from the intelligence analysis indicated that the Iraqi army was repositioning forces to reinforce Baghdad's defenses. At this time, the areas around Baghdad were experiencing major sand storms and the staff believed that the Iraqis were using this period of limited visibility to reposition military forces. Military units are most vulnerable to attack when they are moving in large formations on roads. The commander asked whether any element could physically observe these formations, which was a prerequisite for attack according to the ROE under which the Corps was operating. The storm prevented any friendly elements from confirming that the vehicle formations moving toward Baghdad were military. The commander was facing a stark dilemma: Should he adhere to the ROE, or should he direct an attack on these fleeting, lucrative targets without physical confirmation?

Prior to the start of this operation, planners estimated that the fight for Baghdad would result in heavy casualties and would be long drawn out. If the formations moving south were military, they would strengthen the defenses of Baghdad, which would more than likely result in greater U.S. casualties. The commander had only a small window of opportunity to attack the formations. The commander was thus faced with a tough decision of exceptional moral content. He decided to adhere to the ROE and not to attack the formation of moving vehicles. His decision clearly communicated to his staff and subordinate units that the moral and ethical guidelines governing the Corps' conduct in combat were applicable and that the members of his unit could not violate them. The Corps battle staff was initially frustrated by not being able to engage such lucrative targets, but realized the commander did the right thing. The commander's strong moral leadership solidified the moral and ethical culture in the unit, which enhanced the probability that future combat operations would be conducted in a similarly ethical manner.

Another instance was experienced by the second author of this chapter during the first Gulf War in 1991, when immediately after the end of hostilities his infantry battalion was moved to a position on the military demarcation line (MDL)—the line separating U.S. and Iraqi forces. The rules of the surrender agreement disallowed any hostile action across the MDL unless U.S. forces were directly fired upon. The Iraqis used this limitation to blatantly murder Iraqi civilians, primarily Shiites, who they claimed were "sympathizers" of U.S. forces. These executions, often in the direct view of U.S. forces and at times involving the murder of women and children, were atrocious and demoralizing to American soldiers. The battalion commander in this case talked to his junior leaders candidly about the moral aspects of this issue (thereby promoting the moral development of his junior leaders in the process) and formulated what he determined was the best moral solution given the less-than-perfect choices. He determined that the greater good is served by adhering to the ROE, but made best use of the maximum boundaries of the ROE by firing nonlethal illumination mortar rounds and at times staging feint attacks on Iraqi forces whenever executions were being commenced. These actions greatly reduced the overt executions while also reducing the psychological strain on U.S. troops and their need to take some humanitarian action. By staying within the limits of the ROE under such atrocious conditions, the commander balanced and reinforced both the rules of conduct and also the personal impulses of soldiers to take actions to stop these atrocities.[32]

In contrast to these two positive examples, we shall glance at an incident highlighting the consequences of a commander's decision to break ethical guidelines in an effort to prevent an upcoming attack against his unit. This incident from Operation Iraqi Freedom illustrates the significant impact a commander's behavior has on a unit's moral-ethical culture. In August 2003, a battalion commander received intelligence that he was being targeted for assassination and that the guerrillas were going to ambush elements of his unit in a very short time. The intelligence also indicated that a local policeman was involved with the guerrilla forces. The commander had the local policeman arrested and brought to his headquarters for questioning.[33]

After the interrogators failed to get useful information from the policeman, the commander conducted his own interrogation. He had his soldiers physically rough up the policeman in an effort to get the information about the attack. When this failed, the commander decided to use his weapon for intimidation. The commander fired his pistol into a clearing barrel and then had the policeman placed next to the barrel. The commander then fired his pistol close to the policeman's head, frightening him so badly that he divulged information about the upcoming guerrilla attack, including names of those involved. With this information, the unit was able to capture the guerrillas and prevent the intended ambush. The commander thereupon informed his superior of his actions and was relieved of command after a formal investigation.

The episode brings into bold relief the dilemma of how far a commander should go to protect the welfare of his soldiers in combat. The battalion commander used the threat of deadly force to persuade the prisoner to quickly reveal the information about the upcoming attack. His interrogation technique was successful, the information obtained helped save soldiers' lives, and the prisoner, though terrorized, was unharmed. The foregoing scenario illustrates the tough situation commanders face when they have to ask their soldiers to assume more risk than would otherwise be necessary in order to hew to the moral and ethical path. The scenario also highlights the ramifications of the commander's actions when he or she takes a wrongful path. Unless one is embedded in the situation, he or she cannot fully appreciate the overpowering strength of the bonds of brotherhood that drive commanders to protect their soldiers. In tough, morally and ethically ambiguous situations, commanders are expected to consider all implications—immediate as well as long-term, direct as well as indirect, tactical as well as strategic—of their decisions.

In this case, the commander decided to break the moral and ethical rules to reduce a potential threat to his unit. His desire to protect the welfare of his soldiers was honorable; however, the means used to do it was not. The commander admitted that what he did was wrong, but he did it anyway to protect his soldiers. By breaking ethical rules to get the information about the upcoming ambush, the commander blurred the moral and ethical boundaries for all soldiers in the unit. In addition, his behavior called into question the moral and ethical values of the organization's culture. The commander's actions during the interrogation put his unit on a very "slippery slope" that could lead to moral and ethical lapses in future combat operations. For instance, the next time his soldiers stopped suspected guerrillas and wanted information quickly, they might follow the example of the commander and threaten the use of deadly force. Since the commander's behavior blurred the moral and ethical boundaries pertaining to conduct in combat, soldiers in this unit could very easily have stepped over the line and committed an atrocity in pursuit of a laudable goal. Therefore, to negate the impact of the commander's unethical behavior on the unit's culture, he was properly relieved of command.

All of the foregoing examples highlight the concept of moral complexity. A leader in the often morally ambiguous contexts must be able to conduct moral reasoning through a set of multidimensional lenses that assesses the rules, outcomes, and also the inherent virtues associated with a moral dilemma.

Authentic moral leadership that sets clear and firm moral and ethical boundaries for followers to operate within helps ensure that they will do the right thing in all situations.

AUTHENTIC MORAL LEADERS

The moral values and principles contained in the Cadet Prayer, Cadet Honor Code, and Army values, if internalized by leaders, will lay the foundation for the development of their character. Leaders who live by these values and principles will have the ability to exercise authentic moral leadership. Results from the studies investigating trust and leadership in combat clearly indicate that leaders must have good character to lead effectively. Followers will trust competent and morally strong leaders and allow them a greater degree of influence and latitude under stress. Soldiers will willingly follow trusted leaders of character into the frightening, dangerous, and chaotic environment of combat. For they know that trusted leaders of character will accomplish the mission in an ethical manner and with the least risk to their lives.

Moreover, leaders' moral and ethical values and behaviors have a significant influence on the moral development of their followers by setting the example and establishing a positive moral and ethical culture in their units. The leader's character, coupled with a strong moral and ethical organizational culture, helps establish clear and firm boundaries for conduct. Military leaders serve as moral and ethical guardians to ensure that their units uphold the values of the nation and the Army, thus validating the moral justification for fighting, preserving soldiers' will to fight, protecting followers' psychological well-being, and maintaining the honor of the profession. These actions in turn maintain the American people's trust and respect for their military professionals. Character is the foundation for leadership. This is why character development is so important to leadership, and why West Point takes it so seriously.

CHAPTER SIX

Moral Principles and Moral Reasoning in the Ethics of Leadership

Anthony E. Hartle

General Sir John Hackett once claimed that good soldiers must first of all be good people. His argument for that claim is compelling and one that the Military Academy fully accepts. The further question for a developmental institution like West Point focuses on what it means to be a good person. Over the last 20 years I have had the opportunity to work with the staff and faculty at the Military Academy in pursuing that question as well as the issue of what the Academy should teach cadets to help them become good men and women as well as good soldiers.

When I was a cadet learning about the values of the Academy and of the profession I aspired to enter, all cadets attended chapel on Sundays. Each cadet could choose which religious service to attend, but all participated. A variety of religious services were available, to include Protestant, Catholic, and Jewish. The Academy no longer requires attendance, though many cadets voluntarily participate.

One common element of our lives on Sunday was the Cadet Prayer. I remember reflecting at the time that the virtues identified in the Prayer had a fundamental appeal that easily crossed faith and denominational boundaries—the Prayer expressed what it means to be a good person from a religious perspective, indeed, but it also presented a prescription that held in almost any context. That congruence with our society's views explains to a degree why the Cadet Prayer is consistent with the ethic of the military profession as well. The Prayer's description of what it means to be a good person applies directly to General Hackett's statement that good soldiers are first of all good people.

The Cadet Prayer presents the following exhortations, among others:

> Admire honest dealing and clean thinking.
> Do not tolerate hypocrisy or pretense.
> Live above the common level of life.
> Choose the harder right instead of the easier wrong.
> Do not be content with a half truth.
> Be loyal to all that is noble and worthy.
> Scorn to compromise with vice and injustice.
> Reject fear when truth and right are in jeopardy.

Keep honor untarnished and unsullied.
Manifest the ideals of West Point.

These expectations provide useful insight concerning the character of a good person in terms of development the West Point way. In the ethics of the military profession, you will see that the strictures of the Cadet Prayer, the traditions of the military, and the requirements of the military ethic have much in common for military leaders, and can apply to those in leadership positions outside of the military as well.

WHAT WE TEACH: THE FOUNDATIONS OF THE MILITARY PROFESSION

History plays a major role in cadet education. The Academy has long emphasized the broad moral principles that structure the military ethic and the moral reasoning that characterizes sound decision making by military leaders. The work of the Academy staff and faculty in recent years, as they studied the content and application of the professional military ethic, has guided the actions of leaders in our military services.

Much of what we teach at West Point comes from history and tradition. To understand the substance and depth of the military ethic, one needs to know how it evolved. A part of that understanding comes from knowing how military service developed as a profession. When we look at the historical record, we find that professional military forces emerged during the last two centuries, although a long history of warriors and armies led up to their emergence. Professional armies are not a development peculiar to the modern world. In all probability, ancient Egypt in certain periods maintained well-trained, highly experienced armies of men who made careers of fighting wars, but in the period that we know well, from 900 A.D. to the present, professional armies came into being only during the last two centuries.

Military institutions have evolved into complex organizations that serve the purposes of their political masters, and military culture has become bound by both custom and law. In that culture, professional and moral guidelines limit permissible action by those who exercise military force in the name of the state. In educating cadets at West Point, the faculty has carefully studied the history of the profession and the standards for professional conduct of members of the military that have evolved over time. Understanding that history makes clear that the standards are firmly grounded in both tradition and principle.

Warriors and Soldiers

Historical records show that armed warriors have played a central role in the life of almost all societies, and evidence indicates that was true long before written records appeared. Besides to hunt more effectively, human beings have taken up arms to defend themselves, their families, and their communities from a variety of external threats that often included other people.

Over 4,000 years ago, however, events triggered a momentous change that altered the nature of conflict prevailing in primitive societies. More structured governing organizations, agricultural development that stabilized populations and made land highly prized, and other factors in combination led to the widespread establishment of armies. Expanding societies turned from ritualized combat between warriors to the pursuit of conquest by large, organized military forces. In disciplined, trained military formations, the warriors became soldiers, and over the centuries between 9000 BC and 3000 BC, civilization and politics introduced systematic warfare.

The State

The emergence of the state brought the genesis of armies, which only the state could support. At the same time, the army was essential to the existence of the state. The Roman legions provide a striking example. Historians consider Rome the "mother house of modern armies."[1] Beginning in the fifth century BC, the Roman Empire began to expand, subsequently using the fierce discipline and merciless efficiency of the legions in an ever-widening circle of conquest. In the view of John Keegan, "The Roman centurions, long-service unit-leaders drawn from the best of the enlisted ranks, formed the first body of professional fighting officers known to history."[2] At its height during the second century AD, the Empire, through the legions, controlled provinces stretching from Gibraltar to Hadrian's Wall on the Scottish border, encompassing most of modern Europe and the Middle East, and then extending across all of northern Africa to Morocco. The purposes to which Rome put her professional soldiers may well be questioned, but few question the dedication and sacrifices of the legions.

The "centurionate," the professional core of the legions, provided the great strength of an army that dominated the known world for century after century. The higher-ranking leadership came from the upper levels of Roman society and came in good supply since service as a tribune (a military commander associated with the lower classes) was a prerequisite for political service leading to the ruling consulate and imperial power.[3] Contemporary military forces whose members take pride in their traditions and successes pale in achievement when we consider the record of the legions of Rome over nearly six centuries.

The role the military played in the evolution of Roman society also proved notable. John Keegan emphasizes its centrality: "Rome, unlike classical Greece, was a civilization of law and physical achievement, not of speculative ideas and artistic creativity. The imposition of its laws and the relentless extension of its extraordinary physical infrastructure demanded not so much intellectual effort as unstinted energy and moral discipline. It was of these qualities that the army was the ultimate source. . . ."[4]

While no one makes so strong a claim for the military services in America today, the military remains a repository of some of the primary values that have formed our society and its institutions. John Keegan says of the legionnaire that "[h]is values were those by which his fellows in the modern age continue to live: pride in a distinctive (and distinctively masculine) way of life, concern to enjoy the good opinion of comrades, satisfaction in the largely symbolic tokens of professional success, hope of promotion, expectation of a comfortable and honourable retirement."[5] And throughout, of course, the life of the legionnaire demanded iron discipline and extraordinary loyalty.

From Roman Legionnaires to Modern Military Professionals

Five centuries after the barbarians sacked Rome, men still fought in the same manner, though not nearly as efficiently as had the legions. The swarming horse cavalry of the steppes and the Arab world were ferociously successful, but their contributions to military development were tactical rather than formative. With the Fall of Rome, the disciplined Roman armies disappeared. Standing military organizations serving the state did not reappear for almost a thousand years. Throughout the medieval centuries, the feudal system, in which the mounted man-at-arms was the central figure, dominated Europe. During this period, and especially after the 11th century, chivalry became a dominating feature of Western military culture. While overlaying the brutality of the Crusades with the ideals of chivalry appears suspect at first glance, the influence of the Church and the founding of knightly orders led to refinements in the outlook and conduct of fighting men that remain with us to this day. Enemies in battle (other than heretics, unbelievers, and peasants who failed to adhere to their appropriate class roles, of course) were to be accorded respect and treated in accordance with an elaborate code of honor. Such attitudes provide the moral foundation for the modern international laws of war. To the indispensable virtue of loyalty and the courtesies owed to fellow members of the knightly class, the religious knightly orders such as the Templars and the Hospitallers added the characteristics of discipline in personal affairs as well as in battle and service to a higher cause. Loyalty and service to a higher cause became lasting features of the military culture of the West, though the example of the mercenary soldier obscured that picture for some time. The Roman tradition had relied upon the idea of a citizen army, an arm of the state, and that concept gradually reentered Western institutions, coming to full flower under Gustavus Adolphus of Sweden in the 17th century in the midst of European powers that still relied upon mercenary forces (mercenaries dominated conflict for more than a century). Gustavus Adolphus "successfully developed and applied [the Roman model] on the battlefield, and the system he evolved persisted in its essentials well into the twentieth century."[6] That system involved conscripted soldiers, generally linear formations, smaller units (though larger armies), and more junior leaders who had to exercise some initiative. The Swedish commanders endlessly drilled infantry units in precise formations, prepared them for specific tactical maneuvers, and used cavalry elements for shock action. Sweden's great success was a factor leading to the development of standing armies.

In the Europe of the 17th and 18th centuries, in the midst of the Enlightenment and the flourishing of science and human progress, each state believed that it could ensure its survival only by developing military forces and alliances sufficient to defend against other states pursuing their own interests at the expense of their neighbors. We can find features of the professional military, as we understand that term today, in the European armies of the mid-1700s, even though the professional officer corps came into its own only after the Napoleonic Wars. The officer ranks had begun to develop the characteristics described by Samuel Huntington in his penetrating study of military sociology: corporate unity, career structure, and specialized training.[7] Army and navy officers were about to become not just masters of their trade, as many undoubtedly had been over the centuries, but members of a profession, a distinction that requires some explanation and one that illuminates the status of the military ethic.

Many developments revealed the need for professional skills in managing armed forces, but the enormous increase in logistical requirements in the 19th century provides an obvious one. Large, technologically advanced armies called for professional military logisticians. Amateur soldiers could not meet the demands of the campaigns that followed the Napoleonic era, as the following historical note illustrates:

> Napoleon's artillery at Waterloo [1815] . . . numbered 246 guns which fired about a hundred rounds each during the battle; in 1870 at Sedan, one of the most noted battles of the nineteenth century, the Prussian Army fired 33,134 rounds; in the week before the opening of the battle of the Somme [in World War I], British artillery fired 1,000,000 rounds, a total weight of some 20,000 tons of metal and explosive.[8]

As a result of these and other requirements of combat operations, the military evolved into a profession, if by profession we mean an occupation with "a distinguishable corpus of specific technical knowledge and doctrine, a more or less exclusive group coherence, a complex of institutions peculiar to itself, an educational pattern adapted to its own needs and a distinct place in the society which has brought it forth."[9] This definition conveys some of the most essential aspects of the professional military establishment, and the historical features of military service in the West are still reflected in the guidance for members of the military today.

To become professional, the officer corps of military organizations had to make competence a foundation. Leaders had to be selected on the basis of competence and ability rather than political influence or class prerogatives if military organizations were to assume the characteristics noted above. The Prussians led the way toward professional forces by lowering class barriers for officer appointments, establishing entry standards that officer candidates had to meet, and beginning an educational system for career officers that came to fruition in 1810 with General Gerhard von Scharnhorst's establishment of the famous Kriegsakademie in Berlin. Comprehensive examinations for officers seeking promotion ensured a new level of competence. Other European countries emulated Prussia's success in the decades that followed.

The United States began with an abiding distrust of standing armies and "the man on horseback" that delayed the development of its military as a profession. That distrust was probably the legacy of our experience with the British and the background of European history, with its Caesars, Cromwells, and Napoleons. Thus, not too surprisingly, military professionalism developed later in America than in Europe. Instantly following the resolution of foreign crises requiring the raising and commitment of armed forces, the nation's military invariably declined in strength and readiness, with a corresponding decrease in the prestige and attention accorded the officer corps.

Despite the Revolutionary War against the British, the American military largely adopted the traditions of the British officer corps: an officer is a gentleman, a man of courage and unquestioned integrity. Those who led our forces, after all, had grown up as British citizens. Morris Janowitz claims that the American military inherited four central elements from the British military tradition: gentlemanly conduct, personal fealty, self-evaluating brotherhood, and the pursuit of glory.[10] If by glory we understand not self-aggrandizement but esteem for patriotism, for leadership in combat, and for public service, and if we recognize that 200 years have removed the aristocratic tenor of honor from American officership, Janowitz's observation appears accurate. For the century that followed the establishment of the United States, however, the characteristics of a profession emerged only slowly. During much of the 19th century, America's best educated military officers were graduates of West Point but were better known as engineers than as battlefield leaders. Although the Civil War, 1861–1865, changed that, after the war the Army became little more than a constabulary force in the West, fighting and policing the Native American tribes.

CHARACTERISTICS OF THE PROFESSION TODAY

Not until the turn of the century did the military profession as we know it today in the United States assume maturity. During that period the Army and Navy established permanent schools for advanced military education and began to develop systematic processes for educating and training career professionals.

Relationship to the Parent Society

One indelible characteristic of the American military that emerged from its first century of development remains foundational: the military is entirely subordinate to and responsive to the civilian leadership of the nation. That feature receives little attention when we consider our own military forces because it is so deeply ingrained in our society's consciousness. In Latin America, however, and in the Middle East, Asia, and elsewhere, such subordination is decidedly not the rule, and to note that military cultures differ markedly from one society to another raises few questions because the statement is so obviously true. In a number of countries we can mention, the military is the government. Until recently, the military dominated life in Haiti, Brazil, and Argentina, as it still does in Thailand, Pakistan, and a number of African countries. If we are to understand the military profession, we need to understand why military establishments differ in these obvious ways—and why they nonetheless share so many features. When we recognize the major formative influences on military organizations, we can more readily focus on moral principles and moral reasoning.

Factors Shaping the Military Ethic

The nature and structure of any military organization result in large part from the basic exigencies of warfare. If the military organization is to be effective, both leaders and subordinates must possess competence in the use of weapons, the application of effective tactics, and the provision of support necessary to sustain combat. Such skills represent one of the essential characteristics of any profession: a set of abilities acquired as a result of prolonged training and education that enable the professional to render a specialized service considered essential to society. The weapons, the tactics, and the organizational structures of military establishments may differ radically as a result of different circumstances, but certain commonalities will always exist. Such commonalities are those aspects of the institution unique to the military function. They shape the nature of any professional military group and, in particular, they shape the culture and ethos that together provide direction, purpose, and guidance for the conduct of military affairs.

WARFIGHTING IMPERATIVES

The imperatives of effective combat operations constitute the most obvious shaping influence. Though functional necessities vary greatly in detail over time and in differing circumstances, the general nature of such requirements remains constant. In broad terms, we recognize that any consistently successful military organization must have members who possess physical courage; soldiers who flee the battlefield will not win. Soldiers and sailors must be courageous and physically strong if they are to prevail. Military organizations must also be sufficiently disciplined, with a recognized hierarchy of authority, to ensure that orders are carried out consistently and reliably. Individual soldiers must possess the skills necessary to employ weapons and equipment in the accomplishment of tactical missions, and commanders must possess both character and the tactical skills required to pursue military objectives successfully without excessive losses. These broadly described functional requirements involved in the systematic application of force will be essentially constant from one society to another. Professor Samuel Huntington observed of the military profession—with emphasis on profession—that it

> exists to serve the state. To render the highest possible service the entire profession and the military force which it leads must be constituted as an effective instrument of state policy. Since political direction only comes from the top, this means that the profession has to be organized into a hierarchy of obedience. For the profession to perform its function, each level within it must be able to command the instantaneous and loyal obedience of subordinate levels. Without those relationships, military professionalism is impossible. Consequently, loyalty and obedience are the highest military virtues.[11]

Without disciplined organization, military units cannot maintain obedience. Huntington and others have shown us that the requirements of the military profession demand loyalty, obedience, and discipline no matter what particular nation or society may be involved. As we have noted, the values of technical competence and physical courage also arise directly from the nature of military activity. In some form, over time, such functional requirements will become institutionalized as standards of conduct for members of the armed forces. In the U.S. Army, physical fitness provides a clear example of a functional imperative. Individual soldiers and the institution both recognize that successful armies must be composed of those who are physically fit. Within our military culture, physical fitness has become admirable and expected as well as necessary for Americans in uniform. Functional requirements thus emerge as one of the major factors shaping the ethic of any military organization.

THE LAWS OF WAR

A second factor that shapes a military ethic, the international laws of war, has become progressively more prominent in the last 60 years. With essentially all countries now being signatories to the most important international treaties and conventions governing the conduct of war, all military organizations are affected by the existing laws, and particularly those with a Western heritage. The degree to which a specific military ethic has incorporated the principles manifested in the laws of war may vary considerably, but those existing laws exert a persistent influence that cannot be ignored. Moral principles ground the international laws of warfare as they now exist; to the extent that a military ethic recognizes and incorporates the provisions of the laws of war, it incorporates two underlying humanitarian principles:

1. Individual persons deserve respect as such.
2. Human suffering ought to be minimized.[12]

Both of these principles have become fundamental to the ethics of the military profession in the United States, in part because they also manifest basic values in American society.

VALUES OF SOCIETY

The third and most complex factor that influences the ethic of the military profession, one that further circumscribes and limits the other two, emerges from the dominant values of the society that creates and sustains the military institution. In all societies, the purposes, concerns, and interests of the people involved in an institution give it life and mold its character. And because its members are drawn from the society served, their own society, those members reflect the society's basic cultural values and infuse these into the organization's culture. Military institutions reflect this same pattern of cultural influence—from society to its individual citizens and on to the military institution. But, because societies differ in these cultural values, the military cultures that develop within them will differ as well, despite the common professional exigencies. We can thus understand why subordination to civilian authority, such a dominant feature of the American military, does not characterize the military forces of some other nations.

General Eric Shinseki, former Chief of Staff of the Army and current Secretary of Veteran Affairs, observes that the values of the U.S. Army are not just war-related. He notes that "[t]they are deeper, more universal values. And most importantly, they accord with values we are taught in our families, our schools, our churches, synagogues, and mosques. Only in this way can they be deeply felt, made congruent. . . ."[13] These values are those espoused by all truly moral leaders.

From the values of American society arise enduring principles that characterize the nation's armed forces as well. Americans have long held that human beings have an inherent right to freedom. That principle and others are specified in the foundational document of American society, the Constitution. The fundamental values manifested in the Constitution directly affect the ethic of the military profession through the oath that officers take upon commissioning. That oath makes the commitment of officers clear:

> I do solemnly swear (or affirm) that I will support and defend the Constitution of the United States against all enemies, foreign and domestic; that I will bear true faith and allegiance to the same, and that I take this obligation fully, without any mental reservation or purpose of evasion; and that I will well and faithfully discharge the duties of the office on which I am about to enter. So help me God.

The officer's primary loyalty is to the Constitution, not to an organization or to an individual. We thus turn to the Constitution to identify the most important values that our society imposes on the members of the military services. Preeminent among those values are the following:

1. The principle of individual rights, which states that individuals have certain rights that are not to be denied by the government itself nor by the desires of the majority.

2. The rule of law, which establishes that no person is above the law of the land and that the law applies equally to all. Law secures individual rights.

3. The principle of constitutional authority, which establishes the Constitution as the abiding and foundational structure for the content of law in the United States.

The third principle makes clear why the officer's oath focuses on the Constitution. The other two help explain why the status of the individual takes a central place in the ethic of the military profession and why adherence to law governs military behavior. Within the context of a hierarchical military organization, the principle of individual rights holds that individual soldiers have value because they are human beings and deserve to be treated with respect within the context of military organization and discipline. A further principle enshrined in American institutions because of our constitutional foundation is the moral and legal equality of all American citizens. All members of our society have equal status in these realms until their own transgressions lead to abridgment. That principle also finds expression in the requirement of leaders to protect the welfare of subordinates within the military institution.

As is the case with respect to several moral principles that structure the activity of the American military, the soldier's commitment to defend his/her society's values as well as its people and institutions generates a multilevel moral obligation. Not only must the nation be protected, but it must be protected in a manner consistent with the society's fundamental values. Failure to adhere to the values is a failure to fulfill the oath. The obligation to protect a set of values creates the potential for difficult choices. A military leader has an obligation to treat members of his/her command as autonomous individuals deserving respect in their own right, but leaders also have an obligation to perform with maximum competence in their roles as military professionals. The two requirements may lead to situations in which leaders must decide to choose an action that protects their subordinates or to choose a different action that satisfies tactical requirements. They also have obligations to adhere to the professional standards of their organization. Cases will arise in which they must give a particular professional requirement priority over another. Given such multiple levels of moral obligation, leaders must exercise moral reasoning.

SPECIALIZED EDUCATION AND TRAINING

Despite a few skeptical views of the military's professional status, which include concerns about "a trade devoted to slaughter" and the view that a career soldier is a "paid jack-of-all-trades,"[14] the profession of arms exemplifies the general pattern of specialized education and training that leads to a profession-peculiar body of expert knowledge and associated expertise. Following a diversified basic education, career members of the American military undergo a systematic program of education that extends over a period of 20 years. The officer corps of the services, from which the senior military leadership is ultimately drawn, provides the most obvious example of this aspect of the American military profession.

Junior officers in the Army, following a pattern found in all the services, undergo initial training that includes preparation for service in their branch (infantry, field artillery, signal corps, etc.). They learn fundamental skills, leadership techniques, and small-unit tactics, among many other subjects. During a full career, each officer attends further courses of instruction in preparation for higher command and increased responsibilities. In addition, the majority of the officers in our armed forces earn graduate degrees during the last half of their careers.

Thus a senior professional military officer is one in whom the nation has made a major investment. He or she has an expert knowledge of a complex intellectual discipline that results only from extensive training and education, wide experience, and long application. The commander of an aircraft carrier group or a similar naval command must understand the relationships between tactical alternatives and organizational capabilities, the technological abilities and limitations established by highly complex equipment, and the variety of interpersonal and leadership skills necessary to motivate and lead others. The mastery of complex staff procedures and the competent command of large military formations require capabilities normally achieved only after progression through years of professional preparation and experience.

During the Cold War, Professor Roger Nye of West Point's Department of History observed: "The clear consensus of the American people, whose elected representatives have created and maintained the authorization for military forces, is that a professional officer corps remains indispensable."[15] That observation remains true today. Recent operations in Afghanistan and Iraq have made the competence of our military leadership a subject of intense public interest. Occasional failures in the conduct and character of military leaders cause great concern, if not alarm, and public demands for corrective measures invariably follow. The transgressions of individual soldiers, particularly against noncombatants, cause public concern, but the greatest unease always focuses on the leadership that either fails to prevent war crimes or fails to take swift corrective action.

Two considerations obviously at work are the military's role as the ultimate defenders of freedom and rights and the military's responsibility for the lives and welfare of the sons and daughters of America who serve in military organizations. Those considerations alone establish competence in military duties as a moral imperative for leaders at all levels. Incompetence can result in disaster for serving members of the military and danger to national security. In view of such possibilities, the military's continuous concern about individual skills and performance and the profession's competence in general follow logically. The military services' extensive systems of schooling and focus on professional development reflect such concern.

CORPORATENESS AND AUTONOMY

As Professor Huntington observed decades ago, fulfillment of the functional imperatives over time gives rise to complex vocational institutions that mold officer corps into autonomous social units possessing a collective awareness of their corporateness. Entrance into such a unit is restricted to those with the requisite education and training, and new members usually begin at the lowest ranks. The corporate structure of the officer corps includes not just the official bureaucracy but also societies, associations, schools, journals, customs, and traditions.[16]

Corporateness thus involves characteristics that make a group providing a specialized service to society a distinctive and relatively autonomous entity. By "autonomous" I mean that the group establishes its own criteria for certification of candidates for membership and for the development and application of its expert knowledge, evaluates and judges the conduct and competence of its members, and imposes its own sanctions for failures to meet the professional standards set by the group. Members of the group are the only ones ultimately competent to judge the professional abilities of individual officers. Officers can be judged in terms of the results they achieve, just as medical doctors can be judged by the success of their treatment of patients, but as with the case of doctors this is best done only by other doctors who can accurately judge the technical performance of a member of the medical profession. Thus, the officer corps is a largely self-regulating body that determines the standards of competence and conduct for its members. Such internal standards reflect the institution's relative autonomy and constitute an important aspect of its corporateness.

Another facet of corporateness emerges from the individual's sense of identity with the institution and its values, which we will discuss in more detail shortly, and from the feeling of obligation to further the institution's purposes. Individual members thus share responsibility for maintaining the standards of the corporate group with respect to the performance of other members, and a variety of institutional procedures and mechanisms help safeguard and perpetuate the standards.

In addition to structural indications of corporateness, the military exhibits a strong sense of group identity that is strengthened by and in turn supports the value of loyalty in the professional ethic. This feature reflects the historical significance of loyalty discussed earlier. One sociologist describes the contemporary sense of loyalty for the American military in these terms:

> Loyalty is the quintessential military virtue: loyalty to the country, the Constitution, and the president as commander-in-chief . . . to the [military] itself and its standards and traditions; to the unit in which a soldier serves, and to peers, superiors, and subordinates. In theory the most important of these loyalties is to the United States Constitution; in practice the most important—to a soldier's morale and to his or her willingness to obey orders and assume responsibility—is to comrades.[17]

Loyalty strengthens the sense of identity with the professional calling and the willingness to subordinate one's own interests to the interests of the institution and the client the institution serves. Both developments enhance the corporate nature of the activity.

MORAL PRINCIPLES

When Academy officials studied the content of the ethic at West Point, we recognized that the American military and the individual services had no formally published code of ethics as such (all we have formally common to all is the Uniform Code of Military Justice that establishes military law, which admittedly governs behavior but in an exclusively proscriptive legal fashion). Nonetheless, the military services do have standards of conduct passed on through the education systems previously described and the process of professional socialization. In the view of one outside observer, it appears that "loyalty to this code and to the people with whom it is shared is the essential military quality."[18]

In considering loyalty to one's superiors, many have turned to the classic statement in Shakespeare's Henry V. On the eve of the historic battle of Agincourt, where the English under King Henry won an improbable victory, the disguised monarch walks among his soldiers to assess their temper. Henry hopes to prompt a supportive response by declaring, "Me thinks I could not die anywhere so contented as in the king's company, his cause being just and his quarrel honorable." When one soldier rejects that view by replying, "That's more than we know," another describes the view long held to both justify and excuse the actions of soldiers necessary in war: "Ay, or more than we should seek after, for we know enough if we know we are the king's subjects. If his cause be wrong, our obedience to the king wipes the crime of it out of us."[19] Because the information available to common soldiers had always been so limited, the principle of superior orders held that so long as one was obeying the orders of one's superiors in the military chain of command, one could not be held accountable for those actions.

More recent history in the form of the Nuremberg Trials after World War II, however, has modified this tenet in important ways. In fact, published guidance in military manuals today repeats in emphatic terms the requirement for members of the military to refuse to obey illegal orders. The U.S. Army's The Law of Land Warfare presents an uncompromising position on this point, one that we felt must be emphasized in cadet education: "The fact that the law of war has been violated pursuant to an order of a superior authority, whether military or civil, does not deprive the act in question of its character as a war crime, nor does it constitute a defense in the trial of an accused . . . ."[20] As I noted previously, the international laws of war have strongly influenced the guidance for conduct of members of the military-ethical guidance as well as legal.

As we studied the military ethic, we clarified the elements that guide the conduct of all members of the American military by reconsidering in more detail the three formative influences we discussed earlier. The first and most ubiquitous of these is that set of functional requirements arising directly from the nature of warfare. Courage, competence, and discipline (obedience) were the foremost elements of the ethic we identified in this category.

Second, because they are sworn to uphold and defend the Constitution, soldiers are constrained by Article 6, Clause 2, of that document, which states that international treaties signed by the United States become the law of the land. As *The Commander's Handbook on the Law of Naval Operations* states, "Pursuant to the Constitution of the United States, treaties to which the United States is a party constitute a part of the supreme law of the land with a force equal to that of laws enacted by Congress."[21] Among such treaties are the Hague and Geneva Conventions.

Despite ambiguities that arose from the American response to the terrorist attacks of September 11, 2001, and from the subsequent American experience in Afghanistan and Iraq, when an American serviceman or servicewoman swears to uphold and defend the Constitution, he or she swears to uphold the international laws of war. Any deviation from that obligation will have to have legal justification for modifying what appears to be a constitutional requirement. This second set of constraints on permissible conduct further delineates the officer's commitment to the military ethic, especially when we recognize that commitment to uphold the laws of war logically entails commitment to the two previously cited humanitarian principles that underlie those laws of war, which we repeat here for emphasis:

1. Individual persons deserve respect as such.

2. Human suffering ought to be minimized.

Mission requirements impose duties and dictate actions, but those requirements must always be consistent with the recognition of and respect for these two overarching moral principles.

Our review of the basic elements of the military ethic identified the third major influence on the ethic as the set of fundamental and unique values of American society. We recognized that tension may arise at times between the requirements of military activity (accomplishing the mission most effectively and efficiently) and our fundamental social values. When such conflicts occur in our system and society, the fundamental values of society, respect for the individual as a person, the rule of law, and the authority of the Constitution, provide boundaries on permissible action. While translating those values into specific guidelines may take different forms, the values ultimately do establish the final moral constraints on acceptable behavior by members of the American military. The fundamental values of society and thus the moral constraints for the military normally change and evolve slowly. In any individual's career, they will appear to be constant. The application of those principles may change more noticeably. Thus, the military's treatment of racial issues, the role of women, and the status of homosexuals has evolved relatively rapidly over the past several decades as a result of social practice and legal interpretation.

These three major influences that shape the contents of the American military ethic provide no simple equation for identifying permissible actions, even after we specify the structure and the broad content of the ethic. Recognizing the nature and relationship of the influencing factors merely provides a framework for considered judgment by the individual officer or soldier. Having identified such factors, however, we can more convincingly summarize the central tenets of the American military ethic that has emerged, and continues to do so, from the interaction of these formative influences.

First and foremost, military officers are expected to be loyal to their organization and their country. During the Korean Conflict, for example, under brutal duress numerous American

POWs collaborated with the enemy or performed actions demanded of them that were impermissible under military regulations. Our national dismay at such conduct by captured soldiers and a determination to minimize future recurrences led President Eisenhower to promulgate The Code of Conduct for Members of the Armed Forces of the United States in Executive Order 10631, August 17, 1955, which President Reagan revised in a 1988 executive order.[22] Standards established in that document, reproduced below, grow out of the basic value of loyalty.

CODE OF CONDUCT
for Members of the Armed Forces of the United States

1. I am an American, fighting in the forces which guard my country and our way of life. I am prepared to give my life in their defense.

2. I will never surrender of my own free will. If in command, I will never surrender the members of my command while they still have the means to resist.

3. If I am captured, I will continue to resist by all means available. I will make every effort to escape and aid others to escape. I will accept neither parole nor special favors from the enemy.

4. If I become a prisoner of war, I will keep faith with my fellow prisoners. I will give no information or take part in any action which might be harmful to my comrades. If I am senior, I will take command. If not, I will obey the

lawful orders of those appointed over me and will back them up in every way.

5. When questioned, should I become a prisoner of war, I am required to give name, rank, service number, and date of birth. I will evade answering questions to the utmost of my ability. I will make no oral or written statements disloyal to my country or its allies or harmful to their cause.

6. I will never forget that I am an American, fighting for freedom, responsible for my actions, and dedicated to the principle which made my country free. I will trust in my God and in the United States of America.[23]

A second fundamental element of the military ethic, selfless service, implicit in The Code of Conduct, follows necessarily from the ultimate liability of combat: loss of life. The same principle applies in many contexts, albeit to a lesser degree, in which the military institution often expects the individual to subordinate personal interests to the requirements of military duty. In paying tribute to the heroes of D-Day in World War II, General Gordon Sullivan, then Army Chief of Staff, emphasized selfless service:

> I think these soldiers—the Eisenhowers, the Summers, and the Pinders and all the rest whose names are known only to buddies, loved ones, or God alone—did their duties and made their sacrifices for each other and for us. They epitomized the ethics of *selfless service*, the

> core value of American soldiers and, indeed, everyone in the country's armed forces.[24] [Emphasis added.]

The value of obedience provides a third element in the foundation of the military ethic. In the military context, it follows from commitment to the profession and its purposes. In contrast, obedience that results from fear cannot be relied upon in crisis situations when immediate dangers might otherwise overwhelm the threat of sanctions. Obedience in all circumstances relates directly to loyalty, selfless service, and the overarching emphasis on mission accomplishment (the duty concept). Thus the central place of duty in military values suggested earlier by the passage from Shakespeare also holds today, within clear limits emplaced by law and our fundamental social values. In the Academy's study of the military ethic, we found that all versions of moral guidance for American soldiers include in some form the duty concept, which usually obligates subordination of personal interest and, indeed, personal safety to the fulfillment of professional obligations.

Those four values—loyalty, selfless service, obedience, duty—all basic elements of the American professional military ethic, result from the functional requirements of military service, just as do courage and integrity. Courage needs no further elaboration. Unless subordinates can rely on the honesty and sincerity of their leaders, the basic components of integrity, trust will be elusive. Without trust in the unit's leadership, no combat organization will be nearly as effective as it must be to succeed consistently in combat. For example, without accuracy in reports from subordinate headquarters, no commander can make timely, informed decisions that will maximize opportunities for success in battle. The importance of integrity appears undeniable and uncontroversial as well. At the Military Academy, the principle of integrity finds application in the Cadet Honor Code. Not only are cadets expected to live up to the standards established by the Honor Code, but they are also expected to make those standards part of their own belief systems and to help their comrades do the same by not tolerating their violations of those standards. Only then will they be able to manifest the character necessary for leadership of American forces.

While military organizations have long recognized commitment to the welfare of one's fellows and one's subordinates as a practical benefit, serving as a multiplier of combat effectiveness, such commitment also flows from respect for the integrity and the fundamental rights of individual persons. In the American military, the functional aspect of respect receives strong reinforcement from the core American social value of individualism. In American culture, the worth of the individual has shaped all of our primary social institutions. The religious tradition that posits an immortal soul, the idea of equality before the law, and the principle of protecting individual rights from the power of the state all contribute to the value imputed to individual soldiers, a value that has become fundamental to the American military culture. That tradition buttresses the appreciation of initiative in the American soldier, sailor, and airman. Initiative and independent action, which superficially appear to be directly contrary to the expectations of a hierarchical, authoritarian institution, actually have great practical value.

Initiative, innovative thinking, and adaptability contribute greatly to success on the battlefield, as we see today in operations in Afghanistan and Iraq.

PRINCIPLES OF OFFICERSHIP AND MORAL REASONING

While remembering that any specific articulation of the Army's or the American military ethic will be problematic in view of the penumbra of values that inform the ethic and the complexity of the moral concepts that provide its structure, the staff and faculty at West Point did identify a set of principles for officers to live by, principles intended to guide them as they live out their shared professional identity of being an officer. We believe these principles capture the central features of the military ethic, the values of the military profession, and the underlying moral foundation necessary for an effective Army and other effective leaders.

Officers develop the ability to apply these principles and ethics to their profession. As mentioned earlier, obviously there are no formulas for the moral reasoning required. Even the "rules of engagement" carefully developed for each military operation cannot foresee all situations that leaders will face in combat. If, as one scholar has noted, the professional practice of Army officers is the "repetitive exercise of discretionary judgment while making decisions and taking actions that fulfill their responsibilities under the Commission," how does West Point foster the type of moral reasoning needed for such demands?[25] The first step is to ensure that cadets understand the forms of moral reasoning available. Education in the processes of moral reasoning occurs within the academic curriculum, in the practical lessons presented during the values education program, and in living under the Honor System.

In the classroom, cadets learn the difference between consequentialist systems and nonconsequentialist systems of moral reasoning. Moral reasoning and analysis usually take one of these two forms. Consequentialist systems base moral decisions on the anticipated results of the actions under consideration. For example, utilitarian moral reasoning, one of the consequentialist systems, begins with the assumption that the right action is the one that will produce "the greatest good for the greatest number." The best known nonconsequentialist systems are rule-based, or deontological, to apply the label used in moral philosophy. In that form of moral reasoning, an action is right if it conforms to a specific moral rule or principle. Cadets study various processes for resolving moral questions. They examine numerous case studies in academic courses and in the values education program, often case studies that generate debate and differing opinions. Cadets learn that under the military ethic, consequentialist reasoning has limited application.

In a well-publicized case in Iraq during Operation Enduring Freedom, an officer chose to mistreat a prisoner to extract information about a planned ambush of the officer's unit. The case centered on the actions of Lt. Col. Allen B. West on August 20, 2003 in Taji, Iraq. (Lt. Col. West was a battalion commander in the 4th Infantry Division.) Although he was prosecuted and convicted, the officer declared that he had to choose the welfare of his soldiers over the constraints imposed by regulations and policies concerning the treatment of prisoners. His criterion for his decision was to choose the action that best served the interests of his soldiers. Even though objective analysis suggests immediately that we would not expect a military leader to apply such a standard to all cases, widespread discussion of the case demonstrated that many people, including soldiers, did not understand the guidance established by the military ethic. They found it difficult to accept that the ends do not justify the means, a principle that the officer in Iraq apparently applied. Cadets examine many such case studies and apply the military ethic in the process of analyzing the moral reasoning process. Ideally, they come to recognize the relationships among the various constraints on the actions of military professionals that we discussed earlier.

On reflection, we can see that the American military ethic is rule-based. The actions of those bound by the American military ethic are first constrained by the functional exigencies of military operations, further constrained by the laws of war, and finally by the enduring values of American society—the values that soldiers defend. In addition to regulations and rules established by the profession, the laws of war and the values of American society both limit actions permissible in accomplishing assigned missions. Classroom studies and sessions in the values education program, spread over the entire four-year baccalaureate experience, further cadet understanding in these areas.

Living under the Cadet Honor System also strengthens understanding of and commitment to a set of values that does not justify action solely in terms of results or consequences. The emphasis falls on rules. The Honor Code does not recognize conditions under which violation of the prohibitions against lying, cheating, and stealing are acceptable in the lives of cadets. Although sanctions for violations of the Code have changed over time, the guidance for conduct has remained clear and consistent. The Academy and the Corps expect cadets to be men and women of integrity. In Aristotelian terms, acting with integrity over time builds integrity. Doing strengthens being. Thus the Honor System, which encourages truthfulness, fairness, respect for the property of others, and commitment to professionalism, contributes to the process of character development and moral understanding. Cadets and graduates alike participate in that process through adhering to the duty concept, which establishes limits by applying the active boundary conditions supplied by the Principles of Officership and the military ethic. The strengthening of character must continue throughout an officer's professional life if he or she is to meet the demands of senior leadership.

Under the American military ethic, consequentialist reasoning does not provide final answers, however tempting that formula may be in difficult situations. Extreme circumstances may be the basis for morally excusing some actions, but they do not justify transgressions. Considerations arising from the American value system limit morally permissible actions under the American military ethic. The moral reasoning involved is at bottom nonconsequentialist in nature.

The military ethic clearly functions under a moral teleology, but the purpose of the ethic is to guide the actions of the military in the effort to maintain the nation under the Constitution. The purpose is to uphold a matrix of institutional values.

During their four years at West Point, cadets learn not only the nature of the military ethic and the reasoning involved in applying its mandates, but also the reasons for the limitations on professional conduct. That is why they need to understand the history of the development of the American military ethic and the factors that have shaped it over time. They need to understand the central role that the Constitution plays in both law and morality. When they do, they are much better prepared to apply the military ethic in situations in which grave issues hang in the balance and they as leaders must choose a course of action.

STRENGTHENING MORAL LEADERSHIP AND ACTIONS

The laws of war will change over time, slowly, and the core values of our society will evolve, even more slowly, eventually bringing about changes in our military ethic, but the central features of the code of professional military ethics identified here will guide the conduct of members of the American military profession for the foreseeable future. The critical point to recognize is that stable, enduring standards of conduct do exist. The "Principles of Officership" incorporate them. Those standards of conduct are part of our military heritage, and they can be and have been passed on from one generation of military leaders to another. The processes of professional socialization in all the military services are designed to foster in the officer corps a deep commitment to professional values and to strengthen such values among all members of the armed forces. Americans can depend upon the military institution to carry out its responsibilities largely because of the ethic of the military profession and the institutional commitment to professional military values. At West Point, that commitment takes tangible form in the Cadet Leader Development System.

Many have questioned the efficacy of the military ethic in the face of blatant violations of its tenets. The recent events at Abu Ghraib Prison and at Haditha in Iraq during Operation Iraqi Freedom provide well-known examples. At a 2006 presentation in Austin, Texas, however, by Brigadier General (Retired) Howard Prince to a military audience on the subject of Abu Ghraib, discussion suggested that the ethic remains strong. General Prince asked whether any members of the audience had served in Iraq. Two volunteered that they had served there as junior officers, and in fact were there when the Abu Ghraib revelations of prisoner mistreatment and torture became public. General Prince asked about their reactions to the disclosures. Both related that they were dismayed and ashamed that fellow soldiers in uniform had so egregiously violated the laws of war and Army regulations.

The two former officers saw the actions of the prison staff as betrayals of the trust that Americans place in their military services. Although the investigation proceeded at a deliberate, careful pace, the Army did eventually try eleven military personnel for their actions, to include the officer commanding the prison. The harsh, demanding environment of combat generates the full spectrum of human reaction, from compassion and heroism to brutality and viciousness. The issue central to the moral status of the military profession is the reaction of the institution when violations of the ethic occur. The disposition thus far of Abu Ghraib and other instances of unacceptable behavior indicates that the military ethic described here remains firmly in place and central to the development of leaders of character.

We can identify, explain, and justify the moral guidelines for members of the armed forces; nonetheless, the demand remains for officers to make discretionary judgments, often in the heat of battle, and not all moral decisions will be straightforward. What a specific leader should do in a particular situation, and what we should be willing to excuse should the prohibitions established by law or by the ethic be violated, remain difficult questions. That reality explains the need to develop in cadets an understanding of the capabilities discussed in Chapter 4: an appreciation for moral complexity, a recognition of moral responsibility, and confidence in one's own beliefs.

The Army expects and requires moral reasoning based on moral principles established by the military ethic. The moral landscape of the soldier has always been difficult, perhaps more so now than ever before when we consider that in the long war against Islamic radicals using the techniques of terror among urban populations, situations of moral ambiguity abound. The actions of individual soldiers can affect both subsequent policy decisions and public support for security operations. The American interventions in Afghanistan and Iraq reinforced that conclusion in the context of counterinsurgency and terrorism following initial combat operations. Military losses can often be overcome; however, moral failings constitute greater obstacles to national success, and leadership is the only effective answer to such challenges. The battle against terrorists that now spans the globe highlights not only the important role of the profession of arms but also the military ethic under which it functions. The inculcation of that ethic has become the foundation of developmental systems at West Point.

Conclusion

Don M. Snider

Since the Army was professionalized in the early 1900s, debates have raged within the Academy and the larger Army as to which is more important in military leaders, their character or their competence. Similar debates appear episodically across America as the moral failure of major leaders in the private and public sectors comes to light. Simply stated, the theme of this book is that in leadership of all kinds, the moral character of the leader is most determinative of any success.

In 1924 when Clayton Wheat, the USMA Chaplain from 1918-1924, wrote the Cadet Prayer, he "attempted to compose a petition that would set forth in simple phrases the aspirations of young men who earnestly desired to realize in their own lives the ideals and principles which have long been fostered in the Corps." Consider these phrases, which are at the very core of what it means to be a leader of character:

- "Strengthen and increase our admiration for honest dealing and clean thinking, and suffer not our hatred of hypocrisy and pretense ever to diminish

- Encourage us in our endeavor to live above the common level of life
- Make us to choose the harder right instead of the easier wrong, and never to be content with a half truth when the whole can be won
- Endow us with courage that is born of loyalty to all that is noble and worthy, that scorns to compromise with vice and injustice and knows no fear when truth and right are in jeopardy
- Guard us against flippancy and irreverence in the sacred things of life
- Grant us new ties of friendship and new opportunities of service
- Kindle our hearts in fellowship with those of a cheerful countenance, and soften our hearts with sympathy for those who sorrow and suffer"

These precepts from the Cadet Prayer have informed and motivated the moral character in West Point cadets for almost a century, and they continue to do so today. They have strongly informed who they are, and from that strength of character, what they do. In leadership, being precedes doing!

Throughout this book, we have discussed the moral and spiritual development of these future leaders and how this will affect, or has affected, their lives and actions as leaders, whether they continue with the military as a profession or enter the public and private sectors. While the moral challenges of leading in physical combat are unique, that is not to say that these lessons taught at West Point cannot apply to leaders of any kind. The Cadet Prayer's call for the leader's virtues of integrity, honor, and courage is universal.

Many West Point graduates have gone on to become successful business leaders, including, among many others, CEO Joe DePinto of 7-11 (class of '86), CEO Robert McDonald of Procter & Gamble (class of' 75), CEO of Aptuit Tim Tyson (class of '74), and CEO Alex Gorsky of Johnson & Johnson (class of '82). Others have continued in military service or entered politics. Their success may stem from many factors, but we believe that the values espoused by the West Point experience were essential to their growth.

We have offered here that the Academy has a method of "forging" the moral character of its graduates that is broadly applicable to the development of leaders of all stripes throughout America's public and private sectors. But that development will not just occur, it is the mutual responsibility of both the aspiring leader and the organization within which he or she is studying or working and in so many other ways being developed. And in all such settings the leader's strength of personal character that animates their daily lives is fostered by clearly stated moral precepts to which he or she can aspire. It is to that end that this book has been created.

NOTES

Foreword

1. Richard Cavanagh, foreword to Be-Know-Do: Leadership the Army Way, by the Leader to Leader Institute, with introduction by Frances Hesselbein and General Eric K. Shinseki, USA Ret. (San Francisco, CA: Jossey-Bass, 2004), xi.
2. Ibid.

Chapter 1

1. General Donald V. Bennett, U.S. Army Ret., and William R. Forstchen, *Honor Untarnished: A West Point Graduate's Memoir of World War II* (New York, N.Y: Forge, 2003), pp. 303–304.
2. General George C. Marshall, quoted in Department of the Army Pamphlet 600-63-12, *Spiritual Fitness: Fit to Win* (Washington, DC: U.S. Government Printing Office, September 1987), p. 1.
3. Colin L. Powell, Comments on the Receipt of the USMA Association of Graduates Thayer Award, West Point, NY, September 15, 1998, accessed August 6, 2006, at http://www.aogusma.org/ aog/awards/TA/98Speech .html.
4. John J. Mearsheimer, "The Aims of Education Address, 1997," accessed on January 1, 2006, at http://www.uchicago.edu/docs/education/record /10-23-97/aimsofeducation.html.
5. Andrew Abbott, "Welcome to the University of Chicago," The Aims of Education Address, 2002, accessed on January 11, 2006, at http://www .ditext.com/abbott/abbott_aims.html.

6. This section of the present chapter is an abbreviated version of chap. 1 in Don M. Snider, project director, and Lloyd Matthews, editor, *The Future of the Army Profession*, 2d ed. (Boston: MA, McGraw-Hill, 2005). That chapter deals with how West Point revamped its approach to leader development in the late 1990s.
7. See Don M. Snider, John A. Nagl, and Tony Pfaff, *Army Professionalism, the Military Ethic, and Officership in the 21st Century* (Carlisle Barracks, PA: U.S. Army War College, Strategic Studies Institute, 1999); 10 Office of Policy, Planning, and Analysis, U. S. Military Academy, *Strategic Vision–2010* (West Point, NY, 2000), p. 7. This mission statement has been modified by a few words in subsequent versions.
8. Professor Huntington began his classic treatise as follows: "The modern officer corps is a professional body and the modern military officer a professional man. This is, perhaps, the most fundamental thesis of this book." See Samuel P. Huntington, *The Soldier and the State: The Theory and Politics of Civil-Military Relations* (Cambridge, MA: Belknap Press of Harvard University, 1957), p. 7.
9. USMA Strategic Vision–2010, p. xx.
10. Ibid., 8. I should note that the development of the eight principles was no easy task. They were originally formulated as 12 principles in Don M. Snider, John A. Nagl, and Tony Pfaff, *Army Professionalism, the Military Ethic, and Officership in the 21st Century* (Carlisle Barracks, PA: U.S. Army War College, Strategic Studies Institute, 1999), pp. 36–42, but subsequent vetting within the committee, with Academy leaders, and ultimately with a host of senior retired Army officers including former Chiefs of Staff, eventually reduced the list to eight.
11. CLDS Manual, pp. 21–24.
12. Field Manual 1, The Army (Washington, DC: Department of the Army, 2005), pp. 1–18, 1–19.
13. Scott Snook, "Be, Know, Do: Forming Character the West Point Way," *COMPASS: A Journal of Leadership* (March 2004), pp. 16–20.
14. CLDS Manual, pp. 27–28.

15. Higher Education Research Institute, *The Spiritual Life of College Students: A National Study of College Students' Search for Meaning and Purpose* (Los Angeles: University of California, 2005), accessed June 2005 at http://www.spirituality.ucla.edu.
16. Gilbert W. Fairholm, *Capturing the Heart of Leadership: Spirituality and Community in the New American Workplace* (Westport, CT: Praeger Publishers, 2000), p. 1.
17. CLDS Manual, p. 16.
18. See *Perspectives on Officership: The Commissioned Army Leader*, 3d ed., published by the William E. Simon Center for the Professional Military Ethic, United States Military Academy (New York: McGraw- Hill Publishing, 2005), p. xxxi.
19. Longitudinal data collected voluntarily from incoming freshmen (Plebes) indicate consistently that over 90 percent of Academy cadets do identify a religious preference among the 75 faiths and denominations listed. Data received by author from Office of the USCC Chaplain, West Point, NY, August 18, 2006.

Chapter 2

1. F. J. Bing, "American Military Performance in Iraq," *Military Review* (September/October 2006), pp. 2–7.
2. Department of the Army, Field Manual 1, *The Army* (June 2005), p. iv.
3. Dana Parsons, "Orange County Marine's Death Transcends Tragedy," *Los Angeles Times*, December 14, 2006, accessed December 15, 2006 at http://ebird.afis.mil/ebfiles/e20612144473768.html.
4. *The American Heritage College Dictionary*, 3d ed. (Boston: Houghton Mifflin, 1997).
5. John M. Brinsfield and Peter A. Baktis, "The Human, Spiritual, and Ethical Dimensions of Leadership in Preparation for Combat," in Don M. Snider, project director, and Lloyd Matthews, editor, *The Future of the Army Profession*, 2d ed. (Boston: McGraw-Hill, 2005), p. 464.
6. Samuel A. Stouffer et al., *The American Soldier: Combat and Its Aftermath*, Vol. 2 (New York: John Wiley & Sons, 1965), pp. 105–191.

7. Leonard Wong, "Combat Motivation in the Iraq War," in Don M. Snider, project director, and Lloyd Matthews, editor, *The Future of the Army Profession*, 2d ed. (Boston: McGraw-Hill, 2005), pp. 491–514.
8. Department of the Army, Field Manual 22-100, Army Leadership (Washington, DC: U.S. Government Printing Office, 1999), p. 2–2.
9. *The American Heritage College Dictionary*, 3d ed. (Boston: Houghton Mifflin, 1997), p. 1313.
10. Carl R. Rogers, *On Becoming a Person* (Boston: Houghton Mifflin, 1961), pp. 164–181; and Abraham H. Maslow, *Motivation and Personality* (New York: Harper & Brothers, 1954), pp. 80–96.
11. Jon C. Dalton et al., "Inward Journeys: Forms and Patterns of College Student Spirituality," *Journal of College and Character* (October 2006) vol. 7, pp. 1–22, retrieved November 13, 2006 from http://collegevalues.org/pdfs/dalton.pdf.
12. Ibid.; Rogers, pp. 164–181; and Maslow, pp. 80–96.
13. Christopher Peterson and Martin E. P. Seligman, *Character, Strengths, and Virtues: A Handbook and Classification* (New York: Oxford University Press, 2004), pp. 599–622.
14. Lord Moran, *The Anatomy of Courage* (Garden City, N.J.: Avery Publishing Group, 1987), p. xii.
15. Dalton et al., pp. 1–21.
16. John F. Kihlstrom, Jennifer S. Beer, and Stanley B. Klein, "Self and Identity as Memory," in Mark J. Leary and June P. Tangney, eds., *Handbook of Self and Identity* (New York: Guilford Press, 2003), pp. 68–90.
17. Rogers, p. 170.
18. Ibid., pp. 170–172.
19. Ibid., p. 33.
20. Maslow, p. 92.
21. Rogers, pp. 37–38.
22. Daniel Goleman, *Emotional Intelligence* (New York: Bantam Books, 1995), p. 96.
23. Rogers, p. 34.
24. Ibid., p. 34; and Goleman, p. 100.

25. Maslow, pp. 80–98.
26. Ibid., p. 87.
27. Sharon D. Parks, *Big Questions, Worthy Dreams: Mentoring Young Adults in Their Search for Meaning, Purpose, and Faith* (San Francisco: Jossey-Bass, 2000), p. 90.
28. Stouffer et al., 142–149.
29. Roger W. Little, "Buddy Relations and Combat Performance," in Morris Janowitz, ed., *The New Military: Changing Patterns of Organizations* (New York: Russell Sage Foundation, 1964), pp. 195–223.
30. Franklin D. Jones, "Traditional Warfare Combat Stress Casualties," in The Surgeon General, Textbook of Military Medicine: War Psychiatry (Washington, DC: Walter Reed Army Institute of Research, 1995), p. 38.
31. Stouffer et al., p. 179.
32. Daryl J. Bem, "Self-perception: An Alternative Interpretation of Cognitive Dissonance Phenomena," *Psychological Review* (1967) vol. 74, pp. 183–200.
33. Robert G. Lord and Douglas J. Brown, *Leadership Processes and Follower Self-identity* (Hillsdale, NJ: Erlbaum, 2004).
34. Albert Bandura, *Self-Efficacy: The Exercise of Control* (New York: Freeman, 1997); and Allen E. Kazdin, "Covert Modeling-Therapeutic Application of Imagined Rehearsal," in Jerome. L. Singer and Kenneth S. Pope, eds., *The Power of Human Imagination: New Methods in Psychotherapy—Emotions,* Personality, and Psychotherapy (New York: Plenum, 1978), pp. 255–278.
35. The work of Abraham Maslow was the primary source used to develop the categories of indicators outlined.

Chapter 3

1. Louis W. Fry, "Toward a Theory of Spiritual Development," *Leadership Quarterly* (December 2003) vol. 14, pp. 693–727.
2. William Crain, *Theories of Development*, 4th ed. (New Jersey: Prentice Hall 2000), 113. A complete list of Piaget's periods of development is as follows: Sensory-Motor Intelligence (birth to 2 years); Preoperational Thought (ages 2 to 7); Concrete Operations (ages 7 to 11); and Formal Operations (ages 11 to adulthood).

3. Lawrence Kohlberg, *Essays on Moral Development*, Vol. II: *The Psychology of Moral Development* (San Francisco: Harper Row, 1981), pp. 175–176. Kohlberg's stages of moral development are as follows: Stage 1-Heteronomous Morality; Stage 2-Individualism, Instrumental Purpose, and Exchange; Stage 3-Mutual Interpersonal Expectations, Relationships, and Interpersonal Conformity; Stage 4-Social System and Conscience; Stage 5-Social Contract or Utility and Individual Rights; and Stage 6-Universal Ethical Principles.
4. Robert Kegan, *The Evolving Self* (Cambridge, MA: Harvard University Press, 1982), 87. Kegan's stages of human development are as follows: Stage 0-Incorporative; Stage 1-Impulsive; Stage 2-Imperial, Stage 3-Interpersonal; Stage 4-Institutional; and Stage 5-Interindividual.

Chapter 4

1. Philip Lewis et al., "Identity Development During the College Years: Findings from the West Point Longitudinal Study," *Journal of College Student Development* (2005) vol. 46, no. 4, pp. 357–373.
2. USMA Circular 1-101-1, Cadet Leader Development System for Cadets (West Point, NY: Defense Printing, 2005), 19.
3. Ibid., pp. 29–30.
4. James R. Rest, "Background, Theory, and Research," in *Moral Development: Advances in Theory and Research*, eds. James R. Rest and Darcia Narvaez (New York: Praeger, 1994), pp. 59–88.
5. James R. Rest et al., "A Neo-Kohlbergian Approach to Morality Research," *Journal of Moral Education* (2000), pp. 381–395.
6. Jane E. Dutton and Susan E. Jackson, "Categorizing Strategic Issues: Links to Organizational Action," *Academy of Management* (1987) vol. 12, pp. 76–90.
7. Gordon H. Bower and Ernest R. Hilgard, *Theories of Learning* (Saddle River, NJ: Prentice-Hall, 1981).
8. Alice A. Eagly and Shelly Chaiken, "Attitude Structure and Function," in *Handbook of Social Psychology*, 4th ed., vol. I, eds. Daniel T. Gilbert, Susan T. Fiske, and Gardner Lindzey (Boston: McGraw-Hill, 1998), pp. 269–322.

9. Janet Metcalfe and Arthur P. Shimamura, *Metacognition: Knowing About Knowing* (Cambridge, MA: MIT Press, 1994).
10. H. Lee Swanson and George Hill. "Metacognitive Aspects of Moral Reasoning and Behavior," *Adolescence* (1993) vol. 28, pp. 711–735.
11. Marvin W. Berkowitz, John Gibbs, and John Broughton, "The Relation of Moral Judgment Disparity to Developmental Effects of Peer Dialogues," *Merrill-Palmer Quarterly* (1980) vol. 26, pp. 341–357; and Lawrence J. Walker, "Sources of Cognitive Conflict for Stage Transition in Moral Development," *Developmental Psychology* (1983) vol. 19, pp. 103–110.
12. James R. Rest and Stephen J. Thoma, "Education Programs and Interventions," in *Moral Development: Advances in Theory and Research*, ed. James R. Rest (New York: Praeger, 1986), pp. 59–88.
13. Shelley Chaiken, "Heuristic versus Systematic Information Processing and the Use of Source versus Message Cues in Persuasion," *Journal of Personality and Social Psychology* (1980) vol. 39, p. 752.
14. Ibid.
15. John F. Kihlstrom, Jennifer S. Beer, and Stanley B. Klein, "Self and Identity as Memory," in *Handbook of Self and Identity*, eds. Mark J. Leary and June P. Tangney (New York: Guilford Press, 2003), pp. 68–90.
16. Robert G. Lord and Douglas J. Brown, *Leadership Processes and Follower Self-identity* (Hillsdale, NJ: Erlbaum, 2004).
17. Albert Bandura, *Self-Efficacy: The Exercise of Control* (New York: Freeman, 1997).
18. Dov Eden, "Means Efficacy: External Sources of General and Specific Subjective Efficacy," in *Work Motivation in the Context of a Globalizing Economy*, eds. Miriam Erez, Uwe Kleinbeck, and Henk Thierry (Hillsdale, NJ: Lawrence Erlbaum, 2001), pp. 65–77.
19. Albert Bandura, *Self-Efficacy*.

Chapter 5

1. Headquarters, Department of the Army, Field Manual 22-100, Army Leadership (Washington, DC: U.S. Government Printing Office, 1999), pp. 1–2.

2. Harold Kelley and John Thibaut, *Interpersonal Relations: A Theory of Interdependence* (New York: Wiley, 1978),
3. Kelley and Thibaut, p. 232.
4. FM 22-100, pp. 2-24 to 2-26.
5. USMA Circular 1–101, pp. 16–17.
6. Bernard M. Bass, *Leadership and Performance Beyond Expectations* (New York: Free Press, 1985).
7. Kevin Lowe, K. Galen Kroeck, and Nagaraj Sivasubramaniam, "Effectiveness Correlates of Transformation and Transactional Leadership: A Meta-analytic Review of the MLQ Literature," *Leadership Quarterly*, (1996), vol. 7, pp. 385–425.
8. Robert G. Lord and Karen Maher, "Leadership Perceptions and Leadership Performance: Two Distinct but Interdependent Processes," in *Advances in Applied Social Psychology: Business Settings*, vol. 4, ed. J. Carrol (Hillsdale, NJ: Erlbaum, 1990), pp. 129–154.
9. Olga Epitropaki and R. Martin, "Implicit Leadership Theories in Applied Settings: Factor Structure, Generalizeability, and Stability Over Time, *Journal of Applied Psychology*, (2004), vol. 89, no. 2, pp. 293–310.
10. Bernard Bass, "Does the Transactional-Transformational Leadership Paradigm Transcend Organizational and National Boundaries?" *American Psychologist*, (1997), vol. 52, no. 2, pp. 130–139.
11. Jay A. Conger and Rabindra Kanungo, "Toward a Behavioral Theory of Charismatic Leadership in Organizational Settings," *Academy of Management Review*, (1987), vol. 12, pp. 637–647.
12. Hugh Thompson, "My Lai" (Talk given to United States Military Academy Cadets enrolled in General Psychology for Leaders Course, West Point, New York, in March 2002).
13. Ibid.
14. United States Military Academy, The Cadet Prayer. West Point, NY.
15. Edwin P. Hollander and Lynn R. Offermann, "Power and Leadership in Organizations: Relationships in Transition," *American Psychologist*, (1990), vol. 45, no. 2, pp. 179–189.

16. Gary Yukl, *Leadership in Organizations*, 4th ed. (Upper Saddle River, NJ: Prentice Hall, 1998), p. 178.
17. Fragging is the term used when a leader is killed by his or her own soldiers.
18. Patrick J. Sweeney, "Trust in Combat" (A paper presented at the Academy of Management Annual Conference in New Orleans, August 10-12, 2003).
19. Shelly E. Taylor, Letitia A. Peplau, and David O. Sears, *Social Psychology*, 11th ed. (Upper Saddle River, NJ: Prentice-Hall), pp. 99–124.
20. Sean T. Hannah, Paul B. Lester, and Gretchen R.Vogelsang, "Moral Leadership: Explicating the Moral Component of Authentic leadership," in *Authentic Leadership Theory and Practice: Origins, Effects, and Development*, eds. William B. Gardner, Bruce J. Avolio, and Fred O. Walumbwa, Monographs in Leadership and Management, (Oxford: Elsevier Ltd., 2005), vol. 3, pp. 43–81.
21. George R. Goethals and John M. Darley, "Social Comparison Theory: Self-evaluation and Group Life," in *Theories of Group Behavior*, eds. B. Mullen and G. R. Goethals (New York: Springer-Verlag, 1987), pp. 21–48.
22. Albert Bandura, *Social Learning Theory* (Englewood Cliffs, NJ: Prentice-Hall, 1977).
23. Ibid.
24. Goethals and Darley.
25. R. Glen Hass, "Effects of Source Characteristics on Cognitive Responses and Persuasion," in *Cognitive Response in Persuasion*, eds. Richard E. Petty, Thomas M. Ostrom, and Timothy C. Brock (Hillsdale, NJ: Lawrence Erlbaum Associates, 1981), pp. 141–172.
26. Hass.
27. Edgar H. Schein, *Organizational Culture and Leadership* (San Francisco: Josey-Bass, 1992).
28. USMA Circular 1-101-1, Cadet Leader Development System for Cadets (West Point, NY: Defense Printing, 2005), p. 19.
29. Michael A. Hogg, "A Social Identity Theory of Leadership," *Personality and Social Psychology Review*, (2001), vol. 5, pp. 184–200.

30. Hannah, Lester, and Vogelsang.
31. John Mattox, "The Ties That Bind: The Army Officer's Moral Obligations," in *The Future of the Army Profession*, project directors Don M. Snider and Gayle L. Watkins, eds. Lloyd J. Matthews (New York: McGraw-Hill, 2002), pp. 293–312.
32. Note in Chapter 1 of the present book, in the experiences of General Donald Bennett, that such occurrences, sadly, have been observed by other Americans in combat.
33. Rowan Scarborough, "Army Files Charge in Combat Tactic," *Washington Times*, October 29, 2003, p. 1.

Chapter 6

1. John Keegan, *A History of Warfare* (New York: Alfred A. Knopf, 1993), pp. 263–281.
2. Keegan, p. 268.
3. Keegan, p. 268.
4. Keegan, p. 283.
5. Keegan, p. 270.
6. General Sir John Hackett, *The Profession of Arms* (New York: Macmillan, 1983), p. 58.
7. Samuel Huntington, *The Soldier and the State* (New York: Vintage Books, 1964), pp. 37–39.
8. Julian Thompson, *The Lifeblood of War: The Logistics of Armed Conflict* (London: Brasseys, 1991), p. 38, as quoted in William T. Divale, *War in Primitive Societies: A Bibliography* (Santa Barbara, CA: ABC-Clio, 1973), p. xxi.
9. Hackett, *The Profession of Arms*, p. 9.
10. Morris Janowitz, *The Professional Soldier: A Social and Political Portrait* (Glencoe, IL: Free Press, 1960), p. 218.
11. Huntington, p. 73.
12. Anthony E. Hartle, *Moral Issues in Military Decision Making*, 2d ed. (Lawrence, KS: University Press of Kansas, 2004), ch. 5.

13. General Eric Shinseki and Frances Hesselbein, *Be-Know-Do: Leadership The Army Way* (San Francisco, CA: Jossey-Bass, 2004), p. 26.
14. Lloyd J. Matthews, "Is the Military Profession Legitimate?" Army 44, no. 1 (1994), p. 16.
15. Roger Nye, *The Challenge of Command* (Wayne, NJ: Avery; 1986), pp. 12–13.
16. Huntington, 16.
17. Kim Hays, *Practicing Virtues: Moral Traditions at Quaker and Military Boarding Schools* (Berkeley, CA: University of California Press, 1994), p. 54.
18. Hays, p. 43.
19. William Shakespeare, *The Life of King Henry the Fifth*, vol. IV, no. i, pp. 123–126.
20. U.S. Department of the Army, FM 27-10, The Law of Land Warfare (Washington, DC: GPO, 1956), p. 182.
21. U.S. Department of the Navy, NWP 9, *The Commander's Handbook on the Law of Naval Operations* (Washington, DC: Department of the Navy, July 1987), p. 6-1.
22. U.S. Department of Defense, *The U.S. Fighting Man's Code, DoD Pamphlet 1-16* (Washington, DC: GPO, 6 August 1959); U.S. Department of Defense, DoD GEN 36-A, The Armed Forces Officer (Washington, DC: GPO, 1988), p. 74.
23. The Code of Conduct clearly applies to members of the military today, though it is supplemented by statements such as the Soldier's Creed, the Warrior Ethos, and other publications that receive focused attention upon distribution and subsequently play a significant role in training.
24. General Gordon R. Sullivan, "D-Day Plus Fifty Years," *Army,* (1994), vol. 44, no. 6, p. 26.
25. Don M Snider, "The Multiple Identities of the Professional Army Officer," in *The Future of the Army Profession*, 2d ed., ch. 6.

CONTRIBUTORS

Captain Erica Borggren graduated from the U.S. Military Academy in 2002 as the class valedictorian. A Rhodes Scholar, she spent her lieutenant years at Oxford University, England, where she earned an M.S. degree in Comparative Social Policy in 2003 and a Postgraduate Diploma in Theology in 2004. Since then, she has been stationed in Yongsan, Korea, where she served as the Executive Officer for Headquarters and Headquarters Company, 18th Medical Command, and then as the Management Officer in the Resource Management Division of the 18th MEDCOM. She now commands Alpha Company, 121st Combat Support Hospital, in Yongsan, Korea.

Colonel Donna Brazil is an Academy Professor in the Department of Behavioral Sciences and Leadership at the U.S. Military Academy. She holds a B.S from the Academy and an M.A. and Ph.D. in Social Psychology from the University of North Carolina at Chapel Hill. She has eight years experience on the faculty at the Military Academy, teaching Military Leadership, Group Dynamics, Leadership Theory, and Marriage and the Family.

Lieutenant General F. L. Hagenbeck is the 57th Superintendent of the United States Military Academy at West Point, New York. He was commissioned in the Infantry from the Military Academy in 1971. Later, at Florida State University, he earned a Master of Science Degree in Exercise Physiology and served as an assistant football coach. While assigned to the U.S. Military Academy's Department of Physical Education, he earned a Master of Business Administration from Long Island University. He is also a graduate of the Army War College and the Army Command and General Staff College. General Hagenbeck has commanded at every level from company through division, culminating as Commanding General of the 10th Mountain Division. He has also served in the 25th Infantry Division, 101st Airborne Division, 82nd Airborne Division, including the Grenada operation in 1983, and TRADOC. Before becoming Superintendent, General Hagenbeck served as the Army's Deputy Chief of Staff, G-1, and in numerous staff positions, including Chief of Staff, 10th Mountain Division; Director, Officer Personnel Management Directorate, U.S. Total Army Personnel Command; and Assistant Division Commander (Operations), 101st Airborne Division. General Hagenbeck has served in numerous Joint assignments, including Exchange Officer and Tactics Instructor at the Royal Australian Infantry Center; Deputy Director for Politico-Military Affairs, Strategic Plans and Policy Directorate (J5); and Deputy Director for Current Operations, J33, Joint Staff. General Hagenbeck served as Commander, Coalition Joint Task Force Mountain, Operations Enduring Freedom/Anaconda, and Deputy Commanding General, Combined Joint Task Force 180 in Afghanistan.

Lieutenant Colonel Sean T. Hannah is the Director of Leadership and Management Studies, Department of Behavioral Sciences and Leadership, U.S. Military Academy. He has 20 years' experience leading in infantry units both at peacetime and in combat and at strategic levels working for the Chief of Staff of the Army, and later for the Assistant Secretary of the Army (Financial Management and Comptroller) at the Pentagon. He holds both an MBA and MPA from Syracuse University, an M.A. in Military Science from the Marine Corps University, and a Ph.D. in Leadership from the University of Nebraska. His scholarly research focuses on authentic and moral leadership, and his most recent publications on those topics include "Authentic Leadership: The Heart of High Impact Leadership," in Leadership Lessons from West Point, ed. Doug Crandall (John Wiley and Sons, forthcoming); and co-author, "Veritable Authentic Leadership: Emergence, Functioning, and Impacts," and "Moral Leadership: Explicating the Moral Component of Authentic Leadership," both in Authentic Leadership Theory and Practice: Origins, Effects, and Development (2005), eds. W. B. Gardner and B. J. Avolio.

Brigadier General Anthony E. Hartle, U.S. Army Ret., received a B.S. from the Military Academy, M.A. in American and English Literature from Duke University, and a Ph.D. in Philosophy from the University of Texas at Austin. Commissioned in the Infantry, he served two tours in Vietnam, commanded a battalion in the 101st Airborne Division (Air Assault), taught literature and philosophy and served as Vice Dean at USMA, and retired as the head of the English Department in 2004, 40 years after commissioning. While stationed at the Academy, he also served as a staff member for the Presidential Commission Investigating the Space Shuttle Challenger accident. General Hartle authored *Moral Issues in Military Decision Making* and coauthored *Dimensions of Ethical Thought.* He has also published a variety of book chapters and journal articles. At West Point, he chaired the Superintendent's Honor Review Committee for many years and worked closely with the Center for Professional Military Ethics in the supervision of the Values Education Program for cadets. He was also the chairman of the Executive Board of the Joint Services Conference on Professional Ethics from 1993 to 2002.

Colonel Lloyd J. Matthews, U.S. Army Ret., received a B.S. degree from the U.S. Military Academy, an M.A. from Harvard University, and a Ph.D. from the University of Virginia, and is a graduate of the Army War College and Armed Forces Staff College. His military assignments included command at platoon, company, and battalion levels; advisory duty in the Vietnam War; editorship of *Parameters*, the Army War College quarterly; and an English professorship and the associate deanship at the Military Academy. Following retirement from the Army, he served as a project manager in Saudi Arabia and later Turkey. Colonel Matthews has published well over 100 articles, features, reviews, monographs, and editions on professional topics, including the edition, with Dale E. Brown, *The Parameters of Military Ethics* (Pergamon-Brassey's, 1989); the article "The Need for An Officers' Code of Professional Ethics," *Army Magazine*, March 1994; the entry on American Military

Ideals, Oxford Companion to American Military History, ed. John Whiteclay Chambers (Oxford University Press, 1999); and the edition, with Don M. Snider, *The Future of the Army Profession* (McGraw-Hill, 2d ed., 2005). Colonel Matthews also served on the editorial staff for the August 2004 Final Report of the Independent Panel to Review DoD Detention Operations [at Abu Ghraib] ("Schlesinger Panel Report").

General Eric K. Shinseki, U.S. Army Ret., holds the Class of 1951 Chair for Leadership Study in the Department of Behavioral Sciences and Leadership at West Point. He graduated from the Military Academy in 1965 with a B.S. degree and was commissioned in the Armor branch. He later obtained an M.A. in literature from the University of North Carolina, following which he taught philosophy and world literature at West Point. During his 39-year Army career, he commanded at troop, squadron, brigade, division, and army levels, and among other positions served as the Army's Deputy Chief of Staff for Operations and later as the Vice Chief of Staff. He served two combat tours in the Vietnam War and was twice wounded; served as the Commander of the NATO Stabilization Force during the campaign to pacify Bosnia-Herzegovina; and was the Army Chief of Staff during the period encompassing the terrorist attacks in New York and Washington on September 11, 2001, the Coalition campaign that ousted the Taliban government in Afghanistan in the late fall of 2001, and the campaign resulting in the capture of Baghdad and deposition of Saddam Hussein by Coalition forces in the spring of 2003. General Shinseki retired from the Army at the completion of his tour as the 34th Army

Chief of Staff in June 2003. He became the United States Secretary of Veterans Affairs in 2009. Asked how he wanted to be remembered by history, he replied, "Simply as a soldier."

Professor Don M. Snider, Colonel, U.S. Army Ret., received a B.S. degree from the U.S. Military Academy, an M.A. in Economics and an M.A. in Public Affairs from the University of Wisconsin, and a Ph.D. in Public Policy from the University of Maryland. He was appointed to the civilian faculty of the U.S. Military Academy in 1998. This followed a 28-year military career in the Army, five years in Washington, DC, as analyst and director of political-military research at the Center for Strategic and International Studies, and three years as the Olin Professor of National Security Studies at West Point. Among his most important early publications was a two-part series appearing in the September and December 1987 issues of Parameters, constituting at that time the definitive public explication of the 1986 Goldwater-Nichols legislation. Other publications include "The Civil-Military Gap and Professional Military Education at the Pre-commissioning Level" in *Armed Forces and Society* Winter 2001 (coauthor); and "The Future of Army Professionalism: The Need for Renewal and Redefinition" in *Parameters* August 2000 (coauthor). Most recently he was coauthor of the article "Christian Citizenship and American Empire" in the fall 2003 issue of *Faith and International Affairs*, author of "Leadership by Example," *Army Magazine*, November 2005, and project director, *The Future of the Army Profession*, 2nd ed. (McGraw-Hill, 2005). He is a member of the Council on Foreign

Relations, and serves on the Executive Committee of the Inter-University Seminar on Armed Forces and Society.

Colonel Patrick J. Sweeney is an Associate Professor and the Deputy Head of the Department of Behavioral Sciences and Leadership at the U.S. Military Academy. He is also Director of the Eisenhower Tactical Officer Leader Development Program for the Academy. Colonel Sweeney commanded the 3rd Battalion, 320th Field Artillery, in the 101st Airborne Division (Air Assault) at Ft. Campbell, KY, and served with the 101st during Operation Iraqi Freedom I. He received an M.A. and a Ph.D. from the University of North Carolina at Chapel Hill. Colonel Sweeney was an Assistant Professor in the department from 1992 to 1995 where he served as an instructor of the General Psychology for Leaders course and Executive Officer/Researcher in the Center for Leadership and Organization Research. His research interests include trust and influence in combat, leader development, and cohesion. He currently teaches the Leadership in Combat course at the Academy.

EVOLUTION
SHERRIE LYONS

FILM STUDIES
AMY VILLAREJO

FINANCE (SECOND EDITION)
ERIK BANKS

HUMAN GENETICS
RICKI LEWIS

HUMAN GEOGRAPHY
ANDREW JONES

INTERNATIONAL RELATIONS
PETER SUTCH AND JUANITA ELIAS

ISLAM (SECOND EDITION)
COLIN TURNER

JOURNALISM STUDIES
MARTIN CONBOY

JUDAISM
JACOB NEUSNER

LANGUAGE (SECOND EDITION)
R.L. TRASK

LAW
GARY SLAPPER AND DAVID KELLY

LITERARY THEORY (SECOND EDITION)
HANS BERTENS

LOGIC
J.C. BEALL

MANAGEMENT
MORGEN WITZEL

MARKETING (SECOND EDITION)
KARL MOORE AND NIKETH PAREEK

MEDIA STUDIES
JULIAN MCDOUGALL

THE OLYMPICS
…MIAH AND BEATRIZ GARCIA

Konstantin Stani
twentieth-centur
system of actor
introduction to h

- life and the
- major work
- ideas in pra
- impact on

With furthe
comprehensi
of Stanislavs

Rose Why
the Univer
System of A

The Basics

ACTING
BELLA MERLIN

AMERICAN PHILOSOPH
NANCY STANLICK

ANTHROPOLOGY
PETER METCALF

ARCHAEOLOGY (SECON
CLIVE GAMBLE

ART HISTORY
GRANT POOKE AND DIA

ARTIFICIAL INTELLIGENC
KEVIN WARWICK

THE BIBLE
JOHN BARTON

BUDDHISM
CATHY CANTWELL

THE CITY
KEVIN ARCHER

CONTEMPORARY LITERATU
SUMAN GUPTA

CRIMINAL LAW
JONATHAN HERRING

CRIMINOLOGY (SECOND ED
SANDRA WALKLATE

DANCE STUDIES
JO BUTTERWORTH

EASTERN PHILOSOPHY
VICTORIA S. HARRISON

ECONOMICS (SECOND EDITIO
TONY CLEAVER

EDUCATION
KAY WOOD

EUROPEAN UNION (SECOND
ALEX WARLEIGH-LAC

PHILOSOPHY (FIFTH EDITION)
NIGEL WARBURTON

PHYSICAL GEOGRAPHY
JOSEPH HOLDEN

POETRY (SECOND EDITION)
JEFFREY WAINWRIGHT

POLITICS (FOURTH EDITION)
STEPHEN TANSEY AND NIGEL JACKSON

THE QUR'AN
MASSIMO CAMPANINI

RACE AND ETHNICITY
PETER KIVISTO AND PAUL R. CROLL

RELIGION (SECOND EDITION)
MALORY NYE

RELIGION AND SCIENCE
PHILIP CLAYTON

RESEARCH METHODS
NICHOLAS WALLIMAN

ROMAN CATHOLICISM
MICHAEL WALSH

SEMIOTICS (SECOND EDITION)
DANIEL CHANDLER

SHAKESPEARE (THIRD EDITION)
SEAN MCEVOY

SOCIAL WORK
MARK DOEL

SOCIOLOGY
KEN PLUMMER

SPECIAL EDUCATIONAL NEEDS
JANICE WEARMOUTH

TELEVISION STUDIES
TOBY MILLER

TERRORISM
JAMES LUTZ AND BRENDA LUTZ

THEATRE STUDIES
ROBERT LEACH

WORLD HISTORY
PETER N. STEARNS

STANISLAVSKI

THE BASICS

Rose Whyman

LONDON AND NEW YORK

For Brian Door, with all my love and thanks, as ever.

First published 2013
by Routledge
2 Park Square, Milton Park, Abingdon, Oxon OX14 4RN

Simultaneously published in the USA and Canada
by Routledge
711 Third Avenue, New York, NY 10017

Routledge is an imprint of the Taylor & Francis Group, an informa business

British Library Cataloguing in Publication Data
A catalogue record for this book is available from the British Library

Library of Congress Cataloging in Publication Data
Whyman, Rose.
Stanislavski : the basics / Rose Whyman.
p. cm. – (The basics)
Includes bibliographical references.
1. Stanislavsky, Konstantin, 1863–1938. I. Title.
PN2728.S78W49 2014
792.02'8092 – dc23
[B]
2012023194

ISBN: 978-0-415-49294-2 (hbk)
ISBN: 978-0-415-49297-3 (pbk)
ISBN: 978-0-203-07760-3 (ebk)

Typeset in Bembo and Scala Sans
by Taylor & Francis Books

Printed and bound in Great Britain by the MPG Books Group

CONTENTS

ACKNOWLEDGEMENTS

I would like to thank Victoria Door for much help and support, also Valerie Finegan, Roy Thompson, Janyce Hawliczek and Martin Leach. Other friends and colleagues from the Professional Association of Alexander Teachers have helped in a variety of ways.

Talia Rodgers from Routledge and, for the Basics series, Andy Humphries, Rebecca Shillabeer and Sophie Thomson have been an invaluable source of advice and support.

I am grateful to Matt Turner, Tamara Abrossimova, Bella Merlin, Tanya Lipatova, Suresh Patel, Maggie Gale, Maria Shevtsova, John Warrick and Robert Ellerman.

Lastly, thanks go to my family, John, Lynne, Laurie, Tom, Georgia and Eddie and I would also like to remember the encouragement given me by my parents, Rose and Lawrence Whyman.

A NOTE TO READERS

In the early part of the twentieth century, Konstantin Sergeievich Stanislavski, the Russian director and actor, developed a way of training actors, which is known as the *system*. Though the *system* is very well-known, aspects of Stanislavski's work have been misunderstood and misinterpreted, both in Russia and the West. The first translations of Stanislavski's books into English were heavily edited and contained inaccuracies, which have compounded problems of understanding. New translations have been published only recently: *My Life in Art* (2008a), *An Actor's Work* (2008b) and *An Actor's Work on a Role* (2010). *Stanislavski: The Basics* aims to explain the *system* and the significance of Stanislavski's work for the contemporary actor, using the new translations, as part of a reassessment of the work and evaluation of its continued importance.

Chapter 1 gives a brief biography and indicates Stanislavski's development as an artist, identifying the principles on which the *system* is based. Chapters 2, 3, 4 and 5 analyse the *system*, aiming to offer the student actor a basis for their own use and experiment, providing the tools to explore *truth* in acting conceptually and practically. Chapter 2 begins with a consideration of Stanislavski's ideas about the actor's basic training. The processes of research, analysis, rehearsal and performance of a role are described, with explanations of Stanislavski's key terms and comparisons with the goals of contemporary directors and actor-trainers. The different elements of the *system* that enable the actor to *experience* and to *embody* a role are explained, including key ideas of *action* and *emotion*. Chapters 3, 4 and 5 include approaches to work on a text. The main play text used as an example is Tennessee Williams' *The Glass Menagerie*; there are references to other plays such as Arthur Miller's *Death of a Salesman* and Timberlake Wertenbaker's *Our Country's Good*. You can take exercises from or look at explanations in different places in the book: your reading does not have to be sequential. Chapter 6 looks at how Stanislavski's work influenced, provoked and inspired others in his time and into the present day.

I refer to *An Actor's Work*, which is in two parts, describing the first two years of the course of training for actors that Stanislavski envisaged. I also refer to *An Actor's Work on a Role*, a text which is incomplete in Russian, and this describes the third year of the course. Stanislavski found a way of bringing writing about practice to life, by telling the story of a fictional drama school, where Tortsov is the teacher of the *system* and a famous actor and director of the theatre to which the school belongs. Kostya (the short form of Konstantin, Stanislavski's first name) and Tortsov are each an alter ego of Stanislavski: the teacher of the *system* and the enthusiastic and imaginative student. Tortsov was initially 'Tvortsov', which means, in Russian, the 'creator.'

There are various ways of transliterating Russian words, so there are variations on the spelling of 'Stanislavski'. When referring to other writers' work, I have used their chosen form of the name.

1

STANISLAVSKI'S LIFE AND CONTEXT

Konstantin Sergeievich Stanislavski (Russians have three names, as their middle name is derived from their father's name) is famous throughout the world as the originator of the *system*, a method of training actors, and as a director and actor. He was born in Russia in 1863 and died in 1938. His main work was at the Moscow Art Theatre, which was opened in 1898, with Vladimir Ivanovich Nemirovich-Danchenko. In his groundbreaking work, Stanislavski asked questions about what makes a great actor, and explored this in depth. His work established acting as an art, rather than a craft, and he also developed the art of directing. As a result, Stanislavski's work and the *system* in particular continue to be the most important development in the history of acting in the West and to have tremendous impact on acting and theatre today. Many fine actors in film and theatre still use his actor training method, the *system*, or aspects of it, and his ideas continue to influence and provoke contemporary theory and practice of theatre.

If the actor is to be an artist, rather than someone who can please a crowd, and pull out a bag of tricks in performance, then they need constant practice, as musicians and painters do. Stanislavski often said, 'Nothing comes without work; only that which is acquired with difficulty is worth anything' (Toporkov 1998: 93). Think of the difference between, on the one hand theatre performances you have seen where the actors have performed competently, telling the story of the play, and on the other hand experiences that seem almost magical, where the actors or even just one actor have taken you into the world of the play, drawing you in by the intensity of their performance. Regrettably, these experiences may be few and far between, but Stanislavski himself sought to perform at this level and, most importantly, believed that the way to do this could be taught. Before discussing what the *system* is and how it works, this chapter will trace how it emerged, looking at Stanislavski's life and the context for his work.

KONSTANTIN STANISLAVSKI – EARLY LIFE

Konstantin Sergeievich Alekseiev was born in 1863 in Moscow. He adopted the stage name 'Stanislavski' when he began to act. The Alekseievs were an immensely wealthy manufacturing family: Stanislavski's father, Sergei Vladimirovich, owned a factory that made gold and silver thread. Stanislavski's mother, Elizaveta Vasilevna, was the daughter of a Parisian actress, Marie Varley. Like other wealthy families, the Alekseievs were patrons of the arts. Artists of all kinds visited the Alekseievs' home. The family made regular visits to the circus, theatre, ballet and opera flourishing in Moscow at the time. The young Konstantin was smitten with a girl at the circus, Elvira, who danced on horseback. Once, as she made her exit, passing close to his family's box, he jumped out and kissed her skirt, much to the amusement of his family, who asked him when the wedding was to be. Stanislavski, with his brothers and sisters (ten children were born, nine of whom survived), took part in plays and entertainments with other members of the household, organised by their governess, Evdokiia A. Snopova. They were so enthusiastic about this that Sergei Vladimirovich had a theatre built at the family's country home in Liubimovka, near Moscow. Stanislavski describes his early experiences of acting and the impressions made on him by visits to performances in his autobiography, *My Life in Art*. It was Moscow's Imperial Maly Theatre which influenced him most: he wrote that 'It taught me how to observe and see the beautiful' (2008a: 29). And he discusses the many outstanding actors whom he saw performing there, imitating them in his performances at home as a child.

In 1877, the family formed an amateur theatre company, the Alekseiev Circle, which included members of the household and friends, and Stanislavski worked on productions as an actor and director. They performed operettas and Russian vaudevilles, which were comic plays. He took part in semi-professional productions with members of the Maly Theatre and learned about acting from them. The Maly tradition embraced ideas about truthful, natural acting which were articulated by Mikhail Alexandrovich Shchepkin (1788–1863), who had begun his acting career as a serf or slave in a theatre company owned by an aristocrat but became a star of the Russian theatre. The Maly tradition was an influence on Stanislavski in the development of the *system*.

Stanislavski was educated first of all at home by tutors, and was much more interested in fencing, dance, skating and other forms of exercise than study, an interest that led him to explore many forms of exercise in his later experiments. When he went to school, he disliked it and only passed his examinations with clandestine help: he and his classmates learned sign language so that the best student signed the answers to them all.

FIRST STEPS TOWARDS A CAREER IN THEATRE

As the children grew up, married and had children, the activity of the Alekseiev Circle decreased, though Stanislavski's interest in acting and other kinds of performance did not. During one period, Stanislavski, like several of his young male friends, became a 'balletomane', attending the ballet often and falling in love with one dancer after another. He admired the work of Italian ballerina Virginia Zucchi (1847–1930), and her qualities as a performer influenced Stanislavski in the development of the *system*. In 1881 Stanislavski began work in his father's business, but continued to pursue his interests. Moscow was an important centre for music at the time, with artists such as the famous composer Tchaikovsky based there. Savva Ivanovich Mamontov, a railway magnate related to Stanislavski by marriage, was an artistic entrepreneur who spent much of his fortune producing theatre and opera. Stanislavski already knew much of the standard opera repertoire and learned a great deal more about the Russian repertoire in particular at Mamontov's private opera. He decided to train to be an opera singer, taking lessons from the Bolshoi Theatre's

Fiodor Komissarzhevski, who also taught at the Moscow Conservatoire. Though he soon abandoned this training because of vocal problems, he maintained his love of music throughout his career, directing opera in later life and teaching the *system* to opera singers.

Seeking instead to become a professional actor, he went to the Moscow Theatre School in 1885, but left after three weeks, disappointed with the standard of training. He also visited the Paris Conservatoire in 1888, to study how acting was taught there. In the same year, Maria Petrovna Perevoshchikova (who later took the stage name Lilina) performed with him in a comedy to raise funds for charity, and they married the following year. She was to be a life-long supporter in the development of Stanislavski's work.

At this point, Stanislavski was concealing his theatrical ambitions from his family, as the professional theatre was not considered a respectable occupation for a cultured young man. This is why he adopted his stage name. Of course his family found out eventually, and they accepted his chosen career, though his father bluntly said to him, 'If you want to do some acting in your own free time, then create your own circle and your own repertoire, but don't play any old filth with God knows who' (2008a: 85). In 1888, Stanislavski and other theatricals founded the Moscow Society of Art and Literature. Following the entrepreneurial example of Mamontov and others, Stanislavski subsidised the work of the Society from his own private fortune. He acted in classics like the French playwright Molière's *Georges Dandin* and Russian Romantic writer Alexander Pushkin's *Miser Knight*, gaining valuable acting experience and instruction from seasoned professionals who were involved with the Society. His first directing work was a one-act comedy in 1889.

A significant influence on the development of Stanislavski's thinking about theatre was the famous acting company of the Duke of Saxe-Meiningen, which presented Moscow with a new kind of theatre when it arrived on tour in 1885. Stanislavski did not miss a single show of their second tour in 1890. This company was dedicated to producing the classics, such as Shakespeare and Schiller, with meticulous historical accuracy in set, costume and properties, as opposed to the stock sets and costume on which most theatres relied. The methods of the company's director, Ludwig Kronegk, inspired Stanislavski, and in 1891 he undertook his first major production for the Society – a new play by the great writer

Leo Tolstoy, *The Fruits of Enlightenment*. As well as directing, he played a number of major roles over the next few years, including the lead roles in Shakespeare's *Othello* and in *Uriel Acosta*, a play by Karl Gutskov about a seventeenth-century Jewish community. Stanislavski's new approach to direction and interpretation and his own performances gained much critical comment.

It was a hugely exciting period to be working in theatre in Russia. Venerating the classic writers from the Golden Age of Russian literature such as Pushkin and Nikolai Vasilievich Gogol, Stanislavski engaged with the traditional aesthetic of the Russian intelligentsia, including the ideas of the critic Vissarion Grigorevich Belinski, who believed in the importance of art in bringing about social change, and with Tolstoy's teachings on the spiritual importance of art. And he also encountered new ideas that emerged in the period between the 1890s and the Russian Revolution in 1917 – the Silver Age of Russia – when Russian music, dance, literature, theatre and fine art were celebrated in Europe and America. Fin de siècle movements such as naturalism and symbolism challenged existing ideas, and were thought-provoking for Stanislavski.

At the same time, the new science of psychology was developing. In the period after the publication of Charles Darwin's *On the Origin of Species* in 1859, new ideas, including those about evolution, had changed the way human life was conceptualised in the West and in many other places throughout the world including Russia. All sorts of investigations took place. Studies in physics, sociology, physiology and psychology arose from a fascination with what lies below the surface of life. There was a desire to find out how the human organism could best function. This led to ideas that training and daily work in sport and exercise could open up possibilities for human beings, and these ideas influenced Stanislavski's experiments in the psychology and physiology of acting. He rooted his work, he said, in observations of the realities of human nature.

THE MOSCOW ART THEATRE – BEGINNINGS

Stanislavski's dream was to have a theatre of his own, and in 1897 he met Vladimir Ivanovich Nemirovich-Danchenko, a famous playwright and theatre teacher at the Moscow Philharmonic School. Stanislavski had performed in his play *The Happy Man* with the

Alekseiev Circle and Maly Theatre actors. The two men formulated a plan for a new theatre during a conversation in a restaurant, the Slavyanski Bazaar, which lasted eighteen hours. They rejected much that they saw in the theatre of the time and wanted to create a new kind of theatre, dedicated to high standards of acting and production. They wanted it to be a popular theatre and to keep ticket prices affordable, with the aim of educating audiences. In 1898, the theatre opened, and it gained an audience from the first season. The success of what became known as the Moscow Art Theatre (then as the Moscow Art Academic Theatre from 1919 until recently) was linked inextricably with the work of Anton Chekhov, whose great plays *The Seagull*, in 1898, *Uncle Vanya* in 1899, *Three Sisters* in 1901, *The Cherry Orchard* in 1904 and *Ivanov*, also in 1904, were all produced there, the last three as premieres. Stanislavski performed leading roles in each of these plays, respectively the writer Trigorin, the doctor Astrov, Lieutenant Colonel Vershinin, and the aristocrats Gaiev and Shabelskii, while also directing. These productions were recognised for their 'spiritual naturalism', the fact that they were both true to life and poetic. Nemirovich-Danchenko's role at the MAT was literary manager, in charge of decisions about repertoire, while he also directed plays. Other plays by contemporary writers such as Henrik Ibsen, Gerhardt Hauptmann and French symbolist writer Maurice Maeterlinck, contemporary Russian writers such as Alexei Tolstoy and Maxim Gorky, and Russian classical writers such as Gogol, Pushkin and Alexander Sergeievich Griboiedov, as well as Shakespeare and Molière, were the substance of the Theatre's repertoire over the first twenty years of its existence.

Lilina, Stanislavski's wife, performed in many Moscow Art Theatre plays and was much acclaimed as an actress. She was dedicated to Stanislavski's attempts to investigate acting and was a willing participant in his experiments. Early in their marriage she had to accept that, essentially, for Stanislavski the theatre would always be more important than their family life. Other important figures who were founder members of the MAT included Olga Knipper, who married Anton Chekhov in 1901, and Vsevolod Emilievich Meyerhold. Meyerhold was to become the leading avant-garde director of the revolutionary period in Russia after leaving the MAT in 1902 to pursue his own career. The MAT itself was to become, arguably, the most famous theatre in the world, producing celebrated actors such as Vasilii Ivanovich Kachalov and Ivan Mikhailovich Moskvin.

THE 1905 REVOLUTION

> Down with the old! Long live the new!
>
> (Stanislavski 2008a: 185)

The MAT came into being in a transitional period in Russian history. Two years before Stanislavski's birth, 1861 was the year in which slavery in Russia was banned – the emancipation of the serfs. Russia was until then basically a feudal society, in which the supreme ruler or Tsar governed an empire where the vast majority of people lived in rural areas as peasants, often very impoverished, or as serfs. Serfs or slaves belonged to the local landowners, working for them on the estate or in the home. Currents of rebellion moved through the empire during Stanislavski's lifetime and Tsar Alexander II was assassinated in 1881. There was a revolution in 1905, in the early years of the MAT's existence. On 'Bloody Sunday', peaceful demonstrators were massacred by the Tsar's forces in St Petersburg. The revolution was suppressed at this point but dissent continued to brew.

There was artistic as well as political ferment. Stanislavski resisted relating the theatre directly to politics, stating that biased, utilitarian ideas kill art (2008a: 219); nevertheless, many of the plays put on by the MAT in this period had a resonance for the times, despite the existing censorship. As well as Chekhov's plays, which depicted the stagnancy of Russian social structures with humour and bite, plays by Gorky and Ibsen were produced early in the 1900s. In 1902, Gorky's *The Lower Depths* depicted the terrible conditions and desperation in which poor people lived in Moscow in 1902. In Ibsen's *An Enemy of the People*, Stanislavski played Dr Stockmann, whose stance for principle against corruption appealed in a time of social protest to many who were supporting radical change in Russia. The 1905 'Bloody Sunday' massacre on Kazan Square, outside the Tsar's Winter Palace, took place on a day when the play was on tour in St Petersburg, and that evening Stanislavski, playing Stockmann, was mobbed by the audience.

MODERNISM – THE AVANT-GARDE

In Russia, the period from the late nineteenth century until 1917 – broadly speaking, the modernist period, when new ideas about life were emerging – was reflected in theatre in new artistic ideas, and theories about the relationship between politics and art. The ideas about natural acting that made Stanislavski's work on the Chekhov plays famous were not as appropriate to dealing with symbolist plays and theatre of other emergent avant-garde movements.

In 1905, Stanislavski set up a studio theatre called the Studio on Povarskaia, and invited Meyerhold to work there to develop approaches to acting in the new avant-garde plays. Initially Meyerhold experimented with acting and staging with some success in Stanislavski's view, and work began on Maeterlinck's *Death of Tintagiles*, Hauptmann's *Schluck and Jau* and one-act plays by other writers. But according to Stanislavski it became apparent that in their roles the inexperienced young actors were unable to sustain the new techniques Meyerhold was developing. Stanislavski reacted badly to a dress rehearsal, for which Meyerhold had chosen very subdued lighting, shouting 'Light!' then saying 'The audience cannot take the darkness on stage for long, it goes against psychology, they must see the actors' faces!' (Popov in Gauss 1999: 20). In addition there were financial problems and in 1905, as life in Moscow was made difficult by street fighting, Stanislavski decided to close the Studio.

Stanislavski was to continue to develop his own ideas about the new plays – he produced Knut Hamsun's *The Drama of Life* and Leonid Nikolaevich Andreiev's *The Life of Man* in 1907, Maeterlinck's *The Blue Bird* in 1908 – and he regarded some of his experiments with symbolism and impressionism as successes and some as failures. His friend and collaborator in this was Leopold Antonovich Sulerzhitski, nicknamed Suler, who joined the Moscow Art Theatre in 1906. Formerly a revolutionary, he adopted Tolstoy's philosophies, which were based on Christian principles, but rejected church orthodoxy. He introduced Stanislavski to Raja yoga; Tolstoy was interested in this meditative practice of Hinduism, and concepts from it were to make their way into the *system*. The relationship between Nemirovich-Danchenko and Stanislavski was deteriorating by this point, as they had artistic differences and different views about the direction the theatre should take.

In 1906, drawing on his previous experimental work, his studies of psychology and his own personal struggles – experiences of reaching a dead-end, with both the Studio on Povarskaia and in his own acting – Stanislavski began to formulate what became the *system*. He began to introduce concepts related to the *system* in a production of Gogol's *The Government Inspector* in 1908. In that year, he discovered the work of French psychologist Théodule Ribot and drew from this, particularly ideas about the memory of emotions and sensory experiences, known as *affective memory*. He used exercises from the *system* in 1909 in Turgenev's *A Month in the Country*. By the time he worked on *Hamlet* in 1911, he was attempting to implement the *system* as fully as possible.

Stanislavski's ideas were not entirely well received at the MAT. However, at this point he found two internationally renowned artists who were also breaking ground artistically. One was the dancer Isadora Duncan, who first performed in Moscow in 1905. He recognised in her a kindred spirit in his search for creative expression based on natural principles of how the human organism works. She introduced him to British director and designer Edward Gordon Craig (1872–1966), whom Stanislavski invited to the MAT to work on this production of *Hamlet*. Stanislavski wrote, 'Craig, like me, wanted perfection, an ideal, i.e. a simple, profound, inspiring, artistic, beautiful expression of human feeling' (2008a: 296). These ideals proved hard to realise: there were misunderstandings and difficulties in fulfilling Craig's vision, and Stanislavski viewed his own work with actors as a step on the way towards his vision of acting in plays like Shakespeare's. Despite this, the production was reported as a success across Europe.

THE STUDIOS

Stanislavski's developing ideas about the *system* met with resistance from MAT actors, who, as established professionals, did not see the need for continuous training. His relationship with Nemirovich-Danchenko continued to be problematic. Though the *system* was recognised by the MAT in 1911, in 1912 Stanislavski founded and devoted much of his time to a new studio, the First Studio, where he could experiment with the *system* with young actors. Suler was a key figure and influence on its development. Studio members included

Evgenii Bagrationovich Vakhtangov, Richard Boleslavsky, Serafima Germanovna Birman, Maria Alekseievna Ouspenskaia and Michael Chekhov, who was later to become famous in the West. In 1913, Boleslavsky directed *The Wreck of the Ship 'Hope'* to great acclaim, and in 1915 Vakhtangov directed *The Festival of Peace*, with Suler's help. *The Cricket on the Hearth*, based on a story by Charles Dickens, directed by Suler and Boris Sushkevich, was a great success. Landmark productions included *The Government Inspector* with Michael Chekhov in 1921 and Vakhtangov's production of Strindberg's *Erik XIV* in 1921, also with Michael Chekhov in the lead role.

The studio was a wonderful place to research methods of voice and movement training. The First Studio was small, seating only about fifty people and thus enabling a very intimate actor-audience relationship. It has been described as the 'incubator' of the *system* for its greatest teachers and practitioners, who were to spread knowledge of it to various places in the world (Gauss 1999: 49). Then, in 1916, the Second Studio was formed. This was the year that Suler died, and Stanislavski was devastated to lose his collaborator and friend. Vakhtang Levanovich Mchedlov was the main organiser of this studio, joining forces with some actors from the MAT who had run a private drama school, and he won approval for the studio from Stanislavski. He began to teach the students there, and so did Nemirovich-Danchenko. Maria Osipovna Knebel, later a significant figure in Russian theatre, became a member.

Next, in 1918, Vakhtangov began to work at the Mansurov Studio, which was incorporated into the MAT in 1920 as the Third Studio (later it became the Vakhtangov Theatre). Vakhtangov famously directed Maeterlinck's *Miracle of St Anthony* and Carlo Gozzi's *Princess Turandot* in 1921 and 1922.

A group of young Jewish actors had also approached Stanislavski in 1918, wanting to found a theatre, and the Jewish Habima Studio was formed. Vakhtangov also directed there; his production of Ansky's *Dybbuk* became very famous. In 1919, Stanislavski was invited to teach the *system* at the Opera Studio of the Bolshoi Theatre, Moscow's major theatre, where he gave some important lectures. The studio was named the Stanislavski Opera Studio in 1924 and the Stanislavski Opera Theatre in 1928. A Fourth Studio was opened at the MAT in 1921, later becoming the Realistic Theatre.

The studio movement gained pace in Moscow in the period between 1918 and 1925, with many other studio theatres apart from those connected to the MAT. Young people who worked in factories and offices in Moscow would rehearse late into the night to stage performances for small audiences of like-minded people, family and friends.

THE 1917 REVOLUTION

This experimental studio work was taking place against a backdrop of social and political disruption. Following the 1905 Revolution, World War One broke out in 1914 and a further, major revolution took place in Russia in 1917. A civil war followed in 1918, won eventually by the Bolsheviks. They established communist rule in Russia, sweeping away the old Tsarist system and putting Tsar Nicholas II to death, thus ending the Romanov dynasty. The Revolution in 1917 was not just a revolution in politics and economics; it was thought that everything could be made new: art, philosophy, education. Even what people *were* could essentially be reformed: communism involved an experiment in social conditioning, based on the idea that our environment determines who we are and how we behave. The wealthy Stanislavski, like many of his peers, was stripped of his fortune and his factories were nationalised. After Lenin's death in 1924, Josef Stalin eventually gained power, turning the ideals of the early communists into the harsh reality of a dictatorship under which millions of people were put to death. The fate of Stanislavski and the MAT was subject to much change in the years after the Revolution.

The year 1917 was also a crisis point in Stanislavski's career, as Nemirovich-Danchenko removed him from the role of Rostanev in *The Village of Stepanchikovo* after 156 rehearsals. Stanislavski was mortified by this and continued to act, direct and develop the *system* until his death, but did not test his ideas out on the creation of a new role. In addition to these internal problems for the theatre, times were hard because money was short. The Civil War began in 1918 and a group of actors who toured to Kharkov were stranded there for two years. Many from Russia's cultured and moneyed classes, including some MAT actors, began to emigrate. Attempting to weather the storm, the theatre placed itself at the service of the

Revolution and was required to attract new audiences of people who had not previously had access to it.

As communist rule became established, Russian theatres had to find new repertoires that would match up with the government's views on the purposes of art in Soviet society, but the MAT struggled to fulfil this task. While Meyerhold was recognised as a leading figure in the theatre of the Revolution, it seemed that the MAT was becoming a thing of the past, seen as 'bourgeois', attacked by the avant-garde and extreme left. The government decided that the theatre would tour in Europe and America, and these tours took place from 1922 to 1924. A version of Stanislavski's autobiography, *My Life in Art*, was published in America in 1924. A version that he approved was published in Russia in 1926. Though an important aim of the tour had been to raise funds, the troupe returned to Moscow in debt. The Soviet press said that the company had 'sold out' on the Revolution by going on the tour in the first place.

While Nemirovich-Danchenko toured abroad for two years, Stanislavski began to refashion the theatre's repertoire, developing nine productions between 1925 and 1928, including three new Soviet plays and four operas, working at the Opera Studio at the same time. Mikhail Afanasevich Bulgakov's *The Days of the Turbins*, about a liberal family in the Civil War, was a box office success in 1926, though it was savaged by many critics because of its sympathetic portrayal of a 'White' family, representing those opposing the 'Red' revolutionary forces in that war. In 1927, Vsevolod Viacheslavovich Ivanov's *The Armoured Train No. 14–69*, about the capture of an armoured train from counter-revolutionary forces, was staged. The production marked the change of status of the Second Studio, which had become the Second Moscow Art Theatre. Using aspects of the *system* and his directorial expertise, Stanislavski was able to gain hard-edged performances from the MAT actors in a political play, which was greeted as the MAT's entry into the new era of art and the Revolution.

Stanislavski performed for the last time in 1928, after collapsing with heart problems while playing Vershinin in an excerpt of *Three Sisters*, which was staged for the MAT's thirtieth anniversary. Though his own acting career was over, Stanislavski continued to develop his ideas as a teacher and a director.

STANISLAVSKI AS DIRECTOR

Before Stanislavski's time, many companies had an actor-manager rather than a director, and he was one of the main instigators of the development of the role of the director, as we know it today. His early productions, influenced by Kronegk's methods, prioritised historical accuracy in the look of a play and well-orchestrated crowd scenes. When he began to develop the *system* from 1906, he focused more on the individual actor's process. As a young actor, he experienced his directors telling him what result they wanted but saying nothing about how to achieve it. He recounts that they would just shout 'Experience it, really feel it, live it!' (2008a: 95). His concern was to find the method an actor could use in order to 'experience, feel, live a part'. At the beginning of his work as a director on Chekhov, he wrote detailed production scores, explaining comprehensively what the actor should do, leaving little to the actor's own creativity. The *system* began to develop as a way of teaching actors, rather than instructing them in how to achieve what he, as the director, wanted in a dictatorial way. This was not to say that Stanislavski became any less insistent on attaining the highest standards he thought possible: throughout his career as a director, Stanislavski regularly lost his temper, terrorising many an actor with his response to acting he perceived to lack 'truth': 'I don't believe you!'

The beginning of rehearsals for many years focused on *round-the-table* work, where in-depth analysis of the play took place through discussion, with the company seated around a table, before beginning practical work. The problem with this was that the actor's process could become overly intellectual and the work that had been done was of little use practically, when the actors began to rehearse. In the last period of his work, Stanislavski developed ways of encouraging the actor to work on their feet, using improvisation as a way into a text.

STANISLAVSKI'S LAST YEARS

The Communist Party continued to strengthen its position. The materialistic ideologies of Soviet communism opposed religion and any philosophies that were perceived to be mystical. A campaign against the avant-garde began. In 1928, Michael Chekhov, who held beliefs in anthroposophy, a mystical branch of Christianity, was forced to emigrate. Stanislavski's work was also subject to attack, The Russian Association of Proletarian Writers, who found that Stanislavski's *system* was not materialist or proletarian enough in its emphasis on 'soul' and 'spirit' and use of terms such as 'the magic if' (the way an actor begins to envisage the character, saying 'if I were Romeo, I would … '). Meyerhold was also criticised, at the opposite extreme, for being too 'mechanistic'! Hopes that the Revolution would bring about a just and equal society were shattered for many, as a wave of repression and rule of terror began in the 1930s.

However, despite the attacks on Stanislavski's work, it was revealed in 1932 that Stalin's favourite play was *The Days of the Turbins*. In 1934, Stanislavski was invited to collaborate with the Soviet government, whose cultural branch was seeking to find a Marxist aesthetic, a realist art that would communicate with the masses, and his ideas were seen to be compatible with this. Stanislavski's concepts of truth and realism in art became acclaimed and equated with socialist realism, the doctrine that defined the official form for Soviet art. This was a narrow view of realism, promoting socialist ideals that the Soviets claimed were rooted in nineteenth-century Russian realism. Politics were involved here: action, which along with emotion had always been a lynchpin of the *system*, was seen as more concrete and scientific than emotion, which was hard to define and had 'spiritual' connotations. The Soviets emphasised the importance of action rather than emotion in the *system*, stating that Stanislavski had moved away from his ideas about *affective memory*, including *emotion memory*. Stanislavski strongly denied this in private correspondence. Letters were exchanged about a joint experimental project with Ivan Petrovich Pavlov, the leading Soviet scientist whose theory of conditioned reflexes was lauded, but as Pavlov died in 1936 this did not come to fruition. The project was still publicised, as linking Stanislavski's work on action with what was then cutting-edge science. These political emphases were to cause confusion in understanding the *system* at first in the West, but much has become clearer in recent years. For Stanislavski, emotion was no less important than action; what went on inside the actor, *experiencing*, was just as important as external action.

In 1935, after various crises at the MAT, including problems over a production of Bulgakov's *Molière*, Stanislavski began a new Opera-Dramatic Studio with his sister Zinaida. In 1938, he invited

Meyerhold to work at what was now called the Stanislavski Opera Theatre, after Meyerhold's own theatre had been closed. Stanislavski continued to work but died from a heart attack later that year; the two productions he had been working on – Verdi's *Rigoletto* and Molière's *Tartuffe* – were completed by Meyerhold and Mikhail Nikolaevich Kedrov respectively. In 1936, the American edition of *An Actor Prepares* was published; the Russian first part of *An Actor's Work, Experiencing,* was published in 1938 after his death, the second part, *Embodiment,* was not published until 1955 and *An Actor's Work on a Role* appeared in 1957. Stanislavski died acclaimed as a leading figure in the Soviet Union, with the *system* set to become the official training method for actors.

KEY IDEAS ABOUT ART

Stanislavski made important discoveries early in his artistic career. Though he had much experience as an amateur actor and director from an early age, and then further experience from his work with the Moscow Art Theatre, acting and directing did not come easily to him. He rejected the idea of talent being something you either have or don't have – as he put it, 'the idea that great actors can only have divine inspiration' (2008a: 347). He believed that creativity could be developed: his quest was to discover practical methods of training to act at the highest standard possible.

Following Tolstoy, Stanislavski believed that art is about communication between people and that what is communicated is of spiritual importance. This did not imply religious feeling but that art enables human beings to transcend everyday experience and to envision dimensions beyond it, of truth and beauty. Stanislavski believed that art does not represent or imitate nature: art should be nature. It should be life, or natural truth, and the purpose of theatre is the creation of life on stage. The actor invests something of him or herself into this in order to create 'the life of the human spirit of the role', as Stanislavski put it (2008b: 24).

The tradition of viewing art in this way in Russia was summarised by the critic Belinski: 'As we … become more engrossed in the emotions and fate of other human beings on stage, our egoism evaporates and we become better persons and better citizens' (Senelick 1981: xxviii). The actors in a drama represent humanity and theatre is the art form closest to its audience; as it is live, it can convey more about human life to an audience and communicate on more levels than, for example, music or visual art.

This essentially humanist view – that our shared experience is all-important in art – means that truth of characterisation is based in actual experience. Actors must gain understanding of life and what makes human beings behave as they do. One of Stanislavski's precepts, adopted early on in his career, was 'When you play a bad man, look for the good in him' (2008a: 105–7), that is, characters should be fully rounded, even possessing contradictory characteristics, as human beings do. Art should enable understanding of people in depth and the actor and director must have this understanding themselves. This means that the actor has a mission and is an artist, rather than a craftsperson.

Contemporary British director Mike Alfreds, who acknowledges his debt to Stanislavski, writes, 'If theatre has a purpose, I believe it is this: the revelation and confirmation of the heights, depths and breadth, the multi-dimensional richness, of our shared humanity' (2007: 19).

KEY IDEAS ABOUT ACTING

Stanislavski's study of acting, which led to the development of the *system*, began with his observations of actors and of himself, and in particular his problems in acting. When he first began to ask the question 'what makes a great actor?' he was struck by Zucchi, the ballet dancer he had admired when he was a young man, the 'freedom and looseness of her muscles and the moments of highest emotional intensity' (2008a: 79). He continued to observe great actors and to study acting methods, noting in other actors this quality of 'bodily relaxation, the absence of muscular tension and the total obedience of the physical apparatus' (2008a: 257–58) which brought about the *creative state*, a quality of spontaneity in their work, and facilitated emotional and spiritual expression. He drew comparisons between these great performances and those of actors he did not admire and his own performances: 'I was always stiff on stage' (2008a: 79). As a young actor he was tall, ungainly, gauche and had problems in pronouncing certain letters (2008a: 68).

He experienced stage fright and recognised that his muscular tension onstage was a barrier to feeling and emotion. He found he could not control what was going on when he reached an emotional climax in a role:

> what can the body do when creative feeling is required? The body tenses because the will is powerless, abnormal tensions set in everywhere, in various centres, tying you in knots, creating spasms so that your legs go stiff and can scarcely move, your hands turn to wood, your breath is short, your throat is tight and your whole body goes dead. Or, alternatively, uncontrolled feelings reduce the entire body to anarchy. The muscles involuntarily shorten, resulting in a countless number of movements, meaningless poses and gestures, nervous tics etc. Feeling runs away from this chaos and takes refuge in its secret places.
>
> (2008a: 100)

He wrote that for a young, inexperienced actor to be playing roles which place a great emotional demand on them, like Shakespeare's tragedies, is like being in a lion's cage or having to jump across a chasm; the young actor strains excessively in the effort to find a way to laugh or cry on demand. The only way out is to adopt conventions, which soon become clichés (2008a: 111–12).

So the work on the *system* began with a recognition of the importance of training the body and voice, in order to solve problems of acting: how the actor can overcome stage fright and tension, how he or she can truly *experience* a role. Stanislavski worked to overcome these problems and made progress. Later, as an established actor, he experienced a crisis when he was playing Stockmann in Ibsen's *An Enemy of the People*, in 1905–6. It is ironic that the role in which he had scored such a success was the one in which he was to fail, but this resulted in the beginning of the *system*. In creating the role originally, Stanislavski had found the material he needed from experience and observations from life that were appropriate, or, as he said, 'analogous' to the role (2008b: 19). He drew from memories which had been retained in his subconscious as well as factual research in conceptualising the character, and found that if he thought what the character would think, the external form of the characterisation appeared. As the actor, he had only had to think of Stockmann's cares and worries and the character's stoop and hurried walk appeared instinctively. He wrote: 'Stockmann's mind and body and Stanislavski's mind and body came together as one being'

(2008a: 216). But what he realised in 1906, after playing the role for some years, was that he was going through the motions onstage. His mind was wandering; he had stopped thinking the thoughts the character would think.

> Previously everything had flowed from the beauty and excitement of inner truth. Now all that remained was an empty shell, dust and ashes that had stuck in the mind and the body, which had nothing to do with genuine art.
>
> (2008a: 254)

This is the most important lesson an actor can learn, the difference between mechanical acting and inner *experiencing*. Drawing on all his previous work, Stanislavski set about developing the *system*, to find a method for ensuring that acting could always be spontaneous, so that he was prepared for every creative act.

A different problem occurred later: when playing Salieri in Pushkin's *Mozart and Salieri* in 1915, Stanislavski realised that he was *experiencing* the part and its internal life correctly.

> What I did, I did sincerely; I felt Salieri's heart, mind, his aspirations, his entire inner life. I lived the role while my feeling went from my heart to the motor centres of the body. But once feelings were turned into movement, especially in words and speech, despite myself I was out of joint, out of true, out of tune, I did not recognize the sincerity of my inner feelings in their outer form.
>
> (2008a: 314)

Again, tension and vocal strain resulted. The solution to the problem of preventing a role from degenerating was in the development of the *creative state* and in training the actor in *experiencing* and *embodiment*: the art of the actor.

He drew a distinction between this and *representation*, and also *stock-in-trade*. With what he called *stock-in-trade* acting, the actor reproduces clichés or tricks, the external results of the creative process. These, as Stanislavski explains in *My Life in Art*, are fixed ways of representing characters or emotions (2008a: 111–12). For example, peasants always spat on the floor; aristocrats played with their monocles; and to express despair, actors tore their hair or covered their faces with their hands instead of really crying (2008b: 29).

There are *stock-in-trade* ways of speaking and moving onstage. Stanislavski describes the *bogatyr*, the Russian warrior hero of folk tales: actors playing this role adopt a particular walk and mannerism, a terrible cliché. 'These platitudes have gone so deep into the ears, eyes and the body, that there is no way for the actor to get rid of them' (2008a: 112). In the art of *representation*, the actor observes in themselves typical human traits and reproduces them in the role without involving their own feelings (2008b: 24). This can result in acting that is impressive, but which is not art; the art of acting is in *experiencing*, where the actor recreates the emotional, inner content of the role in each performance.

These experiences and observations led to the development of the *system* as a problem-solving method of acting, where in fact the actor is not 'acting' in the sense of creating pretence, but undergoing a real experience.

THE *SYSTEM*

The *system* is something that every actor must discover for themselves over time, not something they can gain from reading a book quickly. It is based, in Stanislavski's view, on scientific principles, on observation from nature, and was a way of codifying what he had learned about acting from the start. Great artists may work through intuition, without the need for a *system* to create the 'inspiration' that others may need. Despite this, both the great opera singer Chaliapin and a member of the chorus have something in common, 'for both have lungs, a respiratory system, nerves and a physique' (2008a: 347). Though this may be better developed in Chaliapin and less so in the chorus member, each of them produces sound according to physiological laws that are the same for all human beings. Therefore the ways for the great artist and the chorus member to train their voices will have much in common. Similarly, the processes of imagination and memory are the basis of creativity in acting for everyone, and every actor should study how they work. Stanislavski asserts here that there are psycho-physical and psychological laws: the laws of creativity, scientific in the sense that they must be true for all human beings and verifiable practically.

Underpinning the laws of creativity are *action*, *emotion* and the *subconscious*: the *three bases of the system*.

ACTION

In performance, the actor should be involved in *action* internally and externally. The action must be purposeful: Stanislavski relates a story of when he realised as a child what action meant onstage. He was dressed as winter in a tableau of the four seasons. He did not know what to do or where to look and 'unconsciously I felt the embarrassment of meaningless activity'. He then put a stick into the real fire to see it burn, a purposeful activity that made much more sense to him (though it did not go down well with the adults; 2008a: 4–5).

EMOTION

If the actor is 'active', that is, truthfully engaged in purposeful action rather than pretence, the expression of truthful *emotion* will be possible. Pushkin had stated that 'truth of passions, verisimilitude in feelings experienced in given circumstances – that is what our intelligence demands of a dramatist' and Stanislavski applied this to acting (Stanislavski 2008b: 53). This means that the actor must create a real emotion onstage. The actor is constantly *experiencing*, creating the *life of the human spirit of the role*. This may be achieved indirectly, by processes of emotional recall, or the emotion may come if you perform the actions truthfully in the circumstances of the play. Attempting to act an emotional state directly, for example, trying to 'be angry', will not bring about success. This is the difference between *acting in general*, where you are pretending to be angry, and *playing an action*, where the character's anger is apparent because the actor wants to lash out at another character, for example.

THE SUBCONSCIOUS

The third base is the *subconscious*. When the actor applies the *system*, the subconscious will produce material and engender *experiencing*. The 'subconscious creativity of nature itself' can be accessed through the artist's 'conscious psycho-technique' (Stanislavski 2008b: 18). *Emotion memory* and the imagination are the mechanisms for this.

The *system* enables the actor to prepare, researching the play and preparing themselves to develop the ability to pay attention and to

One of Stanislavski's problems as a young actor, as it is for many of us, was learning to cope with an audience. The effect of being watched can result in a number of responses: 'nerves', self-consciousness, corpsing, or 'showing off', which is playing to the audience instead of focusing on your fellow actors. All these mean that you are paying attention to the wrong thing, so that instead of remaining in control of what you are doing on stage you are succumbing to the power of the audience. A scene or monologue that you performed perfectly well, with full attention, when you were rehearsing on your own or with a couple of others, may start to come out quite differently when you are being watched, whether it is by fellow students or actors, the director or an audience. The student actor Kostya in *An Actor's Work* relates how the scene he and other students had prepared in detail goes wrong when performed to an audience and the 'black hole' of the auditorium becomes intimidating:

> It is amazing how the feeling of intimacy can be shattered by the black hole ... our acting turned into mere display, and was a failure.
>
> (Stanislavski 2008b: 87)

[illegible]t is essential to be fully focused on what you are doing as an actor. [illegible]tanislavski told a story of a Hindu Maharaja's test of potential [illegible]inisters by challenging them each to walk around the city on top [illegible] the city wall, carrying a pot full to the brim with milk, without [illegible]lling a drop, despite attempts to distract and frighten them, [illegible]nparing this to the level of attention required by the actor [illegible])8b: 103).

[illegible]e actor has to be trained to respond to the conditions of the [illegible]orium, and to performing in public in order to overcome stage [illegible] in all its manifestations. Work on attention helps to develop [illegible]e on stage when the actor experiences *public solitude*, a state of [illegible]on in spite of the presence of the audience. What is more, if [illegible] able to maintain this, your acting can communicate effec[illegible] the audience. Stanislavski writes that the more strongly the [illegible] create for himself a circle of public solitude and the more [illegible]attention and thoughts are on discovering positively what is [illegible]und him, 'the greater his charm, the stronger the vibrations [illegible]tive work and the more powerful his influence on the [illegible] (Stanislavsky 1967: 123).

be fully alive onstage. By full concentration on the *task* they have onstage, the actor develops and practises the feeling of truth and freeing the muscles, which enables them not to react to the audience, not to stiffen in fear or to show off. Through techniques of *belief* and the *magic if*, all actions are internally *justified*, not carried out externally. Crucial to this is the *task*. The *task* touches the actor's will: the right *task* will evoke internally the actor's emotion. This is the path to the unconscious through the conscious, to *experiencing*.

The following chapters explain in detail the different aspects of the *system* and how the actor can put them to use.

FURTHER READING

Benedetti, J. (1999) *Stanislavski, His Life and Art*, London: Methuen.

Gauss, R. (1999) *Lear's Daughters: The Studios of the Moscow Art Theatre 1905–1927*, New York: Peter Lang.

Ignatieva, M. (2008) *Stanislavsky and Female Actors: Women in Stanislavsky's Life and Art*, Maryland: University Press of America.

Merlin, B. (2003) *Konstantin Stanislavsky*, London: Routledge.

Pitches, J. (2005) *Science and the Stanislavsky Tradition of Acting*, London: Routledge.

Shevtsova, M. (forthcoming) *The Cambridge Introduction to Stanislavsky*, Cambridge: Cambridge University Press.

Stanislavski, K. (2008) *My Life in Art*, London: Routledge.

Whyman, R. (2008) *The Stanislavski System of Acting: Legacy and Influence in Modern Performance*, Cambridge: Cambridge University Press.

BASIC TRAINING

In this chapter, we will look at elements of basic training, *attention*, *muscular release*, *sense and emotion memory*, *action*, *justification*, some of the lynchpins of the *system*, and discuss why they are important in relation to *experiencing*. Exactly how does the actor work on themselves? As Stanislavski put it, how do you 'earn the right to be on stage' (Stanislavski 2008b: 400)? The actor should not step on stage, or even into the rehearsal room, unless they are in the right state of mind – the *creative state*. It isn't any good turning up to work with others or to perform with your mind on other things, in a bad mood or lacking energy. You have to prepare yourself so that you can be committed to the work, whatever distractions you may be experiencing that day in your own life. In Stanislavski's view, preparation is all-important in the actor's work on themselves and on the role.

Sulerzhitski talked about Stanislavski's dream of the whole cast at the Moscow Art Theatre spending time working together to get ready for performance or rehearsal. We now know this as 'the warm up', and because of Stanislavski's pioneering efforts, it has become established as the way to prepare for performance. There are many ways to warm up, but what is crucial is that they result in the actor giving full attention to the work and not being distracted. This is the purpose of much of the basic training work that actors undergo. You can use high-energy exercise and games, and vocal work, in

addition to the most important elements of daily practice and training, which include work on attention, muscular release, sense and emotion memory, action and justification – the actor's building blocks.

ATTENTION

> What can be more appalling than an actor's vacant eyes!
>
> (Stanislavski 2008b: 95)

Stanislavski pointed out that if an actor is fully involved in what they are doing, this will draw the audience into what is going o onstage. The actor's attention is an element of the *creative state* the actor is not 'there', it puts the audience off and they may interest in the stage action as a whole. The disengaged ac one who is on automatic pilot, not really thinking about wh are doing but performing by rote. Alternatively, they are about the role but in the wrong way. It may be that they things mechanically in order to appear full of activity, to fi 'A wagging tongue, hands and feet moving like an auton replace thoughtful eyes that give life to everything' (2

There are many demands on the actor's attention think consciously on stage about how they are actions or delivering the lines, the quality of the voice, what the other performers – their stage p and saying, timing responses and reactions, h reacting, lighting and sound cues, where the ture are and how to use them effectively, an to be thinking about the present moment what is to come next in the trajectory their technique, while sustaining aware role in the particular environment of th actor has to be giving attention to a once. This is by no means impossib for what Stanislavski referred to essential to the *creative state*, and (2008b: 112). For example, you ing, giving attention to what is along to a favourite song.

> The secret is very simple: to divert your attention from the auditorium you must become engrossed in what is happening on stage.
>
> (2008b: 90)

Our brains have to pay attention to something. It is important to choose the right object of attention. The actor has to stop reacting to the audience by instead becoming absorbed in the world on stage, distracting themselves by finding something to capture their attention. It isn't that you are ignoring the audience or pretending that they are not there. After all, if the audience respond to what you are doing, if, for example, you get a laugh, you may have to pause a little before your next line. The eighteenth-century French actor-philosopher Denis Diderot originated the idea of the *fourth wall*, an imaginary demarcation between actors and audience.

You can imagine being in a traditional theatre on the stage set of the interior of a house and that there is a fourth wall where the proscenium arch is. It is not that the actor wants a barrier between themself and the audience. From the point of view of naturalistic theatre, it is as if the audience is looking at a scene on stage with X-ray vision through the wall of a house, and the actors are performing actions as if they were in the house, without reacting to the presence of the audience. For Stanislavski, this has two purposes: first, the stage directions may indicate that the actor is looking out of a window in the *fourth wall*, as, for example, Lyubov Andreyevna Ranevskaya is towards the end of the first act of Anton Chekhov's *The Cherry Orchard*. In that case, the actor has to pay attention to that focal point on the imaginary wall, carefully considering its placement, so that the audience can believe the window is there, and that Ranevskaya is looking through it at the cherry trees, covered in white blossom, and being affected by the memories the orchard holds for her. Second, the actor can create so strongly for herself the illusion that the wall exists that the presence of audience is not a distraction.

The actor must understand the role of the audience so that they are able to perform private, intimate scenes on stage truthfully, not ignoring the audience, but as the actor involving them within the intimacy. Spolin notes that they are a group with whom you are sharing an experience (1999: 13) but you are not reacting to them in an untoward way. Mike Alfreds, the director of the British theatre company Shared Experience, notes that 'The actors offer a suggestion, the audience develops it. The actors initiate a transaction, the audience completes it' (2007: 14).

Stanislavski's exercises in *circles of attention* were devised to help the actor cope with the problem of the audience.

EXERCISE: *CIRCLES OF ATTENTION*

Stand in the playing area and focus on an immediate object. This can be a lamp or a stage prop or a piece of furniture such as a chair. Give all the attention you can to it.

Expand your circle of attention to the playing area. Take note of everything that is in it, on all sides. Keep an awareness of the space behind you and to the sides even if you cannot see it.

Expand your circle of attention to take in the whole of the space, including where the audience would be, without making eye contact with anyone who is there. Let the gaze of your eyes be on stage. Experiment with the idea of the *fourth wall* and see whether you can look at something that might be on that wall without letting your focus be drawn beyond it into the auditorium.

Expanding further, think about the space beyond the theatre to the distant horizon, using your memory and your imagination of what is outside.

Experiment with changes of focus from one circle to another.

Evaluate your experience. How difficult was it to pay attention? To help keep your attention, always keep your eyes in focus, no matter which circle you are in. Notice when you start thinking about something else, and go back to the first circle (*public solitude*). How long can you sustain this? Work on this outside the rehearsal room, when you are sitting on the bus, or walking along the street.

Stanislavski's advice: If you get lost in the large circle, reduce it at once to a small circle (2008b: 105).

This is a useful exercise to repeat within the context of a play, using the relevant series of circles of place. For example, in *The Cherry Orchard*, Act 1, the first circle might involve a chair on the set, the second the whole set for the nursery, and the largest circle the Gayev household, the estate including the cherry orchard and beyond that Russia! In Chekhov's play, this is a Russia at the beginning of the twentieth century when, after centuries of isolation, the rest of the world is beginning to seem closer: telegraph poles bring messages from Paris, Englishmen come and discover white clay on the land to use in British potteries, and the railway system is developing links with Europe – all food for the actor's imagination.

EXERCISE: FOCAL POINT

As a group of actors, fix an imaginary object such as a mirror or a window on the *fourth wall*. Do this by using markers that are really there in the line of vision in the rehearsal space. For example: the window is in the *fourth wall* level with the edge of the rehearsal space; if I imagine looking through the window, what I actually see is the top of the middle seat in the sixth row. Enter in turn into the space and look through the window or comb your hair in the mirror.

Experiment with more than one object and with several actors at the same time. Ensure that all actors are working to the same reference points.

CREATIVE CONCENTRATION AND ATTENTION

Sometimes the term *concentration* is used instead of *attention*. Stanislavski read *Concentration*, a book by Ernest Wood that was very popular in the early part of the twentieth century, on concentration and meditation. It provides exercises in giving one's whole to an object, taking in all its details, and refers to these exercises as 'expansion of concentration' (Wood 1999: 111–13). In the way that a prism disperses light, the actor's concentration must expand to take in many objects of attention. Thinking of it in this way will help to get beyond the problem with the word 'concentration' where, if asked to concentrate, often people will do something other than giving their attention to the thing that is important (Alexander 1996: 63). This is behaviour that we often develop as schoolchildren; when the teacher tells us to concentrate we adopt a furrowed brow, or show tension in other ways in order to appear to be paying attention to what we are reading or being told (when what we are thinking about may be something much more interesting!). Therefore it is important to notice whether you are trying to *appear* to be concentrating

(Stanislavski 2008b: 94), that is, whether you are staring or frowning, which will interfere with, rather than bring about, the *creative state*, as you will be using unnecessary muscular tension.

There are many ways you can train the power of *creative concentration and attention*. 'The habit of devoting his attention to all the manifestations of life on and off the stage will endow the student-actor with the conscious power of observation of everything that is taking place outside and inside him' (Stanislavsky 1967: 123).

EXERCISE: RECALLING THE DAY

Regularly take a few minutes to sit in a chair in the evening and go over the day, remembering the events, what you saw and heard. Remember the thoughts and feelings associated with the events and what people said. You can work on recalling events from the past, seeing what you remember when you bring your attention to bear.

Improving your ability to sustain attention may not be easy. Sometimes people worry when they find it difficult to pay attention. If a group of student actors are asked to focus on what they are doing, they are often aware that their thoughts are elsewhere. They may have anxieties about whether their work in class or on the course will be successful, or they have other worries or stayed up too late last night and are tired. Often this means they think they are inadequate in some way. However, there is an explanation for this in the way the brain works. 'When the brain has had enough of something for the time being, it will "jump". We find ourselves thinking about something else' (Door 2003: 76). As messages are conveyed by nerve cells in the brain, other brain cells are stimulated in what can be a random way, and we find that our thoughts can lead us from one thing to another until we are thinking about something quite different from what we started with. If you find you have stopped paying attention and drifted off, keep bringing your attention back to bear on the exercise or the role and don't worry.

As a young actor at the Moscow Art Theatre, Vasilii Osipovich Toporkov once approached Stanislavski and said that in his experience 'concentration and a serious attitude toward a role do not always give the best results.' He said that other actors had also said to him that if they wanted to give a particularly good performance, to impress someone special or important, they found that they inevitably gave bad performances. 'The actor braces himself but in most cases is a complete failure.' His belief was that a lighter attitude, even indifference, could bring better results. Stanislavski responded by saying that, when Toporkov acted badly, it was not because of his attentiveness and concentration or because his approach was too serious; it was simply that he was concentrating on the wrong thing. He was concentrating on trying to do well. 'When you discarded the false concentration that hindered you, it turned out better. But if you can direct your genuine attention and concentration on fulfilling the concrete task in a scene, it will be very good' (Toporkov 1998: 59). The actor must not adopt an attitude of not caring, being blasé, but work at getting the thought right, paying attention to the right things.

EXERCISES: ATTENTION

1. The leader asks the students to listen, first to everything that can be heard in the workspace, and next to the sounds from the street.

   They ask questions to establish who has heard the subtlest sounds.

2. Ask the students to recall and describe their route into the theatre.

   Give the students the task of studying the street where they live. Ask them to describe it in the next session. How does the street seem different at different times of day?

EXERCISES ON ATTENTION, SYNCHRONICITY AND DEXTERITY

3. The class is divided into two groups. One of the groups place the chairs in a semicircle and sit on them. The task of reorganising them is given: from a semicircle into a circle, facing the centre, then into a diagonal facing one of the corners of the room, into two circles, back to the centre. Ask the students to return to a semicircle again. They can only communicate with their eyes, but should do everything simultaneously. The chairs must be placed

down noiselessly. They should avoid bumping into one another. Instruct them to go round the chairs from the same side, to lift the chairs in the same way: left hand on the back and right on the seat. The main thing is to work all at the same time!

Continue the exercise to add other tasks to the reorganisation: counting the number of different sounds that are made, for example someone putting a chair down with a bang, the sound of a foot on the floor.

4. Individual exercises: each student observes an object, paying attention to all aspects of it, and then describes it to someone else.

   Each student works on giving attention to an imaginary object, and then describes that to a partner.

5. Touch exercises: Whose hands? Three students are asked to study the hands of their fellow students (who are not wearing rings or watches). Three students sit blindfolded at a table and the other students one by one sit with their hands on the table. The group of three attempt to identify whose hands they are by touch.

EXERCISES ON ATTENTION, MEMORY, CO-ORDINATION, SELF-DISCIPLINE

6. The students sit in two rows, observing and remembering what each other is wearing. The leader should state that the calmer the student is, the better they are able to pay attention.
7. The group are asked to mirror the leader's actions. The leader makes various movements, stepping to the side, forwards and backwards, claps, stops and stands still for a moment, encouraging the group to respond rapidly so they move or make the sound at the same time.

   After a few minutes, the leader should point out when members of the group are 'concentrating' too hard, frowning, 'trying'. They need to pay attention to work in synchronicity.

   Carry on. Vary the pace.

   Point out that the focus of attention is communication, not just with the leader but also between the group members, so that everyone is moving together.

Carry on. Ask the group to include the whole space in their awareness.

Point out that giving attention to oneself and to everything around oneself is *multi-level attention*.

8. The leader asks half the group to walk around in the space with eyes closed and asks the other half to watch. Point out as a general note that some people stiffen. Also, those who are at ease begin to have the 'right to be in the space'; they are learning not to hurry, and to maintain equilibrium in front of an audience.

   Ask the group to find partners and, keeping their eyes closed, to walk to meet their partners and shake hands, and to walk so that they meet back to back. Emphasise that the students should begin only when they are as still and calm as possible.

Note that exercises such as 3 are also *sense memory* exercises: see the section on *sense and emotion memory*.

MUSCULAR RELEASE

> Acting demands the co-ordination of the entire organism.
>
> (Stanislavski 2008b: 109)

In order to be attentive and responsive, to be fully present and thinking creatively, the actor must be free, in the sense of being able to direct their attention freely, not trying to do something, not in a state of fear. Integral to this is freedom of the bodily mechanisms. If we are in a state of anxiety or are trying too hard, it can seem impossible to direct our thought. What we refer to as brain and body are one thing; we are psycho-physical beings. 'The body doesn't function without direction from the mind and mind cannot express itself in the world without the body' (Door 2003: 38).

Being free from unnecessary muscular tension is therefore one of the most important things for an actor.

> You cannot imagine how damaging muscular tension and physical tightness can be to the creative process.
>
> (Stanislavski 2008b: 120)

Stanislavski understood the importance of *muscular release*, as he put it, learning to be onstage without stiffening, in fear, or from making an effort. The state of stiffening is counterproductive to the *creative state*, to actors' ability to express themselves freely. It can bring about vocal problems, so that people who are born with good voices become hoarse; many experience problems such as nodules on the vocal cords or lose their voices altogether. Stiffening can impede the respiratory process and cause breathlessness, so that the actor does not have enough breath to 'support' a speech or piece of movement.

If an actor is stiffening, this can be seen in the way they are moving; they will not be 'neutral', but may be bringing their own idiosyncrasies (hunched shoulders, a stoop, toes turned inwards) into the movement of the character, for whom it might be completely inappropriate. If you are playing Henry V after his coronation, as he dissociates himself from Falstaff in Act 5 of Shakespeare's *Henry IV Part 2,* hunched shoulders may give the impression of diffidence, rather than a young man confidently exerting his authority. Stanislavski observed that the facial expression can be affected: if, for example, the actor has a habitual frown, however slight, their facial expression will not correspond to what the actor should be *experiencing* as the character. Voice and movement are the modes of expression of meaning or inner content. The actor needs to be able to convey *experiencing* to the audience by means of *embodiment* of the character.

> All this [tightness] cannot but be harmful to the process of experiencing, to the external, physical embodiment of what is being experienced and to the actor's overall mental state ... There can be no question of true, subtle feeling or of the normal psychological life of a role while physical tension is present.
>
> (Stanislavski 2008b: 120–21)

In the attention exercises, as in everything, it is important for you to notice when you are nervous or trying too hard and creating unnecessary muscular tension. This interferes with your ability to pay attention. If you are tense, you are interfering with the capacity to think. Stanislavski was categorical about this:

> Can I persuade you that physical tension paralyses our whole capacity for action, our dynamism, how muscular tension is connected to our minds?
>
> (2008b: 121)

In *An Actor's Work*, Tortsov, the fictional acting teacher, demonstrates to the students that while they are straining to lift a heavy object, they cannot think straight, remember lines they knew, sing, recall a taste of touch or smell.

In the early years of Stanislavski's career he used to be in such a state of nervousness that muscular tension nearly caused him to go into spasm. His answer to this was that the actor must develop a *controller*, a system of checking for superfluous muscular tension and letting it go. He believed that by the practice of regular self-monitoring, working on himself in his everyday life, he would eventually be able to walk onstage free from tension (2008b: 121). Expressing the subtleties of a character's inner life accurately requires that the actor has 'an exceptionally responsive and outstandingly well-trained voice and body' (2008b: 20).

Training yourself to this level of skill takes time and commitment and it cannot be done just in your acting classes. Stanislavski knew that one of the problems is that people generally do not know how to go about their everyday activities without creating unnecessary muscular tension; it is not just a problem onstage.

The Alexander Technique has been taught to actors since the time of F.M. Alexander (1869–1955), who started off as an actor but had problems with his voice. Alexander developed his technique, which has since been corroborated by principles of anatomy and physiology; it enables you to learn through daily practice to respond to the stimuli of life without unnecessary muscular tension, and maintain what educationalist John Dewey called 'thinking in activity' during even the most difficult situations (Alexander 1985: 42). The actor can use it to overcome the stimulus of performance and be free from what Stanislavski identified as problems, bad habits and shortcomings (2008b: 132).

Maintaining control, so that the actor does not become tense, is important not only at the points where the character is quiet and calm but also in times of excitement. This often comes as a surprise to student actors, because they associate the expression of heightened emotion, of anger or grief, with effort, with trying to achieve what they envisage for the character. Habitually, people tense even more when 'worked up'. Of course, the expression of heightened emotion places a demand on the actor, but it must be without the distortion of muscular tension. As Stanislavski says, 'we know what effect that has on the creative process' (2008b: 122–23). As described in Chapter 1, he studied great actors and dancers and noticed their muscular freedom at the moments of highest emotional intensity, whereas he knew he was always stiff onstage (2008a: 79). As he said:

> You know that in acting we must always start by relaxing the muscles. So first of all sit comfortably and easily as though you were at home ... Ninety-five per cent less tension!
>
> (2008b: 322)

British actress Edith Evans said, 'You only really begin to act when you leave off trying' (Redgrave 1995: xiii).

SENSE AND EMOTION MEMORY

If the actor is in the *creative state*, is attentive and not in a state of tension or anxiety, then they are prepared for *experiencing*, bringing the role to life from within, which encapsulates what Stanislavski prioritised in the actor's emotional expression – that it expresses what makes us human, the human experience. The word *experiencing* (*perezhivanie* in Russian) means to experience, undergo or live through, and has also been translated as 'living the part'. As the writer encapsulates their own human experience in the creation of characters, it is the actor's job, through processes of empathy, to develop and convey genuine human experience, which will in turn convey itself to the audience. The actor should observe and understand how people behave and should reflect on their own behaviour.

One of the keys to understanding and encapsulating human experience is *emotion memory*, a tool that Stanislavski experimented with early in his career. *Affective memory* is a general term which refers to both *emotion* and *sense memory*. *Emotional* and *emotion memory* are the same thing. To explain this, let's start by thinking about a major aspect of acting. In order to achieve *experiencing*, the actor must be able to produce truthful emotion on demand. One problem is that if the character has to cry at a certain point in the role, it may be the case that the tears appear easily at first, but recreating the emotion time and time again in a role can be difficult for many actors. The problem does not just lie with intense emotions: the recreation of tears of sadness, or the recreation of extreme anger, or rage. If you know what is coming next in the role and have repeated it many times before, even at a point where you simply say 'hello' to a character coming into a room, your reaction to the actor's entrance may lack the quality of spontaneity. You may fall back on a mechanical response. In the case of intense emotions, it may be that the actor cannot find a truthful response and may fall back on clichés such as pretending to cry, giving the impression of anger through a raised voice and stereotyped gestures. Stanislavski was highly critical of actors who were prepared to fall back on these tricks. The direct attempt to express emotion often results in cliché, what he referred to as the simple mechanical actor's 'stencil', 'trick' or 'conventional external sign' and what he called 'actor's emotion' (2008b: 31).

In *An Actor's Work*, Tortsov berates his student actors, rather sarcastically, when they are asked to repeat an improvisation where there is a madman at the door of the house. They allow the fact that they know what is going to happen in advance to influence their responses, and the performance lacks spontaneity.

> In that case, why bother to think again, or justify what you were doing using your own experience of life, your feelings, the things you have lived through in the real world?
>
> (Stanislavski 2008b: 197)

He refused to let his actors get away with 'playing the result' in this way: falling back on old formulae, without giving attention to each moment of the improvisation as they did when creating it the first time. When the scene is analysed and discussed, it is clear that the students had convinced themselves that they are experiencing the emotion in the way they did the first time, but their teacher says this is false *experiencing*: they are performing almost mechanically (2008b: 197).

A way out of this problem is to use *affective memory*. Stanislavski understood the problems of trying to find emotion directly, so he placed much emphasis on the role of the subconscious in the creative process. The basic principle of the system is 'the subconscious through the conscious' (2008b: 209). In acting, we are drawing on our human experiences stored, often subconsciously, in the memory. An important part of Stanislavski's training for actors, therefore, is the development of the *sense and emotion memory*, which he believed the actor could develop voluntarily. The significance of *sense memory* is that we can recall emotion often by bringing back other aspects of a particular memory connected to the sensory experience. For example, if as a child you went on holiday to the seaside, recalling playing on the beach, experiencing the sand and the sea, will bring back other aspects of the memories such as what you and your family wore, what you had to eat. And you may be able to recall emotional experience connected with that, such as the disappointment when you dropped your ice cream in the sand, the happiness of building a sandcastle and putting a flag on top.

We are able to relive emotional experiences. It may be that you have had the experience of remembering something funny and laughing out loud, when on your own on the bus or the underground. Or it may have been remembering something you said which you really wish you hadn't and again experiencing embarrassment, the desire for the floor to open and swallow you up. Or it may be that you were angry about something and though the situation is past you experience the anger again, perhaps even more strongly than before. There is no doubt that we are relying on our own previous emotional experience to understand the emotions a character undergoes in a role. *Sense and emotion memory* are very important as this is how we gain understanding of human reactions. The young actor has to draw on their experience and they will have experienced a range of emotions – of love, jealousy, even hatred – at home and in the playground. Stanislavski points out that 'the character is put together by the actor out of the living Elements of his own self, out of his Emotion Memories and so on'. There are a huge range of 'states, moods, feelings' that everyone has experienced, 'enough to last your artistic lifetime' (2008b: 210).

It is not necessary to find a one-to-one correspondence between an emotion you may have and an emotion the character undergoes. If it were, young people would never be able to play roles in which they are a different age or have had different life experiences with any success. Even if you have had an experience that is appropriate for the role, the required emotion may not appear on demand. As Stanislavski noted, 'we can't put the recollections of our feelings in order the way we do the books in our library' (2008b: 207).

Equally, you can't take a shortcut by giving yourself an experience appropriate to the role which you later recall. Stanislavski describes in *My Life in Art* how he had himself locked up in a deserted castle overnight in the attempt to find internal experience for the main character of Pushkin's *Miser Knight* – an old man who lives in isolation in a castle. All that happened was that Stanislavski caught a cold (2008a: 95).

What he found worked was that he could find the seeds for *experiencing* in the role by exploring his *sense and emotion memories*. The important thing is that our previous experience can give us the information we need to develop the character's inner life, and *emotion memory* can be used to help us consider this. As noted, *sense memory* helps stimulate *emotion memory* and the actor needs to work on both:

> Memory is stirred by the five senses ... and there is a tight relationship between the interaction of our five senses and their influence on the things which Emotion Memory recalls.
>
> (Stanislavski 2008b: 200, 203)

Exercises can be used to develop *sense memory*, such as recalling the taste of raspberries or the smell of salmon. These are also exercises in developing *attention*. Your experience of acting eating delicious food should be so vivid when it is conveyed to the audience that their mouths water. In preparation work, actors need to impress on themselves and be able to recall visual and aural images, observing other people's faces, expressions, walks, mannerisms and voices, and reading from that what might be going on internally. Reflection and observation are important: putting oneself in someone else's place. Generally, the actor must work to constantly replenish the stores of *emotion memory*, gathering impressions, feelings, experiences. These can be obtained from the real world and from our imagination, from our recollections, from books, from science and learning, from travelling, from museums and, most important of all, from our relationships with other people (2008b: 226).

We have to exercise a great deal of care in relation to *emotion memory*. In daily life, it may be an unproductive thing to keep going over an experience of being angry about a situation in one's mind, rather than sorting it out in the best way possible. In performing, we have to learn to recreate emotional experiences in a way that means that we can give a shape to a role, the experience of the character, without getting distracted or overwhelmed by personal memories. We do not want to attempt to recreate the past in a way that constrains our present response.

Some of Stanislavski's own colleagues and students found his emphasis on *emotion memory* problematic. Meyerhold and Michael Chekhov both had experiences where recalling their own past in relation to a role was just too difficult for them, as it brought back upsetting associations. See Chapter 6 for a description of Chekhov's preferred approach to infusing a role with emotion, one that he developed as an alternative to Stanislavski's method.

The extent to which you want to recall and use difficult experiences from your past must be up to you; you should never do so in a way that causes you distress or allow anyone else to make you recall things you don't want to. This will not do you any good nor help with acting a role. There are some examples of harrowing experiences from the past that come up in the students' process in *An Actor's Work*, but whether the students use these experiences is a matter of individual choice. One student recalls the death of a friend and tells the teacher Tortsov about this (2008b: 199). Kostya sees a street accident and draws on it for emotional experience (2008b: 203–7). Another student, Darya, performs an improvisation with a baby which is very moving, based on her own loss of a baby (2008b: 339–43).

Emotion memories shift over time. Kostya explores the changes in his emotion over time on recollecting the street accident that he witnessed. Other *emotion memories* – for example when Kostya was moved on seeing a Serb musician, a street performer, crying because his pet monkey had died – become mixed up with other memories. Tortsov explains that *emotion memory* purifies the recollections in the melting pot of time (2008b: 206). Memory crystallises or synthesises and purifies feelings, providing a bank of repeated memories, which, when refined, forms material for the life of characters. These may change and the artist should seek to find new ones.

What does the actor actually think about onstage? You have to create the *emotion memories* of the character when you are performing rather than being aware of your own memories, though these may have informed the character's *emotion memories* in the rehearsal process. Using *emotion memories* is one way to make a personal connection with the character. What is important is how you use them, in preparing the role, to fuse with the life of the character: onstage, 'Get out of your head all concern for your own emotional experiences and feelings' (Toporkov 1998: 54).

Once you have found the appropriate emotions for a role, the danger, as said, is in wanting to repeat the success, where you attempt to take the 'direct route to the feeling itself and try and experience it' (Stanislavski 2008b: 218). Playing anger or sadness directly will result in clichéd acting; you have to recreate every time the process you went through to find the emotion. Stanislavski learned this the hard way in working on the role of Satin in Gorky's *The Lower Depths*. He played the result, 'instead of behaving logically and sequentially and thereby moving quite naturally towards the result, i.e. towards the main idea of the play and of my own creative work as an actor' (2008b: 219).

Because emotion cannot be forced, it requires *lures*. A *lure* is anything that arouses *experiencing*, and one possible lure is *emotion and sense memory – affective memory*. There are many other ways for the right inner content to be stimulated, including action, working with the other actors, and sets and lighting and sound effects, all of which help to 'establish a creative atmosphere, one which correctly stimulates Emotion Memory and experiencing' (Stanislavski 2008b: 216).

EXERCISES: SENSE AND EMOTION MEMORY

1. Recall a family meal – sit with your eyes closed and recreate all the details of the table settings, the food, the room, the time of year, what you were wearing, what the other people were wearing, the atmosphere, what people said, what you experienced. After you've done the exercise notice how recalling the details of what you saw, heard, smelled, tasted and felt is linked with emotions you may have experienced.
2. Recall a toy or ornament that was special to you when you were a child.
3. Consider how you might use these images in creating *emotion memories* for a role. For example, referring to Appendix 1, think about how you could connect your memories with Laura Wingfield's glass animals in *The Glass Menagerie*, or how you could use your memories of a family meal to inform your acting in the meal

scene at the beginning of Act 1, though your memories may be of a much happier occasion.

4. Work with imaginary objects, recreate drinking a cup of fragrant tea, making a snowball, finding a bill you've forgotten to pay. As in Exercise 4 in the attention exercises above (see p. 30), create the object in detail in your imagination.

ACTION

> Acting is action – mental and physical.
>
> (Stanislavski 2008b: 40)

Stanislavski knew that 'feeling' or 'emotion', *experiencing*, is a very slippery thing. He discovered as a young man, performing in A.F. Pisemski's *Bitter Fate*, that the actor cannot judge success by what it feels like to perform the role. He felt good about what he was doing onstage but the director told him he was shouting and pulling faces. It may also be the case that emotion is elusive, even with *lures* such as *emotion memory*. The actor cannot wait until the right feeling occurs – instead, what is needed is to take action (Stanislavski uses the Russian word *deistvovat'*, which means to take action, rather than the word *igrat'*, which refers to 'acting'), emphasising that the *action* required is real, not representational, not pretending or playing at it (2008b: 40). 'It is necessary to go on the stage not to *play* something but to *act*, to conquer. We cannot play calmness, there must be truth in our calmness' (Toporkov 1998: 197). So acting is taking action. This does not mean external action: for a drama to be full of action it does not have to be like an action movie and full of events, deaths, intrigues, confrontations or conflicts. Nor is it about the actor necessarily filling the stage with individual action, or about facial expressions or histrionic representation. Stanislavski wanted to avoid theatricality of all kinds, wanting the actor instead to be 'human' (2008b: 409).

In *An Actor's Work*, Stanislavski devoted a chapter to *emotion memory* and, equally, one to *action*. Sometimes actors find the appropriate emotional experience easily, but very often other routes are necessary. It is important to understand exactly what Stanislavski meant by *action*. Students at Tortsov's drama school are introduced to the concept of *action* in their very first lesson with the director (2008b: Chapter 3). The actor can always rely on *action*, can always choose to give attention to how they are performing the actions onstage, and with this will come the right inner content for the role.

Stanislavski clarifies his notion of *action* by emphasising that it is *dynamic* and has as much to do with internal states and moments as with its external expression. By acting based on *dynamism*, Stanislavski means the actor has to be thinking and acting purposefully, full of intention. This reveals itself in actions and actions convey the essence of a part, the actor's own *experiencing* and the inner world of the play itself. So stage *action* can mean inactivity, for example sitting waiting for something. Stillness can be full of inner action (2008b: 40). The *action* of the actor is made up of the sequence of logical physical actions forming their role. The actor executing such an action is *active*.

EXERCISE: ACTION

Sit onstage in front of a group of fellow students for several minutes. Notice how difficult this is to do. You may experience self-consciousness.

Sit onstage, being watched, but give yourself a concrete *task*, as simple as mentally reciting your multiplication tables. Give full attention to this.

Ask for feedback on the difference between the simple physical action (sitting onstage) and the dynamic one (sitting and thinking about something definite).

In a wonderful example in *An Actor's Work*, showing what Stanislavski meant by stage action and the difference between being theatrical and being 'human', Tortsov asks a student, Marya, to perform an improvisation. The circumstances leading to the improvisation are that Marya is to be thrown out of the drama school as she cannot pay her fees, but a friend has come to the rescue and brought her a brooch to sell to pay the fees. Tortsov says that Marya has at first refused, so her friend has pinned the brooch to the curtains and left the room, followed by Marya, who eventually says she will accept her friend's gift. When she returns to the room she cannot see the brooch. It is possible that one of the other tenants in the apartment could have come in and taken it. This is the point where Tortsov asks Marya to begin the scene. She does so, rushing up and down, tragically clasping her hands in her head, burying her head in the curtains, 'acting' looking for something in a state of anxiety. The other students are secretly highly amused but at the end of the improvisation, she feels that she has been successful, because 'she really felt it'.

Tortsov asks where the brooch is and she realises she forgot about it. Tortsov reminds her that if she finds the brooch she is saved and can continue coming to the school, and if not she will have to leave. Marya now begins to focus on the important things; she gets the thought right, enters into the imaginative situation and begins to look for the brooch. Tortsov comments privately that she is very 'responsive'. She has a completely different effect on her audience, who 'believe that Marya was not wasting a moment, that she was sincerely worried and anxious'. Afterwards, Tortsov tells her that, the first time, she was 'suffering for suffering's sake', whereas the second time she was really looking. The first time, she was indulging in 'theatrical posturing' and the second time was 'perfectly right'. Marya is stunned (2008b: 40–42). Her idea of what acting is has been challenged.

This example demonstrates how action and emotion work together. In the first improvisation, Marya is expressing emotion 'in general'. Tortsov says, 'We don't need mindless rushing about on stage. There should be neither rushing about for rushing about's sake, nor suffering for suffering's sake. On stage you shouldn't perform actions "in general" for action's sake' (2008b: 57). This is 'filling the inner emptiness with an external display of ham acting – with empty words and actions that are not invested with anything' (Stanislavski 2008b: 55). The actions are not experienced and do not communicate anything essential. As Alfreds puts it:

> Actions lead to feeling ... If actors are not in action, what passes for their emotional life will of technical necessity be dredged up, simulated, contrived, strained and often clichéd ... *actions are tactics* we employ to get what we want.
>
> (2007: 68)

Stanislavski writes:

> When the actor suffers for suffering's sake, when he loves for loving's sake, when he is jealous or asks forgiveness for its own sake, when all

> these things are done because they are written, and not because they are experienced in the heart and life of the role, then the actor has nowhere to go, and then 'playing in general' is the only way out for him.
>
> (2008b: 56)

What would give the actor purpose here, instead of thinking, for example, 'I want to look penitent and ask forgiveness', would be to focus on the fact that they really want to get their stage partner to forgive them. *Stage action*, in Stanislavski's meaning, involves the actor as the character, focusing on their stage partner, really wanting to influence them, getting them to do or to think something as you would in your communication with other people in everyday life. The basic principles of *stage action* involve full attention, really seeing your stage partners in their role, listening to what they say, understanding and responding. All too often, actors are 'in their own heads', sometimes even waiting until the other actor stops speaking to say their line, rather than listening to what the other actor says.

For Stanislavski, *verbal action* is the highest form of *stage action* and stage communication. He saw the acting as the task of planting our mental images in someone else. Words are the expression of a thought, the most effective means of influencing the consciousness of the person you are in conversation with – your stage partner.

> Verbal action must involve your partner in your images. To accomplish that it is necessary for you to see everything you tell him clearly and in detail. The sphere of verbal action is tremendous. It is possible to transmit thought simply by intonations, exclamations, words. The transmission of your thoughts is the action. Your thoughts, words, images – everything must be done only for your partner.
>
> (Toporkov 1998: 189)

In the same way that dialogue can either express thought or simply be the mechanical repetition of words while thought is elsewhere, each *physical action* can be performed mechanically or brought to life from within. Then there is *inner action*, experiencing (Stanislavski 2010: 57). A role exists on two levels: inner and outer.

EXERCISES: ACTION AND VERBAL ACTION

1. Walk across the stage:
   Walk as if you were strolling by a river on a sunny day.
   Walk as if you had a train to catch and had no time to waste.

   Get feedback and compare the difference between the first and the second/third actions.

2. Tell a partner everything you did since you got up this morning.

   Recall or invent the details of an important morning in your life – the day you went for an audition in which you were successful, or a day you were getting ready to leave home. Tell a partner everything you did and what you experienced. Want your partner to understand the significance of that day.

   Get feedback about what your partner thought; did you really want them to understand?

JUSTIFICATION

Key to the concept of *action* is that everything that happens onstage must occur for some reason, for a purpose. The actor must believe in the importance of what they are doing every moment they are onstage, and there should be no superfluous actions. In life, we may make gestures such as brushing hair out of our eyes. If an actor does this, especially if is something that is repeated, the audience may think the gesture has significance, or it may be distracting. It may suggest that the character is nervous or uncomfortable, or it may break the illusion that the actor is the character. Nothing should happen accidentally. One way that you can work on this is by means of exercises in justifying action.

TENSION, RELEASE, JUSTIFICATION

The *justification* of poses, a very important exercise in the *system*, is one of *three moments* in any pose or position onstage. The actor comes into the performance space with the rest of the class watching and adopts a pose. First, the actor should note the superfluous tension which comes from adopting a new pose and the stimulus of being watched by an audience; second, they let this tension go with the help of the *controller*; and, third, *justify* the pose if necessary, for example by thinking of *given circumstances*. One example that is given in *An Actor's Work* is where Tortsov stands onstage, raises his arm and justifies this, releasing stiffness in his arm and asking himself 'If I were standing like this and above me there was a peach on a tall branch what would I have to do to pick it?' (2008b: 128).

We can contrast this with unjustified action, where, for example, a student paces up and down during a speech for the sake of filling up the stage with action which does not have a purpose in terms of what the character should be doing.

EXERCISES: JUSTIFICATION OF POSES

1. Students run around the rehearsal space. When the leader claps, they should adopt a pose immediately. On the next clap, they should begin the process of *justification* of the previous pose, by detailed action. For example, if you have randomly thrown both your hands up in the air, you might justify this pose by imagining you are a customer in a bank that is being held up. You could then imagine the robbers instructing the customers to lie face down on the floor and you then carry out that action, justifying the initial pose.
2. As in the first exercise, but on the clap students pose in pairs. They should then work together, without speaking, moving to justify both positions.
3. The leader gives an outline of a sequence of actions, which the students are to fulfil precisely and in the given order. In between each action, the students can add what they want in order to create a logical line of behaviour.

   Examples of sequences of actions:

   1. Come into the room, lie under the table, then get on the table, then run out of the room.
   2. Come into the room quickly, lie on the floor, climb onto the windowsill, run out of the room.
   3. Run into the room, knock on the wall several times, stamp on the floor several times, go out of the room slowly.
   4. Come into the room slowly, lean your back on the wall, quickly jump away from the wall, hop on one leg, slowly leave the room.

Ask students to justify each of these. For example, their justification for the first sequence might be that they are a child playing hide and seek. They first think that hiding under the table might be a good idea, then reject it. Next they get on the table to see whether from there they can climb onto a large cupboard next to it and hide on top of that, but they are not tall enough. They run out of the room to find a better place to hide.

Tortsov gives his students études to work on as part of their training. These are exercises in improvisation that can be performed spontaneously as a one-off or rehearsed and repeated; they can be done solo or in pairs, or as group exercises, and can use words or dialogue. They are also used as part of the rehearsal process on a text, as we will see in Chapter 3. Repeating études enables you to develop skills in analysis of your own performances.

ÉTUDES

EXERCISES: ÉTUDES

1. EXERCISES IN PAIRS, USING WORDS

Place: a street or a square. B is sitting on a bench of chairs and A walks past.

Before you begin, agree whether A will sit, or A or B leave. The rest of the action is improvised.

A: Excuse me, aren't you X?
B: No, you've made a mistake.
C: I'm sorry.
D: That's all right.

2. INDIVIDUAL EXERCISE

Task: Come into the rehearsal space singing a song. React to the group, saying 'Oh, I'm sorry!' and leave.

3. PREPARED EXERCISE IN PAIRS

Taking about twenty minutes to prepare, work in pairs on a score of dialogue, using one of these three variations:

A. Good!
B. Sit down!
A. Well?
B. I don't know.

Or

A. That's funny.
B. It's rubbish.
A. It's time to go.
B. Wait a bit.

Or

A. I don't understand.
B. There's all sorts.
A. There can't be!
B. It's cold.

4. IMPROVISED ÉTUDES

In a group, develop an improvisation situation for one of the following places, taking time to prepare fully:

1. a book shop
2. a forest in November
3. an antique shop
4. morning transport
5. an orchestra playing at a concert

5. ÉTUDES USING AN OBJECT OR SELECTION OF OBJECTS AS STARTING POINTS

Focus on developing situations as in life, rather than trying to tell an exciting story, using the following objects:

1. a telephone book
2. a water dispenser
3. a weapon
4. an old language book
5. a woman's glove
6. rope

6. ÉTUDES USING IMAGINARY OBJECTS

Start with the objects listed above, recalling the experience of actually using them, and then work with objects created entirely in your imagination.

7. IMPROVISATION

Develop an improvisation of a scene from:

1. a silent film
2. a murder mystery

Note the importance of working truthfully with objects. British actress Harriet Walter writes:

> working in the context of Chekhov's plays where the putting down of a book or the stoking of a stove might be all that is happening visually on stage, that action towards an object becomes a vital means of expressing how the character is feeling.
>
> (1999: 157)

FEEDBACK AND ANALYSIS

When you watch each other's études and discuss them, learn to notice what is natural, whether there is truth of behaviour, whether the words and actions are being justified.

In observing yourself and others performing these études, ask questions:

- Did I sustain my attention on what I was doing or get distracted?
- Was I tense unnecessarily?
- Was I 'active'? Did my partners think I was really talking to them, engaged in action with them?
- Can I justify the movements I made?

In seeking to answer these questions honestly, you are 'earning the right to be on stage'. Bear in mind: 'Doubt is the enemy of art' (Stanislavski 2010: 163). It is easier said than done, but actors must learn not to doubt their potential. Stanislavski writes that doubt 'blocks the path to experiencing, destroys it and produces the stock-in-trade'

(2010: 163). You will not perform well if you are thinking about what you perceive to be the faults in your performance at any point onstage. By the same token, the actor must learn to be generous to other performers who are struggling. Don't be a nit-picking critic (2008b: 175).

FURTHER READING

WARM-UP GAMES AND TRAINING EXERCISES

Boal, A. (2002) *Games for Actors and Non-actors*, London: Routledge.

Johnston, C. (2005) *House of Games: Making Theatre from Everyday Life*, London: Faber and Faber.

Merlin, B. (2007) *The Complete Stanislavsky Toolkit*, London: Nick Hern.

Spolin, V. (1999) *Improvisation for the Theater*, Evanston: Northwestern University Press.

ATTENTION

See Merlin (2007: 279–81) for the use of *circles of attention*, also as a relaxation exercise.

Mitchell, K. (2009) *The Director's Craft: A Handbook for the Theatre*, Abingdon: Routledge. See p. 22, on circles of place in *The Seagull.*

See also Stanislavski's 'Concentration' and 'Public Solitude' exercises in (2008b) *An Actor's Work*, pp. 654–5, 656–8.

SENSE MEMORY

See Stanislavski's exercises in *An Actor's Work* on the memory of physical actions (2008b: 653–4) and Spolin's sensory awareness exercises (1999: 53–60).

ACTION

See *An Actor's Work* (2008b), pp. 38 and 662–68.
See also the 'exposure' exercises in Spolin (1999: 51–3).

JUSTIFICATION

See *An Actor's Work* (2008b), p. 656 for justification exercises.
See Gordon (2010), *Stanislavsky in America*, p. 75, for Group Theatre exercises.

3

ANALYSIS OF THE PLAY

In this chapter, we will move on from thinking about training to look at how the actor applies the *system* in working on a role. At the training school of the Moscow Art Theatre (MAT), students did not perform a complete play until the third year, but worked on excerpts and études (though they would have got to know the whole play), as it was considered that two years of training were needed in order for the actor to have sufficient control of their 'artistic apparatus' (Stanislavski 2010: 3) and to understand how to achieve the *creative state*, to be ready to approach work in the right way. But whether the end performance in a course or a rehearsal process is to be a full-scale production or scenes from a play, the principles for analysis of the text and the role remain the same. In getting to know the play, it is important to engage the actor's imagination, so that the analysis of the play is not just an intellectual exercise. Stanislavski gives the actor various ways to engage with the text creatively; the aspects of the *system* that we will look at in this chapter – *if* and *given circumstances*, *bits* and *tasks*, *supertask*, *truth and belief*, the *method of physical actions*, and *active analysis* – are all intended to get the actor thinking and working actively on the text.

ANALYSIS OF THE PLAY

Stanislavski identifies four principal phases in the actor's work on a role:

> getting to know it, experiencing it, embodying it, making it effective
> (2010: 98)

This chapter is concerned with the first phase and how getting to know the role in the right way will bring about the second, *experiencing*.

First impressions are very significant, and so the actor should prepare for the initial reading of the play, so that the first encounter with the text isn't rushed or done in a cursory way (Stanislavski 2010: 102). From the beginning, the actor should be making creative, imaginative connections with the world of the play. It is also important to approach the play without preconceptions, based on incomplete knowledge, as this will prevent intuitive responses (Stanislavski 2010: 8–9). These intuitions or impressions, 'which are often patchy, momentary, often very vivid', set the tone for later work. This is important, though these scattered impressions, however powerful they might be, do not give you a *sense of the whole* of the play. 'You will not know that until you feel its life, not only mentally, but physically' (Stanislavski 2010: 74), that is, until you have got the play 'up on its feet'.

So a rushed first reading or preformed opinions will get in the way of the initial analysis of the play. During the period of work at the MAT in which Stanislavski and Nemirovich-Danchenko used the practice of *round-the-table analysis*, the troupe would sit and discuss the play at length, a practice that Stanislavski later rejected. This was because it involved intellectualising, particularly with complex plays where a lot of work and research was required to understand them. He found that it could give the actors the impression that the play was inaccessible and boring. All the same, the actor should be well-informed, able to form their own opinions about a play and not idly accept other people's (Stanislavski 2010: 11). He insisted that actors should study and engage with literature, language, the world in general, not just plays and criticism.

In his recommendations on approaching the text, Stanislavski warned against actors turning up to first rehearsals having already learned the role by heart (2010: 20). He thought that if actors do this without preparing themselves fully, the way they perform the role could too easily become mechanical. They will portray the character superficially, finding a way to say the lines without fully envisioning the world of the play, creating life onstage. He wrote:

> For that you have to dig deep into the meaning of the words you are saying and feel them.
>
> (2008b: 410)

So, in order to open up the actor's mind creatively before they form judgements about the part, as we will see, Stanislavski advocated approaching a new role in practical ways, with keys to analysing the text and ways to begin improvising in order to approach the play through the basic plot and simplest physical actions (2010: 48). If you use these methods, the exciting thing is that characterisation will emerge, as he put it, 'in such a way that you will know nothing about it'. The director may know more about how and when the actor finds the role and *fuses* or *merges* with it than the actor. This indirect approach to the text will ensure that the actor does not start to regard the character as finalised too soon; this will lead to overacting, or *representing* rather than *experiencing* (Stanislavski 2010: 86). In attempting to achieve characterisation too early, the actor will limit what they could achieve with the role and will inevitably repeat what they have done before in previous roles, using old methods (Toporkov 1998: 203). What is essential is to see the character or role as a process, created afresh each time, and never completely fixed.

There are different layers to the analysis: after the first reading, analysis of the script will be expanded by research. The director may give you tasks, and you may wish to conduct some of your own.

> Research helps you know the play better, clarifies the world you will be building.
>
> (Mitchell 2009: 15)

The elements of the *system* referred to as *if* and *given circumstances, bits* and *tasks* are used to extend the initial analysis. This can also be known as *analysis and evaluation of the facts*. There is also *analysis by action* or, as it can be referred to, *analysis by étude*, an approach that involves improvisation. The *method of physical actions* and *active analysis*

BRIEF SYNOPSIS OF SCENE 1

The Glass Menagerie is set in America in the 1930s, in St Louis, a city in Missouri, on the Mississippi river. Tom Wingfield begins the play with a monologue, explaining that this is a memory play, his memory of events that took place previously in his life. It is set in a tenement apartment, where he lived with his mother, Amanda, and his sister, Laura, as his father abandoned the family some years before the time of the play. Tom works in a factory making shoes, and is frustrated by the narrow life he leads in the period of the Depression. He writes poetry. He is following events in Europe (which are to lead to World War Two) and wants to join the merchant navy. In Scene 1, the tensions in the family are apparent during a meal, where Amanda annoys Tom, talking a great deal, instructing him how to eat his food and telling stories she has told before, of her admirers in her youth in the South. She is convinced that Laura will soon have a 'gentleman caller', a thought that terrifies Laura. Laura has a slight disability as a result of childhood illness and does not work, as she is afraid of the outside world. She creates her own imaginary world with her collection of glass animals.

EXERCISE: FACTS AND INCIDENTS

When you have read the scene, you can make a list of facts and incidents – these could just be about your character to start with, if you wish, rather than about the whole play or all the characters. For example, if you are playing Tom:

- Tom is a young man.
- He lives with his mother, Amanda, and his sister, Laura.
- They live in St Louis now, though his mother is from Blue Mountain, Mississippi.
- His father worked for a telephone company and left the family a long time ago, sending them a postcard from Mazatlan, in Mexico, which said only 'Hello – Goodbye!'
- He smokes.
- He is the narrator of the play.
- He is a character in the play, and, in the first scene, is having Sunday dinner with Laura and Amanda.
- He finds his mother difficult and leaves the dinner table, saying she has spoiled his meal.

are techniques of analysis by action and will be discussed later in this chapter.

IF AND *GIVEN CIRCUMSTANCES* AND THE PLAY

Analysis of the facts establishes the *given circumstances* of the play. These are all the aspects of the play and production that are 'given' to the actor to work with. These include the story of the play, the setting, the director's interpretation, and the design, including props, costumes and so on. So that the actor does not see these just as an objective list of facts, the *given circumstances* and what Stanislavski calls *if*, or *the magic if*, are linked together inextricably. Taking into account the *given circumstances*, the actor says to themselves, '*If* I were in this character's shoes, I would … ' and this sparks off inventive thought.

> If is a spur to a dormant imagination, and the Given Circumstances provide the substance for it …
>
> (Stanislavski 2008b: 53)

The actor has to work on these separately, but when put together they take the actor into the world of the play.

IF

The magic if is the key when you are playing a character who is very different from yourself or who is in a situation that is very different from your own life experience. In *An Actor's Work*, there is a discussion of an étude in which Tortsov's students are inside a house and an insane man who is threatening their lives is at the door. This is not a situation, one would hope, that the students have experienced in their lives, but a hypothetical one. The director does not ask the actors to believe that there really is an insane and threatening person outside the door but to freely accept 'the possibility that such a thing might exist in real life' (2008b: 51). You can then use *the magic if* to begin to work on what you would do in such a circumstance: 'If someone who is insane were outside my door threatening to kill me and my friends, I would … '.

There are a large number of *ifs* in the text created by the author, related to the *given circumstances*, referred to as *multi-storey ifs*. Examples might be: 'if the action takes place in such and such a period, in such and such a country, in such and such a place or house, if such and such people live there, then I would … '. The director and designer in working on the play will add to these *ifs* (Stanislavski 2008b: 49–50).

Keep in mind the idea that *if* is a hypothesis which takes the actor into the world of the play. Sometimes, when student actors are presented with a character behaving in a way that is very different to the way they might behave themselves, they want to use *the magic if* to justify altering the stage directions. For example, your character is annoyed with something another character has said and storms out of the room, slamming the door, whereas you as the actor would never lose control of your temper in such a way. If you ask the question, 'If I were in this situation how would I respond?' and answer, 'Well, I might be annoyed, but I would just leave the room, showing that I was annoyed and I would not slam the door,' you have misunderstood the purpose of *the magic if*. The question should be 'If I were so incensed by a situation that I stormed out of the room and slammed the door, what would that mean?' You should accept the possibility, the hypothesis that you could do such a thing. This will help you to ask more questions and explore ideas in order to find a way to perform the action truthfully. You could think about whether you have ever lost your temper, or been close to it, or when someone has said something so hurtful to you that you have had to put a distance immediately between yourself and that person (this may be a physical distance or simply not speaking to them). You can work from that desire to create a distance in order to find a way to fulfil what is asked of you in the role – storming out and slamming the door – in a truthful way.

American actress Uta Hagen wrote in *Respect for Acting*,

> If I am to play a silly, fluffy creature, and I think I am not such a person, I cannot use myself. I mistakenly believe I can only *indicate* what *she* would do. Yet if I watch myself greeting my dogs with gushes of baby talk and little giggles, *I* am silly. If I talk to a scientist, even to an electrician *I* am stupid, though my cliché image tells me I am brilliant. If a drunken, bigoted doorman gives me a hard time, I appear snobbish and I pull rank, though my self-image tells me I am a humanist, a liberal at all times. I think I am fearless, yet you should see me with a mouse.
>
> (2008: 26)

Essentially, in developing a truthful performance, you should not limit yourself to your opinions of what is true for you; instead search for the seeds of the character's behaviour in something you would do, say or think, though it might be something unusual for you.

GIVEN CIRCUMSTANCES

If brings to life the *given circumstances*. Stanislavski took the latter term from the Russian poet Pushkin, who wrote that 'truth of passions, verisimilitude in feelings experienced in given circumstances – that is what our intelligence demands of a dramatist' (Wolff 1971: 265). *Given circumstances* can also be translated as the 'supposed' or 'proposed circumstances. They are 'given' for the actor as they cannot be altere They include:

> the plot, the facts, the incidents, the period, the time and pla the action, the way of life, how we as actors and directors stand the play, the contributions we ourselves make, the r scène, the sets and costumes, the props, the stage dressing, th effects etc., etc., everything which is a given for the actors rehearse.
>
> (Stanislavski 20

How could we define the *given circumstances* in *The Gl* by Tennessee Williams? (See Appendix 1.)

PLOT, FACTS, INCIDENTS

As you read the play, note what happens. There' you can write a list, or a synopsis like the examp is no need to spend a lot of time on it and you about leaving things out. This is the first re important is to note what strikes you immediate to include everything. But notice that making you with the play, and begins to raise ques more so than simply reading it might do.

- He listens to a story told by Amanda, about a Sunday afternoon when she was young, when she received seventeen gentleman callers, because Laura asks him to let Amanda tell the story.
- He groans when Amanda asks how many gentleman callers Laura is expecting that afternoon.

At this stage you should avoid making judgements about the character – deciding, for example, whether Tom is a good or a bad person – focusing instead on finding out information about him.

Note that if you do not know where St Louis, Blue Mountain or Mazatlan are, these are things you should research.

THE PERIOD, THE TIME AND PLACE OF THE ACTION, THE WAY OF LIFE

The action takes place in a tenement apartment in St Louis in America, in the 1930s, in the period of the Depression, when labour protests or demonstrations, which could be quite violent, are taking place in big cities like St Louis. In Europe, the Spanish Civil War is being fought, dating the play between 1936 and 1939. Tom says in one of his speeches to the audience in *The Glass Menagerie*, 'Adventure and change were imminent in this year. They were waiting round the corner for all these kids. Suspended in the mist over Berchtesgaden, caught in the folds of Chamberlain's umbrella' (Williams 2009: 35, Scene 5). He is referring to the fact that World War Two is imminent, with Neville Chamberlain, the British Prime Minister (the holder of the umbrella), waiting for Hitler (whose mountain residence was in Berchtesgaden in the Bavarian Alps) to make a move.

These *given circumstances* help the actor to gain a sense not only of the atmosphere of the play – the fact that change is in the air – but also of Tom's outlook, and an image of Tom the poet.

HOW WE AS ACTORS UNDERSTAND THE PLAY, THE CONTRIBUTIONS WE OURSELVES MAKE

At this stage, your early understanding and interpretation of the play could involve your views about its *themes* and also about its *genre*.

EXERCISE: THEMES

When you have gone through the play, note any themes or ideas that occur to you. They don't have to be right or exact, and you may change your mind as you continue to work on the play. But you will be thinking creatively, and questions and areas for possible research will occur to you. Possibilities are:

- Families – single-parent families, conflict between generations
- Memory
- Survival
- Creativity
- Work and poverty
- Entrapment and escape
- War, violence
- Guilt
- The power of the past over life in the present

GENRE

What kind of a play is this? How naturalistic is it? There are scenes of everyday life; it is situated in a particular time and place. The stage directions suggest poetic aspects to the play: Tom breaks the *fourth wall* and the eating of the meal in Scene 1 is mimed. Williams writes in his production notes, 'Being a "memory play", *The Glass Menagerie* can be presented with unusual freedom of convention. Because of its considerably delicate or tenuous material, atmospheric touches and subtleties of direction play a particularly important part' (2009: xvi).

Is the play a drama? Is Laura's situation 'tragic' and if so in what sense? Is Amanda's? At the end of the play, Amanda is seen to be silently comforting Laura, and Williams writes, 'Now that we cannot hear the mother's speech, her silliness has gone and she has dignity and tragic beauty' (2009: 86). You could consult Patrice Pavis' (1998) *Dictionary of the Theatre* on definitions of tragedy and the tragic.

THE MISE-EN-SCÈNE, THE SETS AND COSTUMES, THE PROPS, THE STAGE DRESSING

At this early stage, simply see what ideas about the look of the play as a whole come to you (*mise-en-scène* is the term used to refer to the design aspects of the play – the way the themes are expressed visually). They may not be the same as the director's or the designer's, but if you allow aspects of the text to begin to form visual images for you, you are beginning your creative work as the actor. What is the Wingfield's home like? What do we know about the living room? What is the atmosphere of the tenement?

Consider the stage directions:

> Scene: An Alley in St. Louis. The Wingfield apartment is in the rear of the building, one of those vast hive-like conglomerations of the cellular living units that flower as warty growths in overcrowded urban centers of lower middle-class population and are symptomatic of the impulse of this largest and fundamentally enslaved section of American society to avoid fluidity and differentiation and to exist and function as one interfused mass of automatism.
>
> ... At the rise of the curtain, the audience is faced with the dark grim rear wall of the Wingfield tenement. This building is flanked on both sides by dark, narrow alleys which run into murky canyons of tangled clotheslines, garbage cans, and the sinister latticework of neighbouring fire escapes.
>
> (Williams 2009: 3, Scene 1, stage directions)

This description goes beyond realism, suggesting that the inhabitants of the tenements are dehumanised by life in the cramped living spaces, the narrow alleyways. See what is suggested to you by Williams' images of 'hives', 'warty growths', 'slaves' and 'automatism'.

Notice specific aspects of the set:

> The apartment faces an alley and is entered by a fire escape, a structure whose name is a touch of accidental poetic truth, for all of these huge buildings are always burning with the slow and implacable fires of human desperation. The fire escape is part of what we see – that is, the landing from it and steps descending from it.
>
> (Williams 2009: 3, Scene 1, stage directions)

The fire escape figures as a symbol for the theme of entrapment and escape. Note its incidences in the text.

Find pictures to help you imagine settings mentioned in the text, for example the Moon Lake Casino where the shooting that Amanda describes took place.

Find pictures and objects that help you imagine both the props and furniture in the text, such as the upright typewriter, typewriter keyboard chart and Gregg shorthand diagram, the portieres, the sofa bed (note that Laura does not have a room of her own). Of course, if you are working on a full-scale production these will be supplied for you, but if you are working on scenes, you should find these images for yourself and your group.

What clothes do the characters wear? Though you may not have the costume resources to dress exactly as Amanda would, you can still imagine and give some indication of what she would wear, for example a hat, a brooch or a necklace, which will help you create and sustain the character. Tom wears a merchant sailor's uniform.

In Scene 6 Laura has a beautiful new dress, and Amanda, inappropriately, wears a 'girlish frock of yellow voile with a blue silk sash' attempting to re-enact her success in her young days as a Southern belle (Williams 2009: 48, stage directions).

THE SOUND EFFECTS, ET CETERA

The production notes refer to a single recurring tune, 'The Glass Menagerie', which is 'used to give emotional emphasis to suitable passages' (Williams 2009: xvii), such as at the end of Scene 1, after Laura says, 'Mother's afraid I am going to be an old maid.' (Williams 2009: 9, Scene 1.) It was written for the play by composer Paul Bowles. You can find this music on the internet.

Note where else it occurs and consider what emotional emphasis it adds.

Note the other occurrences of music and the reason for their inclusion. For example, ironically, the strains of 'The World Is Waiting for the Sunrise', a popular ballad, are heard coming from the Paradise Dance Hall across the alley while Tom is talking about how the young people who go there are consoling themselves with 'hot swing music and liquor, dance halls, bars and movies, and sex that hung in the gloom like a chandelier and flooded the world with brief deceptive rainbows' (2009: 35, Scene 5), oblivious to the approach of World War Two.

In considering each aspect of the *given circumstances* above, we have moved from facts to the aesthetic. Study and research of the play takes the actor through different levels of analysis from external to internal. Starting from the external level of facts, events, plot and structure, you gain a sense of the next level: everyday life in the epoch of the play, social customs and beliefs. From this, Stanislavski said, you pass onto the aesthetic level, an understanding of how the play works as a piece of theatre in terms of dramatic structure, how it will look, movement and proxemics, and the sound. All this enables you to pass on to the inner psychological level of the role, *experiencing*, and the outer expression or *embodiment*, and lastly the actor's own personal creative level: their state of mind in a role (Stanislavski 2010: 106).

All analysis should be creative. Stanislavski thought that the biggest problem in acting came from insufficient discernment, and so the actor must work hard to gain understanding of the role. If one aspect of work on the given circumstances does not appeal to you, try something else. In a diagram of the *system*, Stanislavski listed *given circumstances* under 'inventions of the imagination' to emphasise that actors and directors should work on them in a creative way. Additionally, if you are working on scenes from a play you should get to know the whole play in as much detail as possible. You have to understand the text in full in order to see how your character fits into the whole.

OTHER APPROACHES TO ANALYSIS OF THE *GIVEN CIRCUMSTANCES*

The director Katie Mitchell uses the term 'precise circumstances'. Her analysis is from the perspective of the director, but if this approach appeals to you as an actor, do use it. She recommends making two lists: the facts of the play and questions.

EXERCISE: LISTING FACTS AND QUESTIONS

Place: The environment the characters are in.

Character biographies: The events in the past that shape the characters.

Immediate circumstances: The twenty-four hours preceding the action of each scene.

Time: The year, or season, or hour the action takes place in, or the effect of the passage of time between acts or scenes.

Events: The changes that affect the behaviour of the characters.

Intentions: The pictures of the future that drive the present action of the characters.
Relationships: The thoughts about others that calibrate the behaviour of the characters (Mitchell 2009: 10).

As you list facts, list all the questions that arise – the things you don't know, as yet.

At the end of this process you have two long lists: one of facts and one of questions. You should then read each of the lists back to yourself and

> consider how your picture of the play has altered as a result. The list of facts will make you feel secure and confident about the certainties preceding the action of the play. It will give you a picture of the world in which the play occurs.
>
> (Mitchell 2009:14)

You can use the questions as a prompt to assess what work needs to be done to answer them. You cannot be expected to answer them yet.

SIX QUESTIONS

One of Stanislavski's ways of getting an actor to work on *given circumstances* was to get them to answer six questions about the character: *who, what, when, where, why, wherefore* (meaning 'for what reason'; 2008b: 116). He introduces this idea in *An Actor's Work* by suggesting that the students individually visit the room of an actual person and ask themselves these questions. He gives the example of visiting the apartment of a famous writer. The questions are as follows:

- Who lives here – what do you know about them?
- What is in the room, what appeals to you, what characterises the owner?
- When was the apartment built? When might the owner have come to live here?
- Where is the apartment situated?
- Why are there a shawl and a tambourine on the sofa?
- Wherefore/for what reason is the furniture arranged as it is?
- What is the purpose of the room, what goes on in it?

There isn't one correct way to put the questions: you can ask any questions that occur to you beginning with a 'w' word. You can use the questions for your character in a particular scene or scenes, or for the play as a whole, or even for a single action (see Stanislavski 2008b: 670–71). A question can provide the key to the whole scene.

EXERCISE: *SIX QUESTIONS*

Ask the *six questions* above or similar questions about the dining room in *The Glass Menagerie.*

The following includes some suggested answers to the questions in relation to the three characters in *The Glass Menagerie*, whereas you may focus on the character you are playing in answering all the six questions. Note that answering one question may spark off other questions.

WHO?

If your character is Laura you might have some of these answers to the question 'Who is Laura?' from Scene 1. You might want to answer them in the first person, to help you begin to think about yourself as the character.

- I am a young woman, living with my mother and brother.
- I have left school.
- I had an illness when I was a child and this has left one of my legs shorter than the other. I wear a brace.
- I don't speak very much.
- I have a collection of glass animals.
- My mother thinks that I should be popular with boys as she was. This makes me very nervous.
- My brother argues with my mother a lot. I love them both and I don't want them to argue.

As well as gathering details on Tom, Laura and Amanda, think about the characters we hear about that do not appear in the play. Note the photograph of the father, 'a very handsome young man in a doughboy's cap. He is gallantly, ineluctably smiling as if to say

"I will be smiling for ever" ' (Williams 2009: 4, Scene 1, stage directions). Gather all the information from what people say about him in the play. At what points in the play might your character in the play be thinking about him? What are they thinking about him?

WHAT?

Returning to Laura: What does she hear? What does she say? What does she do? What does she wear? What are the pieces in the glass menagerie?

Here are some suggestions which you can develop much further:

- I am at dinner with my mother and brother.
- My mother and I have spent a lot of time preparing this meal.
- Mother is telling Tom how to eat and I know he is getting annoyed.
- I am trying to get through the meal, to get on to the dessert.
- I can smell Tom's cigarette smoke.
- Now, Mother is telling her story and Tom is listening, so that makes things a bit better.
- Mother wants me to have a gentleman caller.
- She is afraid I will be an old maid.
- I am a disappointment to her.

WHEN?

When does the scene take place? This was discussed above under 'The period, the time and place of the action, the way of life'. In addition, you can consider the following:

- The stage direction is *Now and the Past*. Williams writes of 'that quaint period, the thirties, when the huge middle class of America was matriculating in a school for the blind. Their eyes had failed them, or they had failed their eyes, and so were having their fingers pressed forcibly down on the fiery Braille alphabet of a dissolving economy' (Williams 2009: 4–5, Scene 1). Work with this image of humanity and evaluate it from your point of view.
- Find out about the civil war in Spain and what Tom might hear about it.
- Find out about the labour disturbances in what are described as otherwise peaceful cities, such as Chicago, Cleveland, St Louis.

- When in your character's life does the play take place? How old are Laura, Tom and Amanda?

WHERE?

- As already suggested, find out about the geographical location of the play.
- The stage directions discussed above give a lot of information about the tenement building in St Louis.
- The Wingfield apartment. The living room is Laura's bedroom; what is it like? What are the portieres and the old-fashioned whatnot like? Note the presence of the typewriter keyboard chart and the Gregg shorthand diagram.

WHY?

Why are the characters here? What in the past has brought them to this present situation?

- Why is Amanda described as 'a little woman of great but confused vitality, clinging frantically to another time and place' (Williams 2009: xv, Characters)? What is her confusion?
- Why is the play set in memory? What could Williams be saying about the way the past affects the present? Look at the more symbolic aspects of the set descriptions that are there to suggest that this is a memory play, for example.

> The scene is memory and therefore non-realistic. Memory takes a lot of poetic license. It omits some details; others are exaggerated, according to the emotional value of the articles it touches, for memory is seated primarily in the heart. The interior is therefore rather dim and poetic.
>
> (Williams 2009: 3, Scene 1, stage directions)

- Why does Williams use the title, *Ou sont les neiges d'antan*? (2009: 8), which has been translated as 'Where are the snows of yesteryear?' This is a quotation of the refrain from a fifteenth-century poem by French poet François Villon, *Ballade des dames du temps jadis* ('Ballad of the Ladies of Times Past'). Villon was fatherless at an early age, living a life of poverty, a thief and a wanderer. The parallels with the characters of the play are evident: Tom, the poet and wanderer, reflects on his ladies of times past, but why does he do this?

WHEREFORE/FOR WHAT REASON?

This question points us towards the future, whereas 'why?' refers to the past of the characters.

- For what reason does Tom say 'I think the rest of the play will explain itself'? He has set the 'social background to the play', mentioned his mother and sister and described the gentleman caller as 'a symbol: he is the long delayed but always expected something that we live for', and his father as 'a telephone man who fell in love with long distances; he gave up his job with the telephone company and skipped the light fantastic out of town'. He tells the audience about the picture postcard his father sent from Mexico 'containing a message of two words: "Hello – Goodbye!" and no address'.
- For what reason does he give these details and images? What is he saying about the direction the play is to go in and the course his life is to take (Williams 2009: 4–5, Scene 1)? Tom is indicating that he, like his father, will leave his sister and mother and go away to travel.

Considering the last two questions may help understand the play and the reasons for framing the play as a memory play, which tells the story of Tom escaping his home life but not what has happened to him since then. Bigsby writes that Tom

> revisits the past because he knows that his own freedom, such as it is, has been purchased at the price of abandoning others. He 'writes' the play more significantly perhaps because he has not effected that escape from the past which had been his primary motive for leaving. The past continues to exert a pull on him, as it does on his mother and sister, as it does on the South which they inhabit.
>
> (1997: 37)

Tennessee Williams drew from his own experience in writing his plays. The director Elia Kazan, who directed much of Williams work, said 'Everything in his life is in his plays and everything in his plays is in his life' (Spoto 1997: 171). Williams worked in a shoe factory, as we learn that Tom does, where his father had a position, and aspects of Laura are based on Williams' sister, Rose. Williams also left his mother and sister to pursue his career as an artist. Williams wrote from very clear images based on actuality, and, through use of *given circumstances*, you as the actor are seeking to recreate for yourself, as far as possible, the facts and images Williams worked from.

Taking into account everything you have learned from investigating the *given circumstances*, you can then work with the *magic if*.

EXERCISE: *IF*

Spend half an hour setting yourself the question 'If I were Amanda ... ?' and seeing what thoughts come to you. Use these questions to start you off. You may not, at the moment, know the answers.

- If I were Amanda, how would I try to remain cheerful?
- If I were Amanda, what would my hopes and dreams be?
- If I were Amanda, aged in my forties, 'a little woman of great but confused vitality' how would I move?
- If I were Amanda, how would I think about the family's financial situation?
- If I were Amanda, when was the last time I enjoyed myself?
- If I were Amanda, why would I be 'clinging frantically to another time and place', and what would that mean in terms of my thoughts and actions?
- If I were Amanda, what would I think might be the reason for my son Tom's attitude towards me?
- If I were Amanda, what would I want for my daughter, Laura?

Return to this exercise later on in rehearsals and see how your perception of the character has developed.

EXERCISE: HOTSEATING

Hotseating is a well-known way to help the actor with work on *given circumstances* and *if*. The group of actors each take turns to ask questions of one actor who is in role, helping him/her to develop the back-story of the character. Return to this exercise throughout the rehearsal process.

APPRAISAL OF THE FACTS

You should build regular appraisal of the facts into your analysis, from an early stage. This is where you review what you know about the play and test these facts out, going back over them to gain further enrichment. Stanislavski pointed out that the actor is not a machine, 'he cannot feel a role the same way every time, be stirred by the same stimuli. He feels the role differently every time and sees the facts that are forever fixed in the play differently from yesterday' (2010: 132–33). List the questions, any questions, that this appraisal raises for you and see what has changed in your analysis of the play. You are then ready to go on to a further stage.

> Now with the work we have done, your image has become much clearer. You have come to understand *when, where, why, for what reason* you are there. You can already distinguish the outlines of a new life, previously unknown to you. You can feel the ground beneath your feet. But this is not enough. The stage demands action. You must evoke it by setting tasks and intentions towards them.
>
> (Stanislavski 2008b: 81)

BITS AND *TASKS*

> There is a creative Task stored in each Bit. The Task arises organically out of its own Bit, or, vice versa, gives birth to it.
>
> (Stanislavski 2008b: 142)

Stanislavski developed a method of analysing the text by means of *bits* and *tasks*, probably first using them in *Hamlet* in 1911 (Senelick 1982: 132). *Bits* are sections of action in the play. Essentially, a *bit* or, as it is also translated, a *unit*, is a section of the play as determined by the actor or director, and the *task* is what the actor wants to do as the character in that section. Working on *bits* and *tasks* is an interim measure, a way into work on the role and the play. Using the idea of *tasks* is a way to help actors by getting them to focus, simply, on what they, as the character, want to do. *Task* is also translated as *objective* and the word 'motivation' is also used in connection with the concept of the *task*. So are 'problem', 'intention', 'want' and 'need'. The main point, whichever words are used, is that the idea of the actor's task involves an inner aspiration to do something. The *task* combines what Stanislavski referred to as *psychological and physical action*, as discussed in Chapter 2. The action must be purposeful – it is directed towards a goal; it is what you want to do as the character, the inner push or stimulus, or motivation, if you like.

For example, in *An Actor's Work*, Tortsov explains what is meant by psychological and physical action with an example from Pushkin's *Mozart and Salieri*. The composer Salieri decides to kill his friend Mozart out of jealousy because he recognises that Mozart's genius is far greater than his own. The actor's *task* in Scene 2 of the play could simply be expressed as 'to poison Mozart'. Tortsov points out that the psychology of Salieri's decision is very complicated. But what the actor playing Salieri actually does is to carry out *physical actions*, as it were, that is, taking a glass, pouring wine in it, putting in the poison and taking it to his friend, the genius whose music is so exquisite. In order for the actor to carry out these actions truthfully as Salieri, he must think as Salieri would at each moment, so these actions are simultaneously all psychological (Stanislavski 2008b: 147).

Tortsov gives his students a graphic example, instructing them: 'Go up to someone and slap him!' (2008b: 147). (Obviously, this exercise is intended to be used with some caution!) In order to carry out that action genuinely, the students would have to find suitable *given circumstances* immediately, inventing a reason for the slap, finding the right psychology for the character in the action.

Stanislavski's use of *tasks* emphasises that the actor in developing work on a role is to answer the question 'what do you want to *do* as the character in *the given circumstances*?' rather than 'how do you *feel* as the character in *the given circumstances*?' Mike Alfreds notes that it is often a source of disappointment or dissatisfaction to an actor that the actions do not deal directly with the emotions implicit in the speech. Stanislavski would ask the actor playing Salieri not what he is feeling but what he is thinking and doing, and, similarly, Alfreds describes working with an actress on Juliet's speech to her Nurse in Act 3, Scene 2 of *Romeo and Juliet*, where she learns that Romeo, whom she has just married, has killed her cousin Tybalt. Again, the director is not so much interested in what the actor is feeling but what she is doing.

> Despite the very obvious intensity of what she's expressing, Juliet is nonetheless executing very ordinary and available actions: *explaining, questioning, declaring* and so on. This is a helpful way into an intense speech so early in rehearsals – the actor is not ready to fulfil the emotional heights the scene will demand of her ... but she can fulfil – play – her actions fully and strongly.
>
> (Alfreds 2007: 139)

In working on a play based on Gogol's *Dead Souls*, Stanislavski tells Toporkov not to think of how Chichikov feels but how he acts (Toporkov 1998: 85), because the right *task* evokes internal *experiencing*. The right inner content will come about if the actor is thinking about what the character wants to do and performing the actions truthfully.

BITS

On first analysing the play, you can divide it into *bits*. The big question is 'how many *bits* should there be?' If you work on this on your own then compare your analysis of a scene into *bits* with those of other actors; you may find differences. This does not matter, as the exercise is about coming up with material rather than getting something right or wrong. You may be analysing the section of the scene from the point of view of your character and the other actors from theirs. The director may have a different breakdown. In discussing your differences of opinion you are engaging with the play, making connections with the characters. It can be fun. Remember, this is a creative process!

Each *bit* should be given a name and the name should be a noun or a noun phrase. For example, these could be names for *bits* in *The Glass Menagerie*, Scene 1 (see excerpt in Appendix 1):

BIT 1: 'Truth in the disguise of illusion' (lines 1–37, Tom's speech).

BIT 2: 'Mastication' (lines 38–61, from 'AMANDA'S *voice becomes audible through the portieres'* to 'AMANDA: You smoke too much').

BIT 3: 'Sunday afternoon in Blue Mountain' (lines 62–127, from 'LAURA *rises*' to 'AMANDA: How many do you suppose we're going to entertain this afternoon?').

BIT 4: 'Old maid' (lines 128 on, from 'TOM *throws down the paper*' to the end of the scene).

You can entitle each *bit* generally like this, or, where possible, each actor who appears in a *bit* can name it in a way that makes their character the subject (Alfreds 2007: 127). So if you were playing Tom, your titles could be:

BIT 1: 'Turning back time'
BIT 2: 'Spoiled appetite'
BIT 3: 'Mother "entertaining" '
BIT 4: 'The unendurable'

As you work on the scene you should find that what you have divided into smaller *bits* can in fact be extended into larger ones. This is a natural progression as you get to know the play, so that you are not dividing it into small *bits* that are hard to remember, but the most important *bits*, which will correspond with the rhythm of the play and help you to remember the sequence of events and what is going on for your character (Stanislavski 2008b: 139). The larger the *bits*, the fewer the number and the more they help us grasp *a sense of the whole* (2008b: 140–42). To begin with, you could consider each scene in *The Glass Menagerie* as a *bit* and give it a title.

TASKS

When it comes to defining a *task*, you should identify what your character is doing in that *bit*. This may take some thought, as you should seek to find a *task* that is right for you as the actor as well as in keeping with the role, and it should be something significant (Stanislavski 2008b: 145). Determining what the *task* should be is a creative process. The most important quality for a *task* is that it should interest, even fascinate, the actor. Stanislavski wrote that the *task* 'has to be pleasing, draw him, make him want to do it. Like a magnet it attracts his will to create' (2008b: 146).

Because *tasks* involve action, they *must* be defined by a verb, whereas it is possible to define a *bit* by a noun (Stanislavski 2008b: 148) or a phrase that does not involve a verb, as in some of the examples above, such as 'Spoiled appetite'. It can be very helpful to think about what 'I want … ', as the character, what 'I want to do' in the *given circumstances* of the *bit* (Stanislavski 2010: 142). Again, this helps the actor avoid falling into the trap of thinking about what they should be 'feeling'. Stanislavski wrote that when actors are asked what the *task* might be they often answer with nouns, for example, 'indignation, certainty, calm, joy, sadness'. These nouns may result in images of actions but not the feelings and actions themselves. If you answer the question 'what would I do in the given circumstances?' you will come up with ideas for actions such as 'I want to run, to shout or to argue'. These are external or physical *tasks*, but there can also be internal, more psychological wants and *tasks*, for example, 'I want to understand a misunderstanding, clarify a doubt, create calm, hearten and encourage' (Stanislavski 2010: 143). The one verb that must not be used is the verb 'to be'. If the actor identifies their *task* as 'I want to be happy' this will lead to acting in general (Stanislavski 2008b: 149).

The *task* must lie within the actor's capabilities. In *An Actor's Work*, Stanislavski writes that Tortsov's students are working on the play *Brand* by Ibsen, which is about a priest with strong views on how to live life. One of the students suggests that Brand's *task* in the play by Ibsen is 'to save humankind'. Tortsov encourages the students not to choose *tasks* like this, which are too grand and place too much of a demand on the actor (2008b: 146). Instead of appealing to and engaging the actor they are likely to frighten the actor and result in their falling back on clichés and stock acting. Breaking down the play into *bits* and manageable *tasks* makes it possible for the actor to work on building the role up into the whole, stage by stage.

EXERCISE: *TASKS*

Identify Tom's *tasks* in the first four *bits* of *The Glass Menagerie*. These are some suggestions: your *tasks* might not be the same. There is no absolute right and wrong here.

BIT 1: 'Turning back time'
Task: 'I want you to understand my life at home.' (Though Tom's speech is directly addressed to the audience, in contrast to in the more naturalistic scenes, there is no reason why you can't use *bits* and *tasks* here.)

BIT 2: 'Spoiled appetite'
Task: 'I want to get through this meal and get out.'

BIT 3: 'Mother "entertaining"'
Task: 'I want to get through listening to Mother's story without losing my temper.'

BIT 4: 'The Unendurable'
Task: 'I want Mother and Laura to shut up.'

THE WRONG *TASK*

As part of the appraisal process, where the actor reflects on what has been achieved, perhaps with the help of the director, you should check whether you are performing your *tasks* as the character really in accordance with the *given circumstances*. Are you performing the wrong *task*? Stanislavski distinguishes between 'living tasks and dead tasks'. Where a living task is genuinely active, the actor's imagination is at work, 'well substantiated by belief in the Given Circumstances' (2008b: 129–30). The acting will have a 'natural' quality, where the actor is not straining in any way. Dead *tasks* are those where the actor is going through the motions.

Another kind of wrong *task* would be if you as the actor were preoccupied with getting a response from the audience rather than thinking about performing the *task* as the character. In the example of the brooch given in Chapter 2, Marya is asked to go on stage and at first is awkward, then tries to do something to impress the audience with her histrionic gestures, forgetting entirely about the simple *task* of looking for the brooch (see pp. 41–42). Alfreds notes that many actors do not play actions and have the wrong objectives, implicitly saying 'look at me acting' (2007: 65). Working with *tasks* helps avoid the trap of 'playing the result', thus enabling the actor to overcome egotism and to get the thought, as the character, right. Stanislavski writes that most actors make the mistake of thinking not about the action but about the result, which means ham or stock-in-trade or forced acting (2008b: 144). Toporkov describes a rehearsal where he performed his monologue as Vanechka in *The Embezzlers* by Kataev, a very emotional speech, for Stanislavski. He is embarrassed that the rehearsal does not go well, and he is not in control of his voice. He says he does not know why 'Nothing will come … At home this monologue turned out well … There was much feeling. I even cried.' His director says

> Exactly! You were afraid of losing those feelings. A completely wrong task. That is exactly what spoiled it. Does Vanechka think of that while speaking to the peasants? No. And you must not think of it either. Why should you cry? Let the audience cry.
>
> (1998: 53–54)

Stanislavski continually emphasises that the actor should focus on how *if* and *given circumstances* lead on to a *task*.

EXERCISES: APPRAISAL OF THE *TASK*

Identify *tasks* for *bits* of the play. Or play an improvised scene with some *given circumstances* and *tasks*.

Ask for feedback on what your *task* appeared to be to the audience. Was there any element of getting the class to guess what the *task* was in order to feel that your improvisation was successful? Or to amuse the group? Or were you fully committed to the *task* and not thinking about the impression you were making on the audience?

COUNTER-TASKS

Of course, the fact that you as the character want to perform a certain *task* in a *bit* does not mean that you will be able to do so. The other characters' *tasks* may well conflict with yours. Mitchell (discussing 'intentions', which can be equated with *tasks*) writes that 'scenes work best when they contain a simple conflict. So ensure that the intentions contradict, or interact dynamically, with each other' (2009: 63). The process of working with your partners on conflicting *tasks* is a creative one. Stanislavski notes that *tasks* take on a new life because of changing *given circumstances* (2008b: 333–35), as in the process of work, you gain more insight into your character when you see what results from the *counter-tasks* and *counter-actions* of other characters and the events in the play.

Consider the following example of *tasks* and *counter-tasks* in Scene 1 of *The Glass Menagerie*:

BIT 1: 'Truth in the disguise of illusion'
Tom's *task*: 'I want to make you understand what it was like for me at home.'

BIT 2: 'Mastication'
Tom's *task*: 'I want to get through this meal and get out.'
Amanda's *task*: 'I want my children to understand that a meal should be a social occasion.'
Laura's *task*: 'I want to get away from the argument.'

BIT 3: 'Sunday afternoon in Blue Mountain'
Tom's *task*: 'I want to get through listening to Mother's story without losing my temper.'
Amanda's *task*: 'I want to relive happy days in the past and tell my children about how I chose their father.'
Laura's *task*: 'I want Tom to listen to Mother without arguing.'

BIT 4: 'Old maid'
Tom's *task*: 'I want Mother and Laura to shut up.'
Amanda's *task*: 'I want to entertain my children and encourage my daughter.'
Laura's *task*: 'I want to hide my embarrassment.'

It appears from this analysis that Tom and Laura want not to be at the table with their mother, whereas Amanda wants to be with them. Their *tasks* are sometimes in conflict with each other; they do not want the same things.

THE MAJOR *TASK* – THE *SUPERTASK*

In *My Life in Art*, Stanislavski gives examples of the *supertask*, which is also known as the *super-objective*, or the *kernel* or main idea, or 'ruling idea' of the play. It is the main aim of the writer, and the *tasks* of all the characters are linked to it. For example, he writes that Chekhov's *supertask* in his work was to struggle against triviality, and Tolstoy's in his was to strive for self-perfection (2008b: 307). This obviously is a large idea and may not be apparent when you begin work on a play, but if you can arrive at an idea of the *supertask* and focus on it this helps you fulfil the large *tasks* of the play, as you can link them into the *supertask* (Stanislavski 2008b: 336). It enables you to have and keep in mind a *sense of the whole* as you perform the play. Like ordinary *tasks*, the *supertask* should not be an intellectual idea but should appeal to the emotions – one which 'stimulates our creative imagination, which attracts our total attention, satisfies our feeling of truth and stimulates our power to believe' (Stanislavski 2008b: 308).

It may be difficult to find the *supertask*. After initial analysis and work on the play it may be useful to think about major, medium and minor *tasks* and make a limit of approximately five major *tasks* in each act in a four-act play, so that there are twenty to twenty-five for the whole play. It may be that further work is required, or that ideas about the *supertask* emerge from this. Stanislavski notes: 'the supertask is the fundamental basis, the essence and must arouse creative wants and striving towards action in the actor, so that finally he can master the *supertask* that aroused the creative process' (2010: 25).

It is possible to think of the *supertask* of the character, as opposed to that of the play. Alfreds describes the *supertask* of the character as informing a character's journey through life, both a goal and a guide to conducting one's life. He notes that, in the play, the *supertask* influences all the choices that characters make and this will include their *tasks*. An example is given of Konstantin in *The Seagull*. Alfreds considers that his *supertask* is 'to win his mother's love and respect' (2007: 58–59).

EXERCISE: FINDING THE *SUPERTASK*

Using the summary and excerpt from *The Glass Menagerie*, or, better still, reading the whole play, simply brainstorm a list of key ideas that seem to inform the text. Don't censor your ideas, but see them as starting points. Then think about what Williams' *supertask* may have beeen in writing *The Glass Manageric*.

What might Williams have intended for the play? Bigsby notes, 'Tom, the narrator, who shares Tennessee Williams' first name, chooses to write the play, in the sense of recalling what seem to him to have been key moments in his past life' (1997: 37). But the *supertask* of the play could be seen to be more than the expiation of guilt, Williams' own guilt at abandoning his own family. Tom leaves partly because he thinks he will never be fully alive, able to write while in the confined existence he has in St Louis. But at the end of the play, we do not know that he has found artistic or any other fulfilment. Perhaps he too has lived with illusions about life abroad, as Laura's lives in a world of glass animals and Amanda clings to the past to escape the realities of Depression America and the world at war.

Consider whether it is possible to find one sentence to summarise the *supertask*.

What relevance does the *supertask*, however you may define it, have for you? What points of connection can you make with the key ideas of the text? If, for example, you think the *supertask* of the play is to show how people are commoditised in a capitalist society, can you think of any examples from your experience of how people are valued for their possessions rather than as human beings?

Russian director Georgi Tovstonogov writes that Stanislavski did not regard the *supertask* as the be-all and end-all, and he in fact widened the concept to that of the *super-supertask*! By this, Stanislavski wanted to emphasise that theatre should 'be a bridge between the stage and the audience, making even an old classic sound contemporary, fusing the thoughts and feelings of actors in a single élan' (1972: 38). From Stanislavski's essentially humanist perspective, the *super-supertask* of the play is to convey something which will help people through life's difficulties, to understand themselves and life better.

TRUTH AND BELIEF OF ACTIONS

In practice, the actor performs *tasks* in *given circumstances* using *the magic if*, generating truthful acting. Having defined your *task* as the actor, you should now perform the actions needed to fulfil the task with *truth and belief*.

In *An Actor's Work*, Marya loses her handbag and the other students help her look for it. When they have found it, the students are asked to perform an étude looking for an imaginary lost handbag. The scene does not work because they do not believe in their *tasks* and they are pretending to look, rather than really looking. Tortsov comments that they have not gone through the process they should to

> transfer the life of the imagination onto the stage ... In this process the magic 'if' and Given Circumstances, when they are properly understood, help you to feel and to create theatrical truth and belief onstage. So, in life there is truth, what is, what exists, what people really know. Onstage we call truth that which does not exist in reality but which could happen.
>
> (Stanislavski 2008b: 153)

In order to understand what truthful acting is, we have to see how easy it is to take shortcuts, which results in being false in acting. It is easy for acting students to fall into 'the habit of lying'. In working with the idea of the *fourth wall*, you may be tempted to glance at an audience member, or your director, instead of focusing on where you should be looking to be truthful in the scene. You may pretend to look at an object onstage but not really see it, focusing instead on how you are delivering your line or the impression you are creating. In working with your stage partners, you may not be looking at them and responding to them as you would someone in everyday life, but be doing something extra because you are performing, or 'be in your own head'. Maybe some mannerisms begin to creep into your speech as the character. If you are working with props, maybe you don't take the trouble to compare how you would handle the object as you would in real life; for example, if you are holding a baby in the scene and have a doll to work with, you will look like you are holding a doll unless you take the trouble to find out how much heavier a baby is than a doll and to convey the right weight in your actions. You may take shortcuts if you are working with imaginary objects, not bothering to be precise about how you would handle those objects in life. It is important in working with imaginary objects to use sense memory every time. Stanislavski's advice is 'Don't neglect small physical actions but learn to use them for the sake of truth and your belief in the genuineness of what you are doing' (2008b: 164).

Exercises with props and imaginary objects are very helpful in this. You do not necessarily want to use props that distract the audience because they are real (Hagen 2008: 76); you have to find that sense of purposeful action within the artificiality of the stage setting. Othello may have to stab himself with a papier-mâché dagger but the actor/human must behave as if it were real, justifying the fact that is it not (Stanislavski 2008b: 154). So, it is essential to give time to working with props in order to get to know them and to justify their use. It is not a good thing, as often happens in student performances, to get all the props together only at the dress rehearsal. Uta Hagen insisted on having the set pieces and props in the rehearsal room from the beginning and would refuse to accept mock-ups: 'I want to have opened and closed that refrigerator door a hundred times before I set foot on the stage' (2008: x).

Work with imaginary objects helps the actor in many ways: a non-existent object 'focuses the actor's concentration first on himself and then on physical actions and obliges him to observe them' (Stanislavski 2008b: 167). It helps the actor, of course, to develop *sense memory* (Chapter 2). In the étude 'Burning Money', Kostya pretends to count money. Tortsov goes through the actions of counting money with him meticulously. 'As soon as I felt the truth of physical action, I felt at home on the stage' (Stanislavski 2008b: 161).

EXERCISES: PHYSICAL ACTIONS AND IMAGINARY OBJECTS

1. Develop a scene where you are at home. Make a phone call, make a cup of tea, do your hair.
2. Develop a scene where you take a walk on the beach, paddle, throw stones in the sea.
3. Develop a scene where you do some gardening in cold weather.

Stanislavski wrote: 'The secret of my method is clear. It's not a matter of the physical actions as such, but the truth and belief these actions help us to arouse and feel' (2008b: 162–63). Stanislavski often used to say to actors in rehearsal 'I don't believe you.' He could be quite tyrannical in this way and some actors would be very upset by it, feeling that they could never achieve what he wanted. But if you spend a little time in a drama school or department while students are rehearsing, just walking past the rehearsal studios listening to what is going on, or looking in, how often do you hear a note of authenticity, something that evokes a response as if you were hearing or seeing something in everyday life, whether it is a naturalistic play or not? A key to achieving the authenticity Stanislavski sought is being meticulous about work with physical actions.

Of course no action is purely physical: 'in every physical action there's something psychological and there's something physical in every psychological action' (Stanislavski 2008b: 180). Physical actions are the outward expression of what the character is *experiencing*. For example, in *The Glass Menagerie* in Scene 1, Tom 'throws down the paper and jumps up with a groan', expressing his disgust at Amanda's playacting, 'flouncing girlishly' in the anticipation of gentleman callers when there will be none (Williams 2009: 9).

'Physical action' is by no means simple physical movement, but is in essence psycho-physical action which includes the psychological task (Chuskin in Toporkov 1998: 16). As Alfreds puts it:

> *actions are what characters do to try to achieve their objectives; therefore actions are what actors play.* Playing actions is the actor's main task. It's what actors do. This is their job ... actions are what characters carry out *to try to get what they want* – to *change their current situation, to improve* or *rectify* it ... Therefore to achieve the desired change, *characters* have to effect a change in *other characters*. Which means that *actors* have to effect a change in *other actors*. They can only achieve this by pursuing actions.
>
> (2007: 65)

Actions have to be directed towards other people and they have to be precise, logical and sequential. Perhaps you have to carry out an action that must be completed at a certain moment in the dialogue, maybe putting some flowers in a vase then turning as someone speaks to you. If you rush the action in order to be on time to turn, the action will not be precise or logical; the character would not rush and the rushing spoils the sequence of actions. The sequence of actions an actor carries out in a role is called the *score* of actions. Like a score in music it guides you through the performance and has to be thought through afresh every time: 'how I carry out the action according to the score here, before *this* audience – that is creativity' (Toporkov 1998: 211).

If the *score* of physical actions in a role is carried out in a precise way as in life, 'truth and belief carries over, of itself into all other fields: thoughts, desires, feelings, words' (Stanislavski 2008b: 169) and together they create '*I am being*'. That means, I am, I live, I feel, I think as one with the role (Stanislavski 2008b: 186), the state where the actor is creative. If something unexpected happens, for example accidentally dropping a prop, the actor can handle the accident as the character in the play and incorporate retrieving the object into the role, as a new creative impulse (Stanislavski 2008b: 163).

To that end, Stanislavski thought that it was worth focusing on the 'physical' as opposed to verbal actions of a scene on their own, as a rehearsal technique to enable the actor to get the thought of the character right and to clarify the *tasks*. He developed new techniques towards the end of his career, which have become known as the *method of physical actions* and *active analysis*.

THE *METHOD OF PHYSICAL ACTIONS* AND *ACTIVE ANALYSIS*

The *method of physical actions* and *active analysis* are techniques that can be used in the rehearsal process. There are varying accounts of their significance, but essentially both techniques enable the actor to get to know and analyse the role practically, to 'get it up on its feet' without too much intellectual analysis.

THE *METHOD OF PHYSICAL ACTIONS*

Stanislavski wrote about what became known as the *method of physical actions*:

> It involves reading the play today and tomorrow rehearsing it on stage ... A character comes in, greets everybody, sits down, tells of events that have just taken place, expresses a series of thoughts. Everyone can act this, guided by their own life experience ... and so we break the whole play, episode by episode, into physical actions.
>
> (Stanislavskii 1999: 655)

Like other elements of the *system* it helps the actor 'go from the simple to the complicated, from simple physical actions to complex psychological emotional experiences, as helps toward the creation of character … ' (Toporkov 1998: 17).

Basically, the actors improvise a scene, working from the *score* of actions, drawing on whatever knowledge they have of the play and the roles at that time. You begin by relating the plot of the play very broadly as a framework, finding the situations, events or experience. Then take a section of text and play the physical actions. In order to do this you will need to think about the given circumstances and use your powers of invention for those you do not know. Use your own words (Stanislavski 2010: 16–19).

You may not be able to remember the lines exactly. You learn as much from seeing what is not there, what you don't know about the role, as from what you do know. You are working at getting the thought right and testing it out and it is a way to draw out the emotion in the role. This may have to be set up carefully, with the director feeding in ideas about the *given circumstances*, as some actors are very insecure about working practically before learning the text by heart and can find the exercise exposing.

EXERCISE: *METHOD OF PHYSICAL ACTIONS*

Using Appendix 1, tell the story, as a group, of the main events in Scene 1 of *The Glass Menagerie.*

Identify *bits* and *tasks.*

Perform the scene, *justifying* the actions by means of *if* and *given circumstances.*

The director can guide all this by asking each actor 'what do you want to do?' (*task*), 'where have you come from?' (*given circumstances*), and 'if you were Tom/Laura, Amanda, would you ... ?' (*magic if*).

As a group, analyse what has happened, keeping the comments and self-commentary creative and helpful. What were the things that you remembered from your reading and telling of the story of the scene that found their way into the improvisation?

Re-read the script. Note the difference between the words you have used and the words in the text and see what has struck you as important in the text. Repeat the process and deepen your analysis. You will find that you remember more than you think you can and that this will help you learn words and actions.

Each actor can then relate in their own words (1) the line of thoughts and (2) the line of mental images, and (3) explain them to their stage partners so as to establish *communication* and the *through-line* of action.

EXERCISE: SILENT ÉTUDES

You can perform the *bit* or section of the play that you are working on as a silent étude, focusing on the physical actions. The first part of *The Glass Menagerie*, the meal scene after Tom's speech, lends itself to silent étude work because the actions are loaded with meaning. In sections where there is dialogue, don't be tempted to start to mime; keep the physical actions as they would be if you were using the dialogue and, instead of speaking, convey the text by thought as much as possible.

Identify the physical actions. For example, in Scene 1, from the stage directions from line 35 to 75 onwards ('TOM *divides the portieres and enters the dining room*' to 'AMANDA *returns with a bowl of dessert*'; Williams 2009: 5–9):

Amanda and Laura are seated at the table.
Tom bows slightly to the audience and withdraws, reappearing in his place at the table.
Tom, Amanda and Laura eat, indicated by gestures without food or utensils.
Amanda lectures Tom.
Tom lays down fork and pushes the chair back.
He rises and walks to the living room.
Amanda reacts.
Laura rises.
Tom remains standing with a cigarette by the portieres.
Amanda rises.
Laura sits.
Amanda crosses out to the kitchenette.
Tom and Laura communicate about their mother.
Amanda returns with the bowl of dessert.

Discuss the scene. Did you really communicate? What were your thoughts, reactions?

ACTIVE ANALYSIS

Maria Knebel, who worked with Stanislavski later in his life, gave this term to Stanislavski's later approaches to work on a text. The terms 'rehearsal by études', and 'analysis by action' mean the same as *active analysis* and the principle is the same as in the *method of physical actions*. The purpose is to engage the actor actively in getting to know the text in a way that will lead to *experiencing* as opposed to 'round-the-table' analysis, where actors can often only make partial use of what is discussed. Getting the thought right before learning the lines is important. The actor identifies facts and events then 'evaluates' them through improvisation and discussion on the improvisation, focusing on interactions with the other characters.

Evaluating the facts takes place through conflict and *counter-actions* or *counter-tasks*. You could analyse the play focusing on the clashes between characters. 'Defining the reasons for these clashes, understanding the motives and the behaviour of the characters is to understand the play, truly to define the idea of the production' (Korkorin 2007: 66–67).

The *method of physical actions* and *active analysis* enable the actor to develop understanding of the play as a whole, to work at understanding the thought behind the text, the author's intentions, the *supertask*. The exercises lead the actor to a deep understanding of the text, hopefully preventing them from developing a mechanical way of saying the words that lacks depth.

EXERCISE: *ACTIVE ANALYSIS*

Using Appendix 1, work through the first scene taking into account what is known about the *given circumstances*. In your improvisations, focus on your *tasks* and how you are interacting with the other characters in this. Then read through the episode or scene being rehearsed, using the author's text to verify everything that you did in the improvisation.

In your discussion and self-evaluation ask questions such as these:

- Were the physical actions truthful? How did you work with imaginary objects?
- Did you keep in mind your *task*?
- What aspects of the *given circumstances* did you incorporate successfully? What could you add?
- How did you work with the other actors and their *counter-tasks*?
- How are your actions directed? How do you want to influence your partner, change their behaviour? What prevents you from achieving your *task* (was it a *counter-task*, even inner conflict)?
- Do any external events influence the scene?
- Did you communicate truthfully?

FURTHER READING

Alfreds, M. (2007) *Different Every Night – Freeing the Actor*, London: Nick Hern Books. See description of physical and verbal actions in the first *bit* of Act 1 of *The Seagull*, pp. 134–35, and also examples of *bits* in Act 1 of *The Cherry Orchard*, pp. 125–26.

Hodge, A. (2000) *Twentieth-century Actor-training*, London: Routledge. See summary of *active analysis* by Carnicke, pp. 26–29.

Mitchell, K. (2009) *The Director's Craft: A Handbook for the Theatre*, Abingdon: Routledge. See Chapter 1, 'Organising Your Early Responses to the Text'.

Stanislavski, K. (2008) *An Actor's Work*, London: Routledge. See discussion of the *six questions*, pp. 80–81 and 669–71. For Stanislavski's exercises on the memory of physical actions, see pp. 653–54.

Stanislavski, K. (2010) *An Actor's Work on a Role*, London: Routledge. Stanislavski explains the *method of physical actions* in 'The Approach to a Role', pp. 88–90.

CONSOLIDATION AND SPONTANEITY

This chapter continues to look at how the actor works on a role. After the initial analysis and work, when the actor is beginning to have a *sense of the whole*, they must consolidate and deepen the work in order to fully *experience* the role. Then, they have to be able to stay in character, and keep the performance fresh and spontaneous each time. Stanislavski discusses aspects of the *system* and techniques that can help the actor to do this: *imagination*, *adaptation*, *communication*, *here*, *today*, *now*, *the through-line* and *the subtext*. As with the *system* as a whole, there are crossovers; the point is that creating and performing a role, looking at what is going on from different angles, helps the actor to sustain insight and inner content, and to develop and deepen the work.

IMAGINATION

> The imagination paints not only things which actually exist but also fantastic worlds which could not actually be.
>
> (Stanislavski 2008b: 107)

In a play text, the writer only provides some of the information, the *given circumstances* for the actor. Plays like *The Glass Menagerie*, by Tennessee Williams, may include a fair amount of description in the stage directions, as the accuracy of the setting is important, whereas a play like *Far Away* by Caryl Churchill, set in a surreal, dystopian future where everything in the world is at war, contains very little detail, relying on those working on the production to create the imaginary world. Even with more naturalistic plays, the author will not provide much detail of the characters' back histories, events before the play begins, what the future will hold for the characters or what is meant to be happening offstage between the scenes when a particular character is onstage (Stanislavski 2008b: 62). We have to supply what the author has not given in the text, using our own imagination. This is important in the interpretation of the play. For example, Chekhov's *Three Sisters* is a play set in the early twentieth century in Russia. The three sisters, Olga, Masha and Irina, are from a cultured and wealthy background but live in a provincial city where they have few outlets for their talents and accomplishments. They long to live in Moscow, the capital city. Because of the way they have been socialised as women in that society they do not take action, pinning their hopes on the men around them to find their way forward in life. The play ends with the death in a duel of the man Irina is to marry, and their brother Andrei sinking into apathy. Some interpretations have seen the sisters as tragically 'doomed' to a sterile future at the end of the play, whereas if the play is seen as ending with a question as to what their future will be, it is left to the actors and the audience to create an answer. The exact interpretation may be the province of the director, but, that aside, it is essential for the actor to create the life of the character in the imagination, 'Otherwise you won't get a continuous "life of the human spirit" in a play from the actor, you'll be dealing with isolated scraps' (Stanislavski 2008b: 288). A bitty approach, where an actor knows the scene and has developed the character's inner life for the scenes, but has not worked sufficiently on the character's life as a whole beyond the play, results in a standard of performance that would be inadequate for Stanislavski. To create 'the life of the human spirit' of the role, the actor must create as rounded a character as possible and inhabit the role in performance.

In order to bring the role to life, the actor has to work not only on the past and future for the character but also their relationships. As Katie Mitchell points out, relationships in real life are a result of events shared between two people over a period of time. 'Actors need to build the relationships between characters in a play in a similar way, by inventing shared pictures of past events that determine the relationship they have in the play' (2009: 19). Stanislavski considered the key to be the creation of images that the actor accesses in the course of playing the role. Mitchell points out that in real life if we mention or hear a reference to a town or a place we know, a 'picture appears in our mind'. This may be just a flash, but if we stop to retrieve the image, we can flesh it out in more detail. If we have a particular view of a place or connect it with past experiences this will colour our expression of what we are imagining in what we say or do. So for example, if you had an enjoyable holiday in Crete one year, when Crete is mentioned in conversation, your thought and response to it will be informed by that experience. It will be a different sort of response if someone mentions a place where as a child you had an unpleasant time at school. What this means is that onstage

> The actor must have a picture in their head for every place their character talks about or listens to – both near and far. If they see the place in their mind, then they will adjust their tone of voice and bodies accordingly. The audience will then have the impression that they are referring to real places.
> (Mitchell 2009: 23)

In a play like *The Glass Menagerie*, your research and work in rehearsal should supply you with mental images of America in the 1930s, of St Louis (see Appendix 1). The actor playing Amanda Wingfield should have seen pictures of the Mississippi Delta, Blue Mountain, Moon Lake, Memphis, Greene County, Jackson, Sunset Hill, Tennessee, if she is unable to go there. Tom's imagination of Guernica, the Basque capital bombed from the air by the Spanish nationalist forces in 1937 during the Spanish Civil War, will have been fed by newspaper images, which the actor should research and think about. The actors playing Laura and Jim, as well as Tom, should create a shared memory of the school assembly hall, the scene of Jim's triumphs as a singer and Laura's humiliation when she regularly comes in late and has to walk up the aisle, self-conscious about the noise she is making with the brace on her leg (Williams 2009: 67, Scene 7)

Similarly, Arthur Miller's *Death of a Salesman – Certain Private Conversations in Two Acts and a Requiem* is also set in America in the

1930s, in New York. Willy Loman, a travelling salesman, aged 60, is married to Linda and has two adult sons, Happy and Biff.

BRIEF SYNOPSIS OF ACT 1

Willy Loman, the Salesman, arrives home at night, laden with suitcases containing his sales samples, and has a conversation with his wife Linda. He says that on his drive home he couldn't drive anymore, couldn't think about what he was doing and had to do the last part of the journey at 10 miles an hour. Linda tries to reassure him and encourages him to go and see his boss Howard the next day and ask to work in New York, where they live, so he doesn't have to drive long distances any more. He says he is going to get a sandwich and some milk. Linda tells him that their sons, Biff and Happy, went out on a double date. Willy refers to the fact that he lost his temper with Biff before he left that morning. Biff has had a number of low-paid jobs since he left school and Willy thinks he is wasting his talent. To distract him from thinking about the row, Linda tells Willy that she has bought a new kind of cheese and he shouts at her about this. He complains that he can't breathe as there is no air and that the neighbourhood has been ruined, as apartment houses have been built and trees cut down, and the number of cars has increased. He decides to try the whipped cheese. Biff and Happy start to listen in to the conversation.

The play is set in Brooklyn, New York. From the beginning there are references to many other places that you should research in order to begin to form mental images of them. Willy has got as far as Yonkers that day, which is less than 25 miles from Brooklyn, though it took him four hours to drive back at 10 miles an hour (Miller 2000: 9). He has recently been to Florida, where Happy sent him on holiday, as we find out later (2000: 9, 15). He is expected in Portland the next morning (2000: 10). In a flashback scene to when the boys were young, Willy talks of being in Providence and having coffee with the Mayor (though this may not be true), Waterbury, which has a famous clock, and Boston, the 'cradle of the revolution', 'other towns in Mass., and on to Portland and Bangor and straight home!' (2000: 23–24). He says he 'knocked 'em cold in Providence, slaughtered 'em in Boston' (2000: 26). Willy's brother Ben died in Africa a couple of weeks before the time of the play, and, in a dream sequence, Ben speaks to Willy about making his fortune there in the diamond mines (2000: 37). Willy had the chance to go to Alaska, another place of opportunity, with Ben, but turned this down because Linda did not want him to go (2000: 66–67). Biff herded cattle in Nebraska, the Dakotas and Arizona and is now in Texas (2000: 16). Many other places are mentioned in the play; the characters have mental images of them, and what they say and how they say it reveals much about the characters. Willy's salesman's bluster presents images of his 'conquering' the towns he goes to, which is far from the truth. The vastness of the landscapes of Africa, Alaska and the West is contrasted with the confined space in which the Lomans live.

The stage directions already supply images of the Salesman's house:

> We are aware of towering angular shapes behind it, surrounding it on all sides. Only the blue light of the sky falls upon the house and forestage; the surrounding area shows an angry glow of orange. As more light appears, we see a solid vault of apartment houses around the small, fragile seeming home. An air of the dream clings to the place, a dream rising out of reality.
>
> (Miller 2000: 7)

This description goes beyond realism, suggesting symbolically that the existence of the Lomans is precarious, under threat from the encroaching neighbourhood.

The actor should imagine what would be surrounding them on all sides of the stage. The stage design may suggest the setting, or aspects of the setting, and the actor has to complete the work. Though the Lomans' house is surrounded by nearby apartment blocks, there is a garden. The urban intrudes on this, stifling nature. Willy says that you cannot grow anything any more; the builders have cut down elm trees to make space for the apartments and the lilac, wistaria, peonies and daffodils are long gone. Instead, 'smell the stink from that apartment house' (Miller 2000: 12).

Stanislavski urges the actor to use their imagination, particularly with a role or play they do not find engaging. So, if you are given a role that does not appeal to you or strike any chords with you immediately, you should involve your imagination. Thinking about what is missing from the *given circumstances* spurs the imagination on. The stage directions in *Death of a Salesman* indicate that the house is sparsely furnished (Miller 2000: 7) but the inclusion of specific items, such as the refrigerator (which goes wrong as soon as it is paid for) and the athletics trophy (a momento of the talents and promise of Biff and Happy when they were young), prompts thought.

Some students are concerned that they are not gifted with imagination. Stanislavski's advice is 'Develop it, or give up the stage' (2008b: 63). The imaginative faculties can indeed be developed. A way to do this is to set our brains a task. It is no good just letting your mind wander, vaguely hoping to conjure something up. To stimulate the imagination, the actor can set themselves questions and use the *magic if*, the tool which enables the actor to enter the world of the play, lifting them out of everyday life (Stanislavski 2008b: 60). The director sets a theme for them and the actors begin to see pictures in the 'mind's eye'; 'In our actors' jargon we call these *mental images, the inner eye*' (Stanislavski 2008b: 73).

The actor should develop these mental images for the whole role, like an internal film reel. This may seem daunting at first, but as the actor works on the *given circumstances* and physical actions for the role, this process and the process of developing the mental images will feed into each other. The story of what the character undergoes throughout the play must be logical: Stanislavski said that with a 'small scrappy supply of material you can't create a continuous series of mental images for the whole scene'. Therefore what is needed is a continuous line of *given circumstances* as the basis for each scene and then the actor should 'illustrate' them: 'we need an unbroken line not of plain, simple Given Circumstances but ones that we have coloured in full' (Stanislavski 2008b: 73–74).

The actor does not recall every single image in detail in performing the role, but when the imaginative backdrop has been created, it remains there as a resource for the performance. In *An Actor's Work*, Tortsov asks his students, as an exercise, to remember their life story, in order to see that they can develop a life story in a similar way for the characters. 'You lived through your entire life and memories of the most important moments remained. Live through the entire life of a role and let the most essential landmarks in it also remain'. He says that the 'film of the mental images' will 'sustain moods … evoke corresponding experiences, impulses, intentions and actions themselves' (2008b: 76):

> every one of our movements onstage, every word must be the result of a truthful imagination.
>
> (2008b: 84)

Asking questions which are used to help establish the *given circumstances*, such as the six discussed in the last chapter – *who*, *when*, *what*, *where*, *why*, *for what reason* – stirs the imagination and generates mental images.

The creative power of the actors' imagination draws the audience into the play.

> Actors and audience bond in a shared act of imagination.
>
> (Alfreds 2007: 14)

Working in a studio setting with the minimum of props or even a classroom can be useful for the student actor. Making use of one's surroundings and investing imagination with belief, the depth of belief that enables children to make a cardboard box into a space ship, communicates intensity to the audience. In *An Actor's Work*, Stanislavski writes that Tortsov's students perform an improvisation of an expedition stranded in the mountains on the set of a cosy sitting room and find that they cease to notice the sitting room props (2008b: 68–69). This state of being fully involved in the imaginary world is '*I am being*', which Tortsov defines: 'I have put myself in the centre of a situation I have invented, that I feel I am really inside it, that I really exist at its very heart, in a world of imaginary objects, and that I am beginning to act as me, with full responsibility for myself' (2008b: 70).

Stanislavski always said that if you are playing a bad man you should look for his good side (2008a: 105–7). Developing fully rounded characterisations will place a demand on your imagination and may take some time to develop. If you are playing a character who is much older than you, or you are a female playing a man, for example, rather than settling for an external portrayal of age or gender, seek to bridge the gap between yourself and the character by working on what they are thinking, using your imagination to find age, or masculinity.

It sounds like a cliché to talk about the imagination being creative, but the significance of this is that our imaginations are an aspect of the whole of us and interpret information about the world that comes to us through the senses. Director Declan Donellan writes, 'Our imaginations make us human and they toil every millisecond of our lives. Only the imagination can interpret what our senses relay to our bodies. It is imagination that enables us to perceive' (2005: 9). A lot of the work of interpreting images and creating meaning with them goes on at a subconscious level, and we can develop our imaginations by working consciously with *tasks*, paying attention.

EXERCISES: FINDING IMAGES IN *DEATH OF A SALESMAN*

1. VISUAL

Lying down or sitting comfortably as a group, apply the *circles of attention* exercise from Chapter 2 (see p. 26) to envisage the 'circles' of the environment of the play. The widest circle could be the America of the 1930s, as noted above, a wide circle the immediate neighbourhood, the medium circle the house and garden and the smallest circle your proximity as an actor to an object in the play (for example Linda and the refrigerator, Willy and the suitcases that he uses to carry his goods). Afterwards, share the most significant images that came to you with the group.

2. AURAL

Use the idea of sounds and music to spark your imagination. Think about this: 'A melody is heard, played on a flute. It is small and fine, telling of grass and trees and the horizon' (Miller 2000: 7, Act 1, stage directions). See what occurs to you. There is no right or wrong sound or image. Willy's father made flutes, which he sold as he travelled with his family (Miller 2000: 38). The play ends with a car crash: 'the music crashes down in a frenzy of sound, which becomes the soft pulsation of a cello string' (Miller 2000: 108, Act 2, stage directions). There are about twenty minutes' worth of music in the play; what does that suggest about how atmosphere is created in the play as a whole?

3. SHARED IMAGES

As you get to know a play, work on shared images of objects important in the action of the play. In *Death of a Salesman*, Willy drives a Studebaker but realises he has been thinking that he was driving a red Chevy, a car Biff used to 'simonise' (Miller 2000: 9, 13). Find images of these types of cars and think about their significance to the characters.

4. USE OF IMPROVISATIONS

Develop improvisations on the back-story to the text, generating shared experiences and images, for example what happened when Willy was driving that day. Collect all the information on *given circumstances* from his speeches (Miller 2000: 8–9) and determine your *tasks* as the actor.

Improvise the argument between Willy and Biff on that day, before he set off driving.

Stanislavski wrote: 'We filter all the material the author and the director have given us through our own personalities. We reshape it, give it life, fill it with our own imagination' (2008b: 54). The shared vision of the play developed by the director and actors results in truthful action based on the most important ideas in the play.

THROUGH-LINE OF ACTION

The *through-line* of action is the journey through the play. The combined *through-lines* of the characters make the plot. Mental images and the physical actions of the scene constitute the *through-line*. If the actor gives their attention to actions and images in sequence, this enables them to stay in character. In order to *experience* you must have as continuous as possible a line in a role. For Stanislavski, it is important that the actor stays in role throughout the whole performance, even when offstage. He thought that for the actor to come offstage and start laughing with the other actors or for actors to play jokes on each other between scenes was unprofessional and would create a gap in the *through-line*, disturbing the actors' focus and attention. 'You know that such gaps are of no use to the role and no help to you. That means you must not break the line even in the wings' (2008b: 289). If the actor does allow these gaps to happen in the life of the role, then they are indulging themselves as actors, acting without rooting the role in truth and *experiencing*. Stanislavski's strict views on this indicate how he prioritised the text over the actor and thought the actor should show respect for the play they are working on.

Stanislavski's emphasis on the *through-line* was part of the reason why, when the Moscow Art Theatre toured to America for the first time, the acting was recognised as achieving a standard of ensemble acting that had not been witnessed before. Previously, actors had often conceptualised their roles as having dramatic moments that they worked towards. But with the Moscow Art Theatre,

> Their interactions seemed fresh and startling, not elaborately pre-planned or carefully plotted. The actors' feelings and thoughts arose sequentially moment by moment, rather than in conscious dramatic flares, followed by long 'dead' spots in the action. And because of their inner preparations, finer and more detailed emotions registered on the faces of Stanislavsky's performers.
>
> (Gordon 2010: 9–10)

The reason Stanislavski placed so much emphasis on the work of the imagination and recreating what the author has imagined is so that the actor can develop the *through-line*, including the character's back history. He wrote that an actor playing a role such as Salieri in *Mozart and Salieri* should create not only the fragment of the character's life that the writer has provided, which we see onstage, but also his entire past that is merely hinted at by a word here and there. He creates using his own feelings, memories, his own body, so that when the character is recalling the past, the actor has images that he or she has created to recall (Stanislavski 2010: 96–97).

Alfreds defines the *through-line*: 'It is the character's essential plot-drive through the play. In the Aristotelian sense, this is what gives the drama its cohesion – the character's pursuit of an all-encompassing goal, which they may (comedy) or may not (tragedy) achieve' (2007: 56). It informs every scene the character appears in and therefore each *task*: 'The through-line both generates plot and functions in response to the circumstances of the plot' (2007: 56). In plays that are neither tragedies nor comedies, the *through-line* remains important. Olga and Irina in *Three Sisters* do not achieve their goal of going to Moscow and it is questionable whether it is really what they want to do, and whether life in Moscow would make their lives fulfilling, but their thoughts and desires in relation to the goal form part of the *through-line* for each of them.

Character is defined by *tasks* and the *supertask*, and the *through-line* defines the plot. The *through-line* of the role must be carried out in relation to the *supertask* of the play or the character. So, if you define Tom's *supertask* in *The Glass Menagerie* as 'to escape … ' then his *through-line*, his mental images and actions, all have that aim in view: the images the actor has of the factory, the temporary escape found at the movies and in drinking or writing his poetry. Tom's *supertask* conflicts with Amanda's; hers could be 'to create a secure future for her children'. The *counter-action*, the clash between the characters' *supertasks*, drives the plot. Amanda recognises that Tom wants to leave and finds his application to join the merchant navy. She tells him that he can leave so long as he finds a 'gentleman caller' to secure Laura's future. He does in fact escape from St Louis and his family, fulfilling his *supertask*, but the *counter-action* with the other characters means that he never truly escapes. Laura is always in his mind. Tom describes how he catches sight of the coloured glass of perfume bottles in a shop window at night: 'Then all at once my sister touches my shoulder. I turn around and look into her eyes. Oh Laura, Laura, I tried to leave you behind me, but I am more faithful than I intended to be!' (Williams 2009: 86, Scene 7).

In *Death of a Salesman*, the essential plot drive through the play is Willy's *through-line* – the series of actions that lead to his suicide. Willy has worked as a salesman all his life, subscribing to the idea that success for individuals in a capitalist society is represented by accumulating wealth. His brother Ben was a success in those terms, and became rich. In those terms Willy is a failure and is in conflict in the play, still attempting to present himself as a successful businessman, while increasingly unable to carry out his work. He loses his job and, realising that some good can come from his life if he dies as he can leave the insurance money to Biff, he commits suicide. The events of the play lead to this conclusion and his *supertask* can be viewed in this way.

Miller writes, 'I think the tragic feeling is evoked in us when we are in the presence of a character who is ready to lay down his life, if need be, to secure one thing – his sense of personal dignity. From Orestes to Hamlet, Medea to Macbeth, the underlying struggle is that of the individual attempting to gain his "rightful" position in his society' (Worthen 2010: 868). Willy's name, 'Loman', suggests an ordinary man, an everyman, unlike the protagonists of classical tragedy, but his *supertask* impels the play as in classical tragedy. The attitudes of the other characters to Willy's search for something to make sense of his life are important. Happy subscribes to the prevailing mythology, declaring to Biff after his father's death, 'All right, boy. I'm gonna show you and everybody else that Willy Loman did not die in vain. He had a good dream. It's the only dream you can have – to come out number one man. He fought it out here and this is where I'm gonna win it for him' (2000: 111, Requiem, lines 48–52). Biff rejects this but does not seem to have an alternative set of beliefs to replace it.

LOSING THE *THROUGH-LINE*

Vasilii Osipovich Toporkov, the famous Moscow Art Theatre actor, describes his experience as a young actor when he lost the *through-line*, playing the role of Vanechka in Valentin Kataiev's Soviet play *The Embezzlers* at a point when he had performed in the role many times and considered it polished. Stanislavski took a rehearsal in preparation for a new run of the play. In one scene Toporkov had to run on as Vanechka. Stanislavski stopped the rehearsal and told him he was terrible, and the next four hours were spent working with Toporkov running on, until Stanislavski got what he wanted. At a meeting the next day, Stanislavski explains to Toporkov the difference between what was in the role and what he had made of it. Stanislavski tells him that he had formerly found in the role its *through-line* of action and went along it from event to event, aiming to fulfil his *tasks*. However, he became used to a reaction from the audience to particular successful moments. Then Toporkov began to think about those moments, 'seized them' and in performance

> began to underline them. You grew fond of them, their intonations, their mise en scènes, and ignored all the rest; you waited with impatience for those moments where you won cheap laurels, and, of course, the

> role degenerated, it fell apart, lost its wholeness, its purpose. Earlier it seemed to you that you were playing insipidly.
>
> (Toporkov 1998: 69)

Stanislavski advises Toporkov that, though he might have thought that something was lacking in his earlier performances, he was then playing truthfully. He should have fixed the truthful moments of the role and strengthened the *through-line* of action of the role instead of chasing the audience's reaction to different moments. The actor needs to

> Regard the role as one entity. Let the audience follow the development of the logic of your conflict, interest them in your fate, so that not taking their eyes off you, they follow you fearing not only to applaud but to make even the smallest movement which could hinder them from observing all the subtlety of your behavior. This is the playing of an artist; it does not entertain, it reaches deeply into the heart of the audience.
>
> (Toporkov 1998: 70)

In this way, the actor is a channel for the work; they must set aside ego in playing the role and keep a *sense of the whole*, and the way to work on this is by keeping to the *through-line* of the character. The right *tasks* for the character and the *through-line* take time to develop. Working through the play bit by bit, using tools of analysis and evaluation, the actor gradually clarifies for himself the whole line of his behaviour, of his logic during the entire course of the play. Once the role is defined, the line 'starts for the actor far in advance of the beginning of the play; it finishes for him long after its end. It must not be interrupted in the moments of his absence from the stage. Its embodiment must be accurate, clear and completely truthful' (Toporkov 1998: 215). *Through-lines* can be changed or adjusted as the work develops.

EXERCISE: BODILESS REHEARSAL

This is the process of rehearsing scenes, by oneself, in the imagination.

Sit comfortably and think through the *through-line* of a role. You don't need to include all the dialogue. Thinking through the whole role in a play might take 10–15 minutes. Notice what stands out to you and repeat this throughout the rehearsal process, noting what is different each time.

SUBTEXT AND *THROUGH-LINE*

> What we call Throughline in action, we call Subtext in speech.
>
> (Stanislavski 2008b: 402)

The *through-line* has to be considered with the *subtext*, what is going on 'below' the text, behind the dialogue, what the characters are thinking, which may be quite different from what they are saying. If you cook a meal that doesn't turn out well and your friend compliments you on giving him the best meal he has had in ages, the *subtext* is joking or being sarcastic. How he says what he says makes the meaning clear, not the words themselves, and defines something of his relationship to you. The meaning of a work of art lies in its *subtext*. Without it words are ineffectual onstage (Stanislavski 2008b: 403). If you are gabbling the words, speaking mechanically, there is no *subtext*. The *subtext* justifies the dialogue and brings the words to life. It can be related to irony in a play: in Scene 4 of *The Glass Menagerie* Amanda makes Tom promise he will never be a drunkard. He '*turns to her grinning*', and makes the promise, the irony and the *subtext* being that he came home drunk only a few hours earlier, unknown to Amanda (Williams 2009: 27, Scene 4, lines 87–92).

There is a complex *subtext* to Willy's response in *Death of a Salesman* when he sees Linda darning stockings. He takes them away from her angrily, saying, 'I won't have you mending stockings in this house! Now throw them out!' (Miller 2000: 31). The silk stockings acquire a metaphorical significance, as Willy has given new stockings to his lover, while his wife has to mend her old ones. The next stage direction is 'Linda puts the stockings in her pocket'. The actions performed with the stockings tell the story of the relationship, of Willy's feelings for Linda, his guilt and Linda's devotion to him and acceptance of his behaviour. She is the one to take practical steps, mending and preserving the stockings, while he has the grand but impossible idea that his wife should not have to mend stockings. Linda's *through-line* involves continual making do and mending – in Act 1 she is mending Willy's jacket (Miller 2000: 42) in her continued care for her husband.

In staging a play, the writer supplies the words, and the actor must supply the *subtext*.

The actor can explore this by asking, as the character, 'what is on my mind?' Often in life, we are forming thoughts that we do not speak aloud. Stanislavski wrote, 'Only when the whole line of the Subtext runs through our feelings, like an underground spring, can we create the Throughaction of the character and the play. This is effected not only through physical movement but through speech. You can take action not only with your body but with sounds and words as well' (2008b: 402). When you have developed a series of mental images of what the character is thinking in the play, it becomes easier to maintain the line of the *subtext* and the *through-action*. When we observe our mental images we are thinking about the *subtext* of the role, stimulating the *emotion memory*, and we can therefore *experience* it (Stanislavski 2008b: 410). This is similar to using physical actions to stimulate *emotion memory*; actions performed truthfully can be a *lure* for feelings and experiences. Now mental images are a *lure* for feelings and experiences in words and speech.

The following example of Chekhovian *subtext* is from Act 4 of *The Cherry Orchard*. Lyubov Andreyevna Ranevskaya has suggested on various occasions that Lopakhin, a former serf on the estate and wealthy businessman, and Varya, her adopted daughter who works as the housekeeper, marry each other, but he seems unable to propose. She gets others to leave the room so that she can suggest to Lopakhin again that he proposes to Varya. This will be the last opportunity before the characters all go their separate ways. He says he is prepared to marry Varya. Lyubov finds Varya and sends her into the room. We know from the stage direction '*Behind the door a stifled laugh, whispering, finally* VARYA *enters*' (Chekhov 2005: 368) that she is expecting Lopakhin to propose. She enters and begins to look at the luggage. Lopakhin says nothing so she continues to pretend she is looking for something in the baggage. Lopakhin asks her about her plans to go to the Ragulins', where she has an engagement as housekeeper, and talks about his plans to go to Kharkov. He says 'So ends life in this house' and she reiterates this. He then starts talking about the weather and how cold it is, there are 'three degrees of frost'. The scene ends as someone calls him from outside the door and he leaves as quickly as he can (Chekhov 2005: 368–69).

The dialogue is simple in some ways, typical Chekhovian chit-chat with poetic resonances. There is a pregnant pause on the line 'So ends life in this house'. But the actors must *experience* the inner turmoil of the characters, a rich, full, *subtext*. Varya says on more than one occasion that she loves Lopakhin. Marrying him would mean becoming the wife of a millionaire, with status, perhaps sharing her husband's work to build a new Russia where people from serf backgrounds such as he and Varya can enjoy some of the pleasures granted until recently only to the privileged classes. Instead of that, her future is to be a housekeeper. All these thoughts and desires are part of the *subtext* for her words. In the event, Lopakhin cannot bring himself to propose and the actor must find the *subtext* of what he does not say. Perhaps Lopakhin is afraid of committing himself or does not want to marry someone he is fond of but does not love. Perhaps his inability to propose is rooted in an unconscious desire to resist Lyubov's attempts to arrange his marriage, which was the prerogative of the gentry until Lopakhin's generation were freed from serfdom. His love and affection for Lyubov may also be a factor in the *subtext*. Characters may have *subtext* that is subconscious, of which they are not aware themselves.

The *subtext* informs the physical actions and the way the words are spoken; the words do not, in fact, indicate what is going on for Lopakhin and Varya in this fraught situation.

As British actress Harriet Walter writes,

> A man burns with desire for a woman in the room. He cannot declare it so he reads a book instead. If she must not see his love, then to be truly 'life-like' the actor playing the man must not give it away to us. To signal it to the audience would be to break it away to us. But we do not show our feelings only consciously ... our subconscious can betray us and Stanislavski made his actors think about these physical betrayals. Maybe the lover caresses the back of his book as he blindly stares at the pages, thinking only of stroking his loved one's hair.
>
> (1999: 158)

EXERCISES: *THROUGH-LINE* AND *SUBTEXT*

1. Take a small section of text and identify the physical actions. For example, the first part of *Death of a Salesman*:

    Willy arrives home with his sample cases, comes into the kitchen and puts the cases down. He closes the door then

> goes into the living room. In the meantime, Linda stirs in bed then gets up and puts on a dressing gown, listening. She calls him and he comes into the bedroom. He sits on the bed beside her and they converse. She takes off his shoes. Willy relates what happened when he was driving and presses two fingers against his eyes (Miller 2000: 7).

Work on the *tasks* and physical actions for this scene to get them precise, then identify the *through-line* of what the characters are thinking. Keep in mind Willy's *supertask*, note the lines in the text about his distracted thoughts, and consider Linda's anxiety and care for him.

2. In Scene 4 of *The Glass Menagerie*, after a quarrel the evening before, Amanda has said that she will not speak to Tom until he apologises. The *subtext* for this *bit*, set in the morning, is the characters' thoughts and *tasks* in relation to the quarrel of the previous evening. Initial *tasks* might be: Amanda wants to get Tom to apologise by not speaking to him, Laura wants to persuade Tom to apologise, Tom perhaps wants to get out of the situation. They are enacting a ritual of family behaviour.

   Look carefully at the stage directions and identify the physical actions:

   > As Tom comes listlessly for his coffee, she turns her back to him and stands rigidly facing the window ... Tom glances sheepishly but sullenly at her averted figure and slumps at the table. The coffee is scalding hot; he sips it and gasps and spits it back in the cup. At his gasp, Amanda catches her breath and half turns. Then she catches herself and turns back to the window. Tom blows on his coffee, glancing sideways at his mother. She clears her throat. Tom clears his. He starts to rise, sinks back down again, scratches his head, clears his throat again. Amanda coughs. Tom raises his cup in both hands to blow on it, his eyes staring over the rim of his cup at his mother for several moments. Then he slowly sets the cup down and awkwardly and hesitantly rises from the chair.

   Amanda's response to Tom's apology indicates more of the *subtext*: she 'draws a quick shuddering breath. Her face works grotesquely. She breaks into childlike tears' (Williams 2009: 27, Scene 4, stage directions).

Identify specific thoughts that are flashing into the characters' heads in this scene.

3. Explore, by means of *active analysis*, each of the characters in relation to their own *subtexts* and the *subtext* of *The Glass Menagerie* in Scene 1. We know more about Tom's thoughts from the text, as he is the narrator, whereas identifying the *subtext* for Amanda and Laura will need more of your imaginative resources.
4. In Scene 4 of *The Glass Menagerie*, Laura falls on the fire escape. By means of *active analysis* (see Chapter 3, pp. 81–84), explore the *subtext* for Laura's fall (Williams 2009: 26, Scene 4, lines 65–69). She has been sent out of the way so that Amanda can speak to Tom about Laura and ask him to find a gentleman caller for her; she is rushing because her mother is shouting at her; she is dreading the expression on the storekeeper Mr. Garfinkel's face when she has to ask for the butter on account when the family already have an unpaid bill. What is Laura thinking and what makes her fall? How does the *subtext* for Laura as regards the fire escape differ from the *subtext* of the play: what significance does the fire escape have for Laura? Try the exit and fall with a variety of *tasks* for Laura.

COMMUNICATION

In Russian, the word for 'communication', *obshchenie*, also means 'communion', that is, it can have a spiritual (though not necessarily religious) connotation. For Stanislavski, art has a spiritual purpose in enabling communication between people about the important aspects of human experience. For the performers to communicate fully with the audience they have to be communicating with each other and, as he put it, in communication with themselves. How the actor communicates is not just through speaking or performing actions which the audience listens to and watches, but also through *experiencing*. If the actor is truly *experiencing*, the *subtext* of the role and the play as a whole and its wider meaning will be communicated to the audience.

Communication and attention are interlinked and, as with attention, the problem with communication onstage is the actor's usual human weaknesses. Stanislavski notes, 'You can look, see and understand what's happening, but you can also look, see and understandnothing'. The actor's problem is, 'when he goes onstage he naturally carries with him his thoughts, personal feelings, his ideas from the real world. His own humdrum, daily life is still there, and takes the first opportunity to slip into the character he is experiencing' (2008b: 231–32).

Often an actor will only give himself wholeheartedly to the role when it 'takes him over'. Then he *fuses* or '*merges* with the character and undergoes a creative transformation'. But if the actor is distracted, he is once again caught up in his own personal life, which carries him away beyond the footlights, outside the theatre. Maybe your tooth hurts and you are longing for the painkillers that are in the dressing room. Maybe you, the actor, have had a row that morning with your partner and part of you wishes to be in contact with him or her, to carry on the row or apologise. In this situation the actor will convey the role externally, mechanically, relying on habit. But though the actor may be able to carry on with the habitual line of the role, these distractions break the lifeline, the *through-line*, of the character and break communication. What happens at this point is that 'the gaps are then filled in by details from the actor's personal life, which have nothing to do with the role he is playing' (2008b: 232).

The *through-line* is an unbroken line of attention. To emphasise the intensity of attention and communication that is needed Stanislavski uses a concept he borrows from Ernest Wood's (1999) book on communication and suggests that the actor has to have a *grip* on what is going on that is like a bull-dog sinking its teeth into something. *Grip* is necessary onstage

> in the eyes, the ears, in all five sense organs. If you are listening, then listen and hear. If you are smelling, then smell. If you are looking, then look and see, don't let your eyes slide over the object without latching on to it, just visually licking it. You must, so to speak, sink your teeth into the object.
>
> (Stanislavski 2008b: 251)

The actor must understand how to do this: to really work at communicating without trying, without tension. Instead of tensing, what is required is intensity of communication, which is different from communication in everyday life precisely because it is continually intense. This is the nature of theatre, which is entirely based on the relationships among the characters. The relationships are concentrated into the brief timespan of a play and are powerful because of that.

Stanislavski defines three kinds of communication: direct communication with object and indirectly with audience, self-communication, and communication with an imaginary object (2008b: 242). What he means by self-communication is that the actor must constantly be aware of what is going on; the *through-line* of attention must not be broken. Michael Chekhov explains this in a useful way with the concept of the actor as 'receiver'. The actor 'can receive his surroundings specifically or in general as required by the play. He can also receive the atmosphere in which he finds himself, or he can receive things or events' (2004: 19). The actor should be aware of what he is receiving from his stage partners, dealing with the actuality of the person he is onstage with at that moment, the atmosphere of the play which is beginning to be created and the events as they take place onstage. Constancy of communication with the other actors is essential. Mike Alfreds refers to the actors moving the play forward through 'seamless active contact with their partners' (2007: 65). This is achieved by really making eye contact with the other actors, not avoiding this or doing it in a cursory way (Stanislavski 2008b: 234) and by ensuring that when you speak as the character, you are wanting to speak your thoughts to your fellow actors as if for the first time, though you may have said the lines many times before. They in return are working on 'receiving', really listening to what you are saying and paying attention to what you are doing. This isn't always easy, but it is essential. 'To play actions truthfully, actors have to be in genuine contact with one another. They must truly affect each other, not merely as character to character *but as actor to actor* – no polite pretence at contact. Actors have to have the courage to engage with one another' (Alfreds 2007: 67–68).

As an example of communication with imaginary objects, Stanislavski refers to the ghost of Hamlet's father (2008b: 236). Similarly, actors playing the characters in *The Glass Menagerie* (except Jim O'Connor) are in communication with the father. Tom even introduces him as a character in the play. 'There is a fifth character in the play who doesn't appear except in this larger-than-life-size photograph over the mantel. This is our father who left us a long time ago' (Williams 2009: 5, Scene 1). It is clear later in the text that Laura and Amanda continue to think about him, to communicate with him, as Stanislavski would say, when Laura plays the phonograph records that belonged to her father on the Victrola. Also, Amanda turns to the photograph in Scene 2, when she is urging Laura to develop charm and vivacity to 'make up for' her disability and says, 'One thing your father had plenty of – was charm!', indicating, as happens on more than this occasion, that he still features strongly in her thoughts (Williams 2009: 16). Through the imaginative work they do, the actors playing Laura and Amanda should have a shared image of the father, though Laura's nostalgic and probably romanticised thoughts about her father and the mixed emotions of loss, hurt and the attraction that Amanda always had for him may involve thoughts of a different kind.

In *Death of Salesman*, Willy is often in communication with Biff or Ben, though these characters may not be in the scene.

If the actors are really communicating with each other, and with imaginary objects, this truthful contact will communicate itself indirectly to the audience. The audience becomes involved in the characters' words and actions involuntarily, 'caught up in other people's experiences' (Stanislavski 2008b: 232). If the communication is unbroken, the actors will be able to maintain a *grip* on a large audience (2008b: 232–33).

Stanislavski used the idea of *prana rays* as a way to help the actor achieve the level of communication onstage that he considered necessary. Facial expressions, movement and vocal tone are the normal means of creating character interaction outside the overt meanings of the dialogue, but the most intense form of communication is the radiation of *prana rays* (Gordon 1987: 233). This was an idea he got from his study of yoga, where *prana* is the word for 'life force', and the idea of people radiating signals has a basis in the psychology he read. *Sending rays out* and *receiving rays* is what conveys *experiencing*, it is what grips and *infects* an audience (Stanislavski 2008b: 245–51). Michael Chekhov adopted and used the idea of radiating in his work. He emphasises that radiating is both giving and receiving: 'To radiate on the stage means *to give*, to send out. Its counterpart is *to receive*. True acting is a constant exchange of the two' (2004: 19). You can think of the rays as a current flowing from your eyes, fingertips, skin. This helps the actor to understand that communication takes place with the whole of themselves: with the eyes, face, movements of hands and fingers and body (Stanislavski 2008b: 261).

Another important aspect of Stanislavski's view of communication is *orientation*. The point of *orientation* is where you establish the object of your communication. As he pointed out, when we go into a room we observe the people in it and try to understand what is going on. We don't 'make an entrance' unless there is a particular reason for doing so. If you are at home and your family are all in the kitchen, you walk into the kitchen, see what is going on and judge the situation. If there is a heated argument going on you might choose not it interrupt immediately, but if everyone looks at you and someone asks how your audition has gone today you would respond to that. 'Using transmitting and receiving, we, as subject, on our arrival, establish contact with the object we have selected' (Stanislavski 2008b: 623). Animals do the same thing: a dog comes into a room, sniffs and looks to find its master or mistress, then starts to communicate with him or her. So an actor should not 'make an entrance' thinking about the impression they are making on an audience – the 'object' of the stock-in-trade actor – or just walk on and deliver lines without regard for the other actors as they are at that moment.

Stanislavski identified five phases in the process of communicating (2008b: 624–25): (1) find your bearings and select an object of attention (usually another person), (2) get their attention, (3) make contact with them ('delving into his/her mind'), (4) create images and make one's partner see them as if with their own eyes by what one says and how one says it, *radiating* and *adaptations*, (5) respond to their response. He emphasised that the moment of *orientation*, before the dialogue begins, is a very interesting moment and should not be rushed (Toporkov 1998: 195, 123–24). For example, when Jim enters in Scene 6 in *The Glass Menagerie*, the actor needs a moment, as Jim, to orientate himself, as he steps inside the door, to the fact that Tom has a sister, which he did not know (Williams 2009: 52). If the first thing you do when you step onstage is to give your attention, in the here and now, to specific objects and what is going on onstage as a whole then you will be taking action, rather than 'acting', and opening up the possibility of *experiencing*. Mental, invisible communication is essential and the real sign of dynamism, whereas many people think that it is visible movements, which can be a sign of 'acting' (Stanislavski 2008b: 239).

In summary, the actor has to give full attention to communication with a range of objects when performing and, in doing so, will draw the audience in. This is an ideal and all actors will admit to finding it a challenge to maintain this level of attention. But Stanislavski emphasised that this should always be the actor's aim.

EXERCISES: COMMUNICATION

1. Contact. Work with a partner on improvisations involving

   a) a quarrel
   b) a declaration of love
   c) planning a party

   Assess how well you communicated with your partner – was it as in life, or did it seem like 'acting'?
2. *The Glass Menagerie*. Using Appendix 1, play Scene 1 with *tasks*: Laura scarcely speaks but what is she attempting to communicate or not communicate to her mother and brother? Is she in communication with anyone/anything else?

   Perform improvisations, having determined the *given circumstances*. For example, Tom walks home from the factory where he works through the alleys in order to appear at the beginning of Scene 4. You can use the description of the alleyways and the tenements at the beginning of the play along with your research to set the scene in your imagination. With what or whom is Tom in communication?
3. *Death of a Salesman*. Similarly, consider with whom or what Willy is in communication on his arrival home – the physical actions are detailed in the text.
4. Perform the same scenes including the idea of radiating.

ADAPTATIONS

Another element of the *system* is *adaptation*, also translated as 'adjustments'. Stanislavski defines *adaptations* as ways that people use their ingenuity to adjust their behaviour in order to influence their stage partners (2008b: 259); the devices an actor might use to adapt to working with other actors in a particular scene at a particular time in order to ensure full communication or simply to perform an action appropriately in the *given circumstances*. A basic example of an *adaptation* is where an action such as closing the door can be performed for different reasons: to keep out a draft, or to keep out a persistent door-to-door salesman. The actor adapts the way the action is performed in the particular *given circumstances*. A short phrase can be said in a multitude of different ways. 'It is possible to say, "How wonderfully this actor is playing!" with admiration, with indignation, with contempt, with rapture … even with tender emotion' (Toporkov 1998: 193).

In *An Actor's Work*, Tortsov's students work on the idea of *adaptations* through improvisation. Their *task* is to find a convincing reason why they should be able to get out of the class. Vanya finds the right *adaptation* for the *given circumstances*. His audience are convinced by his performance and believe that he has accidentally hurt his leg during his improvisation, until he starts to laugh (Stanislavski 2008b: 259). This improvisatory quality in acting should be taken into the rehearsal and performance processes. The same *tasks* and actions can be played over and over again with different *adaptations*, however minute, resulting in spontaneity in performance. But if an actor tries to define and pin down an *adaptation*, a cliché results. If an actor defines a *task*, *experiencing* results. What this means is that the actor must come onstage to perform a *task* but exactly how they perform it must be thought through in the moment, not in advance. Thinking in this way, not predetermining exactly what is going to happen onstage, stimulates *experiencing* and means that you are prepared to communicate fully with your stage partners (Stanislavski 2008b: 293). So *adaptation* is a very important technique in communication.

Adaptations enable you to convey nuances of feeling and reveal new interpretations of well-known passages, bringing out hidden meanings (Stanislavski 2008b: 263–64). You may have the problem, in repeating a role, when a scene that has worked goes stale and a moment where you and your fellow actor have truly communicated in the past has stopped working. For example, a scene where you raise your hand to strike another actor starts to become routine; you have ceased to 'believe' that you are going to hit them and the other actor has ceased to 'believe' that they are going to be hit. If you work at an *adaptation*, a new way of thinking about the action, you will be able to regain spontaneity. Moments like this could occur in *The Glass Menagerie*: in Scene 2, after the confrontation with Laura about Rubicam's Business College, Amanda thinks of another way out of her daughter's plight and decides she will get married to some nice man:

> (*She gets up with a spark of revival.*) Sister, that's what you'll do!
> (*Laura utters a startled, doubtful laugh. She reaches quickly for a piece of glass*).
>
> (Williams 2009: 16)

The actor has to find ways to adapt the action 'getting up with a spark of revival' in order to communicate to the actor playing Laura what is needed for her to respond in a 'startled, doubtful' way.

HERE, TODAY, NOW

Another idea that Stanislavski gives the actor in order to work on spontaneity, to achieve *experiencing*, is *here, today, now*. He poses the question: 'Can the actor ask himself and answer truthfully – am I taking action genuinely, productively and towards a purpose? What would I do if I were in given circumstances analogous to the role here, today, now?' (Stanislavskii 1955: 411–12, 445). This is a way to help the actor who struggles with keeping the *through-line* going while offstage. They think about

> what they would do *that day* if they found themselves in the situation the character is in. The actor must answer that question and others, in every show. That's the reason why an actor comes to the theatre to perform. If the actor leaves the theatre without having answered the questions he has to ask on that day, he has not done what he should.
>
> (2008b: 289)

This was a technique Stanislavski introduced while working with the Moscow Art Theatre troupe on Ivanov's *The Armoured Train No. 14–69* in 1927. The cast were struggling with a pro-revolutionary play that required the actors in some scenes to show an aggression alien to many of them as people. He added new *given circumstances* appropriate to the time and day, for the actors by appearing as an important person from the Soviet government who had come to investigate a rumour that the Art Theatre actors were refusing to stage the play. The suggestion that they had to demonstrate their loyalty to the Soviet state was enough for the actors to overcome their block to the scene (Benedetti 1999: 313).

FURTHER READING

Alfreds, M. (2007) *Different Every Night – Freeing the Actor*, London: Nick Hern Books, pp. 183–95.

Chekhov, M. (2004) *To the Actor on the Technique of Acting*, London: Routledge, Chapter 2, 'Images and the Incorporation of Images'.

Gordon, M. (1987) *The Stanislavski Technique: Russia*, New York: Applause Theatre Books, pp. 69–70.

Mitchell, K. (2009) *The Director's Craft: A Handbook for the Theatre*, Abingdon, Routledge. How to use visualisation exercises, p. 165.

Stanislavski, K. (2008) *An Actor's Work*, London: Routledge. See imagination exercises, p. 655, and exercises on contact, pp. 660–61.

5

EMBODIMENT OF THE ROLE

In the last two chapters, we've discussed how to use the *system* to develop the inner content of the role, *experiencing*. In this chapter, we will turn our attention to the outer characterisation of the role, ways of developing the role by working on this and, finally, how the two aspects work together as a whole. The second year of the training undergone by the Moscow Art Theatre students in *An Actor's Work* is introduced to them as the 'transition to physical embodiment' (Stanislavski 2008b: 351–54). The Russian word for this, *voploshchenie*, is translated as 'embodiment' or 'incarnation' or 'outer characterisation'. Stanislavski thought training was necessary for 'outer work' and, in his view, systematic daily exercise and vocal training were essential for the actor throughout their whole career.

Therefore, in order to train the body and voice, in *An Actor's Work, Part 2*, the students engage in various forms of physical education, such as gymnastics, acrobatics and dance, with the aim of developing the expressiveness of the body. They have voice and speech training, which includes singing. Topics for other classes include physical characteristics (or characterisation), *the finishing touches*, the *perspective* of the actor and the role, *tempo-rhythm, logic and consistency* and the *creative state*. These extend and develop understanding of the *system*. The acting teacher in the book, Tortsov, also lectures on ethics and discipline and charisma or stage charm, technique and professionalism.

The overall aim of the second year's work is to assist the actor in the third and fourth phases of work on a role identified in Chapter 3: after *getting to know* the role and *experiencing* it, the actor must *embody* it and *make it effective*. *Embodiment* is an extension of the work done on *experiencing*, not something distinct from it. Mike Alfreds expresses it this way:

> By *embodiment* I mean that the actors and the text take total possession of each other and become one. Think of it like this: at the start of rehearsal you have the text; at the end of rehearsal you have the text *embodied*.
>
> (2007: 142)

Sometimes the way Stanislavski writes implies that these internal and external processes of acting, *experiencing* and *embodiment*, are separable in some way, but this cannot be true in practice. He makes it clear in other places that the understanding of the play that comes from analysis of it, the actor's *experiencing* and the *embodiment* of the role are completely interlinked. One of his actors explains:

> As for outer characteristics, they appear as a result of a deep penetration into the inner world of the character. These special outer characteristics will be more easily found by the actor when the logical line of the behavior of the character has been assimilated, has become his own. The outer characterization completes the work of the actor.
>
> (Toporkov 1998: 202–3)

These *outer characteristics* may be the character's accent, or a particular vocal or physical mannerism, and so on. It can happen that the external characteristics may not be the last thing to emerge in developing a role; sometimes a gesture or vocal characteristic that emerges serendipitously in rehearsal may be a spur to the imagination, enabling *experiencing* to take place, as we will see.

Making the role effective means putting *the finishing touches* to a role and then maintaining it truthfully in performance. Stanislavski's ideal actor works on themselves continuously: 'It's not enough just *to know* the "system". You must be *able to use it*. For that you need daily training and drill throughout your whole acting career' (2008b: 347–48). Stanislavski viewed systematic daily exercise and vocal training as essential to the actor and experimented with a variety of movement and exercise forms in order to refine his ideas about the best methods for the actor. Similarly, a role is never finished but must always be kept alive, by the actor's daily work and by thinking about it afresh.

Using all the elements of the *system* enables the actor to *fuse* or *merge* with the role. All this adds up to the *creative state* in performance, the right to be onstage, also known as *I am being*.

TRAINING: PHYSICAL EDUCATION

Stanislavski experimented with a number of physical education and physical culture methods in order to develop expressiveness of the body. These included acrobatics, dance, *plastique* (developing expressiveness in movement) and Swiss music educator Émile Jaques-Dalcroze's rhythmic gymnastics. He was never fully satisfied with any system. He identified a number of problems with physical training. In relation to ballet, he asked 'Does a dramatic actor need these external, expressive actions which have no content?' (2008b: 364).

He was looking for a solution to the fundamental problem:

> People don't know how to use the equipment nature has given them. They can't even keep it in good condition or develop it. Slack muscles, a distorted frame, poor breathing are common occurrences in life. These are all the result of our inability to educate and develop our physical apparatus. No wonder then if the work nature assigns it is performed in an unsatisfactory way.
>
> (Stanislavski 2008b: 356)

Stanislavski's description of himself as a youth is that he was 'tall, clumsy, graceless and mispronounced many letters'. He therefore set himself a programme of work to train his body in front of a mirror. He would return in the evening from his office work as director of the Russian Musical Society and work, it is claimed, from 7 p.m. until 3 or 4 a.m. He had some success, he writes, in developing expressiveness, in getting to understand his body (2008a: 68).

He noted that often when people step onstage they begin to move in a mannered way:

> Is there a special way of walking for the stage which is not the way we walk in ordinary life? Indeed it is not as in life precisely because none of us walks properly, whereas *walking onstage should be as nature intended in accordance with all her laws* ... Let's talk about this and the possibilities of developing it, so that we can rid the stage once and for all of that grand, actorish, theatrical way of walking which is so common in the theatre at the present time.
>
> In other words, start learning to walk onstage from scratch, just as we do in life.
>
> (Stanislavski 2008b: 372)

He saw that people do not stand or move in the best way possible and so the main purpose of physical education for Stanislavski was for the actor to learn how to control movement, so that it was efficient and purposeful. He saw it as necessary for the actor to study how to do so in accordance with the principles of anatomy and physiology. He wanted to cultivate the actor's voice and body on the basis of nature. Kostya, his fictional student, notes, 'As a result of paying this increased attention to our movement we came, through our conscious mind, to appreciate all the subtlety and complexity of the mechanism of the leg' (2008b: 378). Stanislavski did not have access to all the scientific information we have today and did not have access to the Alexander Technique, which would have supplied answers for him. This was originated by F.M. Alexander (1869–1955), who developed problems with his voice when he was performing. After he lost his voice during an important show, he worked to train himself using mirrors (as Stanislavski also did) so that he could stand, move and speak with good 'use', without doing the harmful things he had done which brought about his loss of voice. The Technique enables the actor, when practised properly, to attain flexibility and command of vocal mechanisms and expressiveness, in order to realise the character fully.

Tortsov also talks about the problem of meaningless movement onstage, the danger of repetitive, false gesturing, gesturing for gesturing's sake. He warns the actor that the embodiment of the character can go wrong, resulting in artificiality in the characterisation. 'While really typical *movements and actions* bind actors more closely to a role, *gestures and gesticulation* distance them from it.' Economy of movement is emphasised: 'Don't make gestures or unnecessary movements. Set yourself the task of conveying the score of a role with the minimum of movement and no gestures at all' (2008b: 538–39). Stanislavski notes that it can take months, years even, to gain *technical control.*

VOICE AND SPEECH

> Voice, voice and still more voice!
>
> (Stanislavski 2008b: 381)

Stanislavski stated that he discovered in 1915, at the age of 52, that he had not really 'mastered the art of speaking on stage, that his voice did not express properly his sincere inner feelings' (2008a: 314–15). He was a pioneer of voice training, deciding that it was as necessary for the actor as for the singer. He identified a number of vocal problems: not being 'on voice', either temporarily or permanently, so that vocal expression is poor, having a good voice but no strength in it so the actor cannot be heard at the back of the auditorium (these actors are in danger of vocal strain as they tend to 'push' the voice), voices which are limited in range in some ways or have an unpleasant timbre. There may be some medical reason for the problem but often the problem results from 'tightness and tension, pushing, faulty breathing and articulation of the lips' (Stanislavski 2008b: 382). The actor needs their maximum vocal range onstage and to be able to meet the demand of being onstage, being loud enough to be heard at the back of the auditorium. Stamina is required to maintain this. Stanislavski knew that in seeking vocal power, the actor should not strain. Physical tension does not 'produce power only yelling and shouting, constriction and hoarseness within a limited vocal range' (2008b: 423).

The actor should begin by thinking about how they speak in everyday life. 'Most people speak badly, poorly in daily life but aren't aware of it. We are used to our faults' (Stanislavski 2008b: 400). So it is most important for the actor to work on voice in everyday life and onstage. 'Work on your diction every day, every hour, not for fifteen minutes once a week' (Toporkov 1998: 188–89). Student days are obviously the best time to work on your speech so that you can go onstage fully equipped, and the voice is the most important part of the actor's creative ways and means. Stanislavski was against actors declaiming, using any way of speaking that is particularly theatrical, and asserted that following the laws of speech results in speech onstage that has a natural quality. Stanislavski also thought that actors who speak consistently in a regional accent or in an idiosyncratic way may appear to have a certain charm but, unless the way of speaking the lines of the role arises from the character, it is not a good thing. The actor who speaks well and can vary the way they speak as appropriate to the character will have more charm, in the long run, for the audience (2008b: 382–83, 418).

Again, the Alexander Technique enables the actor to develop a resonant voice and to use it without risk of injury.

When the actor understands the technique for effective voice production without strain they can work on text, developing clear diction, articulation, intonation, pronunciation, varied pitch, use of stress or emphasis and vocal tempo-rhythm. We are used to the way we speak and we hear ourselves differently from the way our speech is received by others. 'We must study it attentively so as to hear ourselves naturally' (Stanislavski 2008b: 389).

PAUSES

> Inflexions and pauses exercise a strong emotional effect on the listener in their own right, irrespective of the words.
>
> (Stanislavski 2008b: 422)

Stanislavski also stressed the importance of pauses. He draws a distinction between what he calls 'logical pauses', which are essentially the pauses indicated by punctuation marks, and 'psychological pauses which are always dynamic and rich in inner content' (2008b: 419). The actor is communicating something and therefore these pauses result from interpretation in a way that logical pauses do not. They reveal the *subtext*. *Psychological pauses* involve the gaze, facial expression, *sending out rays*, hints, scarcely perceptible movements and subconscious means of communication. Much can be conveyed without words. For example, as discussed in Chapter 4, there is a scene in *The Glass Menagerie* where Tom and Amanda are not speaking to each other but there is a great deal going on between them (see Appendix 1 and Williams 2009: 24–27, Scene 4).

EXERCISE: *SUBTEXT*

Go through a section of play text and pay attention to the pauses. Define what the *subtext* is.

Examples from Timberlake Wertenbaker's *Our Country's Good*:

This is a play set in Australia in 1789 in a penal colony where the governor has the idea of the convicts performing in a play, a radical idea in a society where convicts are considered lower than animals.

1. Ralph, the officer directing the play, *The Recruiting Officer*, reads a speech to Dabby and Mary, two of the convicts who are to be in the play. He is reading the part of Justice Balance, the father of Silvia, Mary's character, and is discussing with her the likelihood of her brother, Owen, recovering from illness.

   > Ralph: We have but little reason to expect it. Poor Owen! But the decree is just; I was pleased with the death of my father, because he left me an estate, and now I'm punished with the loss of an heir to inherit mine.
   > *Pause. He laughs a little.*

   Dabby and Mary say nothing as they do not understand the speech out of context. Ralph laughs to demonstrate that the speech is comic and then explains why to them, a little condescendingly. He reads a further line, where Justice Balance says that Silvia will inherit twelve hundred pounds (a huge fortune), then Dabby turns the tables, making a joke of her own.

   > Dabby: Twelve hundred pounds! It must be a comedy.
   > (Wertenbaker 2009: 14, Act 1, Scene 5)

   What is each of the characters thinking in the pause? Play the scene (having determined *bits* and *tasks*) including these thoughts in the *psychological pause*.
2. Towards the end of the play, the company are getting ready for the performance. Sideway (another convict) says that he is going to start a theatre company and will hold auditions tomorrow. Dabby, Duckling, Mary and Liz each say 'Tomorrow', one after another. Then, '*A long silence. (Un ange passe.)*' (Wertenbaker 2009: 86,

Act 2, Scene 11). Literally, this means 'an angel is passing'; the phrase indicates an awkward silence.

Again, what is each of the characters thinking in the pause? Play the scene (having determined *bits* and *tasks*) including these thoughts in the *psychological pause*.

While the actor should study intonation, pausing, stress and so on, Stanislavski always emphasises the need to go deeply into the true meaning of the words (2008b: 449). Antarieva, a student at the Bolshoi Opera Studio, records Stanislavski as saying,

> It is absolutely wrong to do any of the exercises laid down in my system mechanically and unthinkingly. It is absolutely wrong to speak your words to no purpose. You must acquire the habit of putting the greatest possible meaning into every word you utter.
>
> (Stanislavsky 1967: 128)

It is so easy for the actor to begin to say the lines mechanically, after repeating them in rehearsal and performing them frequently, and to pretend to be listening as the role goes on, destroying true communication.

ACCENTS

Some people are good at accents and, of course, getting the right accent is important for cadences of text. In *The Glass Menagerie*, Amanda Wingfield's Southern accent is part of her personality and the way she expresses herself. In a play like *Our Country's Good*, the way people speak and the language of the play in general are important on many levels: Wisehammer is Jewish, Black Caesar is from Madagascar, James Freeman (Ketch) is Irish, Dabby is from Devon, Sideway and Lizzie Morden from London, and therefore they all have different accents. The voice of each of the characters indicates their identity: their class and background and their attitude to life. There are big differences between the way the convicts and the officers speak but also individual differences. Governor Phillip thinks that it is important that the convicts take part in the play as they 'will be speaking a refined, literate language and expressing sentiments of a delicacy they are not used to. It will remind them there is more to life than crime, punishment' (Wertenbaker 2009: 21, Act 1, Scene 6). Lizzie's use of cant, or criminal talk, when she talks about her past in her monologue, signifies her identification of herself as a criminal (Wertenbaker 2009: 53–54, Act 2, Scene 1) and the transition from this to seeing herself in a different way is signalled by the way she speaks to Governor Phillip:

> Liz: Your Excellency, I will endeavour to speak Mr Farquahar's lines with the elegance and clarity their own worth demands.
>
> (Wertenbaker 2009: 83, Act 2, Scene 10)

Before the play she would not have spoken up for herself, indeed hardly spoken at all, as her experience was that there was no point in doing so as no one listened to her. The way other characters' speech changes is also important. Mary Brennan is at first inaudible, as she is ill at ease and wants to efface herself when Ralph speaks to her (Wertenbaker 2009: 13, Act 1, Scene 5). But she too finds her voice, in actuality and metaphorically, through participation in the production, speaking out in the last scene, giving a note to Arscott about how he should carry her, helping Caesar overcome his stage fright (Wertenbaker 2009: 86–88). The development and work on accents has to be rooted in the understanding of the class and background of the characters and what it means to adopt a new way of speaking. Accents must be *justified*.

OUTER CHARACTERISTICS

The actor may have established the *through-line* of action and the *subtext* for the role, but there remains the question of the outer characteristics: how does the character speak and how does the character move? What gestures or actions might typify the character? In *An Actor's Work*, the drama student Kostya tells Tortsov his concern: that he thinks he understands the process of *experiencing* as developing and fostering how he as the actor should think as the character but he does not fully understand how to *embody* the role. What should he do, how should he speak or walk as the character in order to 'convey the life of the human spirit' of the role (Stanislavski 2008b: 24)? It is not enough to have good ideas about the character's inner experience; this has to be conveyed to the audience by means of the actor's external expression, which illuminates the character's personality and what they are thinking (Stanislavski 2008b: 516).

The *embodiment* of the character may not be effective, if, for example, the actor uses gestures for their own sake, resulting in a mannered, artificial performance. On the other hand, if the actor does not find external characteristics for the character, they may act truthfully, but may be seen as an actor who always 'plays themselves', limiting their range. Stanislavski writes: 'while really typical *movements and actions* [of the character, not the actor] bind actors more closely to a role, *gestures and gesticulation* distance them from it' (2008b: 538). An important aspect of the *system*, therefore, is how it enables the actor to develop appropriate and truthful external characteristics.

Stanislavski himself was a wonderful character actor, who was very skilled in *embodiment*. He emphasised that the art of *embodiment* was not separable from the art of *experiencing* and that his students should not play *feelings*: they must always play *images*. For Russians, the *image* of the character is very important. The word for 'image' (*obraz*) is often translated as 'character', which does not necessarily convey the importance of a clear image of the character having developed in the actor's imagination. The phrase used by Stanislavski translated as 'playing the character' is in Russian *deistvovat' v obraze*, meaning literally to 'take action in the image' (of the character). If you have worked on the image of the character in detail, this will include all aspects of the external expression of the character, not just how the character feels and what they say or do. Toporkov reports that Stanislavski said, 'Of course you cannot act without feeling, but it isn't worthwhile to worry and fret about it. It will come of itself as a result of your concentration on live action in the given circumstances.' The outer characteristics will appear as a result of a deep understanding of the inner world of the character (Toporkov 1998: 202). The actor will find that the more they repeat the so-called line of physical actions, or, rather, the inner impulses to action, the more involuntary movements appear (Stanislavski 2010: 59). These can appear spontaneously when the right inner content has been created. Stanislavski used as an example the character of Stockmann in Ibsen's *An Enemy of the People*: he created the right frame of mind, the thought of the character and then the rapid walk, the body leaning forward, the two fingers jutting forward and other features appeared out of nowhere (2008b: 516).

Often ideas that help create the external image come as the actor is developing the role. Sometimes the ideas seem to occur quite by chance. Stanislavski relates a story of how a mistake in make-up, where half his false moustache was glued on higher than the other, gave him the idea of slyness for a character in Alexander Fedotov's play *The Rouble*. In Pisemski's *A Law unto Themselves*, a play about social injustice in which he acted as a young man, he created the character of a general-in-chief. The image just appeared; he did not know where it came from. 'Technique had pushed me towards the truth and a sense of truth is the finest spur to experiencing, inspiration and creativity' (Stanislavski 2008a: 106). In the role of Paratov in A.N. Ostrovski's *Bride without a Dowry*, he writes that his imagination began to work, 'details began to appear spontaneously, Paratov's little ways, his character traits, for example his military bearing, his dash' (2008a: 107).

In *An Actor's Work*, Kostya relates in detail how he develops the image of 'the critic', a surreal, carping and unpleasant figure, which begins, as in Stanislavski's example of *The Rouble*, with a mistake in make-up. A fully-fledged characterisation appears: Kostya seems to 'know' how to speak and move and how to interact with people as the critic, intuitively. Kostya is delighted because this means he knows what *transformation* and *physical characterisation* are (Stanislavski 2008b: 526). Tortsov similarly develops the character of an Englishman starting with the outer characteristic of shortening his upper lip. Kostya comments, 'There had undoubtedly been a mental change to match the physical appearance and everything that followed from it, because the words he now spoke, as far as we could see, weren't his own, and not in his usual style, although the ideas he expressed were genuine and natural' (Stanislavski 2008b: 519).

Kostya's intuitive creation of the critic comes from something within his own self. It is a 'seed in his psyche out of which a repulsive person could grow' (Stanislavski 2008b: 534); the seed is in his own doubts about himself and his habit of criticising himself too harshly. In this way, characterisation is a kind of *mask* that allows the indirect revelation of personal aspects of ourselves. 'When we are masked we can reveal the most intimate and spicy details about ourselves' (Stanislavski 2008b: 535). Physical transformation is an essential part of this.

Sometimes such intuitive characterisations happen, where inner content and outer expression are found simultaneously; at other times the actor has to keep working. The physicalisation must always be driven by *tasks*. Kostya's *task*, as the critic, though it was not something he planned, was to find fault with everything and everyone he encountered. If you are playing an old woman, for example the nurse in *Romeo and Juliet*, how the character moves and speaks will be very different to how a woman of the twenty-first century would. You may, as the actor, be much younger than the nurse. Miriam Margolyes in Baz Luhrmann's *Romeo and Juliet* portrays her as a character who moves in a bustling way. As an actor, you might experiment with a way of walking, moving about quickly. But the outer image will emerge most successfully from the character's internal life. Find the actor's *tasks* as the character that bring about *experiencing* and what the nurse wants to do to help Juliet: these may bring about outer characteristics of a bustling old woman, or there may be other mannerisms.

The use of costume and props in rehearsal is very helpful in developing the external elements of characterisation, as is rehearsing with the set in the space you will perform in, or whatever is as close as possible to this. Rehearsal clothes are important. Uta Hagen (2008: 71) notes that you can't do Blanche DuBois from Tennessee Williams' *A Streetcar Named Desire*, a play set in the 1940s, in jeans (Blanche is a Southern belle) or St Joan (a saint of the Catholic church, a peasant girl of the fifteenth century who led the French army to victory in the Hundred Years' War) in high heels. Ideally, you need clothing in keeping with the epoch of the play in the rehearsal period and, even if you are a student performing an assessment in blacks, finding a long skirt or a shawl is not difficult if you are playing a female role in a classic play. Wearing tight clothes or a low-cut top will not help you find the outer characteristics.

Nigel Hawthorne, in rehearsing for the role of the king in Alan Bennett's *The Madness of King George*, which opened at the National Theatre in 1991, found that costume was one of the ways he could realise the character's story: George III becomes increasingly mad, but then with treatment begins to recover. Hawthorne wore the clothes that were the trappings of kingship, the regalia, askew. On one occasion he appeared in a very unkingly way, in a nightshirt, bandaged, indicating George's problems as a private person.

> I asked at the very first rehearsal for an assortment of clothes. I said 'I want some slippers and some stockings, and a dressing gown, and a nightshirt and a cap, and something to simulate a uniform and a sash. And as we went from day to day, I'd start to think about what I would be wearing. I'd start off wearing the uniform and then start stripping bits off ... he was sometimes better and sometimes worse and the clothes indicated that. I just had an old cotton wig in rehearsal, but the way he wore the wig was on one side or back to front, and then I'd pick it up and throw it at somebody. All those things were part of the madness that people saw in him. Whether the stockings were wrinkled or whether they were down around his ankles or pulled up tight, and whether his trousers were unbuttoned, all these things indicated very much the way the King was moving.
>
> (Riley 2004: 257–58)

Hawthorne had begun with extensive biographical, political and medical research supporting the imaginative and experimental work he did for the character with the director in rehearsal. The idea for the clothes emerged from his imagination and fed into the character's *experiencing*.

THE FINISHING TOUCHES

Michael Chekhov distinguishes between the character as a whole and the *characterisation*, which can be defined as

> a small, *peculiar feature* of the character ... a typical movement, a characteristic manner of speech, a recurrent habit, a certain way of laughing, walking or wearing a suit, an odd way of holding the hands, or a singular inclination of the head and so forth.
>
> (Chekhov 2004: 83)

These are *finishing touches* that the actor 'bestows on his creation'. It makes the character 'more alive, more human and true'. The audience warm to it and it must be born out of the character as a whole (Chekhov 2004: 83). Chekhov gives examples of an obstinate person, who might have an unconscious habit of slightly shaking his head as though preparing a negative reply. A person who is sly or not quite sincere might acquire the habit of throwing quick glances at the ceiling while speaking or listening. David Suchet as Hercule Poirot in the popular British television series uses a characteristic gesture, where Poirot points upwards with his index finger when he is saying something important, as a *finishing touch*.

EXERCISES: CREATING AN IMAGE

OBSERVATION

Stanislavski often points out the importance of taking time to observe, to draw from oneself, others, life, pictures, books or chance in developing ideas for characters (2008b: 519). Take time to sit in a café and observe people around you; imagine what their lives are like and how you might develop your observations and thoughts in developing a characterisation. Study an image of a person in a picture or a book and, similarly, work on ideas of how the character might speak and move.

CREATING AN IMAGE

Create an external image of a character or characters from a play of your choice, using any descriptions you can find of the way they speak and move. In *Our Country's Good*, for instance, you can use descriptions of the way the convicts hold themselves and move to help you visualise how the difference in status between convicts and officers is expressed externally.

For example, on first meeting Ralph, Mary Brenham is brought on by Dabby 'shrinking', and Sideway, the former pickpocket, steals Ralph's handkerchief, then bows to Ralph and also 'scuttles off' (Wertenbaker 2009: 12, Act 1, Scene 5, stage directions). Major Ross and Captain Campbell, who oppose the play as they view the convicts as irredeemable and treat them sadistically, come to a rehearsal: 'The convicts slink away and sink down, trying to make themselves invisible' (2009: 50, Act 1, Scene 11, stage directions). Dabby and Liz, vying for status in the early period of rehearsals, 'stare at each other, each holding her ground, each ready to pounce' (2009: 16, Act 1, Scene 5, stage directions). Ralph has to get Liz to stand differently, as a 'rich lady' would, when she as Melinda is looking at the character of Silvia 'with a certain assurance' (2009: 47, Act 1, Scene 11).

Work on how a rich lady, as opposed to a convict, might stand.

TEMPO-RHYTHM

Tempo-rhythm is an important way in which the external life of a play is expressed and a useful way to develop insight into the role. In *An Actor's Work*, Tortsov explains the difference between tempo and rhythm using a metronome. You can hear the difference between the rhythm of beats in a bar of music (for example, 3/4 time, which is the rhythm of a waltz, or 4/4 time, which is the rhythm for a piece of marching music) and the tempo or speed of the beats Stanislavski 2008b: 465). It could be a fast or slow waltz or a fast or slow march. In relation to action onstage, we can think of the tempo (or speed or pace) of the external movement and action or speech, and rhythm as the internal state. Internal and external are inextricably bound within the human being so there is one concept: *tempo-rhythm*. External *tempo-rhythm* is visible to the spectator in physical actions, audible in verbal actions, and the internal *tempo-rhythm* is an important element of the *creative state* (Stanislavski 2008b: 463). Maria Knebel used to say that every life situation has its corresponding *tempo-rhythm*. The *tempo-rhythm* of a person changes depending on changes in circumstances and the effect this has on them.

Apparently, Stanislavski had a 'tempo-rhythm machine' for use in rehearsal in the 1930s, an invention of Soviet engineers! 'When MAT performers moved or spoke according to the rhythmic underpinnings of the play, Stanislavsky pressed a button that lit up a blue bulb on an electric board; actions that the old director perceived of as imprecise or out-of-step sparked a red light' (Gordon 2010: 59).

EXERCISE: *TEMPO-RHYTHM*

What is your *tempo-rhythm*?

A *tempo-rhythm* of someone who tends towards nerviness, excitability, panic is different to the *tempo-rhythm* of a calmer, more laid-back individual.

With a partner, agree *given circumstances* and some instructions you are going to give your partner. For example, you are telling your son/daughter what jobs you want them to do around the house while you are away. Perform the same scene first in a rush, because you have to get to the hospital as a relative has had an accident. Then change the situation: you are on your way out to meet a friend, looking forward to it, and you have plenty of time.

How do the two scenarios compare with your own normal *tempo-rhythms*? Do you generally speak slowly, in a measured way, or perhaps you don't talk much at all, or are you a talkative person, who speaks quickly? Does it vary and, if so, in what circumstances?

While the *tempo-rhythm* of a character in a play may vary between scenes and speeches, they may have a characteristic *tempo-rhythm* that is different from yours. In *The Glass Menagerie,* Tom tells Jim of his desire for adventure, for experiences of exotic far-off places and his perception that Americans are simply sitting in a darkened room watching adventure movies while war is approaching. He says, 'But I'm not patient. I don't want to wait till then. I'm tired of the *movies* and I am *about* to *move*!' He adds, 'I'm starting to boil inside. I know I seem dreamy, but inside – well, I'm boiling!' (Williams 2009: 55, Scene 6). In contrast, Laura is 'too exquisitely fragile to move from the shelf' whereas Amanda is more energetic but 'a little woman of great but confused vitality clinging frantically to another time and place' (Williams 2009: xv, The Characters). You can use these ideas about the characters ('boiling inside', 'too fragile to move', 'great but confused vitality') to develop your concept of the characters' *tempo-rhythm*.

The play as a whole has its own *tempo-rhythm*, which can also be discussed as pace or dynamics. The *tempo-rhythm* of the play depends on the *through-line* of action and the *subtext*, in accordance with the *supertask* of the author. Toporkov describes Stanislavski's application of *tempo-rhythm* when he was working on V.P. Kataiev's *The Embezzlers*, which opened in 1928. He discusses how there used to be a universal word 'tone'; actors would talk about finding or missing the 'tone' for the part or the play. The performance might be running in a 'lowered tone' and the actor coming onstage might be asked to 'raise the tone'. But, he says, no one knew how this could be done; the actor would usually just start talking louder. Rejecting this vague idea, Stanislavski did a great deal of research in order to define his idea of *tempo-rhythm*. As a result of the use of this idea, Toporkov writes, 'I saw long, drawn-out rehearsals transformed miraculously into full-blooded conflicts of great intensity' (1998: 60).

There are differences between the *tempo-rhythm*, the dynamics, of plays like *Death of a Salesman*, *The Glass Menagerie* and *Our Country's Good*. *The Glass Menagerie* is a memory play: it begins with Tom's narration, remembering his past life, and the story then unfolds. The author intended it to have a dream-like quality, with its wistful, painful ending where Tom is unable to let go of his memories of Laura. The action in *Death of a Salesman*, on the other hand, despite the fact that it has dream scenes such as Willy's encounters with his brother Ben and memory sequences of his times with The Woman, moves inexorably and urgently towards Willy's suicide. *Our Country's Good* also has a dream aspect, as the play is framed by the appearance of the Aborigine who believes until the end of the play that the British colonising officers and convicts are from Dreamtime, ghostly ancestors who have returned to earth. However, he comes to realise that they are part of a present-day reality, and the play ends badly for him as the settlers have given him smallpox. As a whole, *Our Country's Good* ends on a triumphant note as the performance of *The Recruiting Officer* goes ahead, asserting the humanising power of theatre. The end upholds the compassionate point of view of the officers who have maintained that the convicts are human beings with potential, rather than hopeless, debased creatures. The dynamic is that of the inner struggles and conflicts of the characters as understanding is reached and the play ends on a celebratory note. The actors must find the *tempo-rhythm* in the play so that emotion builds up to the ending, and transformation takes place.

Katie Mitchell indicates how internal and external are linked within this concept. She discusses how to get actors to find the right pace for the play. If, for example, the director tells an actor to speed up what they are doing, the new speed will last for a couple of performances and then the director will probably have to give the note again. If the director gives a concrete instruction about the *given circumstances* it will speed up the scene and last over more performances. For example, the director might remind the actor playing

Nina in Act 1 of *The Seagull* that Nina needs to leave at 9 p.m. so that her father and stepmother do not find out that she has been over to the Sorin estate (Mitchell 2009: 35). If her father and stepmother were away, as they are in Act 3, her whole demeanour would be different. It is easier for the actor to remember the note in relation to her *tasks* rather than as general note to speed up. Her concept of pace, like that of *tempo-rhythm*, includes internal and external.

The characters in *Our Country's Good* are in two groups: the convicts and the officers. As groups, the convicts and the officers have conflicting *tempo-rhythms* and, in addition, neither group coheres together at the start, especially the convicts, who

> begin as a broken, brutalized and dispirited bunch who are united in their subjugation but are shown to be much more viciously antagonistic towards each other than the officers are. Under the influence of their play, they become a group, sympathetic and supportive of each other.
>
> (Wertenbaker 1999: xxv)

You could use the idea of *tempo-rhythm* to explore the differences between the two groups and how the convicts move towards being united as a group. The group dynamic changes as they work on the play together and as individuals assert themselves and adopt more positive attitudes to life and to others.

The most important point about *tempo-rhythm* is that, if the idea is used properly, it can be a way into inner *experiencing*. It requires use of the imagination: the actor must be thinking in the right way rather than performing movements and speaking mechanically. 'Correctly captured temporhythm helps the actor to evoke true feeling, supports it, facilitates its fullest expression' (Korkorin 2007: 160–61). *Tempo-rhythm* can stimulate *emotion memory*, and bring visual memory and mental images alive (Stanislavski 2008b: 473). Like the *through-action* and the *subtext* 'it runs like a thread through every action, spoken word, pause and experience' (Stanislavski 2008b: 501). Toporkov writes that you cannot master the *method of physical actions* if you do not master rhythm. Each physical action is inseparably linked with the rhythm that characterises it. If you always act in the same rhythm, then how will you be able to embody a variety of characters convincingly (1998: 170)?

Toporkov describes one *task* he has as his character in *The Embezzlers*. He is to try to keep another character from getting back onto a train. He only has one line: 'Philip Stepanovich!' From the point where it becomes necessary to prevent Philip Stepanovich from getting back on the train, though he has nothing to do and so little to say, he has to stand in a different rhythm. The way this is achieved is not by working from outside in, mechanically changing the way one is moving, but fulfilling a *task* (1998: 60–63): keeping Philip Stepanovich off the train. In *Onibaba*, a Japanese film by Kaneto Shindo, set in the time of the civil war in Japan, two peasant women kill and rob Samurai passing through their area in order to survive. After one killing they return to their hut and eat a meal. The actors' *task* as the characters, is simply to satisfy their hunger, but their *tempo-rhythm*, as they stand and eat, indicates the intense and awful experience they have just undergone.

Often there is a contradiction between inner and outer *tempo-rhythm*. Many Chekhov characters appear outwardly calm while in a state of almost constant inner anxiety and unrest (Stanislavski 2008b: 482). For example, Masha in *Three Sisters* scarcely betrays her unhappiness in her marriage and her boredom with her life in the first act. She whistles, and recites some lines from a poem, distancing herself from the conversation around her. These are clues to her inner state. In Act 3, she finally reveals her passionate love for Vershinin to her sisters. It is not that she has been passive inwardly to this point, but that her outer *tempo-rhythm* has been adopted to mask her inner *tempo-rhythm*.

EXERCISE: INNER AND OUTER *TEMPO-RHYTHM*

Develop an étude where you are inwardly suspicious of, angry with or in love with a stage partner. You are having dinner with this person, or working with them in an office. Define your *tasks* and use the idea of contradictory inner and outer *tempo-rhythms* to help develop the dynamic of the scene.

Within permissible limits, the *tempo-rhythm* of a performance can vary from night to night. Stanislavski describes how some of the great Russian actors (he names Shchepkin, Sadovski, Shumski, Samarin) always went to the wings long before their entrance so they could tune into the *tempo-rhythm* of the performance. 'That is why they always took life, truth and the right note for the play and the character on with them' (2008b: 486).

PERSPECTIVE

In order to *embody* the character and make it effective, the actor should maintain various *perspectives* on the role. The teacher Tortsov in *An Actor's Work* analyses a speech from Shakespeare and after each phrase gives an account of his thought processes on the technical use of stress, intonation and the other laws of speech. The student Kostya is confused and upset. He does not understand how there can be such technical and professional calculation where he expected inspiration (Stanislavski 2008b: 456). Tortsov explains that this technical expertise, the ability to assess aspects of his performance dispassionately, does not mean that he is performing mechanically. Tortsov explains to Kostya about the difference between the *perspective of the role* or character, and the *perspective of the actor* (2008b: 459). The actor is both performer and observer of their performance. Kostya understands this from experience: 'while I was living the Critic I still didn't lose contact with myself, Kostya … One half was the actor, the other watched like an audience' (2008b: 527).

The actor's perspective is like a small road that runs alongside a highway, the perspective of the role. This is the '*harmonious relationship and arrangement of the parts of the entire play and the role*' (Stanislavski 2008b: 458). There can be no acting, action, movement, thought, speech, words, feeling, etc. without the right kind of perspective. The simplest entrance or exit, sitting down in any scene, and so on, must be in line with the *supertask*. 'Large physical actions, the expression of great thoughts, experiencing great feelings and passions which are composed of many small parts, indeed, a scene, an act, a play cannot be carried out without a perspective, an ultimate goal (Supertask)' (Stanislavski 2008b: 458). The character knows nothing about perspective, or their future, while the artist must always have it in view.

The *perspective* of the role depends on having a sense of the whole play. This is important even if your character does not appear in the whole play. Maybe an actor in a role such as that of Luka in

Gorky's *The Lower Depths*, or Mercutio, who is killed in Act 3, Scene 1 of *Romeo and Juliet*, might be tempted not to work on or even read the last act of the play because they do not appear in it. As a result, the actor does not have the right perspective and cannot play their role as well as possible. The beginning depends on the end. In Gorky's play, the last act is the result of the old man's speech. The actor playing Luka must always have the end of the play in view, and lead the other actors, whom he influences, towards it.

LOGIC AND SEQUENCE

Part of maintaining a *perspective* on the role is that the actor should check the *logic and sequence* of both actions and feelings. 'Train your powers of concentration to observe your inner and outer creative mechanisms' (Stanislavski 2008b: 510). For young actors, it is easy to forget the logic and sequence of even the simplest actions when onstage, as there is so much to think about. Performing actions in a natural manner onstage with cardboard props, for example, takes work and practice. Drinking from a cup or glass that is empty needs careful rehearsal; so does using a doll for a baby, the former being so much lighter. This is why the MAT students in the first year work with imaginary objects and start with simple *tasks* such as counting bank notes, with the outer logic and sequence of actions. These exercises teach you to explore the logic and sequence of the individual, constituent, small actions, which create one large action (Stanislavski 2008b: 508).

CONTROL AND FINISH

Maintaining perspective enables the actor to have *control and finish*. Tortsov relates how a person undergoing an emotional crisis cannot describe it without their voice giving way or crying, but in time can speak calmly and logically about the past event, while it is those who are listening who are moved. In the same way, the actor, who has been moved during rehearsals, calms down from the level of superfluous emotion that would get in the way of describing to the audience what has been *experienced* with the actor's own feelings. The period of *experiencing* can be stormy or even agonising, if, for example, the actor realises that what they are doing is excessive, 'over the top', but as the work continues, they gain control of their emotions, getting rid of what is excessive or inessential and they are able to go onstage and convey the *experiencing* to the audience with clarity and *finish*, warmth and inner richness.

Outer technical control enables the actor to convey *experiencing* with nothing excessive in terms of movement or gesture. One exercise can be to set yourself the task of conveying the *score* of a role with the minimum of movement and no gestures at all. It can take months, even years to master this and make *outer technical control* second nature (Stanislavski 2008b: 539).

Finish requires a *sense of truth*. The more *control and finish* acting has, the calmer the actor, the more clearly the shape and form of the character comes across and the more it affects the audience, and the greater success the actor has (Stanislavski 2008b: 543).

CREATIVE STATE

The first year of the syllabus is devoted to establishing what Stanislavski calls the general (or working) *creative state*, and providing opportunities for the students to maintain this state in front of an audience (2008b: 594). The training in *embodiment*, facial expression, voice, inflexions, speech, movement, bodily expression, physical action, contact, adaptations, with the inner aspects, adds up to the *creative state*, where every feeling, mood, experience you have created is *reflected* externally. The actor can work on elements of the *creative state*, inner and outer, separately and then put them all together. 'For example, combine muscular release with a sense of truth, objects of attention with transmitting, action with physical tasks, etc. In doing so, one leads on to another' (Stanislavski 2008b: 587). The inner and outer creative states add up to the *creative state*, which is a process, which can be referred to as *I am being*.

I AM BEING

This is the culmination of the actor's work. Kostya experiences this in an étude called 'Burning Money', which is one that the students work on over time.

> Before I had fumbled my way through the scene ... Now it was as though my inner eye was open and I understood everything completely.

> Every detail onstage and inside me took on a different meaning. I was aware of feelings, representations, appraisals, mental images in the role and in myself. I was in fact performing a new play.

He is told, 'you have found yourself in the role and the role in you' (Stanislavski 2008b: 325). This perception of the same identity in yourself and the role is also referred to as *fusion* or *merging*, where both the everyday character of the hero and the character of the actor themselves are expressed in the creative act of performing the role. The state of *I am being* is 'I exist, I live, I feel and I think identically with the role.' In the state of *I am being*, the actor feels that they really exist in the world of imaginary objects they have created and that they are beginning to act as themselves with full responsibility for themselves (Stanislavski 2008b: 70). It is also described as 'living the truth on stage' (Stanislavski 2008b: 158). Working at individual physical actions truthfully builds up to this experience, where all aspects of the role are truthful (Stanislavski 2008b: 186).

Uta Hagen describes working on a role, beginning with the difference between 'she' and 'I'. 'My aim is to give myself new roots, to make all of the elements of my life up to the play's beginning as concrete as I can, until I know as much as possible about the new me and more than she knows about herself.' The intensive study of the *given circumstances* and what the character wants and doesn't want is crucial. 'Later all this should fill up and feed what I contact inwardly, as well as what I actually see and hear, and whatever may move in on me. This should make me understand what I do, and why I must do it. And it should give me the faith that "I" *am*!' She discusses the actor's use of emotional memories as 'complete *only* when they have become synonymous with *this* actor, *this* play's events, *these* objects you are using in your stage life and produce a significant action. You may even forget your original source – *fine*!' (Hagen 2008: 42, 153).

In the state of *I am being,* even when something goes wrong onstage, the actor can turn it to their advantage:

> If the actor has his wits about him, if he doesn't get confused or try to ignore this incident but, on the contrary, makes it part of the play then it becomes a tuning fork for him. It provides one true living note in the midst of the convention-bound theatrical lies, it recalls the real truth, it draws the whole line of the play to itself and obliges you to believe and

> to feel the thing we call 'I am being'. All this leads the actor to his natural, subconscious, creative powers.
>
> (Stanislavski 2008b: 338)

Mike Alfreds writes similarly about performances being 'open-ended'. In a performance that is not 'open-ended', if something goes wrong such as a hat falling onto the floor, the actors will pretend that this hasn't happened. Doing so is 'sucking all the energy out of the moment, a dumb but embarrassingly expressive condemnation of the falsity and deadness of this performance in which spontaneous life had been denied' (2007: 23). If the actors adapt to this new, accidental *given circumstance*, responding in character, this will enhance the life onstage, not detract from it.

THE *SUBCONSCIOUS* AND *I AM BEING*

Where there is *truth and belief*, the state of *I am being* arises of itself, naturally, though the *subconscious*. The actor has to learn to trust subconscious processes. Stanislavski drew from yoga to formulate his ideas about this. The yogis' advice is to take a bundle of thoughts and throw them into a subconscious sack. Then you go for a walk and when you come back you ask: 'ready?' The answer might be 'no' at first, but eventually the subconscious will say 'ready' and return to you what was entrusted to it (Stanislavski 2010: 166, Stanislavsky 1967: 207–8). This is an experience we all have; we forget a name and, if we don't try too hard to remember, often at some point later in the day or the next morning it will come into our heads. If we set our brain a problem it will work on it subconsciously and will work creatively to synthesise material. The yogis' approach to the unconscious through conscious preparatory methods, from the bodily to the spiritual, was a profound influence on Stanislavski's thinking.

The aim of the *system* is to enable the actor to access subconscious creativity by means of conscious psycho-technique. The work the actor does consciously on the elements of the *system* will lead to *I am being*. Morris Carnovsky wrote:

> The key that Stanislavski placed in the hands of the actor was – the actor's own consciousness. What does this include? Everything. Everything that comes within the grasp of his five senses and is subject to his will. The

use of his body, his voice, his inner gifts, sense of rhythm, response to imagery, his sympathies, even his moral point of view. Always, his *conscious recognition* of these things.

(Carnovsky in Cole and Chinoy 1970: 617)

FURTHER READING

Door, B. (2003) *Towards Perfect Posture*, London: Orion.

Door, B. (forthcoming) *An Actor's Guide to the Alexander Technique*.

Johnstone, K. (2007) *Improvisation for the Theatre*, London: Routledge. See chapter on status, pp. 33–72.

Spolin, V. (1999) *Improvisation for the Theater*, Evanston: Northwestern University Press. See Chapter 12 'Character'.

Stanislavski, K. (2008) *An Actor's Work*, London: Routledge. See section on stress, pp. 434–46, also *tempo-rhythm* exercises, pp. 671–74.

For information on the Alexander Technique, see www.paat.org.uk

6

STANISLAVSKI'S INFLUENCE AND LEGACY

Stanislavski's work became famous throughout Russia and Eastern Europe in his lifetime, influencing training and production methods in theatres. His ideas became known further afield, and during 1922–24 the Moscow Art Theatre toured in Europe and America with A. Tolstoy's *Tsar Fiodor*, Gorky's *The Lower Depths*, Chekhov's *Three Sisters*, *Uncle Vanya* and *The Cherry Orchard* and Turgenev's *A Provincial Lady*, and, in a second tour to Paris and New York, with Ibsen's *An Enemy of the People*, Goldoni's *La Locandiera* and an adaptation of Dostoevsky's *Brothers Karamazov*. Altogether, they gave 380 performances, appearing in Berlin, Prague, Zagreb, Paris and New York, Chicago, Philadelphia and Boston, Pittsburg, Cleveland, Chicago and Detroit.

Émigré actors settled in America and began to teach others, building on the wave of excitement created in New York by what was recognised as a new standard of acting set by the company. The MAT's work had a profound impact on the history of American acting. Lee Strasberg, Sanford Meisner, Stella Adler and others made versions of the *system* famous, the most famous being Strasberg's Method. Ideas about this spread to the UK and Europe, where Stanislavski's work was known but more diffusely than in America. French directors such as Jacques Copeau and Charles Dullin, and in Germany Max Reinhardt, contemporaries of

Stanislavski, recognised the importance of his work. Poland's Jerzy Grotowski acknowledged the profound influence Stanislavski had upon him and Odin Teatret's Eugenio Barba continued the tradition of in-depth experiment in theatre pioneered by Stanislavski. In Britain, practitioners such as actor Michael Redgrave and director Joan Littlewood have affirmed Stanislavski's importance to them.

Despite confusions and misinterpretations, over the twentieth century Stanislavski-based methods have dominated Western acting, and in other parts of the world – Japan, for example – the work was increasingly recognised and used in the later part of the twentieth century. It is important to understand what Stanislavski wrote himself, because there has been so much misunderstanding, starting with the Soviets. As described in Chapter 1, after the 1917 Revolution the Soviet regime espoused a materialistic philosophy, and presented the work of their figurehead theatre director in a way that played down the spiritual and emotional emphases of the *system*. In recent years, there have been studies attempting to clarify some of the misunderstandings, going back to original sources.

STANISLAVSKI'S INFLUENCE AND LEGACY IN RUSSIA

There were points of agreement and difference on artistic principles between Stanislavski and Meyerhold, Evgenii Vakhtangov and Michael Chekhov, who also worked in Europe and America. All three were directed and taught by Stanislavski, all developed their own ways of working in counterpoint to the *system* and all have had a lasting influence on acting. Meyerhold developed a system of actor-training very different to the *system*, in its emphasis on movement and technical skill, called *biomechanics*. Building on the *system*, Vakhtangov developed the concept of *imaginative realism*, and Michael Chekhov went a step further in emphasising the importance of the actor's imagination, as opposed to Stanislavski's emotional truth. These questions continue to be debated today: questions of emotion and action, whether the actor should work from 'inside out' or 'outside in', *representation* versus *experiencing*, what theatricalism is, what naturalism or realism are and what the role of the audience is.

MEYERHOLD

Vsevolod Emilievich Meyerhold (1874–1940) was born in Penza, Russia. His work inspired many revolutionary artists and film-makers. By the time of the Russian Revolution in 1917, he was considered the leading avant-garde director in Russia. His impact was such that it has been claimed that Meyerhold's work is the foundation of what has come to be known in the West as physical theatre, where there are priorities other than scripted text, such as movement as expression. Meyerhold was executed in the Soviet Union in 1940. As with so many avant-garde artists, his work was seen to be in opposition to the prevailing Soviet view of art as a political tool and he was judged to be an enemy of the Soviet Union under Josef Stalin, its dictator from the 1920s until 1953. There has been a wide resurgence of interest in Meyerhold's work since his rehabilitation. This began in the 1950s but it was only after the breakdown of the Soviet Union in the early 1990s that more information on him and how the tradition of his work has been conveyed has become available. Meyerhold objected to Stanislavski's preoccupation with the creation of life on stage and preferred stylised theatre.

THE AVANT-GARDE

The Symbolist movement in Russia, following on from movements in Europe, began in the late 1890s, led by poets such as Alexander Blok. It drew from French Symbolist poets and playwrights. While writers such as Hauptmann, Ibsen and Chekhov were influenced by symbolism, their plays, many of which were directed by Stanislavski at the Moscow Art Theatre, were predominantly naturalistic, taking the lives of ordinary people as their subject. In 1902, Valery Briusov, an avant-garde poet and leading spokesman for Symbolism, published an article attacking the Moscow Art Theatre for what he called 'unnecessary truth'. He criticised the realism of the sets, props and costumes and the acting style, which aimed to be truthful in Stanislavski's sense of the word. Bryusov said this limited the imagination of the audience, 'the unnecessary truth' of objects cluttering the stages obscured the spiritual side of life on stage, the performer's creative emotion.

Symbolist theatre dealt with the mystical, the supernatural, and required a new kind of acting and mise-en-scène.

Stanislavski rose to the challenge and appointed Meyerhold to work in the studio theatre he created in 1905 on Povarskaia Street, to find ways to develop an acting style that would be appropriate for new drama, the work of symbolist writers such as Maurice Maeterlinck. The project came to an end rather swiftly: Meyerhold attempted to find a new form of stylisation, but though the look of the productions was interesting, the actors were uncertain and looked amateurish. He experimented with lighting, but at a dress rehearsal Stanislavski shouted 'The audience cannot take the darkness on stage for too long, it goes against psychology, they must see the actor's faces!' (Popov in Gauss 1999: 20). Stanislavski went on to conduct some of his own experiments, producing the work of Maeterlinck himself, but it was Meyerhold who continued to focus on the development of avant-garde work.

MEYERHOLD'S EXPERIMENTS: THE SEARCH FOR A STYLISED THEATRE

Meyerhold continued to explore a stylised theatre linked to the Symbolist movement, producing plays such as Blok's *The Puppet Booth* (1906). He wanted his new theatre to be a popular theatre, a theatre that could assist in social and political change, and also worked on productions influenced by the fifteenth-century popular theatre form of commedia dell'arte, which involved improvised performances with character types, many masked.

Theatre-makers, in general, were reassessing the medium of theatre because of the emergence of film (the first motion pictures were shown in 1895) and the challenges it offered to current conceptions of naturalism. As theatre could not compete with film in terms of verisimilitude, there was the question of whether 'truth as in life' should be theatre's aim. Should art perform a different function to 'holding a mirror up to nature' and depicting life? The emergence of photography had previously posed similar questions about visual art: why should painters depict landscapes when photography could do so much more accurately? The movements of expressionism, impressionism and cubism offered new ideas in visual art. The way in which art is perceived, what is conveyed and how it relates to life became central, rather than the content.

Instead of reflecting reality, art signified it. In literature, Russian Formalist critics prioritised the form and not the content of artistic works. They suggested that the purpose of the artist was to make the familiar unfamiliar, to 'alienate' the reader or spectator by making the artwork strange, making the reader or spectator want to look at it again. This process, *ostranenie*, is comparable with Bertolt Brecht's alienation effect, where the intention is to distance the audience from the stage action in order to make them think about it. The Formalists were interested in intertextuality: how a work of literature can refer to other works and comment on them, 'defamiliarising' them. This was a literature and theatre of devices, art that is self-conscious, reflecting overtly on its own conventions. Meyerhold's theatre was 'conventionalised' theatre (also translated as 'stylised'), and, in this way, drew attention to the fact that the audience was watching a play. For example, *The Fairground Booth* used props such as a window of cardboard and paper that a character jumped through, drawing attention to the fact that this was theatre and the window was not meant to appear 'real'. This was very different from Stanislavski's emphasis on props being as authentic as possible.

In 1913, Meyerhold set up a studio under the pseudonym Dr Dapertutto (taken from a story by Hoffman) in St Petersburg, publishing a journal called *The Love for Three Oranges* (named after an Italian eighteenth-century play based on commedia dell'arte). He explored an interest in Eastern performance forms, for example Japanese theatre and Peking Opera. He became interested in Futurism, making links with the poet Vladimir Mayakovsky. Meyerhold researched other popular forms and like many of his contemporaries he was interested in circus, and his productions comprised elements of circus performance. Generally speaking, Meyerhold embraced theatricalism, a theatre that celebrated itself rather than being true to life, though this did not mean it was not about life. One aspect of the revival of commedia dell'arte throughout Europe, and particularly for Meyerhold, was that the metaphor of theatre itself was used to explore the human condition. What was human was emphasised through types of characters, such as lovers, doctors, servants, and these included characters such as Harlequin and Pierrot. The class differences between characters had resonance for Russia, which was undergoing revolution and throwing off the rule of the aristocracy. He directed productions that celebrated the Revolution and were landmarks in avant-garde art, such as Lermontov's *Masquerade* (1917) and Crommelynck's *The Magnanimous Cuckold* (1922).

MEYERHOLD'S DIFFERENCES FROM STANISLAVSKI

The major differences between Meyerhold's and Stanislavski's views on theatre were regarding the role of the audience, the role of the director, character and training.

Regarding the audience, using the idea of the *fourth wall*, Stanislavski taught that, in order to avoid the fear induced by the 'black hole' of the auditorium, the actor should have a focus of attention on stage. Meyerhold held that the actor should not exclude the spectator from his awareness in this way and should be a trained and conscious artist, rather than one whose feeling or emotion hypnotised the actor themselves and the audience (Hoover 1974: 1). He rejected many of the lynchpins of the *system*, such as *sense and emotion memory*, truth and the significance of the subconscious.

As a director, Meyerhold asserted the Theatre of the Straight Line. In this concept, the director assimilated the work of the playwright, then inspired the actors, who presented this to the audience. Meyerhold as the director was in control; it was said that he used the actors as puppets. His productions were often adaptations of play texts where the director's artistic vision was paramount. Stanislavski emphasised fidelity to the text and the writer's artistry, and *supertask* was most important, though the creative process of director and actor was fundamental.

In Meyerhold's productions the actor did not have to *experience*, like Stanislavski's actor, to create a role based on human personality, but represented a 'type' or 'emploi'. The use of commedia characters was a way to experiment with this approach, the servants representing the lower classes, outwitting their masters, the doctors, lawyers and so on.

After the Revolution, Meyerhold developed a method for training actors, *biomechanics*, which was very different from the *system*. *Biomechanics* means 'the study of the mechanics of movement of living creatures'. In developing the theory of *biomechanics*, Meyerhold studied the work of two key figures. The first was American time-and-motion expert Frederick W. Taylor, who explored how manual work could be done most efficiently, and the second was famous Russian scientist Ivan Pavlov, who researched how behaviour can be conditioned. Meyerhold studied many artistic ideas of movement, from expressive gesture – drawn from influential French acting theoretician and teacher François Delsarte – to circus acrobatics. Before the Revolution, part of Meyerhold's training for actors included études. Unlike Stanislavski's improvised études, these were set scenarios, some of which were based on commedia. By learning to perform the études precisely, the actor would learn the skills they needed as a performer in general. *Biomechanics* was understood to work from the outside in: Meyerhold saw movement itself as expressive of emotional, inner content, and thought that movement could generate the emotion for the performer. *Biomechanics* was a physicalised theatre language. It was a style that subsequently influenced Brecht's *Gestus*, the physical theatre techniques of Jacques Lecoq and much other work.

Meyerhold embraced the Revolution fervently. But he swung in and out of favour with the Soviet government. In 1923, he was appointed People's Artist of the Russian Socialist Federation of Soviet Republics, which was a great honour. He was denounced in 1939, as the government under Stalin sought more and more control of art, and Formalist and other avant-garde movements became seen as anti-revolutionary. In the last months of Stanislavski's life, he met on several occasions with Meyerhold and they were said to be discussing a possible synthesis of Stanislavski's later approaches to rehearsal and Meyerhold's *biomechanics*. It is possible that Stanislavski, in his position of prestige in the Soviet Union, was trying to protect Meyerhold.

VAKHTANGOV AND CHEKHOV

Evgenii Vakhtangov and Michael Chekhov were both members of the First Studio of Moscow Art Theatre. Vakhtangov was instructed in the *system* by Stanislavski and then took on teaching responsibilities, while Chekhov joined the Studio later. Each were to take the *system* as a starting point and to develop their own ideas about acting. Chekhov left Russia in 1928 and worked in various other countries, settling in America. His teaching there and his writings have become increasingly popular in the West, whereas Vakhtangov's influence has been less well known.

VAKHTANGOV

Evgenii Bagrationovich Vakhtangov was born in Armenia in 1883 and died in 1922, as his work as a director was gaining acclaim in Russia. He was one of the founder members of the First Studio, under Sulerzhitski's leadership, in 1912. He performed in First Studio productions, for example as the miser Tackleton in 1914 in *The Cricket on the Hearth*, based on Charles Dickens' novella, with Michael Chekhov as Caleb, a toymaker. Despite his talents as an actor and Stanislavski's protests, he was only ever given small parts in the main house shows at the MAT. His work in his own studio was very significant.

Vakhtangov came into conflict with Sulerzhitski and Stanislavski as he developed his own approach. In his production of *The Festival of Peace* by Hauptmann in 1913, Vakhtangov imbued the atmosphere with 'questioning unease', heightening the 'nervousness and excitement of the dialogue' (Rudnitsky 1988: 21). For some, this production created a great impression, but Stanislavski lost his temper, accusing Vakhtangov of taking his actors to the point of hysteria in their performances. For example, he directed *The Flood* by Henning Berger in 1915. The play is about a group of money-orientated people who are in a bar when they hear that their town is to be flooded. In the face of imminent danger, they change their behaviour towards one another and qualities of kindness and consideration emerge, but as the flood is averted they return to their norm of defensive hostility. Suler wanted to use the play to demonstrate the innate goodness of people in a way that would touch the audience, whereas Vakhtangov saw the balance between good and evil as expressive of something essentially human. Stanislavski supported Suler. However, Vakhtangov's innovative approach presaged the expressionism and exploration of the grotesque characteristic of his later work.

In developing his ideas, Vakhtangov also drew from Nemirovich-Danchenko, the co-founder, with Stanislavski, of the Moscow Art Theatre. In 1922, Vakhtangov wrote to Nemirovich-Danchenko, saying,

> I learned to combine yours and Konstantin Sergeyevich's [approaches]. You revealed to me concepts such as 'theatricality' and 'the mastery of acting'. I saw that in addition to 'emotional experience' (you did not like this term) you demanded something else from an actor. I learned to understand what it means to 'speak of feeling' on stage and what it means to feel.
>
> (Vakhtangov in Malaev-Babel 2011: 326)

The logic of behaviour and actions is determined by the nature of the character rather than by the actor's own personality, as with the *system*. Michael Chekhov also took this point of view.

Vakhtangov emphasised the concept that 'theatre is a festival', indicating the heightened, enjoyable experience he wanted to create. Rather than the actor behaving on stage as in life, he sought to create truth through embracing theatricalism. For him the actor should acknowledge the artificiality of the stage setting but behave as if it were real, rather than seeking to behave as in life, without that acknowledgement, like Stanislavski's actor. Boris Zakhava, who was a member of his studio, describes how Vakhtangov sought to resolve the contradiction of the artificiality of being on stage and the need to create something 'real' in performance (Zakhava 1982: 51–53). Vakhtangov asked, if an actor is playing Romeo with an actress he finds unattractive 'what must he *see* on stage, the actress who is unattractive to him who is in front of him or a beauty, whom he can create in his imagination?' Encouraging the actor to see not what is there but what is in his imagination, as Stanislavski indicated, is to encourage him to hallucinate. Instead, Vakhtangov came up with a formula. 'I apprehend everything as it is given, I relate to everything as it is set.' This means that the actor acknowledges his situation, that he is not attracted to his fellow performer, but as is required of him in the role he relates to her as if he is. This was a new way of conceptualising Stanislavski's *magic if*.

As opposed to Stanislavski's actor who defines his *task* by what they, as the character, want, Vakhtangov taught that there were two stages. The first is where the actor has recognised what the character needs to do and say. The actor may describe this in the third person, that is, s/he wishes, s/he speaks, s/he does, s/he needs … Next, the actor must make this need his or her own, feeling the necessity of the given words, action and behaviour not only for the character but for him or herself as the character. The actor identifies with the character through what the actor/character needs (Whyman 2008: 161–62). This is instead of *fusion* or *merging* with the character in Stanislavski's sense. By means of these ideas, Vakhtangov sought to bring together the performer's internal truth so crucial to the *system* with a theatrical style in which the performer could acknowledge another truth: the fact that he or she is on stage, performing to an audience.

IMAGINATIVE REALISM

Stanislavski's solution to the problem of the actor's belief in what they are doing on stage was to work on giving attention to the *given circumstances* in order to overcome the unnatural state induced by performance, creating the *fourth wall* (see Chapter 2). Vakhtangov rejected this, instead emphasising *justification*. He developed Stanislavski's formulation of this and said that the actor must justify everything they do on stage, but not necessarily in a way that fits with the *given circumstances* of the play or the character. The actor could use ideas and experiences that seemed to work, so long as the character's behaviour remained logical.

In *Princess Turandot*, which demanded a stylised form of acting, Vakhtangov moved the *fourth wall* over the footlights into the last row of the orchestra and gallery. He reformulated *the magic if*: 'If you were an actor of the People's Theater, creating the role of Kalaf, how would you behave in the given circumstances of the play?' (Simonov 1969: 163). This enabled the actors to acknowledge in their performances, self-referentially, that they were a commedia troupe presenting Gozzi's play, celebrating and enhancing the theatricality of the production.

Vakhtangov had successfully created a bridge between two styles of performance – Stanislavski's truth as in life, and Meyerhold's theatricalism – proving that the *system* had much wider application than had previously been believed. He demonstrated unequivocally that the *system* and 'theatricality' need not be mutually exclusive (Gauss 1999: 114) but could be outwardly stylised and internally realistic. This is *imaginative* or *fantastic realism*, 'a form that would capture the carnivalesque atmosphere of popular theatre; and in the form of commedia dell'arte with its carnivalesque spirit, Vakhtangov saw the reconciliation of theatrical anti-illusionism with fantastic realism' (Listengarten 2000: 95).

Vakhtangov's work significantly influenced Grotowski, Barba and American practitioners including Lee Strasberg.

MICHAEL CHEKHOV

Mikhail Aleksandrovich Chekhov was Anton Chekhov's nephew. He was born in 1891 in Russia and died in Los Angeles in America, when he had become known as Michael Chekhov, in 1955. Michael Chekhov was trained by Stanislavski, and was a member of the First Studio from 1912 to 1921, but, like Vakhtangov, he began to develop his own direction. He started his own studio, working with it from 1918 to 1921. After Vakhtangov's death, Chekhov became the leader of the First Studio. After the MAT tour of Western Europe and America in 1924 the First Studio became the Second MAT. In that period, Chekhov was developing exercises in rhythmic movement and in *communication*. He explored archetypal images as a basis for characterisation. He experimented with techniques that were very innovative at the time, such as getting the actors to throw balls at each other, as they spoke the dialogue, exploring the connection of movement with words (Chekhov 2005: 107).

Chekhov always stated that his methods were a development of Stanislavski's work. He sought spirituality in theatre, going in the opposite direction to Meyerhold, who sought the brilliance of technical skill as the key to all aspects of performance. At the beginning of the 1920s, he adopted a religion called anthroposophy developed by Rudolf Steiner, and borrowed concepts from this for his acting method. He conducted experiments in *eurhythmy*, Steiner's form where colour and sound are translated into movement. He explored the idea of the *higher self* or *ego*, which gives us 'individuality', as opposed to personality, giving rise to Chekhov's concept of the actor's 'creative individuality'. In *To the Actor*, Chekhov describes the difference between the *lower ego* and the *higher ego* in relation to acting. In acting, we can overcome the *lower ego*, the everyday 'I', which is egotistical and insignificant, and we can experience something higher, more spiritual:

> with the appearance of this new *I*, you felt first of all an influx of power never experienced in your routine life. This power permeated your whole being, radiated from you into your surroundings, filling the stage and

> flowing over the footlights into the audience. It united you with the spectator and conveyed to him all your creative intentions, thoughts, images and feelings.
>
> (2004: 86)

When the creative, *higher ego* has become active, the actor is in the *creative state* of inspiration. Creative individuality draws not on everyday, personal feelings but on more spiritual feelings, which are purified, freed from egotism and therefore aesthetic, significant and artistically true. Stanislavski drew from psychology, believing that only past personal experience could bring truth to acting. For Chekhov, previous personal experience is a trap. He found recalling his own personal past painful. Chekhov observed in a lecture demonstration to members of the Group Theatre in 1935 that the Stanislavskian actor has been taught to build his role on the similarities between his personal history and that of the character in the play. But this constant 'repetition of the actor's own nature', in Chekhov's view, in creating different parts over the years, causes a progressive 'degeneration of talent' (Gordon, introduction in Chekhov 1991: xxvi–xxvii). Instead, inspired by his religious beliefs, he asserted that the actor could transcend their everyday personal experience and convey more universal, elevated experience.

Chekhov was viewed as extremely talented as an actor, able to convey *imaginative realism*, inner truth and outer theatricality, in Vakhtangov's sense. Vera Soloveva wrote:

> The thing was that Chekhov never had to worry about emotions. He only needed to imagine a character he was to play to see him. He used to say he could find in himself, without any trouble, all the feelings of the character. Not everybody had that ability.
>
> (Soloveva in Edwards 1965: 122)

Whereas Stanislavski's *system* arose from his personal problems as an actor, including his experiences of stage fright and his belief, drawn from Tolstoy, that the actor communicates feeling and emotion to an audience by *experiencing* it themselves, Chekhov and Vakhtangov had different perspectives as actors and different aesthetic views.

IMAGINATION

Chekhov's *feeling of the truth* was validated by what was generated by the imagination, not personal experience. He had to leave Russia in 1928 because his spiritual beliefs were considered counter-revolutionary. He met Stanislavski in Berlin in 1928 and writes of this meeting,

> Both points of our conversation, in essence were one thing: *should an actor separate from or bring in to creative work, his personal, unworked-through feelings?*
>
> (Chekhov in Whyman 2008: 195)

Chekhov admonished Stanislavski for the harmfulness of his *system* and told him to replace emotion memory with *imagination*. The *system*, he said, limits the character to the personality of the actor. Stanislavski, of course, did not deny but prized the *imagination*, though he had a different view of it, devoting a chapter in *An Actor's Work* to it: 'Every one of our movements on stage, every word must be the result of a truthful imagination' (2008b: 84).

Imagination feeds into improvisation:

> as soon as an actor develops the *ability* to improvise and discovers within himself this inexhaustible well from which every improvisation is drawn, he will enjoy a sense of *freedom* hitherto unknown to him, and will feel himself much richer inwardly.
>
> (Chekhov 2004: 36)

The actor's capacity for spontaneous response is released.

IMITATION OF THE IMAGE

Chekhov's idea is that, as the character is developed in the actor's imagination rather than from their previous experience, the actor then imitates the image, the internal and external qualities of the character in performance. By this means the actor begins the process of *transformation* into the character. Therefore, *imitation of the image* is a central concept in Chekhov's method (M. Chekhov 2005: 214, 216). Stanislavski's actor 'goes from himself' but it is possible for the

Chekhovian actor to 'go beyond' not just the playwright and the play but also his own *lower ego* into the realms of the *higher ego*, another consciousness. Chekhov was insistent on the separation of the actor from the role. It is the image's *experiencing* that is important, not the actor's. The character is different from the actor and has a different body and psychology – quite different from Stanislavski's teaching. The actor trained in the Chekhov technique does not ask, '"How would *I* behave if I were in this situation?" but "How does the *character* behave in these circumstances?" It might be the case that we would behave in the same way as the character – that is perfectly possible – but the first question must be about the character's behaviour, not our own' (Chamberlain 2004: 40).

ATMOSPHERES

Other ideas of Chekhov's differed from those of Stanislavski, as the former believed in otherworldly forces, atmospheres that surround us, as the source for creativity and food for the imagination. In working on Chekhov's exercises with *atmospheres*, the actor has to pay attention to what is going on for them in the role and the wider atmosphere of the scene, which, as Chekhov explains, may be in complete contrast. He gives an example of a street catastrophe and four different responses to it: the person who is untouched by it, the person who is glad they are not the victim, the policeman concentrating on his job, and the person who is full of compassion (2004: 51). The overall atmosphere is the fraught one of an accident, but each person involved has their own *atmosphere*. *Atmospheres* are a way for the actor to expand their attention from the character's situation to the whole of the scene and to include the audience as well. 'The atmosphere inspires the actor. It unites the audience with the actor, as well as the actors with one another' (Chekhov 2004: 61).

PSYCHOLOGICAL GESTURE

Chekhov developed the idea of *the psychological gesture*, which had its roots in work he did with Stanislavski. Stanislavski was aware of the synthesising and creative power of the brain, and emphasised the role of the *subconscious* in creativity. But he did not want to put full trust in it, relying instead on the certainty of past experience. In *Lessons for the Professional Actor*, Chekhov writes that it is wrong to analyse a role, as art is a process of synthesis, not analysis. In developing a role, a gesture may emerge intuitively and 'if we are patient enough … then this gesture will soon give us so many things that the whole character of Don Quixote, including his speech, his inner characterization, etc. will grow before our eyes and our imagination – our mind's eye – and in our inner emotional life' (Chekhov 1985: 110–11).

RADIATION

Chekhov developed the idea of *radiating*, which was developed from Stanislavski's use of the idea of yogic *prana rays*, the idea that the actor's life force can be communicated to the audience. He used this idea to help the actor overcome self-consciousness and fear and develop stage presence. Imagining a stream of power radiating from the centre 'beyond the boundaries of the body and into the space around you. This power must not only precede each of your movements but also *follow* it so that the sensation of freedom will be bolstered by that of power' and the actor will gradually 'experience more and more of that strong feeling which may be called … presence on the stage' (Chekhov 2004: 8).

STANISLAVSKI'S LEGACY IN RUSSIA AFTER HIS DEATH

Mikhail Kedrov, Maria Knebel and Vasilii Toporkov participated in Stanislavski's classes with the Opera Studio from 1926, where the techniques that became known as the *method of physical actions* and *active analysis* were developed. In the late period of Stanislavski's life and after his death, Soviet science was materialistic. The work of Nobel Prize winning scientist Ivan Pavlov (1849–1936), investigating the conditioning of behaviour, was embraced as the science of the Revolution. Pavlov's work was on dogs, but the Soviets used it to claim that human beings were essentially complex machines. The principle by which behaviour was learned was by the establishment of reflex responses to stimuli from the environment. They hoped this would establish principles by which people, and society, would change for the better and by which a communist society, based on the ideals of Karl Marx, would eventually come about. This meant that ideas of spirituality and emotion, which could not be defined in materialistic terms, were therefore suspect. As far as acting was concerned, it was judged that physical action was central, as it was observable, less nebulous than emotion. The Soviet authorities claimed that Stanislavski had moved away from his belief in *emotion memory* as a lynchpin in acting and was working with action in a way that corroborated Pavlov's science, a claim that Stanislavski denied. The propaganda that emerged about the significance of the *method of physical actions* has caused much confusion in the Stanislavski tradition; for example, Sonia Moore, who founded the American Centre for Stanislavsky Theater Art, propounded the *method of physical actions* in her books on Stanislavski, drawing on Soviet sources while not fully recognising the politics involved. It was not, as she and others believed, the culmination of Stanislavski's work but a rehearsal technique enabling the actor to find inner content through action in the *given circumstances*.

MIKHAIL KEDROV

Mikhail Nikolaevich Kedrov (1893–1972) joined the MAT Second Studio in 1922, then the MAT troupe from 1924. He took over the running of the Opera-Dramatic Studio after Stanislavski's death, until 1948. After the death of Nemirovich-Danchenko and other senior members of the Theatre he became the main director of the MAT from 1949 to 1955, remaining part of its artistic directorate after that. Kedrov saw himself as preserving the theory of Stanislavski's work and took part in scientific research into *the method of physical actions*.

MARIA KNEBEL

Maria Osipovna Knebel (1898–1985) worked with Michael Chekhov in the Chekhov studio from 1918. After the studio closed, Knebel joined the Second Studio, then was a member of the MAT troupe from 1924 to 1950. She was fired from the Art Theatre by Kedrov in 1949, after a dispute over the significance of the *method of physical actions*. 'She fought against what she called the Marxist "vulgarization" of Stanislavski's last technique' (Carnicke 2009: 107).

In 1935 she began her career as a director in the Studio in the name of Yermolova, which became a theatre. In 1950, she joined the Moscow Central Children's Theatre, becoming the main director in 1955, working on classic and fairy tale productions. In *The Magic Flower* in 1958 she used dance and pantomime skilfully to convey the narrative. She is viewed as having preserved the bases of Stanislavski's *system* as a teacher and as having developed Russian directing. She taught from 1948 in the directing faculty at the main Soviet acting school, GITIS, working with people who were to become famous Soviet directors, such as Anatoly Efros, Oleg Yefremov and Georgi Tovstonogov. Thanks to her efforts, the works of Michael Chekhov began to be published in the Soviet Union. Chekhov was more or less deleted from Russian theatre history after he left in 1928, and Knebel was one of the first people to publish work on him, when some relaxation of state censorship made this possible. Her own writing was suppressed in the Soviet Union and her books *On the Active Analysis of Plays* and *The Word in the Art of the Actor* are not yet translated into English.

VASILII OSIPOVICH TOPORKOV

Vasilii Osipovich Toporkov (1889–1970) joined the MAT in 1927 and was directed by Stanislavski as Vanechka in Kataiev's *The Embezzlers* in 1928 and as Chichikov in Gogol's *Dead Souls* in 1932, proving an excellent student of the *system*. He continued to act and direct at the MAT, working with Kedrov. His book, *Stanislavski in Rehearsal*, is an important document of Stanislavski's work.

STANISLAVSKI AND AMERICA

Stanislavski's work was handed on in America initially through the teaching of the émigré actors from the MAT who settled there and through Stanislavski's writings. *My Life in Art* was published in America in 1924 before it was published in Russia in 1926. Unfortunately, there were problems with the editing and translation (see Benedetti's introduction to *An Actor's Work*; Stanislavski 2008b), as there were with the British editions of Stanislavski's books, published as *An*

Actor Prepares, *Building a Character* and *Creating a Role* – the three books intended to form a comprehensive manual. In 1949, thirteen years after *An Actor Prepares*, the main topic of which was inner experience, *Building a Character* appeared. It was in *Building a Character* that Stanislavski's views about the equal significance of *experiencing* and *embodiment* are made clear, but by then the impression that the *system* prioritised inner experience had taken hold. Stanislavski did not want this separation to occur, but rather that the first two books of the actor's manual be published as a single volume. The first book was published in Russia in 1938, as *An Actor's Work on him/herself; Part 1, Work on oneself in the Creative Process of Experiencing*, and in 1946 after Stanislavski's death, *An Actor's Work on him/herself; Part 2, Work on oneself in the Creative Process of Embodiment* appeared. These two books are now available in one volume in English as *An Actor's Work*. The third was more simply entitled *The Actor's Work on a Role* and was published in 1957.

The first MAT actors teaching Stanislavski's ideas in New York were Richard Boleslavsky and Maria Ouspenskaia. Boleslavsky had joined the MAT in 1908 and had been an original member of the First Studio, with Vakhtangov and Chekhov. With Sulerzhitski's help, he directed Herman Heijermans' *The Wreck of the Ship 'Hope'*, the Studio's First Production in 1913. This production was seen as demonstrating the success of the *system*; the directors had used improvisation and *affective memory* work to good effect. Boleslavsky fled the Soviet Union in 1920, working in Europe and then America. He worked with the MAT on their tour in 1923, and gave a lecture series on the Art Theatre and Stanislavski's work. In the same year, Boleslavsky published *Acting – The First Six Lessons*. These lessons were concentration, memory of emotion, dramatic action, characterization, observation, and rhythm. He founded the American Laboratory Theatre with Maria Alekseievna Ouspenskaia, a MAT actress who remained in America after the tour. The Lab lasted until 1930, training, at various times, Lee Strasberg, Harold Clurman and Stella Adler.

THE GROUP THEATRE

The Group Theatre was founded by Strasberg, Clurman and Cheryl Crawford in 1931, and was the most influential company to be founded in America in the 1930s, launching the careers of writers such as Clifford Odets, and director and actor Elia Kazan. Previously, Cheryl Crawford had worked as a casting director at the Theatre Guild, where she and Clurman had met. The Guild was a group of actors and writers in New York who had come together to develop theatre work that was not dominated by the priorities of commercial theatre. Stella Adler, from a Jewish theatrical family, trained with Boleslavsky and joined the Group in 1931. Its aim, influenced by Boleslavsky and Ouspenskaia, was to work as a permanent ensemble, like the MAT, using Stanislavski's training, working to high artistic standards and producing new American plays. Twenty-eight actors joined, to become the permanent company. The theatre's Russian cook, Mark Schmidt, translated and read material from Vakhtangov and Chekhov and other books about Russian theatre not available in English. They called their system of training 'the Method', passionately advocating the importance of inner technique, relaxation, *emotion memory* and improvisation.

In the ten years of the Group Theatre's existence, they produced twenty-two plays by contemporary writers, many commenting on America in the Depression; some Group members were very politicised, but artistic value was seen as essential. They had successes with plays like Paul Green's *The House of Connelly*, about the decline of an old Southern family and the end of an epoch, also Sidney Kingsley's drama set in a hospital, *Men in White*. Four plays by Clifford Odets were produced on Broadway. The acting was recognised as emotionally truthful and as having a rare intensity. Famous actors John Garfield and Franchot Tone, Morris Carnovsky, Sanford Meisner, Margaret Barker, Ruth Nelson, Phoebe Brand, Art Smith were all involved. Arthur Miller wrote, 'I had my brain branded by the beauty of the Group Theatre's productions' (1999: 230).

Strasberg found that Vakhtangov's variations from Stanislavski and his ideas about *justification* were important. He wrote, 'In certain circumstances the Stanislavski approach does not work. The Stanislavski formulation often does not lead the actor to seek the kind of reality which the author conceived and which underlies the lines he wrote' (Strasberg 1965: 309). He adopted Vakhtangov's innovation of *if*, where, instead of the actor saying 'If I were such and such a character, what would I do in the *given circumstances*?', they ask 'If I am playing Juliet, and I have to fall in love overnight, what would I, the actor, have to do to create for myself belief in this kind of event?' (Strasberg 1965: 308). This double layer of thought where the actor has to *justify* their own *tasks*, not just those of the character, countered Stanislavskian *fusion* and went further. 'Justification took the actor out of the play and its internal logic into a private realm. Instead of seeking the character's emotional truth, the performer could conjure up any substitute experience that gave him or her an appropriate sentiment' (Gordon 2010: 54). Any memory at all could be *substituted*; it did not have to relate to the scene or the character so long as it had the right effect. *Substitution* is particularly useful if the actor has difficulty with a part of the role where working with the *given circumstances*, *if*, *tasks* does not bring about the experience, and something extra is needed to stimulate the imagination and bring about spontaneous action. If the character is deceiving their wife or husband and having an affair, the actor can think of a situation in their own life where they have been deceitful and superimpose that on the character's actions. Strasberg thought that the director's skill lay also in enabling the actor to find appropriate *substitutions* and in suggesting ways that sense memory could evoke *emotion memory* (Gordon 2010: 54–55).

Strasberg thought with Stanislavski that an actor should be able to create emotion on stage but it had to be '*the right kind* of emotion' (Strasberg 1988: 90). Strasberg recognised that the actor might have habitual modes of expression of emotion. He wrote that the actor 'is conditioned to express his feelings and emotions not by nature, character, and strength of his own emotional responses, but by what society or his environment will permit' (Strasberg 1988: 95). Strasberg used relaxation, concentration and *emotion memory* exercises in order to overcome blocks to what he saw as the correct *expression* of emotion. This view of emotion was in the context of a society influenced by the Freudian model of the unconscious, the growth movement and the idea that the releasing of emotion was therapeutic, but Strasberg's methods led to a view of him by some as cruel in his attempts to break down actors' inhibitions and he has been a controversial figure in acting history.

In the early period of the Group Theatre's work, Strasberg's version of the Method was dominant. Strasberg, Adler and Clurman visited Moscow in 1934. The MAT productions in 1934, when the Theatre was seeking a new direction, did not, in Strasberg's opinion, live up to the work seen in 1924–25, whereas Adler was enchanted by the productions she saw. Strasberg met Meyerhold and became keen to experiment with visually exciting theatricalism, while maintaining emotional depth, which he did, introducing aspects of Meyerhold's work to the Group Theatre. Later on, in 1934, Clurman and Adler went to Paris, and French director Jacques Copeau introduced them to both Stanislavski and Olga Knipper, who had been Anton Chekhov's wife. Adler, who struggled with Strasberg's view of emotion, as she related, rebuked Stanislavski for ruining her acting with the emphasis on *emotion memory*. He offered to help her to find a different way to think about accessing emotion, using the *method of physical actions*. There are differing reports of Adler's encounter with Stanislavski. Stanislavski was reported as saying he had worked with her to restore his reputation. In fact, he told others that what she had learned about *emotion memory* was correct (Gordon 2010: 155), though Adler did not see or admit this.

On her return to America, she and Strasberg had a dispute which was to have serious repercussions for the understanding of Stanislavski in the West. Adler emphasised action, thinking that Stanislavski had moved away from *emotion memory*. Strasberg asserted that if Stanislavski had done this he was wrong, and he, Strasberg, was right to continue to assert the significance of *emotion memory* and *affective memory* in general. Adler challenged Strasberg's position in the Group and the work done by the American Laboratory Theatre. She maintained that *emotion memory* was harmful, asserting that you could not be on stage thinking about your personal life.

Adler and Strasberg's disagreement over action and emotion led to a split in the Group Theatre in 1934. While Strasberg continued to teach his acting classes with emphasis on *emotion memory*, Adler began her own classes emphasising the *given circumstances* and imagination. Gordon concludes 'Adler did not really understand Affective Memory' (2010: 152).

The Group Theatre carried on until 1940. Odets' *Waiting for Lefty* in 1935 was successful, but in 1936 *Johnny Johnson: A Legend*, which combined song and dance with internal realism and initially a success for Strasberg, ceased to attract audiences. After a while, in 1937, the Group actors stated that they wanted powers over decision-making in the Theatre, as a result of which Strasberg and Crawford resigned. Odets' *Golden Boy*, directed by Clurman, was successful in 1937, running on Broadway for 250 performances. The Group Theatre inspired much experimental work in other groups, and in 1937 Robert Lewis and Elia Kazan set up the Group Theatre Studio. But the Group Theatre itself came to an end, never having gained enough financial investment. Strasberg, Adler, Sanford Meisner and Morris Carnovsky continued to be influential in teaching acting after the close of the Theatre and many actors went to work in Hollywood or other theatres.

OTHER ÉMIGRÉ TEACHERS

Russian ideas of acting were taught and spread by others than those who influenced the Group Theatre. A further influx of émigré actors who trained at the MAT came to America in the 1920s and 1930s. Tamara Daykarkhanova, who was at the MAT school from 1907 to 1911, with Nikita Baliev's *Chauve Souris* in Paris and from 1922 in New York, worked with Ouspenskaia and then with Andrei Jilinsky and Vera Soloviova at the School of Stage Art, teaching Stanislavski's work. Soloviova had trained at the MAT, was in main house productions, the First Studio and at MAT 2, then worked in Lithuania, Paris then New York with Michael Chekhov. Her husband, Andrei Jilinsky, a Lithuanian, worked at the MAT First Studio from 1918. He returned to Lithuania in 1929, inviting Michael Chekhov to Kaunas in 1932, then travelling with his wife in Chekhov's troupe. Their work in New York was significant in offering a combination of Stanislavski's, Vakhtangov's and Chekhov's methods. Others included Leo and Barbara Bulgakov, who founded a studio of theatre art in 1938.

CHEKHOV IN AMERICA

Michael Chekhov arrived in America in 1939. After leaving Russia in 1928, he travelled to various places in Europe, trying to find a more supportive environment for his work. He established a theatre studio at Dartington Hall in England then relocated it to Connecticut, in view of the onset of World War Two. In 1941, he opened a studio in New York, working with famous actor Yul Brynner. Chekhov appeared in a number of Hollywood films in small roles, the most significant being as a psychiatrist in Alfred Hitchcock's *Spellbound*. He continued to coach actors, including Marilyn Monroe, Anthony Quinn and Mala Powers, while writing his books.

THE ACTOR'S STUDIO

In 1947, Crawford, Lewis and Kazan founded the Actor's Studio, which 'became the crucible in which the Russian System became the American Method, moving from the tributary fringe to the center of US film and theatre' (Carnicke 2009: 51). The Studio opened as Kazan was directing Brando in the film of Tennessee Williams' *A Streetcar Named Desire*. Strasberg was not invited to be part of the venture at first because of his 'paternalism' (Carnicke 2009: 54). However, he joined the Studio in 1948, when Lewis resigned after a conflict with Kazan, and the demands on Kazan as a director on Broadway meant that he had little time to run the Studio. By 1951, Strasberg was the artistic director and remained so until he died in 1982. Lewis and Kazan had avoided use of the more emotion-based techniques that Strasberg had emphasised and he himself did not force these methods. The use of the Method in American film was pioneered by Kazan. His film of Tennessee Williams' *A Streetcar Named Desire* won twelve Oscars.

In the 1950s, Strasberg's Method also went beyond the confines of the Studio, and was used in a production of the musical *West Side Story*. Strasberg lectured in America and Europe and, in 1973, acted in Francis Ford Coppola's *Godfather Part II* and in other films. Carnicke notes that 'Whereas Boleslavsky had been Stanislavsky's first spokesperson, Strasberg at the Actor's Studio became Stanislavsky's most famous. The Studio also proclaimed its parentage through its name, recalling both Stanislavsky's "First Studio" and the Group's earliest venture as "The Guild Studio" ' (2009: 52). Students included Marlon Brando, Montgomery Clift and Beatrice Straight. Stanislavski-based work was taught in universities from the late 1960s and there were collaborative programmes with the Moscow Art Theatre School (Carnicke 2009: 56).

Though Strasberg's emphases in directing and training the actor did not differ as radically from Stanislavski's as has been thought, it is important for the sake of clarity to look carefully at what each of them wrote.

STANISLAVSKI AND EUROPE

JERZY GROTOWSKI: POLAND

In Eastern Europe, Jerzy Grotowski (1933–99), a controversial figure – who ranks as one of the greatest and most influential directors of the twentieth century, though he may not be as well known as Stanislavski or Brecht – acknowledged his debt to Stanislavski. He was born in Poland and trained as an actor, then became a director in recognised theatre schools in Poland and the Soviet Union, where Stanislavski's work was the basis for training. His career as a professional theatre director began in Opole, in Poland, in 1959, and his work went through several phases: the Poor Theatre phase (1959–69), the Paratheatrical phase (1970–83), Objective Drama Research (1983–86) in America, and Art as Vehicle (1986–99) in Pontedera, Italy.

Grotowski took from Stanislavski an emphasis on 'searching' and the notion of experiment. His theatre was called Teatr Laboratorium (Theatre Laboratory); in an article written in 1935 entitled 'October and the Theatre', Stanislavski refers to the need for a theatre laboratory, a place of experiment (Whyman 2008: 9). Grotowski directed plays at the beginning of his theatrical career but with little success. Only when he began his own experiments did he start to gain some recognition. He worked with failing actors, seeking to discover for himself, in a different context to Stanislavski, how the theatrical experience could be an important one, essential even, for actors and audiences. Following Stanislavski, he wanted the theatrical experience to be a 'real' one, rather than representational theatre or craft. His search in fact led him to reject theatre altogether at one point: the Paratheatrical phase of his work was a series of group 'happenings', often outdoors, involving participants who were not necessarily actors.

Like Stanislavski, he aimed to purify theatre by ridding it of the traditions and clichés. These made much theatre of the twentieth century, in his view, little more than an evening's entertainment, an experience that no longer had the cathartic and cohesive function for its audience which historically had been the primary role of theatre. He aimed to establish a theatre that was necessary for contemporary society, in the same way that ritual had been essential in former times, in ancient Greece, in primitive societies, as opposed to entertainment.

For both Stanislavski and Grotowski, theatre had a quasi-religious significance: art had transcendental power in its communication with an audience for Stanislavski, and Grotowski developed the notion of 'Holy Theatre'. Dedication and spiritual qualities were to be demanded of its practitioners and a spiritual awareness would be awakened in its audience. This purification meant that theatre was to be distilled to its essence: 'We are seeking to define what is distinctively theatre, what separates this activity from other categories of performance and spectacle' (Grotowski 1975: 15). This led to the notion of the Poor Theatre, where the actor is central and the traditional trappings of the stage are secondary. For Grotowski, the actor must go far beyond what is expected of them traditionally. They must not seek either to represent the role or to give a 'natural' performance but to be genuine. They must use the text as an instrument for self-exploration: the actor must analyse themselves and externalise their discoveries about themselves as a human being by means of their encounter with the text.

Grotowski describes the use of *emotion memory* in Stanislavskian terms for a character in a play who must kill his mother. But it is not sufficient for Grotowski for the actor to find concrete events from their own life. The actor must find a reality that is more difficult: they must find intimate memories and associations which they as a person resist revealing to others. To do this has a purging effect on the actor, and the effect of their breaking down barriers within themselves will be to break down the barriers they normally erect between themselves and other people in their contact with the spectator (Grotowski 1975: 191–92). The employment of all the actor's mental and physical resources in this spontaneous act of self-revelation is known as the Total Act.

THE UNITED KINGDOM

Stanislavski's influence in Western Europe and the United Kingdom was not so direct, though it was nonetheless important, and what happened in the UK has begun to be fully examined only recently. Certain key figures espoused his work and the work became established in a number of theatre conservatoires.

Stanislavski met and shared ideas with Jacques Copeau (1879–1949), who is generally acknowledged to be the major influence on French theatre in the twentieth century. Copeau's nephew Michel Saint-Denis saw the MAT production of Chekhov's *The Cherry Orchard* in 1922, which had a huge impact on him. Saint-Denis moved to London in 1935, founding the London Theatre Studio, acknowledging the inspiration of Stanislavski, while developing his own work from French traditions. After the war Laurence Olivier invited him to form the Old Vic Theatre School.

In Stanislavski's own time, key figures such as Herbert Beerbohm Tree (1853–1917) – actor and theatre manager – visited the MAT. Tree went there in 1911. He established an Academy, which became the Royal Academy of Dramatic Art, but it was much later, in the 1960s, that Stanislavski's work became really established there. Now, it is fundamental to much British theatre training. Harley Granville Barker (1877–1946) – actor, playwright, director and critic who exerted considerable influence on the development of the repertory theatre movement in Britain – also visited Stanislavski and the MAT, in 1914.

Stanislavski's work also became known through a number of individuals, who often combined it with their own ideas.

FYODOR FYODOROVICH KOMISSARZHEVSKY

One of these individuals was Fyodor Fyodorovich Komissarzhevsky (1882–1954), a notable figure who knew Stanislavski in Russia. In 1919, he left Russia for Britain and worked there for twenty years, teaching at RADA and directing and designing productions in London, Stratford-upon-Avon, Rome, Paris, New York and Vienna of Russian classical dramas and operas, as well as Shakespeare and more contemporary dramas. He was one of the first people to introduce Chekhov's plays to British theatre. His father, a famous opera singer, had been Stanislavski's singing teacher and had worked with him in the Society of Art and Literature. While in Russia, Komissarzhevsky was very interested in Stanislavski's work and approached him several times, wanting to join the

Moscow Art Theatre, a request that was not granted. In 1916, Komissarzhevsky infuriated Stanislavski by publishing *The Actor's Creative Work and Stanislavski's Theory*, which was critical of the *system*'s subjective approach while containing some inaccuracies. In fairness, Stanislavski by this point had written nothing himself on the *system* that could have clarified it for others passionate about the development of acting. Komissarzhevsky developed his own methods of working and there is little substantial information about his actual practice. There were various themes to his work, which can be compared with Stanislavski's, Michael Chekhov's and Meyerhold's ideas, including 'Analysis and Preparation, Images and Imagination, Developing Ensemble' (Pitches 2012: 23). British actress Peggy Ashcroft summarised his work in Britain by saying, 'he introduced us to the Stanislavsky system, made us take a fresh look at Chekhov's plays and showed us previously unknown possibilities of the theatre' (Borovsky 2001: xix). As a result of Komissarzhevsky's work, 'new ways of thinking about "character" and alternative approaches to rehearsal enthralled this country's theatre community and clearly had a lasting impact on many of the period's most celebrated actors including Peggy Ashcroft, John Gielgud, Rachel Kempson, Charles Laughton and Michael Redgrave' (Shirley in Pitches 2012: 38).

MICHAEL REDGRAVE

The famous actor Michael Redgrave (1908–85) in his book *The Actor's Ways and Means* espoused the *system*, paying tribute to Stanislavski's influence through Europe and in America and hailing the work of Stanislavski as 'the only successful attempt which has ever been made to come to terms with the fundamentals of the actor's art' (1995: 62). He emphasised the use of Stanislavski's work to go beyond the actor's personality, distinguishing, as French actor Louis Jouvet had done, between *acteur* and *comedien*. The *acteur* or personality actor plays themselves, whereas the *comedien* is 'the actor who, by sinking his own personality or by, as it were, translating or in some cases exceeding it, brings, according to Jouvet, something of the same creative process to bear on his part as the author has brought to the creation of his character' (Redgrave 1995: 6). The actor/*comedien* has to sublimate the ego, and working with

Stanislavski's *given circumstances* (which Redgrave calls 'offered circumstances') is a way to do this:

> I know from experience how difficult it can be sometimes to persuade actors to accept these 'offered circumstances' ... The faults of many actors derive from the fact that they are forced to consider their own aims and ambitions and forget those of the author.
>
> (Redgrave 1995: 76–77)

This focus on the *given circumstances* helps the actor who is good in certain ways but is tempted to rely more and more on what comes easily to them. 'A well-placed, resonant and pleasing voice has been the downfall of many. It can be almost as fatal as an exquisite face and a beautiful body. When the actor has gained some mastery of the essential qualifications, his difficulties have only just begun' (Redgrave 1995: 113).

Redgrave understood that the aim of the *system* was to develop in the actor the *creative state*, 'to clear the decks for action', and was not an invention but a 'codification of ideas about acting which have always been the property of most good actors of all countries whether they knew it or not' (1995: 45, 79). He notes that stage fright is not conducive to the *creative state*, but that, as Stanislavski would have wanted, the actor must not be tense, though their 'state of relaxation or calm must be charged with purpose … By "*cette grace*" (this grace) … the actor can surpass himself. Its chief characteristic is the ease with which everything can be done' (Redgrave 1995: 46).

All in all, Redgrave gives an excellent summary of the main aspects of the *system* and indicates how the actor can use it to overcome ego and establish the particular intensity which is required in communication on stage. *The Actor's Ways and Means* continues to be valuable for the actor.

JOAN LITTLEWOOD

Joan Littlewood (1914–2002) became famous as a director and creative force in Britain from the 1950s. Her Theatre Workshop company at the Theatre Royal, Stratford, East London, was established after World War Two and lasted from 1945 to 1952. Like others, she wanted to challenge low standards in theatre, but she also had overtly political aims. She was part of the Workers' Theatre Movement with Ewan MacColl, forming the Theatre Union in 1936. She intended to 'revolutionize British theatre and re-connect with a large working-class audience' (Holdsworth 2006: 56–9). The idea of a theatre ensemble which was part of Stanislavski and Nemirovich-Danchenko's vision for the MAT was not known before Littlewood in British theatre.

She researched training; the active engagement of the actor was essential. In her early work in Middlesbrough and Manchester, she drew a great deal from *An Actor Prepares* and lectured on concentration, *bits* and *tasks*, *if* and *given circumstances*, imagination and truth. She used *bits* and *tasks* with the aim of uncovering what the character was doing, also working to discuss the *supertask* (Holdsworth 2006: 56–91). Actors were also required to prepare for at least an hour before performance.

Her popular theatre productions combined Stanislavskian 'living the part' with physical theatre techniques drawn from Meyerhold, Rudolf Laban's movement work and Émile Jaques-Dalcroze. In contrast to the productions of more famous companies at the Edinburgh Festival in 1952, audience members, cited by Holdsworth, found in Theatre Workshop 'a group of dedicated players, led by a producer of genius. Here was something fresh, delightful and stimulating. The old techniques of Stanislavsky, Eisenstein and of the commedia dell'arte had been revived, and all the elements of artistic creation excitingly fused into one' (Holdsworth 2006: 17). Her most famous production was *Oh What a Lovely War!* created at the Theatre Royal, Stratford East in 1963, a documentary satire about World War One, set within the framework of a seaside concert party.

As a whole, actor-trainers in Britain have drawn on Stanislavski from a range of different sources and from the *system* alongside other methods. Shirley comments, 'Rather than absorb Stanislavski's principles wholesale, it seems that British actor-trainers have consistently sought new ways of adapting and applying his techniques to a diverse range of teaching and rehearsal situations' (Shirley in Pitches 2012: 59). Stanislavski has been taught in many drama schools and universities for years but a range of interpretations of what the *system* is have existed, including those which have equated the *system* with the American Method.

CONCLUSION: STANISLAVSKI TODAY

Stanislavski's dedicated work to discover the principles of great acting resulted in the *system*, which remains of tremendous importance in acting today. He did not claim that his work was definitive and his true legacy could be said to be that of experiment. His experiments have inspired others to research acting and to search for new methods in theatre.

In Russia, political emphases led to prioritising aspects of the *system* after Stanislavski's death and to a belief that found its way abroad that Stanislavski rejected his earlier work in favour of an approach by action, the *method of physical actions*. In fact, Stanislavski maintained the centrality of *affective memory* in his work, while also stating that there are different routes for the actor to *experiencing*. In American theatre and film, the Method continues to be important, and research has demonstrated the extent to which Strasberg understood the significance of *affective memory*, while working within his own particular context. Grotowski's emphasis on the actor's *experiencing* is comparable, while he also developed the work in his own way.

Meyerhold's opposite stance to Stanislavski, and Vakhtangov's and Michael Chekhov's desire to stretch what they perceived to be the boundaries of the *system* within naturalism have enriched the scope and understanding of actor-training, and interest and research in and teaching of their work continues to increase in Eastern and Western Europe and America. At the same time, exploring what Stanislavski actually taught and the differences between that and the other traditions continues to be fruitful for scholars and practitioners, demonstrating the importance of the questions he asked about acting and his life-long work on the art of the theatre.

FURTHER READING

STANISLAVSKI IN RUSSIA

Braun, E. (1991) *Meyerhold on Theatre*, London: Methuen.

——(1998) *Meyerhold, a Revolution in Theatre*, London: Methuen.

Chamberlain, F. (2004) *Michael Chekhov*, London Routledge.

Chekhov, M. (1977) *To the Director and Playwright,* London, Greenwood Press.

——(1985) *Lessons for the Professional Actor*, New York: Performing Arts Publications.

——(2004) *To the Actor on the Technique of Acting*, London: Routledge.
——(2005) *The Path of the Actor*, London: Routledge.
Leach, R. (1989) *Vsevolod Meyerhold*, Cambridge; Cambridge University Press.
Malaev-Babel, A. (2011) *The Vakhtangov Sourcebook*, London: Routledge.
Pitches, J. (2003) *Vsevolod Meyerhold*, London: Routledge.
Toporkov. V. (1998) *Stanislavski in Rehearsal: The Final Years*, London: Routledge.

STANISLAVSKI IN AMERICA

Adler, S. (2000), ed. Kissel, H. *The Art of Acting*, Canada: Applause Books.
Boleslavsky, R. (2003) *Acting – The First Six Lessons*, London: Routledge.
Carnicke, S.M. (2009) *Stanislavsky in Focus*, 2nd edn, London: Routledge.
Clurman, H. (1983) *The Fervent Years*, New York: Da Capo Press.
Gordon, M. (2010) *Stanislavsky in America: An Actor's Workbook*, London: Routledge.
Krasner, D. (2000), *Method Acting Reconsidered*, London: Macmillan.
Strasberg, L. (1988) *A Dream of Passion*, London: Bloomsbury.

APPENDIX 1: *THE GLASS MENAGERIE*

SYNOPSIS

The Glass Menagerie is set in St Louis, a large city on the Mississippi in America, in the 1930s. Amanda Wingfield was brought up in the Old South, where she was a beauty with many admirers. She married but was abandoned by her husband. Her son Tom narrates the play and it is set in his memory. At the beginning of the play, Tom, Amanda and her daughter, Laura, live in a tenement apartment. Tom works in a shoe factory and Laura, who has a slight disability as a result of childhood illness, does not work, as she is afraid of the outside world. She creates her own imaginary world with her collection of glass animals. Tom writes poetry and is frustrated by the narrow life he leads in the America of the Depression. He closely follows the Spanish Civil War and the events in Europe leading to World War Two and wants to go become a sailor.

In Scene 1 the tensions in the family are apparent during a meal, where Amanda annoys Tom, talking a great deal, instructing him how to eat his food and telling stories she has told before of her admirers in the South. She is convinced that Laura will soon have a 'gentleman caller', a thought that terrifies Laura. In Scene 2 Amanda has found out that, rather than attending the course at Rubicam Secretarial College to learn typing and shorthand Amanda had enrolled her for, Laura has been spending the day walking in the park. She had been unable to cope with the course but also unable to tell her mother. Amanda is humiliated and angry but at the end of the scene convinces herself that Laura's future will be to marry a nice man. She becomes more obsessed with the idea of Laura getting a gentleman caller and takes on extra work, getting subscriptions to a women's magazine, to buy clothes for Laura and things for the apartment. In Scene 3 she and Tom row, revealing her anxiety about him. She thinks the books he is reading are unsuitable and that when he says he is going to the movies he is out drinking. She thinks he is jeopardising his job and therefore their financial security. Tom feels trapped and cannot face spending his life working for Continental Shoemakers.

In Scene 4 Tom comes home drunk and Laura lets him in. In the morning Amanda and he are not speaking to each other. Eventually he apologises and he and Amanda make up. She acknowledges that her anxieties about him and Laura are at the root of how she drives them. Laura has told her how unhappy Tom is and that he goes out to escape the apartment. She cannot stop herself from lecturing Tom and his resentment resurfaces, but at the end of the scene she has made him promise to invite a young man from the warehouse home to meet Laura. In Scene 5 he says he has asked a young man for dinner and Amanda goes into a frenzy of preparation. Tom warns her not to expect too much of Laura but she does not want to listen. In Scene 6 Tom brings Jim home for dinner. He had attended the same school as Tom and Laura and, in fact, Laura had a crush on him. Amanda has refurbished the apartment and dressed Laura up. Amanda puts on a dress she used to wear as a girl and does her hair in ringlets. Laura is terrified. When Jim appears, it is clear that he did not know Tom had a sister and that he has been invited to meet her. He takes in his stride Amanda's appearance and gushing social chit-chat and the fact that Laura is in too much of a state to sit at the table with them. After dinner, Amanda and Tom go into the kitchen to do the washing-up and leave Jim to talk to Laura. He realises how nervous she is and decides to try to boost her confidence. They recall the school assembly hall, the scene of Jim's triumphs as a singer and Laura's humiliation when she regularly came in late and had to walk up the aisle, self-conscious about the noise she was making with the brace on her leg, and Jim tells Laura he never noticed it. They talk and dance together and a glass animal is accidentally broken. Laura takes his attentions for something other than kindness and opens her heart to him. Jim reveals that he is engaged. Laura is desolate. Amanda believes that Tom has invited Jim knowing this, to play a cruel joke, whereas he was unaware that Jim had a girlfriend. She accuses Tom of selfishness and he smashes a glass and goes out. In an epilogue, Tom reveals that he left home soon after and travelled but could never leave behind him the haunting memories of his fragile sister.

EXCERPT: *THE GLASS MENAGERIE*, SCENE 1

CHARACTERS

AMANDA WINGFIELD (the mother), a little woman of great but confused vitality clinging frantically to another time and place. Her characterization must be carefully created, not copied from type. She is not paranoiac, but her life is paranoia. There is much to admire in Amanda, and as much to love and pity as there is to laugh at. Certainly she has endurance and a kind of heroism, and though her foolishness makes her unwittingly cruel at times, there is tenderness in her slight person.

LAURA WINGFIELD (her daughter), Amanda, having failed to establish contact with reality, continues to live vitally in her illusions, but Laura's situation is even graver. A childhood illness has left her crippled, one leg slightly shorter than the other, and held in a brace. This defect need not be more than suggested on the stage. Stemming from this, Laura's separation increases till she is like a piece of her own glass collection, too exquisitely fragile to move from the shelf.

TOM WINGFIELD (her son), and the narrator of the play. A poet with a job in a warehouse. His nature is not remorseless, but to escape from a trap he has to act without pity.

JIM O'CONNOR (the gentleman caller) A nice, ordinary, young man.

SCENE 1

The Wingfield apartment is in the rear of the building, one of those vast hive-like conglomerations of cellular living-units that flower as warty growths in overcrowded urban centers of lower middle-class population and are symptomatic of the impulse of this largest and fundamentally enslaved section of American society to avoid fluidity and differentiation and to exist and function as one interfused mass of automatism.

The apartment faces an alley and is entered by a fire escape, a structure whose name is a touch of accidental poetic truth, for all of these huge buildings are always burning with the slow and implacable fires of human desperation. The fire escape is part of what we see – that is, the landing of it and steps descending from it.

The scene is memory and is therefore non-realistic. Memory takes a lot of poetic license. It omits some details; others are exaggerated, according to the emotional value of the articles it touches, for memory is seated predominantly in the heart. The interior is therefore rather dim and poetic.

At the rise of the curtain, the audience is faced with the dark, grim rear wall of the Wingfield tenement. This building is flanked on both sides by dark, narrow alleys which run into murky canyons of tangled clotheslines, garbage cans, and the sinister latticework of neighboring fire escapes. It is up and down these side alleys that exterior entrances and exits are made during the play. At the end of Tom's opening commentary, the dark tenement wall slowly becomes transparent and reveals the interior of the ground-floor Wingfield apartment.

Nearest the audience is the living room, which also serves as a sleeping room for Laura, the sofa unfolding to make her bed. Just beyond, separated from the living room by a wide arch or second proscenium with transparent faded portieres (or second curtain), is the dining room. In an old fashioned whatnot in the living room are seen scores of transparent glass animals. A blown-up photograph of the father hangs on the wall of the living room, to the left of the archway. It is the face of a very handsome young man in a doughboy's First World War cap. He is gallantly smiling, ineluctably smiling, as if to say "I will be smiling for ever." Also hanging on the wall. near the photograph, are a typewriter keyboard chart and a Gregg shorthand diagram. An upright typewriter on a small table stands beneath the charts.

The audience hears and sees the opening scene in the dining room through both the transparent fourth wall of the building and the transparent gauze portieres of the dining-room arch. It is during this revealing scene that the fourth wall slowly ascends, out of sight. This transparent exterior wall is not brought down again until the very end of the play, during Tom's final speech.

The narrator is an undisguised convention of the play. He takes whatever license with dramatic convention is convenient to his purposes.

TOM *enters, dressed as a merchant sailor, and strolls across to the fire escape. There he stops and lights a cigarette. He addresses the audience.*

TOM: Yes, I have tricks in my pocket, I have things up my sleeve. But I am the opposite of a stage magician. He gives you illusion that has the appearance of truth. I give you truth in the pleasant disguise of illusion.
To begin with, I turn back time. I reverse it to that quaint period, the thirties, when the huge middle class of America was matriculating in a school for the blind. Their eyes had failed them, or they had failed their eyes, and so they were having their fingers pressed forcibly down on the fiery Braille alphabet of a dissolving economy.
In Spain there was revolution. Here there was only shouting and confusion. In Spain there was Guernica. Here there were disturbances of labor, sometimes pretty violent, in otherwise peaceful cities such as Chicago, Cleveland, Saint Louis ... This is the social background of the play.
(*Music begins to play*).
The play is memory. Being a memory play, it is dimly lighted, it is sentimental, it is not realistic. In memory everything seems to happen to music. That explains the fiddle in the wings.
I am the narrator of the play, and also a character in it. The other are my mother, Amanda, my sister, Laura, and a gentleman caller who appears in the final scenes. He is the most realistic character in the play, being an emissary from a world of reality that we were somehow set apart from. But since I have a poet's weakness for symbols, I am using this character also as a symbol; he is the long-delayed but always expected something that we live for.
There is a fifth character in the play who doesn't appear except in this larger-than-life-size photograph over the mantel. This is our father who left us a long time ago. He was

a telephone man who fell in love with long distances; he gave up his job with the telephone company and skipped the light fantastic out of town ...
The last we heard of him was a picture postcard from Mazatlan, on the Pacific coast of Mexico, containing a message of two words: "Hello – Goodbye!" and no address.
I think the rest of the play will explain itself ...

(AMANDA's *voice becomes audible through the portieres.*)
(*Legend on screen*: "Ou sont les neiges?")

(TOM *divides the portieres and enters the dining room.* AMANDA *and* LAURA *are seated at a drop-leaf table. Eating is indicated by gestures without food or utensils.* AMANDA *faces the audience.* TOM *and* LAURA *are seated in profile. The interior has lit up softly and through the scrim we see* AMANDA *and* LAURA *seated at the table.*)

AMANDA: (*Calling.*) Tom?

TOM: Yes, Mother.

AMANDA: We can't say grace until you come to the table!

TOM: Coming, Mother. (*He bows slightly and withdraws, reappearing a few minutes later in his place at the table.*)

AMANDA: (*To her son.*) Honey, don't *push* with your *fingers*. If you have to push with something, the thing to push with is a crust of bread. And chew – chew! Animals have secretions in their stomachs which enable them to digest food without mastication, but human beings are supposed to chew their food before they swallow it down. Eat food leisurely, son, and really enjoy it. A well-cooked meal has lots of delicate flavors that have to be held in the mouth for appreciation. So chew your food and give your salivary glands a chance to function!

(*TOM deliberately lays his imaginary fork down and pushes his chair back from the table.*)

TOM: I haven't enjoyed one bite of this dinner because of your constant directions on how to eat it. It's you that make me rush through meals with your hawklike attention to every bite I take. Sickening – spoils my appetite – all this discussion of animals' secretion – salivary glands – mastication!

AMANDA: (*Lightly.*) Temperament like a Metropolitan star!

(TOM *rises and walks toward the living room.*)

You're not excused from the table.

TOM: I'm getting a cigarette.

AMANDA: You smoke too much.

(LAURA *rises.*)

LAURA: I'll bring in the blanc mange.

(TOM *remains standing with his cigarette by the portieres.*)

AMANDA: (*Rising.*) No, sister, no, sister – you be the lady this time and I'll be the darky.

LAURA: I'm already up.

AMANDA: Resume your seat, little sister – I want you to stay fresh and pretty – for gentlemen callers!

LAURA: (*Sitting down.*) I'm not expecting any gentlemen callers.

AMANDA: (*Crossing out to the kitchenette, airily.*) Sometimes they come when they are least expected! Why, I remember one Sunday afternoon in Blue Mountain –

(*She enters the kitchenette.*)

TOM: I know what's coming!

LAURA: Yes. But let her tell it.

TOM: Again?

LAURA: She loves to tell it.

(AMANDA *returns with a bowl of dessert.*)

AMANDA: One Sunday afternoon in Blue Mountain – your mother received – seventeen! – gentlemen callers! Why, sometimes there weren't chairs enough to accommodate them all. We had to send the nigger over to bring in folding chairs from the parish house.

TOM: (*Remaining at the portieres.*) How did you entertain those gentlemen callers?

AMANDA: I understood the art of conversation!

TOM: I bet you could talk.

AMANDA: Girls in those days knew how to talk, I can tell you.

TOM: Yes?

(*Image on screen:* AMANDA *as a girl on a porch, greeting callers.*)

AMANDA: They knew how to entertain their gentlemen callers. It wasn't enough for a girl to be possessed of a pretty face and a graceful figure – although I wasn't slighted in either respect. She also needed to have a nimble wit and a tongue to meet all occasions.

TOM: What did you talk about?

AMANDA: Things of importance going on in the world! Never anything coarse or common or vulgar.

(*She addresses* TOM *as though he were seated in the vacant chair at the table though he remains by the portieres. He plays this scene as though reading from a script.*)

My callers were gentlemen – all! Among my callers were some of the most prominent young planters of the Mississippi Delta – planters and sons of planters!

(TOM *motions for music and a spot of light on* AMANDA. *Her eyes lift, her face glows, her voice becomes rich and elegiac.*)

(*Screen legend: "Ou sont les neiges d'antan?"*)

There was young Champ Laughlin who later became vice-president of the Delta Planters Bank. Hadley Stevenson who was drowned in Moon Lake and left his widow one hundred and fifty thousand in Government bonds. There were the Cutrere brothers, Wesley and Bates. Bates was one of my bright particular beaux! He got in a quarrel with that wild Wainwright boy. They shot it out on the floor of Moon Lake Casino. Bates was shot through the stomach. Died in the ambulance on his way to Memphis. His widow was also well provided for, came into eight or ten thousand acres, that's all. She married him on the rebound – never loved her – carried my picture on him the night he died! And there was that boy every girl in the Delta had set her cap for! That beautiful, brilliant young Fitzhugh boy from Greene County!

TOM: What did he leave his widow?

AMANDA: He never married! Gracious, you talk as though all of my old admirers had turned up their toes to the daisies!

TOM: Isn't this the first you've mentioned that still survives?

AMANDA: That Fitzhugh boy went North and made a fortune – came to be known as the Wolf of Wall Street! He had the Midas touch, whatever he touched turned to gold! And I could have been Mrs. Duncan J. Fitzhugh, mind you! But – I picked your father!

LAURA: (*Rising.*) Mother, let me clear the table.

AMANDA: No, dear, you go in front and study your typewriter chart. Or, practice your shorthand a little. Stay fresh and pretty! – It's almost time for our gentlemen callers to start arriving. (*She flounces girlishly toward the kitchenette.*) How many do you suppose we're going to entertain this afternoon?

(TOM *throws down the paper and jumps up with a groan.*)

LAURA: (*Alone in the dining room.*) I don't believe we're going to receive any, Mother.

AMANDA: (*Reappearing, airily.*) What? No one – not one? You must be joking!

(LAURA *nervously echoes her laugh. She slips in a fugitive manner through the half-open portieres and draws them gently behind her. A shaft of very clear light is thrown on her face against the faded tapestry of the curtains. Faintly the music of* "*The Glass Menagerie*" *is heard as she continues, lightly.*)

Not one gentleman caller? It can't be true! There must be a flood, there must have been a tornado!

LAURA: It isn't a flood, it's not a tornado, Mother. I'm just not popular like you were in Blue Mountain ...

(TOM *utters another groan. Laura glances at him with a faint, apologetic smile. Her voice catches a little.*)

Mother's afraid I'm going to be an old maid.

(*The scene dims out with the "Glass Menagerie" music.*)

APPENDIX 2: *DEATH OF A SALESMAN – CERTAIN PRIVATE CONVERSATIONS IN TWO ACTS AND A REQUIEM*

SYNOPSIS

ACT 1

The setting is America in the 1930s. One night, Willy Loman, a 60-year-old travelling salesman, returns to his family home, where Linda, his wife, is waiting for him. Willy has problems; he has been away all day but did not make his sales appointments; he was unable to concentrate on his driving and has 'strange thoughts'. Linda encourages him to go to see Howard, his boss, and ask whether he can work in New York, where they live, so that he does not have to drive any more.

His adult son, Biff, is visiting his parents from Texas. He and his brother, Happy, are in the bedroom they used to share as boys: Biff and Happy have been out for the evening together and Happy has returned home with him rather than going to his own apartment. They hear the conversation and Happy expresses anxieties about his father, who talks to himself (often addressing Biff). Biff tells his brother that he feels he is wasting his life; he has had twenty or thirty jobs since leaving home, from shipping clerk to farm work. Happy says he is also discontented though he has his own apartment, a car and plenty of women. They talk about buying a ranch together; Biff is very keen on this idea but it becomes clear that Happy is not really committed to it.

The scene flashes back to the boys' childhood: Willy has come back from a sales trip and brought them a punch bag. The boy from next door, Bernard, calls for Biff; they were meant to study together today and Bernard is worried that Biff is going to fail his exams. Willy gets angry; he thinks his sons, who are 'like Adonises', are the type who will get on in the business world, like him. He says he has 'knocked 'em dead' on his sales trip. His conversation with Linda when the boys go with their friends reveals, however, that his claims of his business success are exaggerated; there are money problems and in fact Willy fears that people do not like him and that he is seen as a ridiculous figure. Linda soothes and flatters her husband.

Another flashback reveals the character of The Woman with whom the younger Willy is having an affair. He gives her silk stockings. The scene returns to Willy's home, where Linda is darning stockings. Displacing his guilt, Willy gets angry and tells her he won't have his wife darning stockings. It is revealed in this conversation that Biff steals.

The action returns to the setting of the first scene and Happy comes downstairs to talk to his father. Willy asks himself why he didn't go to Alaska with his brother, Ben, who later made a fortune from diamond mining. Charley, Bernard's father, comes into the kitchen and signals for Happy to go. Charley cannot sleep either and he and Willy play cards. Charley offers Willy a job, but Willy takes this as an insult.

Ben, whom Willy has longed to see for years, appears in a dream sequence. Willy tells Charley that he heard a fortnight ago that Ben had died in Africa. Willy is quarrelsome with Charley, who leaves. Willy's dream conversation with Ben continues with an appearance from Linda, and Biff and Happy as boys.

In the original setting, Linda tells Willy to go to bed. He goes for a walk. Biff and Happy talk to Linda. Linda defends Willy to his sons and charges them with neglecting him. She says he is exhausted and that they have turned their backs on him. They do not even know that his salary has been stopped so he is now earning only commission. She tells them he has been trying to kill himself; she has found a length of rubber hose which could be connected to the gas pipe.

Willy returns; Happy comes up with a plan to sell sports goods with Biff. Biff says he is going to ask Bill Oliver, a former employer, for a loan to do so. The conversation ends on a note of optimism but the act ends as Biff finds the rubber tubing.

ACT 2

Willy is having breakfast. Biff and Happy have left and Linda tells him the boys have invited him to meet them for dinner that evening. Willy leaves in high spirits to see Howard.

Howard Wagner does not want to listen to Willy; he is engrossed with the tape recorder he has just bought. He brushes off Willy's request to work in New York. Willy reminds him that he has been with the firm since before Howard was born and claims Howard's father was his friend. Selling was the greatest career a man could have. He talks in a grandiose way about his achievements as a salesman, which Howard knows are untrue. Howard says there is no longer a place for him in the firm.

There is a flashback to when Ben invited Willy to come and work for him in Alaska. Linda, who was frightened of Ben, says Willy has a good job here and Ben leaves.

In a further flashback, Biff is about to play in a baseball championship; he has scholarships promised at three universities. Bernard is to accompany him to the match; Willy argues with Charley.

Back to the original scene; Willy is now at Charley's office, where Bernard is. Jenny, the secretary, asks Bernard to get Willy to leave; he apparently comes there regularly and upsets Charley. Bernard is a lawyer, married with two boys, and despite his unpromising start with sport, plays tennis well. Willy asks Bernard what went wrong with Biff; he flunked the exam and refused to go to summer school to make up the grade. Willy borrows money from Charley but refuses a job, arguing with him again.

Willy meets Biff and Happy for dinner, but Happy is preoccupied with organising a date for Biff and himself. Biff has gone to see Bill Oliver, who was considering the idea Biff proposed but Biff rushed out, stealing Oliver's fountain pen. Willy tells them he has been fired but is convinced Biff will have succeeded with Bill Oliver and does not listen. Biff tries to tell him what happened.

The scene is intercut with a flashback, which reveals what happened when Biff failed his exam; he went to see his father in Boston and found him in a hotel room with The Woman.

Biff and Happy leave with their dates. Later, they return home where Linda is furious with them for abandoning their father in the restaurant. Willy is planting seeds in the garden. Biff decides the best thing he can do for his father is to leave and not contact him any more. They argue and Biff confronts Willy with the rubber tubing. Other lies are exposed: Happy's claims about the importance of his job; Biff's stealing. Biff says that the truth is that he is a 'dime a dozen', not the leader of men Willy has expected him to be. Biff cries, holding onto Willy, and Willy realises that Biff does care for him. In the mood of reconciliation, Happy says he is going to marry and settle down.

Ben appears. Willy takes the car and drives away; there is a frenzy of sound. He has decided that the best thing he can do for Biff is to kill himself, so that the family can have his life insurance money.

REQUIEM

Charley, Linda, Happy and Biff are at the grave. No one else has been to the funeral. Linda says that she has made the last payment on the house and after thirty-five years their debts have been cleared. She cannot understand why Willy killed himself. Happy continues to talk in an aggrandising way about the Loman Brothers; Biff says he knows who he really is.

CHRONOLOGY

1858	Birth of Nemirovich-Danchenko.
1860	Birth of Anton Chekhov.
1861	Emancipation of the serfs in Russia.
1863	Birth of Stanislavski.
1870	Birth of Lenin.
1874	Birth of Meyerhold.
1877	Formation of the Alekseiev Circle.
1879	Birth of Stalin.
1879–88	Important work on naturalism in European theatre: Ibsen, Strindberg, Zola, Antoine's Théâtre Libre.
1881	Assassination of Tsar Alexander II. Alexander III becomes Tsar.
1888	Formation of the Moscow Society of Art and Literature.
1889	Stanislavski marries Maria Petrovna Perevoshchikova (Lilina) and directs for the first time at the Society for Art and Literature – a one-act comedy.
1890	Meiningen troupe in Moscow.
1892	Maeterlinck and Hauptmann's work is performed in Russia.
1894	Death of Alexander III. Nicholas II becomes Tsar. Famine, strikes, unrest.

1895	In January Stanislavski directs and stars in Gutskov's *Uriel Acosta*. Meets Nemirovich-Danchenko. Foundation of Art-Popular Theatre, which becomes Moscow Art Theatre. First motion pictures.
1898	Theatre opens with A. Tolstoy's *Tsar Fiodor Ioannovich*, Chekhov's *The Seagull* and other plays. Leo Tolstoy's *What is Art?* published.
1899	Directs and acts in Ibsen's *Hedda Gabler*, A. Tolstoy's *The Death of Ivan the Terrible*, Chekhov's *Uncle Vanya*, Hauptmann's *The Lonely Ones*, Shakespeare's *Twelfth Night*.
1900	Directs and acts in Ibsen's *An Enemy of the People* and Ostrovski's *Snow Maiden*.
1901	Directs and acts in Chekhov's *Three Sisters*, Ibsen's *The Wild Duck* and other plays.
1902	Briusov's *Unnecessary Truth* published. Meyerhold leaves the MAT. Directs and acts in Gorky's *The Lower Depths* and other plays.
1903	Acts in *Julius Caesar*.
1904	Directs and acts in Chekhov's *The Cherry Orchard* in the year that Chekhov dies, and Maeterlinck plays. Scientist Ivan Pavlov is awarded the Nobel Prize. The Russo-Japanese war begins.
1905	Directs Ibsen's *Ghosts* and Gorky's *Children of the Sun*. The Studio on Povarskaia founded with Meyerhold as director. First Russian Revolution and the 'Bloody Sunday' massacre.
1906	Directs and acts in Griboiedov's *Woe from Wit*. Tour of the MAT to Berlin and other places in Europe. Begins to develop what becomes known as the *system*. Asks Sulerzhitski to be his directorial assistant at the MAT. Row with Nemirovich-Danchenko about this.
1907	Experiments with emotion in Hamsun's *The Drama of Life* not successful as the work is too internally focused. Directs and acts in Andreiev's *The Life of Man*.
1908	Studies the psychology of Théodule Ribot. Begins to discuss the *system* at the MAT.

1909	Directs and acts in Turgenev's *A Month in the Country*.
1910	Directs and acts in Ostrovski's *Enough Stupidity in Every Wise Man*.
1911	At rehearsals of *Hamlet* and Tolstoy's *The Living Corpse* works with the actors on the *system*.
1912	Directs and acts in Turgenev's *A Provincial Lady*. First Studio formed – led by Suler. Michael Chekhov joins.
1913	Directs and acts in Molière's *Malade Imaginaire*. Production of *The Wreck of the Ship 'Hope'*, in the First Studio.
1914	Russia allied with France and England against Germany and Austria-Hungary in World War One. Directs and acts in Goldoni's *La Locandiera*.
1915	In March directs and acts in Pushkin's *Mozart and Salieri* and *The Siege During the Plague*.
1916	Second Studio formed. Death of Suler.
1917	General strike, abdication of Tsar Nicholas II, Lenin leads the Revolution and establishes Bolshevik rule. Theatres are placed under Soviet jurisdiction of Narkompros. Nemirovich-Danchenko removes Stanislavski from his role in a Dostoevsky adaptation and Stanislavski never creates a new role after this. *Twelfth Night* in First Studio.
1918	Civil war until 1922. Meyerhold appointed head of Petrograd Theatre Section of Narkompros. Formation of the Bolshoi Opera Studio and the Habima Studio.
1919	Stanislavski works at the Bolshoi Opera Studio and in other studios. All Russian theatres nationalised.
1920	Directs Byron's *Cain*. Third Studio formed.
1921	Gogol's *The Government Inspector* at the First Studio, with Mikhail Chekhov. Fourth Studio formed.
1922	Directs Tchaikovsky's *Evgeni Onegin*.
1922–24	The MAT tour in Europe and USA. Meyerhold develops *biomechanics*.
1924	*My Life in Art* published in America. First Studio becomes MAT 2. Second Studio incorporated into main theatre. Death of Lenin.

1926	Stanislavski and Sudakov direct Ostrovski's *Burning Heart* and Bulgakov's *The Days of the Turbins*. Directs other plays and opera. *My Life in Art* published in Russia.
1927	Directs opera at the MAT and Ivanov's *The Armoured Train No. 14–69.*
1928	Stanislavski's last performance. Directs opera and Kataiev's *The Embezzlers.*
1929	Trotsky is expelled from the Soviet Union. Stalin consolidates his power.
1932	Stalin states that *The Days of the Turbins* is his favourite play. Directs opera and Gogol's *Dead Souls.*
1933	Directs Ostrovski's *Artists and Admirers* and Rossini's opera, *The Barber of Seville.*
1934	Socialist Realism begins to be the dominant form of art in the Soviet Union. Stanislavski visits Paris, meets Copeau and Dullin.
1935	Forms Opera-Dramatic Studio with sister Zinaida. Directs Bizet's *Carmen.*
1936	American edition of *An Actor Prepares*; second Russian edition of *My Life In Art.* Directs Bulgakov's *Molière* and opera.
1937	Continues to work, though increasingly bed-ridden.
1938	Invites Meyerhold to work at the Stanislavski Opera Theatre. Stanislavski dies. *An Actor's Work on him/herself; Part 1, Work on oneself in the Creative Process of Experiencing* published in Russia.
1939	Two productions Stanislavski began work on are completed after his death: Verdi's *Rigoletto,* by Meyerhold, and Molière's *Tartuffe,* by Kedrov.
1940	Meyerhold executed.

GLOSSARY

Action The performer should be involved in *action* internally and externally – they must be *active*. All action is purposeful; everything you do onstage must be for a reason. Physical action can refer to things the character does such as opening a door but this will have a purpose and an internal aspect, for example the character opens the door not knowing he is to be told his wife has been in an accident. The actor opens the door (physical action) for a purpose (to see who is ringing the bell); the inner action is not knowing who is there.

Active Analysis This is also called *analysis by action* or *rehearsal by études* and the principle is the same as in the *method of physical actions*. It is used in the rehearsal process and involves the actors improvising part of a scene, using whatever information they have about the *given circumstances* at that point.

Adaptation or *Adjustment* This is the way an actor can adapt their behaviour to influence a stage partner, keeping a role fresh.

Attention This is an essential element of the *creative state*. If the actor is not fully attending to what is going on onstage, there will be a loss of quality and the acting may seem mechanical. Stanislavski discusses *multi-level attention*, where the actor can pay attention to more than one thing at once, such as the stage partners, the internal action of the character and the quality of voice and precision of movement.

Bit/Unit This is a chosen section of text, varying in length, in which you identify a *task* or *tasks* for the character or characters. You should give the *bit* a title, which helps you begin to learn the text. A change in dynamic or thought or a new event can start a new *bit*, for example when a character's *task* or *objective* is achieved or prevented, or a character enters or leaves the scene or a dialogue between characters takes a new turn.

Control and Finish During rehearsals the actor, when *experiencing*, may not always be in control of emotion but should have full control in performance.

Likewise, they should be *embodying* the character with full technical control of movement and voice by the time of performance.

Controller/Muscle Controller/Monitor This is where the actor develops a system of checking whether they have superfluous muscular tension and let it go.

Communication The actor must be in communication with something onstage, their own thoughts or the other characters. If the actor is *experiencing*, this will be communicated to the audience.

Creative State The inner *creative state* is a readiness to work and *experience*. The outer *creative state* is where every feeling, mood, experience you have created is *reflected* externally, or *embodied*. The actor can work on elements of the *creative state*, inner and outer, separately, and then put them all together. For example, combining muscular release with a sense of truth, objects of attention with transmitting, action with physical tasks. The inner and outer *creative states* add up to *the general or working creative state*, to *I am being*.

Embodiment The outer characterisation of the role; the outer expression of the actor's *experiencing*.

Emotion The actor must create real emotion onstage, but this is not achieved directly by going straight for an emotional state, for example 'being angry'. Sometimes *emotion memory* will help the actor, but by playing the *actions*, fulfilling the *tasks* of the character in the *given circumstances*, the emotion will be generated.
See **Sense and Emotion Memory**

Experiencing This is bringing the role to life from within. The actor must be active, must create the role afresh on each performance and must experience the role as in life in order to convey what makes us human, the human experience. The word *experiencing* (*perezhivanie* in Russian) means to 'experience', 'undergo' or 'live through' (see Stanislavski 2008b: 19).

Fusion or *Merging* This is where the actor has created the character fully, identifies with the character, while being truthful to themselves. The external image or *embodiment* of the character emerges from inner *experiencing*.

Given Circumstances These are all the aspects of the play and production which are 'given' to the actor to work with. These include the story of the play, its setting, the interpretation given by the director and the design, including props, costumes and so on.

Here, Today, Now A way for the actor to work on spontaneity is to ask 'What would I do here, today, now, if I found myself in the situation the character is in?' so that the role is fresh in every performance.

I Am Being The state of *I am being* is where the actor can say 'I exist, I live, I feel and I think identically with the role.' It is also described as 'living the truth onstage' and *fusion* or *merging*. Working at individual physical actions truthfully builds up to this experience of all aspects of the role being truthful.

If/Magic If This is an important tool for the actor; asking yourself 'If I were in these *given circumstances* what would I do?' is a way to begin to create the role truthfully.

Imagination The writer will only provide some of the information needed by the actor in a play and the actor must use research and their *imagination* in order to create the world of the character in full.

Justification Everything that happens onstage must be for a reason; all actions must be *justified*. You should never pace up and down just to be dramatic, only if the pacing is true to what the character would do.

Life of the Human Spirit of the Role The actor should create 'life' onstage, drawing on their own human experiences and observations.

Logic and Consistency The logical sequence of actions carried out by the actor as the character.

Lure A lure is anything that arouses *experiencing*; it can be *emotion memory* or performing *tasks* truthfully in the *given circumstances*.

Method of Physical Actions A practical rehearsal process geared towards creating a 'score of physical actions', where beginning with simple actions in the *given circumstances* begins to unlock *experiencing*.

Muscular Release or *Relaxing the Muscles* Unnecessary tension will detract from the actor's performance, even at times of heightened emotion in the role.

Public Solitude A state of muscular relaxation in spite of the presence of the audience.

Rays A way to help the actor achieve communication onstage is by thinking of sending rays out to the audience and receiving them back.

Sense and Emotion Memory or *Affective Memory* This is the tool for *experiencing*. Acting can be truthful when we use sense and emotion memory in order to inform the role so that what we do is true to life.

The Six Questions These questions help you begin to develop the *given circumstances* of the character and play:

1. Who am I?
2. What is happening?
3. When is it happening?
4. Where am I?

5. Why am I here? (What has happened in the past to bring me here?)
6. For what reason/wherefore am I here? (To do with the *task* or *objective* – what do I want now and in the future?)

Subconscious Much of the actor's creative work takes place in the *subconscious*. If you apply the *system*, analyse the *given circumstances*, use the *magic if*, play *tasks* and so on, stimulating your imagination, ideas about the character and how to play him or her will come to you.

Subtext This has to be considered with the *through-line*; it is what is going on 'below' the text, behind the dialogue – what the characters are thinking, which may be different from what they are saying.

Supertask or *Superobjective* This is the main idea of the play, what the writer is aiming for with the play overall, and the characters' *tasks* are all linked to it.

Supertask of the Character The ultimate objective towards which each character journeys throughout the play. Again this will be individual to each character.

Task/Objective The *task* or *objective* is what you want to do within a *bit* of the play. It can be expressed as 'I want to … '. This is what motivates the behaviour of the character and is directed towards the other characters onstage. Each character will have their own *tasks or objectives*, *counter-tasks* or *counter-objectives*, which may be opposite to those of other characters.

Tempo-rhythm There is inner and outer *tempo-rhythm*. *Tempo* refers to the speed of physical actions and *rhythm* to the inner promptings. There may be a contradiction – the inner agitation of a character may be masked by slow movements in the attempt to appear in control. A play may also have a *tempo-rhythm*.

Three Bases of the *System* *Action*, *emotion* and the *subconscious* are the foundation of the *system* as a whole.

Through-line of Action This is the character's journey through the play, the line of thought and action of the character which the actor must fulfil without losing it. The combined *through-lines* of the characters make the plot.

Truth and Belief The actor fulfils the *tasks* of the character with *truth and belief of actions*. Using *sense and emotion memory* is important here so that you perform actions – handling props, looking at objects onstage and moving in the performance space – as you would in life, not taking short cuts or being overly dramatic.

BIBLIOGRAPHY

Adler, S. (2000), ed. Kissel, H. *The Art of Acting*, Canada: Applause Books.

Alexander, F.M. (1985) *The Use of the Self*, London: Victor Gollancz.

——(1996) *Man's Supreme Inheritance*, London: Mouritz.

Alfreds, M. (2007) *Different Every Night – Freeing the Actor*, London: Nick Hern Books.

Benedetti, J. (1991) *The Moscow Art Theatre Letters*, London: Methuen.

——(1999) *Stanislavski, His Life and Art*, London: Methuen.

Bigsby, C. (1997) *The Cambridge Companion to Arthur Miller,* Cambridge: Cambridge University Press.

Boal, A. (2002) *Games for Actors and Non-actors*, London: Routledge.

Boleslavsky, R. (2003) *Acting – The First Six Lessons*, London: Routledge.

Borovsky, V. (2001) *A Tryptych from the Russian Theatre: An Artistic Biography of the Komissarzhevskys*, London: Hurst.

Braun, E. (1991) *Meyerhold on Theatre*, London: Methuen.

——(1998) *Meyerhold, a Revolution in Theatre*, London: Methuen.

Carnicke, S. (1998) *Stanislavsky in Focus,* Amsterdam: Harwood Academic Publishers.

——(2009) *Stanislavsky in Focus*, 2nd edn, London: Routledge.

Chamberlain, F. (2004) *Michael Chekhov*, London: Routledge.

Chekhov, A. (2005), ed. and trans. Senelick, L., *Selected Plays*, London: W.W. Norton and Company.

Chekhov, M. (1977) *To the Director and Playwright*, London: Greenwood Press.

——(1985) *Lessons for the Professional Actor*, New York: Performing Arts Publications.

——(1991) *On the Technique of Acting*, New York: Harper Perennial.

——(2004) *To the Actor on the Technique of Acting*, London: Routledge.

——(2005) *The Path of the Actor*, London: Routledge.

Clurman, H. (1983) *The Fervent Years*, New York: Da Capo Press.

Cole, T. and Chinoy, H. (1970) *Actors on Acting*, New York: Three Rivers Press.

Donellan, D. (2005) *The Actor and the Target*, London: Nick Hern.

Door, B. (2003) *Towards Perfect Posture*, London: Orion.

——(forthcoming) *An Actor's Guide to the Alexander Technique*.

Edwards, C. (1965) *The Stanislavski Heritage*, New York: New York University Press.

Gauss, R. (1999) *Lear's Daughters: The Studios of the Moscow Art Theatre 1905–1927*, New York: Peter Lang.

Gordon, M. (1987) *The Stanislavski Technique: Russia*, New York: Applause Theatre Books.

——(2010) *Stanislavsky in America: An Actor's Workbook*, London: Routledge.

Grotowski, J. (1975) *Towards a Poor Theatre*, London: Eyre Methuen.

Hagen, U. (2008) *Respect for Acting*, Hoboken: John Wiley & Sons.

Hodge, A. (2000) *Twentieth-century Actor-training*, London: Routledge.

Holdsworth, N. (2006) *Joan Littlewood*, London: Routledge.

Hoover, M. (1974) *Meyerhold: The Art of Conscious Theatre*, Amherst: University of Massachusetts Press.

Ignatieva, M. (2008) *Stanislavsky and Female Actors: Women in Stanislavsky's Life and Art*, Maryland: University Press of America.

Johnston, C. (2005) *House of Games: Making Theatre from Everyday Life*, London: Faber and Faber.

Johnstone, K. (1997) *Improvisation and the Theatre*, London: Routledge.

Korkorin, A. (2007) *Vam Privet ot Stanislavskogo*, Moscow: Boslen.

Krasner, D. (2000) *Method Acting Reconsidered*, London: Macmillan.

Leach, R. (1989) *Vsevolod Meyerhold*, Cambridge: Cambridge University Press.

——(2003) *Stanislavsky and Meyerhold*, Oxford: Peter Lang.

Listengarten, J. (2000) *Russian Tragifarce, Its Cultural and Political Roots*, London: Associated University Presses.

Malaev-Babel, A. (2011) *The Vakhtangov Sourcebook*, London: Routledge.

Merlin, B. (2001) *Beyond Stanislavsky: The Psycho-Physical Approach to Actor Training*, London: Nick Hern Books.

——(2003) *Konstantin Stanislavsky*, London: Routledge.

——(2007) *The Complete Stanislavsky Toolkit*, London: Nick Hern.

Miller, A. (1999) *Timebends: A Life*, London: Methuen.

——(2000) *Death of a Salesman*, London: Penguin.

Mitchell, K. (2009) *The Director's Craft: A Handbook for the Theatre*, Abingdon: Routledge.

Pavis, P. (1998) *Dictionary of the Theatre: Terms, Concepts and Analysis*, Toronto: University of Toronto Press.

Pitches, J. (2003) *Vsevolod Meyerhold*, London: Routledge.

——(2005) *Science and the Stanislavsky Tradition of Acting*, London: Routledge.

——(2012) *Russians in Britain*, London: Methuen.

Redgrave, M. (1995) *The Actor's Ways and Means*, London: Nick Hern.

Riley, K. (2004) *Nigel Hawthorne on Stage*, Hatfield: University of Hertfordshire Press.

Rudnitsky, K. (1988) *Russian and Soviet Theatre*, London: Thames & Hudson.

Senelick, L. (1981) *Russian Dramatic Theory from Pushkin to the Symbolists: An Anthology*, Austin: University of Texas Press.

——(1982) *Gordon Craig's Moscow Hamlet*, Westport: Greenwood Press.

Sher, A. (2004) *Year of the King*, London: Nick Hern Books.

Shevtsova, M. (forthcoming) *The Cambridge Introduction to Stanislavsky*, Cambridge: Cambridge University Press.

Simonov, R. (1969) *Stanislavsky's Protégé: Eugene Vakhtangov*, New York: DBS Publications.

Spolin, V. (1999) *Improvisation for the Theater*, Evanston: Northwestern University Press.

Spoto, D. (1997) *The Kindness of Strangers: The Life of Tennessee Williams*, Cambridge, MA: Da Capo Press.

Stanislavski, K. (2008a) *My Life in Art*, London: Routledge.

——(2008b) *An Actor's Work*, London: Routledge.

——(2010) *An Actor's Work on a Role*, London: Routledge.

Stanislavskii, K. (1955) *Sobranie Sochinenii*, Vol. III, Moscow: Iskusstvo.

——(1999) *Sobranie Sochinenii*, Vol. IX, Moscow: Iskusstvo.

Stanislavsky, K. (1967) *Stanislavsky on the Art of the Stage*, London: Faber and Faber.

Strasberg, L. (1965) *Strasberg at the Actor's Studio,* New York: Viking.

——(1988) *A Dream of Passion*, London: Bloomsbury.

Toporkov, V. (1998) *Stanislavski in Rehearsal: The Final Years*, London: Routledge.

Tovstonogov, G. (1972) *The Profession of the Stage Director*, Moscow: Progress Publishers.

Walter, H. (1999) *Other People's Shoes*, London: Viking.

Wertenbaker, T. (2009) *Our Country's Good*, London: Methuen.

Whyman, R. (2008) *The Stanislavski System of Acting: Legacy and Influence in Modern Performance*, Cambridge: Cambridge University Press.

Williams, T. (2009) *The Glass Menagerie*, London: Penguin.

Wolff, T. (1971) *Pushkin on Literature*, London: Methuen.

Wood, E. (1999) *Concentration: A Practical Course with a Supplement on Meditation*, Adya, Chennai: The Theosophical Publishing House.

Worrall, N. (1996) *The Moscow Art Theatre*, London.

Worthen, W.B. (2010) *The Wadsworth Anthology of Drama*, Boston, MA: Thomson Wadsworth.

Zakhava, B. (1982) *Vospominania. Spektakli i roli. Stat'i.*, Moscow: VTO.

INDEX